T0334033

Constructing Crisis

There is no such thing as a crisis. Rather than an actual, corporeal thing, a crisis is a claim asserted from a position of power and influence, intended to shape the understanding of others. A constructed crisis by a leader may or may not be legitimate, and, legitimate or not, the content of a claim alone does not determine whether people decide to believe it. Rather than viewing crises as the result of objective events, Spector demonstrates that leaders impose crises on organizations to strategically assert power and exert control. Interpreting crisis through a critical lens, this interdisciplinary book encompasses not just management and organizational literature, but also sociology, history, cognitive science, and psychology. The resulting wide-ranging, critical, and provocative analysis will appeal in particular to students and academics researching leadership and crisis management.

Bert Spector is Associate Professor of International Business and Management at D'Amore-McKim School of Business, Northeastern University, Boston. His research interests include organizational change, leadership, business model innovation and management history. His previous book *Discourse on Leadership: A Critical Appraisal* (Cambridge, 2016) received the 2017 Choice Award for an Outstanding Academic Title.

Constructing Crisis

Leaders, Crises, and Claims of Urgency

Bert Spector

Northeastern University, Boston

CAMBRIDGE
UNIVERSITY PRESS

CAMBRIDGE
UNIVERSITY PRESS

University Printing House, Cambridge CB2 8BS, United Kingdom

One Liberty Plaza, 20th Floor, New York, NY 10006, USA

477 Williamstown Road, Port Melbourne, VIC 3207, Australia

314–321, 3rd Floor, Plot 3, Splendor Forum, Jasola District Centre, New Delhi – 110025, India

79 Anson Road, #06–04/06, Singapore 079906

Cambridge University Press is part of the University of Cambridge.

It furthers the University's mission by disseminating knowledge in the pursuit of education, learning, and research at the highest international levels of excellence.

www.cambridge.org
Information on this title: www.cambridge.org/9781108427357
DOI: 10.1017/9781108551663

First published 2019

Printed in the United Kingdom by TJ International Ltd. Padstow Cornwall

A catalogue record for this publication is available from the British Library.

Library of Congress Cataloging-in-Publication Data
Names: Spector, Bert, author.
Title: Constructing crisis : leaders, crises and claims of urgency / Bert Spector, Northeastern University, Boston.
Description: Cambridge, United Kingdom ; New York, NY, USA : Cambridge University Press, 2019. | Includes bibliographical references and index.
Identifiers: LCCN 2019008019| ISBN 9781108427357 (hardback) | ISBN 9781108446082 (paperback)
Subjects: LCSH: Crisis management in government. | Political leadership.
Classification: LCC JF1525.C74 S74 2019 | DDC 352.3–dc23
LC record available at https://lccn.loc.gov/2019008019

ISBN 978-1-108-42735-7 Hardback
ISBN 978-1-108-44608-2 Paperback

To

Harper Elaine

Riley Morgan

Lily Kathleen

Contents

Tables

Preface

The central assertion of *Constructing Crisis* is that there is no such thing as a crisis. It's an observation I came to at a moment when the United States, indeed much of the Western world, seemed to be engulfed in upheaval. It sure felt like crises were real. And they were everywhere.

In the second half of 2016, just as I started writing, a wave of migration convulsed Europe. With ninety people a week drowning on the Mediterranean Sea in a desperate attempt to seek refuge, US President Barack Obama addressed the United Nations' Leaders' Summit on Refuges. This was a crisis of "epic proportions," he declared, a dire situation that posed "one of the most urgent tests of our time."[1] In June, citizens of the United Kingdom voted to exit the European Union. Brexit advocates insisted that their country faced a crisis due to unconstrained immigration, not to mention attempts by faceless bureaucrats in Brussels to deprive England of its traditional identity. In the United States, competing claims of crisis dominated the presidential campaign. From one side of the political divide came an assertion that the country faced "carnage." From the other came an insistence that a constitutional crisis loomed.

As I continued my project, urgent situations appeared to multiply. We learned the details on how Russians had hacked the 2016 US presidential election, and deadly conflict raged in Syria. Terrorists struck Turkey while Recep Tayyip Erdogan's government cracked down on opposition. Humanitarian catastrophes spread across the Middle East and Africa, a hurricane ravaged the island of Puerto Rico, and US immigration officers separated children and parents on the country's southern border. #BlackLivesMatter and #MeToo movements demanded accountability from, among many, police officers, amateur sports coaches, and Supreme Court nominees. Agents of a US ally apparently murdered a US-based journalist. The president announced an immigration emergency at the

---

[1] Available at https://obamawhitehouse.archives.gov/the-press-office/2016/09/20/remarks-president-obama-leaders-summit-refugees.

country's southern border that presented "a crisis of the heart, a crisis of the soul." Critics insisted that the "crisis at the border" was nothing more than a claim made by the president to advance an anti-immigrant agenda. The Earth continued to warm, the polar caps continued to melt, and storms regularly devastated communities around the globe.

It sure felt like crises were real things.

I do my work at a school of business, focusing largely on the role of corporate leaders, mainly CEOs, and the outsized impact they are said to exert on their organizations. As I continued to work through *Constructing Crisis*, numerous urgent performance crises threatened the viability of companies. The Limited, Toys R Us, and Radio Shack were among the many US corporations forced to declare bankruptcy in what came to be called the "retail apocalypse of 2017."[2] Then, in the next year, Sears and Brookstone joined the ranks of the bankrupt. *That* sounded like a crisis.

Videos of a bloodied passenger being dragged down the aisle of a United Airlines flight to make room for staff members and a black customer being led off in handcuffs from a Starbucks by police made for some very difficult moments for corporate leaders. Facebook founder and CEO Mark Zuckerberg faced embarrassingly uninformed – "How do you sustain a business model when people don't pay for services?" – but righteously angry senatorial inquisitors demanding to know how "private" user data had made its way into political campaigns. Japanese authorities arrested the chairman of Nissan Motors on charges of under-reporting his income to the tune of more than $44 million. The credit-reporting firm Equifax admitted that a hack had exposed private data – social security numbers, credit card numbers, and other personal information – of 143 million customers. The Italian fashion house Dolce & Gabbana angered nearly the entire Chinese retail clothing industry with an advertisement deemed to be culturally insensitive and insulting. And accusations of sexual harassment and abuse shook the entertainment industry at its very highest levels.

So, what am I *thinking* when I insist that there is no such thing as a crisis? Let me explain. First, I believe that we seriously, even dangerously, misconstrue the nature of crises and the role played by leaders – CEOs no less than presidents and prime ministers – in asserting that a crisis exists. Crises aren't things at all, but constructions made by leaders, claims that insist that their social unit faces an urgent situation. Second, I think that claims of urgency are not neutral,

---

[2] Derek Thompson, "What in the World Is Causing the Retail Meltdown of 2017?" *The Atlantic* (April 10, 2017).

scientifically objective readings of the external environment. Rather, they are exercises in power and assertions of interests on behalf of the claims makers. There are times, certainly, when claims-maker interests are coincident with the aims of the larger social unit, but not always. Third, while some of these claims of urgency are undoubtedly legitimate, not all are. It would be useful to devise an approach for sorting through the claims with which we are regularly bombarded. And finally, I think that the spreading phenomenon of post-truth claims making demands exploration with attention to the dynamics by which people come to believe or disbelieve claims.

As I considered those points, I knew I needed to address the larger question that my hypothesis raised. If crises aren't *things*, what, then, are they? My own academic background directed me to look for answers in certain places. There is, not surprisingly, a considerable literature on crisis management within business organizations. That's where I turned first. The titles were intriguing, even promising: *What Were They Thinking? Crisis Communication – The Good, the Bad and the Totally Clueless*; "Crisis Communication: Lessons from 9/11"; "Healthy Leadership during Organizational Crisis"; *Crisis Proofing: How to Save Your Company from Disaster*; *When It Hits the Fan: Managing the Nine Crises of Business*; *Why Some Companies Emerge Stronger and Better from a Crisis: Seven Essential Lessons for Surviving Disaster*; and *Transforming the Crisis-Prone Organization: Preventing Individual, Organizational, and Environmental Tragedies* among them.[3] This body of work held out promise that the overlapping dynamics of crisis and leadership were discoverable and could be codified in a way that would direct more effective responses in the future. It was, as it turned out, a largely unfulfilled promise.

Don't get me wrong. There are plenty of lessons to be learned and advice to be considered in that reading. But on a conceptual level, I was

---

[3] Steve Adubato, *What Were They Thinking? Crisis Communication – The Good, the Bad and the Totally Clueless* (New Brunswick: Rutgers University Press, 2008); Paul Argenti, "Crisis Communication: Lessons from 9/11," *Harvard Business Review* 80 (2002), 103–119; Joseph Grant and David Mack, "Healthy Leadership during Organizational Crisis," *Organizational Dynamics* 33 (2004), 409–425; Tony Jacques, *Crisis Proofing: How to Save Your Company from Disaster* (New York: Oxford University Press, 2017); Gerald Meyers with John Holusha, *When It Hits the Fan: Managing the Nine Crises of Business* (Boston: Houghton Mifflin, 1986); Ian Mitroff, *Why Some Companies Emerge Stronger and Better from a Crisis: Seven Essential Lessons for Surviving Disaster* (New York: American Management Association, 2005); Thierry Pauchant and Ian Mitroff, *Transforming the Crisis-Prone Organization: Preventing Individual, Organizational, and Environmental Tragedies* (San Francisco: Jossey-Bass, 1992).

disappointed. There was a noticeable lack of critical analysis, and little acknowledgment that crises could be claimed by various leaders for their own purposes. The lessons being offered in the crisis management literature were almost entirely tactical ones: crises could be managed by communicating constantly and positively to all stakeholders, planning ahead, facing facts, being prepared to make tough decisions, paying attention to your employees, and so on. Sound advice? Perhaps. But what about the nature of the claim itself?

I was, of course, aware of a number of what might be thought of as meta-theories of crises: explanations offered as to how and why urgency becomes a regular disturbance in human affairs. Perhaps the best thought-out meta-theory of crisis comes from Karl Marx and subsequent Marxist economists who posited a law for capitalist economies – the "tendency of the rate of profit to fall" – as a prelude to inevitable decline.[4]

Another well-known meta-theory is attributable to sociologist Charles Perrow. Focused more specifically on "high-risk technologies" than on the economic system in which those technologies were embedded, Perrow noted how complex, tightly coupled components of a technological system rendered crises – or, to use his term, system "accidents" – normal.[5]

As radically different as they were, Marx and Perrow both offered meta-theories of the dynamics of urgency. They were, in other words, not simply offering a hypothesis on a particular situation of urgency – say, the failure of a bank or the meltdown of a nuclear power plant – but a broader notion of why urgent situations are inherent in the institutions that govern and shape the human condition.

People, a number of thinkers have suggested, may well carry in their very being a propensity toward crisis. Sigmund Freud, for instance, suggested an ongoing tension between a primal need for a strong father figure and a tendency to become overly dependent on and subservient to that same figure. Sociologist Howard Becker posited another such tension: between "Us" and the "Other." Anthropologist Ernest Becker pointed to a universal human "terror of death" as the constant driver of a desperate search for meaning. Existential philosophers, Jean-Paul Sartre in particular, found in that acknowledgment

---

[4] Michael Heinrich, "Crisis Theory, the Law of the Tendency of the Profit Rate to Fall, and Marx's Studies in the 1870s," *Monthly Review* 64 (2013), 15–31.
[5] Charles Perrow, *Normal Accidents* (New York: Basic Books, 1984), p. 3.

of death's certainty a source of constant absurdity inherent in the act of living.[6]

My intended focus, however, was on the micro-dynamics of claims making: how particular leaders in specific circumstances called on the dynamics of crisis, to what end, and to what effect. My original academic training is as a historian, so I examined how historians dealt with crisis.

No surprise here, historians adopted a far broader view than what is on offer from crisis management experts. Now, the titles – *The Crisis of Multiculturalism in Europe*; *The Cuban Missile Crisis*; *The Crisis of German Ideology*; *A Nation Forged in Crisis*; and *The Origins of the Urban Crisis* among them – make clear the value of a long view.[7] Management writers are often trapped by a presentist assumption that "now" – whatever "now" they are writing in – is a uniquely uncertain time besieged by crises that dwarf anything that people experienced in the past. Historians help us understand why this assumption is nonsense.

Claims of crises have been with us forever. Urgent dynamics are not the special province of any one age or place. No time is more or less prone to urgent contingencies compared with any other. All communities at all times experience "humor, and art, and passion, and love, and tenderness, and sex," noted historian Jill Lapore, along with "fear, and terror, and the sublime, and cruelty."[8] To assume otherwise is sheer folly.

In past research, I worked with the philosophy of time literature.[9] That work helps explain why the present – anyone's present at any point in history – is experienced as confounding and unsettling with myriad opportunities for claims of urgency. When it comes to the way people

---

[6] I discussed Freud's cautionary exploration of paternal leadership in Spector, "Carlyle, Freud, and the Great Man Theory More Fully Considered," *Leadership* 12 (2015), 250–260. See also Ernest Becker, *The Denial of Death* (New York: Free Press, 1997); Howard Becker, *Outsiders: Studies in the Sociology of Deviance* (New York: Free Press, 1973); Jean-Paul Sartre, *Being and Nothingness: An Essay on Phenomenological Ontology* (New York: Washington Square Press, 1943/1966).

[7] Rita Chin, *The Crisis of Multiculturalism in Europe* (Princeton: Princeton University Press, 2017); Alice George, *The Cuban Missile Crisis: The Threshold of Nuclear War* (New York: Routledge, 2013); George Mosse, *The Crisis of German Ideology: Intellectual Origins of the Third Reich* (New York: Grosset & Dunlap, 1964); Jay Sexton, *A Nation Forged in Crisis: A New American History* (New York: Basic Books, 2018); Thomas Sugrue, *The Origins of the Urban Crisis: Race and Inequality in Postwar Detroit* (Princeton: Princeton University Press, 1996).

[8] Quoted in Alex Carp, "History for a Post-Fact America," *NYR Daily* (October 19, 2018).

[9] Bert Spector, "Using History Ahistorically: Presentism and the Tranquility Fallacy," *Management & Organizational History* 9 (2014), 305–313.

experience time, the present is always at an extreme disadvantage, particularly relative to either the past or the future.[10] The present is experienced in all its complex, turbulent, and troubling dynamics. The past, conversely, is remembered. It was experienced when it was the present, but now it is remembered.

Caught up in a confounding present, facing an uncertain future, and looking back on a past filtered through memory and nostalgia, people *always* find their present time to be one of disorienting turbulence. Urgent dynamics are not the special province of any one age or place. No era is more or less prone to urgent events compared with any other.

It is precisely the inevitable disorientation of a complex present – anybody's present at any time in any place – that is mistakenly called upon by crisis experts as evidence of a uniquely turbulent present. The present *is* turbulent. That reality, however, is not unique. So were past "presents." This historical-philosophical rejection of presentism shapes my approach to crises.

As I moved from philosophers of time to political scientists, especially those who explored state leaders, US presidents among them, I learned how these scholars identified patterns of leaders using claims of crisis for a specific purpose. In particular, it is noted that political leaders leverage crises to advance an agenda: to support entering a war or avoiding one, for instance.

Sociologists working in the fields of knowledge, social problems, and criminology focus on a claims-making process, always sensitive to the exercise of power and the assertion of interests inherent in that process of staking a claim. Management theorists have noted the role of leaders in making sense of a confusing world to their organizational stakeholders. Discourse experts pay attention to the role of rhetoric in asserting meaning. Philosophers consider ontological questions dealing with the nature of being. Experts studying narrative theory pay heed to the structural underpinnings of storytelling employed to attract and appeal to an audience. Mathematicians seek to identify a rigorous application of the notion of plausibility in constructing an argument. Psychologists look into the belief formation process, often joining cognitive scientists

---

[10] My philosophical guides on time are John Bigelow, "Presentism and Properties," *Philosophical Perspectives* 10 (1966), 35–52; Roderick Chisholm, "Referring to Things That No Longer Exist," *Philosophical Perspectives* 4 (1990), 545–556; Neil McKinnon and John Bigelow, "Presentism, and Speaking of the Dead," *Philosophical Studies* 160 (2012), 253–263; Francesco Orillia, "Dynamic Events and Presentism," *Philosophical Studies* 160 (2012), 407–414.

in seeking to explain why people may believe misleading or inaccurate claims.

By integrating these multiple streams – and *Constructing Crisis* is explicitly cross-disciplinary – I was able to derive the hypothesis that there is no such thing as a crisis. To state the argument with more fullness, I developed four propositions:

1. *A crisis is not a corporeal thing. It is rather a claim constructed by a leader from a position of power and influence and intended to shape the understanding of others.*
2. *The construction of a claim of urgency by a leader does not mean that it is necessarily legitimate; a claim may be legitimate, or it may not be.*
3. *The construction of a claim of urgency, even if legitimate, is not determinate of how people decide whether to believe the claim. Factors external to the content of the claim always help shape belief formation.*
4. *Finally, all claims, regardless of their legitimacy and believability, are attempts to enhance the power and advance the interests of the claims maker.*

A crisis, in other words, is *not* a thing to be managed, *not* an objective threat to be responded to with a special form of heroic leadership. Crisis, rather, is a claim awaiting critical appraisal.

To advance these propositions, the arguments of *Constructing Crisis* will be laid out in the following manner: Chapter 1 introduces the conceptual infrastructure of *Constructing Crisis*. The argument throughout the text is offered as a critique of the field of crisis management rather than a criticism of any particular approach. As such, it aims to reshape the way people think about crises and crisis leadership and to influence their response to various claims of urgency.

Chapter 2 analyzes the process by which crises came to be constructed as objective events, calling on the notion of reification to explore the human tendency to translate ideas, concepts, and beliefs into physical entities. Crises aren't things, but we usually think of them as such.

A big part of why we think of crises as things is that there is a crisis management industry constantly promoting that reification. Chapter 3 focuses attention on that industry as the conceptual carrier of the idea that crises are, in fact, things. By adopting uncritically that reified notion of crisis, a professional field of experts has emerged to help organizations and other social units manage through a crisis situation. Leaders are seen as the key respondents to objectively real crisis situations: planning, communicating to employees and external stakeholders, and learning from experienced experts.

The goal of *Constructing Crisis* is not simply to critique the existing dominant model of crises – what I call the "crisis-as-event model" – but to offer an alternative model. Chapter 4 begins the process of building that alternative conceptual model – what I label the "crisis-as-claim model" – by visiting the theories and thinkers who have provided a conceptual foundation for my interpretive effort.

Rather than evaluating events – what type of crises are they? – the crisis-as-claim model advocates for sorting claims of urgency. Chapter 5 offers a classification system in the form of a typology for doing just that. The assertion of urgency by a leader is not taken as per se evidence of legitimacy of the claim. But what are the appropriate criteria for evaluation?

Claims may be legitimate or not. They may be believed or not. Chapter 6 takes the position that those two processes – determining legitimacy and forming beliefs – are not the same. The content of a claim influences belief. It is not, however, decisive. Post-truth claims come under special scrutiny in this chapter.

Claims of urgency come embedded within a story constructed by a leader. Chapter 7 introduces the construct of narrative, noting how narrative structure serves to make a claim compelling to its intended audience. Leaders create a crisis narrative that serves a purpose. It informs the audience: here is how *I* would like *you* to understand the crisis that *I* am asserting. Narratives are constructed to amplify that intended purpose.

The crisis-as-event model positions crises in the negative: as threats to be avoided if possible and minimized when necessary. Chapter 8 ventures even further afield from that traditional approach and suggests an alternative narrative in which a claim of urgency is framed as an opportunity for liberation and an enabler of progress. Rather than navigating their units *through* crisis, some leaders consciously lead their units *to* crisis to serve a higher purpose.

Chapter 9 makes an accounting of leaders as claims makers. Rather than divvying up leaders into effective and ineffective crises managers, the chapter suggests that all leaders, effective or otherwise, follow a recognizable pattern.

How and why does the formation of alternative conceptual models matter? Chapter 10 concludes my analysis by addressing that question directly. Special analytic attention will be paid to the significance of appreciating how an understanding of crises impacts the behaviors of both leaders and followers. The chapter ends with a bottom-line assessment of the implications of adopting a new crisis model.

As a reflection of my micro-theoretical focus on the dynamics of claims making in situations of urgency, I build my chapters on case studies. Starting with Chapter 2, I offer a detailed presentation of a particular situation at the beginning of the chapter, followed by numerous specific examples throughout. To be clear, I do not offer these instances as empirical proof of *anything*. They are intended only as illustrations that, I hope, are helpful in following my reasoning. *Constructing Crisis* is *not* intended as an empirical work. My goal is not to prove something. It is, rather, to provoke thought.

I take full ownership of the argument presented here. At the same time, I am greatly appreciative for all the help and guidance I have received. Let me start my acknowledgments with my colleagues from the Northeastern University community: Nick Athanassiou, Ellie Banalieva, Allan Bird, Paula Caligiuri, Mark Huselid, Maureen Kelleher, Jamie Ladge, Anna Lamin, Harry Lane, Valentina Marano, Jeanne McNett, Dennis Shaughnessy, and Alan Zaremba. For colleagues far and wide, thanks to Joanne Ciulla (Rutgers University), David Collinson (Lancaster University), Margaret Collinson (Lancaster University), Robert Freeland (University of Wisconsin), Keith Grint (University of Warwick), Andrew Kolodny (Brandeis University), Stephan Kozak (Springfield Clinic), Naomi Laventhal (University of Michigan), Albert Mills (Saint Mary's University), Fred Niederman (St. Louis University), José Santos (INSEAD), Andrew Shuman (University of Michigan), Kayte Spector-Bagdady (University of Michigan), Dennis Tourish (University of Sussex), Christian Vercler (University of Michigan), and Suze Wilson (Massey University).

Allow me to call out the above-and-beyond invaluable assistance of two people. Joel Best (University of Delaware) was my expert guide as I worked through the world of social constructionist theory. And Milorad Novicevic (University of Mississippi) was ever-ready with support, clarity, and a relevant citation or two. Thanks to both.

Erica Kleckner, the administrative assistant for the International Business and Strategy Group, was indispensable for helping me navigate the lingering mysteries of Word and Power Point. I am pleased to have worked with Lia Petronio, who helped design the book's graphics.

I also want to take the opportunity to acknowledge Bryan Keogh, my collaborative editor at *The Conversation*. Somehow, we managed to turn out essays ("don't call them blogs!") that have reached nearly half a million readers. I still find that amazing.

At Cambridge University Press, my great appreciation to both my original editor, Paula Parish, and my current editor, Valarie Appleby. There are a great many others, of course, who are involved in producing and marketing this book. I thank you all and want to tell you how pleased I am to be part of the Cambridge University Press team.

1   Undertaking a New Interpretive Effort

Constructing Crisis is about an idea, and that is the idea of crisis. What do we mean when we use or hear that term? What suggestions or thoughts are communicated when our leaders deploy the word? And how does that deployment impact the dynamics that unfold within our business organizations, our communities, and our societies?

Most usually, the idea of crisis conjures up images of threatening events, occurrences that present a serious risk. A business crisis, for instance, may take the form of a public revelation of maleficence on the part of key executives or flawed product design that led to injuries or deaths. Unwelcomed takeover bids and serious financial losses might also trigger what we refer to as a crisis. Will the business survive? In that way, we may understand crisis to be not just a risk but also an existential threat, placing the very future of the company in jeopardy.

We also understand the need to think about the possibility of crises that threaten our communities: an out-of-control wildfire racing toward our homes in California, or the devastating aftermath of a Category 5 hurricane on our island territory. Whole continents may come under threat in periods of great migration sparked by nature, perhaps, or war.

We may take a more conceptual approach to the idea of crisis. Perhaps it isn't a specific social unit or institution at risk. Crises, rather, may be seen as threatening to abstractions: democracy, the rule of law, liberal capitalism, even civilization itself. There is, even in such cases, an event – perhaps an accumulation of events – that is said to trigger the threat.

The variety of events prompted in our thoughts by the use of the term "crisis" is virtually endless. Acts of nature, acts of humans, and acts of humans in response to acts of nature can all generate a crisis, we think. So can system breakdowns, global dynamics, and economic downturns. In all their variety, however, the idea of crisis suggests events that objectively and undeniably pose a threat.[1]

---

[1] The idea of crisis can also be deployed in a more individualistic sense: mid-life crises, identity crises, developmental crises, anxiety crises, and the like. *Constructing Crisis* will not be examining the use and implications of the idea at this level.

Our common notion of what is meant by the idea of crisis carries our thought process even further. We are convinced, for example, that we live in a time – right here and right now – that is especially, even uniquely prone to these types of traumatic upheavals. And as we are buffered by these seemingly endless disruptions, we expect our leaders to step up, navigate the tumult, and help ensure that we emerge, once the crisis has passed, stronger and more resilient than ever. It is precisely this capacity to navigate through crisis, in fact, that we suppose separates the great leaders from the middling or incompetent ones. Leadership, *great* leadership, is forged in crisis.

When crisis hits, those of us who are not leaders have a role to play as well. We rally together, following those heroic leaders as well as responding as a community. We know that not everyone will go along, get on board, and pull together. When US presidents declare a state of war – for example, the country has been attacked and must respond – we tend to respond with support; national unity; and, let's admit it, more than a bit of intolerance for naysayers.[2] And when the CEO of our corporation insists on the need for an urgent response to a threatening situation, employees receive the message loudly and clearly: it's time to join together. Business organizations aren't democracies, after all, so for employees who are not willing to contribute to the leader-defined crisis response, perhaps they should consider leaving. Get on the bus or get off.

It is a powerful idea, in other words, this idea of crisis. The explicit intention of *Constructing Crisis* is to upend these ideas, each and every one of them. Crises are no more, or less, frequent now than at any other historical moment. Crises are not events. Events have no objective meaning. Leadership is not something that is forged in response to crisis. And the leader-follower dynamic that unfolds in the face of crises declarations can be unhealthy, even potentially dangerous.

It's an argument built on a single assumption, that ideas have consequences. How we conceptualize a subject influences how we react and behave in relation to that subject. Given that the proposition that ideas have consequences has become the major theme of my work, it is worth exploring just how it is that ideas generally come to matter. And given that I am offering a new interpretive effort of the idea of crisis, it is also worth asking "how and why might such a reinterpretation of an idea so old and often examined as crisis have value?"

---

[2] It is true that the US Constitution reserves the right to declare war to the Congress, not the president. But as Michael Beschloss has shown, that provision is more often violated than heeded. See Beschloss, *Presidents of War* (New York: Crown, 2018).

In a culture and context in which empiricism is expected and application is preferred to interpretation – that is, the context in which I work at the contemporary university and, with even greater emphasis, at a professional school of management – the governing norm is that ideas should either be grounded in data or have immediate utility. Preferably both. Otherwise, who cares?[3]

And yet, the undertaking of *Constructing Crisis* is not grounded in data. Nor does it offer any suggestions for how to apply in an immediate way lessons to practice. So again, why should anyone care?

Just to be clear, what I am presenting here is a new interpretative effort of the idea of crisis, one that intends to upend traditional notions of a crisis and of the role played by leaders in responding to urgent situations. In doing so, my goal is *not* to offer immediate utility. I do not provide a deep dive into some big database or offer a "new-and-improved" how-to formula to help leaders negotiate urgent situations. Yet, I still insist that, yes, ideas have consequences and matter to both other scholars and practitioners.

This is, I realize, a suspicious posture to assume. Why bother, for instance, with an idea that doesn't directly, even immediately impact practice? Just asking that question reflects a current that runs deeply throughout American thought: an ideology of usefulness.[4]

The Ideology of Usefulness

Consequences and usefulness are not precisely the same notions. Consequences may be long term and indirect, with no immediate or obvious payoff. Certainly, consequences are not necessarily positive. Usefulness, on the other hand, speaks to a far more utilitarian impulse, the desire to apply thought directly to action, to make an immediate difference in practice. That difference is assumed to be positive: to repair a damaged image and to help improve performance at the individual and/ or collective level.

A utilitarian impulse, although not confined to any one culture or single country, has deep and significant roots in American thought. It is a belief system that evolved within a specific temporal and historical context, so it is important to appreciate the interplay between that context and that belief system.

[3] Murray S. Davis, "That's Interesting! Towards a Phenomenology of Sociology and a Sociology of Phenomenology," *Philosophy of Social Sciences* 1 (1971), 311.
[4] The term is from Alvin Gouldner, *The Coming Crisis of Western Sociology* (New York: Basic Books, 1970).

All too often, we take widespread and generally accepted constructs for granted, mistaking historically influenced assumptions for commonsense wisdom, or even more problematically as the "truth." To sidestep that trap, I visit the historical forces that both shaped and amplified that profound preference for the "useful" over the "useless."

The Dominance of Practicality

A doctrine of practicality runs deep and wide through American culture, a conviction forged on the western frontier and in the pervasive mythology that shaped Americans' understanding of that frontier experience. The land that lay beyond settled America helped mold not just a country but also that country's mythology. Frontier settlers engaged in a process of "perennial rebirth" as they moved westward.[5] That was the observation of Frederick Jackson Turner, the prominent frontier historian and popularizer (although not necessarily the originator) of the American frontier myth.

Myths are stories intended to help explain the world and the human condition within that world. They may be accurate, but not necessarily. Turner's frontier myth, though highly distorted as history, communicated how entry into and settlement of the frontier became the ever-unfolding origin story of eighteenth- and nineteenth-century America and its prevailing culture. The myth went like this. The vulnerability of settlers within the wilderness demanded an immediate response from them. And they were nothing if not practical, these hardy settlers. On the frontier, the guiding question was "what works?" With self-constructed implements, the pioneer emerged as a crude farmer, clearing and fencing in land, building a home with available materials, and raising enough crops to allow for subsistence. These folks did what was necessary, nothing more or less.

Pioneer ideals focused not on what settlers *should* do (that is, normative values), but on what they *could* do (that is, practical lessons) to survive and thrive. Past traditions and previously formed heuristics were abandoned. In shedding old concepts and adapting to new realities, the frontier myth insisted, pioneers created a new country. In that way, the practical nature of a unique and exceptional American character was formed at the juncture of settlement and wilderness.

The idea that settlers left all mental baggage behind when they crossed the Mississippi River is, of course, a myth laden with much

---

[5] Frederick Jackson Turner, *The Frontier in American History* (New York: H. Holt, 1920), p. 2.

distortion.[6] As white Americans set a westward course, their preestablished beliefs and values persisted.[7] While aspiring to expand the empire ever westward, Americans maintained an abiding belief in the innocence of their project.[8] They were not conquerors, they believed; rather, settlers were taking advantage of opportunities for self and national improvement. And it was that belief that erected a profound blindness to some not-so-innocent realities. Westward settlement involved more than improvement and opportunity. It inherently required the trespassing on and ruin of occupied land and established institutions and led to the deaths of more than 50 million indigenous people, chiefly through the spread of diseases carried by those pioneers to an unprotected population.[9]

Building empire by ever-westward expansion necessitated violent conquest, in particular, white conquest over Native Americans and Mexicans. Far from adapting to the "new" land, American settlers imposed upon it racial, ethnic, and gendered assumptions. Those prejudices significantly reduced contact with the native population that might have produced wise practical advice for survival based on generations of experience. Rather than shedding ideology and embracing unencumbered practicality, American pioneers carried predetermined views concerning how the world should work.[10] And yet, the myth persisted. Americans accepted the curated narrative of western settlement and, with it, adopted practicality as a foundational principle.

An Undercurrent of Anti-intellectualism

In that adoption of the myth of frontier utilitarianism, it is possible to locate a residue of anti-intellectualism. The ideology of usefulness conveyed a disposition to suspect and resent the output of an active but not immediately practical mind.[11]

---

[6] I am using the Mississippi only metaphorically here. Well before the 1820s, the frontier consisted of lands east of the Mississippi: the Berkshire Mountains, Atlantic tidewaters, Shenandoah Valley, and Mohawk River, for example.

[7] Patricia Limerick, *The Legacy of Conquest: Unbroken Past of the American West* (New York: Norton, 1987), p. 36.

[8] Paul Frymer, *Building an American Empire: The Era of Territorial and Political Expansion* (Princeton: Princeton University Press, 2017), p. 1.

[9] Jill Lepore, *These Truths: A History of the United States* (New York: Norton, 2018).

[10] Richard Slotkin, *Regeneration through Violence: The Mythology of the American Frontier, 1600–1860* (Middletown: Wesleyan University Press, 1973); Margaret Walsh, "Women's Place on the American Frontier," *Journal of American Studies* 29 (1995), 241–255.

[11] Richard Hofstadter, *Anti-Intellectualism in American Life* (New York: Knopf, 1966).

Consider this oration delivered at Yale in 1884 where undergraduates were told,

The age of *philosophy* has passed and left few memorials of its existence. That of *glory* has vanished, and nothing but a painful tradition of human suffering remains. That of *utility* has commenced, and it requires little warmth of imagination to anticipate for its rein lasting as time, and radiant with wonders of unveiled nature.[12]

In the main, Americans took their stand with utility and its proclaimed radiant wonders rather than with fanciful ideas whose practical usefulness was not readily apparent.

Glorification of utility hardened over time into "unreflective instrumentalism": a devaluation of thought, or at least any forms of thought "that do not promise relatively immediate practice payoffs."[13] Pervasive instrumentality worked to erode any passion for critical reflection on the ends to which useful actions were aiming. That thinking seeped into institutions of higher learning as well.

Universities and the Embrace of Utilitarianism

In their continuous need to subdue the wilderness, American settlers relied on the "school of experience."[14] A popular frontier maxim – "Any fool can put on his coat better than a wise man can do it for him" – captured a fundamental unease with educated and detached wisdom. In their desire to be taken as something other than remote cloisters of wise people with little to add to the pursuit of daily life, American universities adapted.[15]

Although often denounced as elitist institutions that functioned in ivory-tower isolation from the "real world" – crossword puzzle clue: "place removed from reality," answer: "ivory tower" – universities became carriers of the same ideological bias for useable truth and against useless imagining that defined the broader culture.[16] That was a trend most prevalent at professional schools such as business colleges attached to universities, but it was also apparent in liberal arts and humanities

---

[12] Ibid., 239.

[13] Daniel Rigney, "Three Kinds of Anti-Intellectualism: Rethinking Hofstadter," *Sociological Inquiry* 61 (1991), 444.

[14] Turner, *Frontier in American History*, 271.

[15] This was a trend that worried Turner. The university must be allowed to be "left free . . . to explore new regions and to report what they find; for like the pioneers, they have the ideal of investigation, they seek new horizons" (Ibid., 287).

[16] That clue and answer appeared in the *USA Today* daily crossword of September 9, 2018.

departments that proclaimed their connections to and support of the national economy.[17] The ideology of usefulness triumphed.

Usefulness expected "applied research" intended to address and solve real-world problems. This is research that, by definition, seeks to improve an existing system. To be sure, applied research can and does offer possibilities for advancement in how diseases are treated, for instance, or how to better measure transaction costs across firm boundaries. It is *not* designed to question the system itself.

"Flights of imagination" that might provide researchers with a less embedded view of systems and practices do not sit comfortably within the applied research paradigm.[18] The work of imagining intends to undermine accepted reality and create counter-narratives. That's what imagining does. Yet, American universities created a climate where such acts were largely marginalized.

It should be no surprise, really, that utilitarianism came to dominate the culture of American universities. Business titans provided the lion's share of university endowments. Nineteenth-century tycoons including Cyrus H. McCormick, John D. Rockefeller, and Marshall Field "took a particular interest in higher education."[19] The end game of a university education bent toward teaching the skills that would repay corporate generosity and help develop the future in a way that supported industrial growth.[20]

In the period roughly spanning 1870 to 1930, academic leaders fundamentally reorganized their institutions to promise upper- and upper-middle-class families that their children, mainly sons, would be well trained for entry into the world of commerce.[21] To enhance the appeal of college life to the "sons of wealth" as well as their (it was surely hoped) philanthropically inclined parents, the university experience was

---

[17] Alan Hughes et al., *Hidden Connections: Knowledge Exchange Between the Arts and Humanities and the Private, Public, and Third Sectors* (Cambridge: Arts & Humanities Research Council, 2011). I purposefully provided this citation – a survey of British universities – to suggest that the turn toward usefulness even among liberal arts schools is hardly unique to the United States.

[18] Rigney, "Three Kinds of Anti-Intellectualism"; Nils Roll-Hansen, *Why the Distinction between Basic (Theoretical) and Applied (Practical) Research Is Important in the Politics of Science* (London: London School of Economics, 2009).

[19] Daniel Wren, "American Business Philanthropy and Higher Education in the Nineteenth Century," *Business History Review* 57 (1983), 324.

[20] Henry Giroux, *The University in Chains: Confronting the Military-Industrial-Academic Complex* (Boulder: Paradigm Publishers, 2007); Mark Learmonth et al., "Promoting Scholarship that Matters: The Uselessness of Useful Research and the Usefulness of Useless Research," *British Journal of Management* 23 (2011), 35–44; James March, "A Scholar's Quest," *Journal of Management Inquiry* 20 (2011), 355–357.

[21] Harold Wechsler, *The Qualified Student: A History of Selective College Admission in America* (New York: John Wiley & Sons, 1977).

reshaped to be "more athletic, more masculine, and more fun."[22] The sciences and the professions would be counted on to supplement classic studies associated with a traditional university education to fulfil the mission co-defined by business sponsors and willing administrators.

Writing in the late 1960s, Alvin Gouldner worried that utilitarianism had begun to erode the space allocated to less obviously pragmatic roads of academic inquiry. It was his concern that the ideology of the useful would do more than find a place within the academy; it would drive out more abstract theorizing that provoked his warning of a "coming crisis." And it was not, in Gouldner's telling, a new or even uniquely American phenomenon.

Taking a broader view than Turner's frontier thesis, Gouldner traced the ideology of usefulness back to the eighteenth-century overthrow of aristocratic privileges in Western Europe. "With the growing influence of the middle class in the eighteenth century," Gouldner wrote, "utility emerged as a dominant social standard."[23] And, to be fair, there was much to celebrate in the glorification of middle-class achievement over aristocratic privilege that marked this transformation.

The rise of a European middle class brought with it an assumption that society's rewards should be allocated not "on the basis of birth or of inherited social identity," observed Gouldner, "but on the basis of talent and energy manifested in individual achievement."[24] Usefulness became more than a philosophy. It was a value system: a deeply entrenched notion, reinforced by a newly emergent middle-class culture, of what *ought* to be. What individuals accomplished rather than their parental lineage became the central tenet for judgment. Utility "became a claim to respect rather than merely a basis for begrudging tolerance," Gouldner noted.[25]

Looked at with the perspective of the eighteenth-century middle class, usefulness represented a liberation from aristocratic privilege. But there was – and is – a rub. "In focusing public interest on the usefulness of the individual," worried Gouldner, the emerging ideology favored "a side of his life that had significance not in its personal uniqueness but only in its comparability, its inferior or superior usefulness, to others."[26] This would inevitably result in a contest over who was *more* and, by implication if not explicit condemnation, *less* useful.

Any tournament that seeks to separate winners from losers must have some metric, some ribbon to be burst through at the end point of

[22] Mitchell Stevens, *Creating a Class: College Admissions and the Education of Elites* (Cambridge, MA: Harvard University Press, 2007), p. 248.
[23] Gouldner, *The Coming Crisis of Western Sociology*, 61.   [24] Ibid., 63.   [25] Ibid., 62.
[26] Ibid., 64.

the race. There could be no capacity to construct measures unless and until "usefulness" was defined. But defining use*ful*ness leads to a residual construct, one that identifies use*less*ness as its counterpart. Fortunately, we have folks who are willing to do the hard work of identifying uselessness for us.

Take the Golden Fleece awards. Between 1975 and 1988, William Proxmire, the Democratic senator from Wisconsin, presented monthly "awards" – really nothing more than acts of public humiliation – to government-funded university professors said to be conducting useless research at taxpayer expense.[27] Projects investigating emotions, the relationship between sexual arousal and marijuana use, and prisoners' motivation to escape were among the many singled out for ridicule. A renowned behavioral scientist studying biological causes of aggression sued Proxmire for damages (and won) after being mocked for researching "why rats, monkeys, and humans clench their jaws."[28] The jeering continued for thirteen years, a testament to the powerful appeal of identifying useless activities unfolding in the ranks of university researchers.

Beyond the inane posturing of a politician, definitions of "useful" and "useless" must be amenable to some sort of comparative assessment that allows for differentiation. If the definition of usefulness is measurable – show me how you improve individual income, overall productivity, streams of innovation, and so on – so much the better. The Obama administration supported a measure of university educational effectiveness that calculated the relationship between the cost of a college degree and the impact on future earnings of each student.[29] What could be more useful than an improved return on investment?

The "B" School Experience

Professional schools of business management, which appeared in the United States concurrent with the emergence of a managerial tier asserting itself between "worker" and "owner," bought enthusiastically and unapologetically into the ideology of usefulness.[30] In the early days, experienced executives taught business school classes: "good ole boys" who dispensed "war stories, cracker barrel wisdom, and the occasional

---

[27] Occasional awards went to government agencies said to be engaged in wasteful spending unrelated to university research.

[28] Robert Irion, "What Proxmire's Golden Fleece Did for and to Science," *The Scientist* (December 12, 1988).

[29] Kelly Field, "Obama Plan to Tie Student Aid to College Ratings Draws Mixed Reviews," *Chronicle of Higher Education* (August 22, 2013). These recommendations were not implemented.

[30] Martin Parker, *Shut Down the Business School* (London: Pluto Press, 2018).

practical pointer."[31] Even when appended to elite, rarefied Ivy League universities – Dartmouth, the University of Pennsylvania, and Harvard initially in the United States – business colleges operated as sanctified trade schools, emphasizing the transference of competencies and skills.

Early pioneers of management theory – Frederick Winslow Taylor, Mary Parker Follet, and Elton Mayo among them – sought to "solve any problems companies and administrative organizations might possibly have."[32] They and their students were meant to be organizational doctors, tending to the health and well-being of their institutional patients. That was the assumed payoff of their applied research: helping practitioners solve real-world problems with their specialized knowledge.

Academics at business schools can and often do act as consultants to business. Oxford University provides a helpful Internet portal that invites outsiders to seek out "experts from all disciplines" who are "available to work with you as consultants through Consulting Services at Oxford University Innovation. We also have specialized consultancy services in statistics and museums and collections, as well as free student and researcher consultancy services."[33] See, even an institution as esteemed as Oxford generates useful knowledge that can be applied to practice.

There is a perfectly legitimate *raison d'être* for applying knowledge to practice: to "provide solutions to problems that are presented to us, or to legitimate solutions that have already been reached."[34] I'm quoting here from Michael Burrawoy, who added that the academic expert can and should supply "true and tested methods" and even conceptual frameworks as a way of orienting thought and legitimizing conclusions. It is a relationship that can be enacted with rigorous attention to constructed knowledge, awareness of prevailing theories, and personal (and interpersonal) integrity.

It is, however, an engagement that unfolds within parameters defined by the client. The end game of applied research and collaborative engagement is to improve organizational performance.[35] The implicit foundations of both parties as well as their relationship are not scrutinized, critiqued, or reconceptualized. Performance is defined by the organization and its agents, a definition that is not up for debate and amendment.

---

[31] Warren Bennis and James O'Toole, "How Business Schools Lost Their Way," *Harvard Business Review* 83 (2005), 98.

[32] Barbara Czarniawska, *Writing Management: Organization Theory as a Literary Genre* (Oxford: Oxford University Press, 1999), p. 3.

[33] www.ox.ac.uk/research/innovation-and-partnership/expertise-and-knowledge/find-academic-consultant?wssl=1.

[34] Michael Burawoy, "For Public Sociology," *American Sociological Review* 70 (2005), 9.

[35] André Spicer et al., "Critical Performativity: The Unfinished Business of Critical Management Studies," *Human Relations* 62 (2009), 537–560.

Perhaps more troubling than that, certainly from the perspective of working to build an academic career, direct engagement with practitioners is not likely to help construct a case for tenure.

From Organizational Doctor to Rigorous Scientist

Chaffing against the early trade school image, mid-twentieth-century business schools sought to embrace academic respectability, an adaptation imposed in strong measure by university-wide tenure and promotion (T&P) committees. Those committees were dominated by faculty from "across the river" in a literal sense at the Harvard Business School and a metaphorical sense elsewhere. The social and hard scientists on T&P committees imposed academic rigor and counted elite publications as the currency of career advancement. Harvard University President Derek Bok issued an especially stinging rebuke of the Harvard Business School in his 1979 annual report, demanding that professors there devote increased attention to rigorous research.[36]

As a response to this intense pressure, usefulness needed to be redefined. Rather than thinking of utility in terms of training practitioners to "do" management better, T&P committees found an alternative measure. The value of business school professors would be established by positivist social science and measured by publications in elite "A" list journals and citations in equally prestigious academic work. These were the criteria applied first to the hard sciences and then to the emerging social sciences. Now, business school researchers could demonstrate their merit "by making small twists on existing academic theory or empirical work, or trying to find 'gaps' in the literature that can be readily resolved conceptually or empirically."[37] Reliance on "large, survey-based data sets and hypothetico-deductive research" – that is, research that starts with a hypothesis that is amenable to either verification or falsification through the application of data – became the defining characteristics of academic rigor.[38] The researcher has no particular commitment to any outcome save one that can be demonstrated quantitatively.[39]

---

[36] Larry Kramer, "Harvard Fights Fiercely Over the Business School," *Washington Post* (June 8, 1979); Duff McDonald, *The Golden Passport: Harvard Business School, the Limits of Capitalism, and the Moral Failure of the MBA Elite* (New York: Harper Business, 2017).

[37] Sandra Waddock, *Intellectual Shamans: Management Academics Making a Difference* (Cambridge: Cambridge University Press, 2015), p. 274.

[38] Sverre Spoelstra and Peter Svensson, "Critical Performativity: The Happy End of Critical Management Studies?" in *The Routledge Companion to Critical Management Studies* (London: Routledge, 2016), p. 70.

[39] There is evidence that positive empirical results – that is, results supporting an earlier hypothesis – are far more likely to be published by elite journals than negative results

Academic "rigor" – the need to be "precise and thorough in the development of the theory, in the design and execution of the study, and in reporting the results and drawing implications" – is, of course, vital to the functioning of university research.[40] There should be no reason to choose between research that generates hypotheses and research that meticulously tests those hypotheses. Big data analysis offers new approaches to understanding the world, from helping online dating sites engineer better matches to allowing public health agencies to identify and react quickly to emergent trends. Empirical research represents the final steps of the theory-building process, converting propositions into hypothesis with empirical indicators that can then be subjected to meticulous testing.[41]

The academic table should offer an honored seat to both imaginative conceptual work and rigorous empirical testing. The worry comes when empirical research is taken as a substitute for rather than a supplement to more conceptual pursuits. There will always be a requirement for new interpretative efforts. But there's that measurement system – publication in empirically, quantitatively oriented journals – that mitigates against engaging in flights of imagination.

Although the trend toward academic rigor was applauded by many, it was roundly denounced by others. Research was becoming something far less "relevant" to managers, these critics worried. "Instead of measuring themselves in terms of the competence of their graduates, or by how well their faculties understand important drivers of business performance," complained Warren Bennis and James O'Toole, "they measure themselves almost solely by the rigor of their scientific research."[42] That debate between applied and pure research, as intense as it often seemed, was more smoke and mirrors than substance.

In a utilitarian culture, the specific definition of usefulness can and will be contested; the underlying need to define and measure the useful and to separate out the useless is accepted. The ideology of usefulness may value ideas based on their capacity to contribute directly to practice improvement. It may, conversely, value a kind of empiricism that can be useful to fellow academic scholars in search of the best measurement

disproving earlier hypotheses. The hurdles for having negative results accepted by reviewers are simply higher. It is a publication bias that can lead to distortions in knowledge. See Y. A. de Vries et al., "The Cumulative Effect of Reporting and Citation Biases on the Apparent Efficacy of Treatments: The Case of Depression," *Psychological Medicine* 1–3 (2018), 1–3.

[40] That definition is from Devi Gnyawali and Yue Song, "Pursuit of Rigor in Research: Illustration from Coopetition Literature," *Industrial Marketing Management* 57 (2016), 12.

[41] Robert Dubin, *Theory Building* (New York: Free Press, 1978).

[42] Bennis and O'Toole, "How Business Schools Lost Their Way," 98.

instrumentation and experimental design. Either way, the trap is set. Research must be directly useful and applicable to someone. Otherwise, why bother?

To frame a response to the why bother question, I'll start with reference to a book by seventeenth-century German physician Johann Joachim Becker titled *Foolish Wisdom and Wise Foolishness*.[43] I take that title to contain a plea for rethinking definitions of the useful and the useless, opening up the possibility that what is labeled as "foolish" by some might, in fact, offer a path to wisdom.

A New Interpretive Effort

The idea that *Constructing Crisis* wants to consider is crisis, a concept both overused and much abused. The crisis label is overused in that it is applied indiscriminately. It is abused in that it is applied incorrectly. My argument is that traditional discourse on crisis gets the idea itself wrong.

This is not a criticism of the traditional approach to crisis. Criticism invokes an examination of a construct – say, a concept, text, or argument – through a consideration of its flaws and imperfections. I could criticize a book on crisis management, for instance, by insisting that the author somehow got the recommendations for how to respond to a crisis wrong. That would be criticism. Criticism can be valuable. Wise, practical counsel is important. It is not, however, what is on offer here.

What I propose instead is a critique of how crisis is conceptualized. Critique focuses not on the particulars of a construct but on the grounds upon which the construct is built.[44] In his 1781 *Critique of Pure Reason*, Immanuel Kant insisted that everything must be subjected to critique to ensure that no institution – especially but not exclusively a religious institution – reject fundamental scrutiny.[45]

By virtue of taking a position "at the edge of established knowledge," critique is inherently seditious of accepted wisdom.[46] *Constructing Crisis* offers critique with the goal of provoking a new interpretive effort

---

[43] The book, subtitled *Or a Hundred or So Political and Physical, Mercantile and Mechanistic Concepts and Propositions*, is referenced in Alfred Kieser, "Rhetoric and Myth in Management Fashion," *Organization* 4 (1997), 49–74.

[44] My definition of critique and its distinction from criticism comes from Barbara Johnson and Jacques Derrida as presented in Joan W. Scott, "History-writing as Critique," in *Manifestos for History* (London: Routledge, 2007), pp. 19–38.

[45] Sverre Raffnsøe, "What Is Critique? Critical Turns in the Age of Criticism," *Critical Practice Studies* 18 (2017), 28–60.

[46] The quote is from Raffnsøe, "What Is Critique?" 42.

concerning crisis. There will be no scripted journey intended to take leaders from the onset of a crisis event to a successful response, recovery, and improvement.[47] No solutions will be proposed, no best practices described so as to be emulated. Rather, an alternative model – a set of concepts and integrating propositions – will be offered built fundamentally on a set of ontological assumptions that veer sharply away from the traditional take on crises.[48]

Ontology of the New Model

What exists? What are those things that can be said to have material being, and what is excluded from that construction? These are the central problems that occupy the discipline of ontology.[49] There is a story told about two famed theoretical physicists, Albert Einstein and Niels Bohr, engaging in an ongoing debate about the question of objective reality. Einstein once asked Bohr if he really thought that if no one were looking at the moon, it would not exist. Einstein, a believer in objective reality, said he would like to think that it did. Bohr countered by insisting that if no one were looking at the moon, it would be difficult to prove that it existed.[50]

I come down firmly on the side of an objective reality: there is a moon regardless of whether anyone is looking at it. Nonetheless, I insist that ontology distinctions reside at the heart of both the dominant model of crisis and the reconstructed model presented here.

I want to be clear in what I mean to suggest, and what I mean not to suggest, in adopting an ontological viewpoint that crisis is not a *thing*. What I mean is captured by Alfred Lord Whitehead's notion of a thing as a "fact of concrete nature." To view crisis as a thing, we must assume that it can simply be observed as existing in the world within a finite duration of time and space apart from any interaction with or intervention by

---

[47] The term "scripted journeys" is taken from Keith Grint, *Management: A Sociological Introduction* (Cambridge: Polity Press, 1995).

[48] I take this definition of a conceptual model from Jo Rycroft-Malone and Tracey Bucknall. In that definition, "conceptual model" and "conceptual framework" are interchangeable. See Rycroft-Malone and Bucknall, "Theory, Frameworks, and Models Laying Down the Groundwork," in *Models and Frameworks for Implementing Evidence-Based Practice: Linking Evidence to Action* (Somerset: John Wiley, 2011), pp. 23–50.

[49] Dale Jacquette, *Ontology* (London: Routledge, 2002). Ontological questions quickly turn to metaphysics as a way of appreciating not just what is but also what "the most general features and relations of these things are." Thomas Hofweber "Logic and Ontology," *Stanford Encyclopedia of Philosophy* (2017).

[50] This story, and other slightly different versions, may be apocryphal. But a form of it is referenced by David Mermin, "Is the Moon There When Nobody Looks? Reality and Quantum Theory," *Physics Today* 38 (1985), 38–42.

human interpretation.[51] To reference the Einstein-Bohr debate, when crisis is taken to be a thing, it is thought of as made up of the same material realness as the moon. Crisis, like the moon, is a fact of concrete nature. It is *that* view of crisis that I will critique.

I do not mean to contest the existence of threatening, dangerous, or potentially calamitous contingencies. Of course there are such dynamics. But dynamics are not things.

Taking crisis to be a fact of concrete nature, a material thing, lies at the heart of the crisis-as-event model. A thing is something that "can be categorized, located in time and space, and given a name."[52] That notion that crisis fits the definition of a thing has become the "intellectual carrier" of the assumptions shared by crisis researchers and expert crisis consultants.[53]

My counter-assertion insists that rather than being a thing, crisis is a claim of urgency made by a leader. There is no real meaning to the dynamics of the world absent human interpretation. Facts never speak for themselves. This is the basis of the crisis-as-claim model.

"A theoretical model starts with things or variables, or (1) *units*, whose interactions constitute the subject matter of attention," wrote Robert Dubin. A model goes on to specify "the manner in which these units interact with each other, or (2) the *laws of interaction* among the units of the model."[54] Constructors of theoretical models always need to ask: what is the focal unit of analysis. Why build a model on this unit rather than that one?

The crisis-as-claim model shifts analysis away from the event and to the claim (Table 1.1). That shift allows analysis that surfaces the blind spots – say, the insufficient attention paid in traditional crisis analysis to power and control or the expression of interests embedded in each and every claim of urgency – in the crisis-as-event model.

I am not building the crisis-as-claim model from scratch. Far from it. Several decades ago, sociologists David Berliner and Bruce Biddle warned against "manufactured" crises generated by a sense of nostalgia and confusion about an idealized past and an uncertain present. The authors were analyzing a manufactured crisis of school inferiority in the United States compared with Japan. The critics of American schools and

---

[51] Alfred North Whitehead, *Science and the Modern World* (Cambridge: Cambridge University Press, 1925), pp. 64, 72.
[52] Robin Wagner-Pacifici, *What Is an Event?* (Chicago: University of Chicago Press, 2017), p. 1.
[53] The term "intellectual carrier" is from Mike Reed and Gibson Burrell, "Theory and Organization Studies: The Need for Contestation." *Organization Studies* (2019), 39–54.
[54] Dubin, *Theory Building*, 7–8.

Table 1.1 *Shifting the unit of analysis*

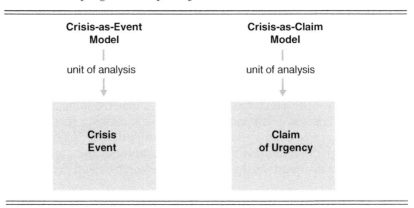

their lack of "competitiveness," argued the sociologists, were explicitly intending to deflect attention away from underlying problems of wealth distribution and inequality.[55] Communications scholars have adopted a social constructionist perspective to note that "crises are symbolic and subjective, not simply objective events" and that "what might be considered a crisis in one situation may not be considered a crisis in another."[56]

As these critiques suggest, the crisis-as-event model errs when it mistakes the content of claims for descriptions of objective truths. Crises are not things that await first being recognized and then being managed; they are claims that assert urgency, insisting that the social unit faces immediate and

[55] David Berliner and Bruce Biddle, *The Manufactured Crisis: Myths, Fraud, and the Attack on America's Public Schools* (Reading, MA: Addison-Wesley, 1995).

[56] Brenda Berkelaar and Mohan Dutta, "A Culture-Centered Approach to Crisis Communication," a paper presented at the annual meeting of the National Communication Association 93rd annual convention (2007). There is a steady stream of linguists and communications and discourse specialists who have tied social constructionism to claims of crisis. See Antoon De Rycker and M. D. Zuraidah, "Discourse in Crisis: Crisis in Discourse," in *Discourse and Crisis: Critical Perspectives* (Amsterdam: John Benjamins, 2013), pp. 3–65; Jesper Falkheimer and Mats Heide, "Multicultural Crisis Communication: Towards a Social Constructionist Perspective," *Journal of Contingencies and Crisis Management* 14 (2006), 180–189; Jesper Falkheimer and Mats Heide, "Crisis Communicators in Charge: From Plans to Improvisation," in *The Handbook of Crisis Communication* (Hoboken, NJ: Wiley-Blackwell, 2010), pp. 511–526; Keith Hearit and Jeffrey Courtright, "A Social Constructionist Approach to Crisis Management: Allegations of Sudden Acceleration in the Audi 5000," *Communication Studies* 54 (2003), 79–95; Loizos Heracleous, *Discourse, Interpretation, Organization* (Cambridge: Cambridge University Press, 2006); Dermot O'Reilly et al., "Introduction: Leadership in a Crisis-Constructing World," *Leadership* 11 (2015), 387–395; Richard Vatz, "The Myth of the Rhetorical Situation," *Philosophy & Rhetoric* 8 (1973), 154–161.

significant threat. The thing under analysis in the crisis-as-claim model is the claim itself.

So, we return to the observation that there is no such thing as a crisis. And yet we persist in thinking of crises as things: events that objectively pose real, even existential threats. That assumption is core to the crisis-as-event model. The critique offered through the crisis-as-claim model is that a crisis is not a thing. It is, rather, a label applied to a set of contingencies that may be confusing, complex, and ambiguous. To refer to these contingencies as crises requires an act of human intervention.

How and why did we come to think otherwise?

2 Crisis as a Reification of Urgency

When Stanford University's Larry Diamond worried about a "crisis in the liberal democratic order," he called attention to a "zeitgeist" in which "around the world, many democracies were hanging by a thread and aspiring autocrats were preparing more savage assaults on what remained of freedom."[1] Diamond's argument was powerful and, perhaps to some, persuasive.[2] But let's face it. Zeitgeist is not a thing, not a material object. Like its first cousin, culture, zeitgeist is a conceptual shortcut for offering an interpretation of a prevailing spirit or mood. Deploying the term "zeitgeist" amounts to an attempt to amass the thoughts and behaviors of individuals into a coherent whole and then to proceed as if that whole was a real thing.[3] It isn't and can never be.

A flash flood warning for southeastern New York State issued by the National Weather Service may seem like a more concrete example of a real thing. The warning cautioned, "DO NOT DRIVE YOUR VEHICLE INTO AREAS WHERE THE WATER COVERS THE ROADWAY. VEHICLES CAUGHT IN RISING WATER SHOULD BE ABANDONED. MOVE TO HIGHER GROUND IMMEDIATELY."[4] No zeitgeist here, no ambiguous contingencies. And it seems like solid advice, well worth heeding.

---

[1] Larry Diamond, "The Liberal Democratic Order in Crisis," *American Spectator* (February 16, 2018).

[2] And he was not alone in that interpretation. See, for example, Michael Gould-Wartofsky, "The Crisis of Liberal Democracy," *Huffington Post* (December 6, 2017); Ronald Hunt, "The Crisis of Liberal Democracy," *Polity* 13 (1980), 312–326; Ziya Öniş, "The Age of Anxiety: The Crisis of Liberal Democracy in a Post-Hegemonic Global Order," *The International Spectator: Italian Journal of International Affairs* 52 (2017), 18–35; Ganesh Sitaraman, "The Three Crises of Liberal Democracy," *The Guardian* (March 7, 2018). The fact that my earliest citation comes from 1980 should suggest caution about making presentist assumptions. Still, no matter how many people believe that liberal democracy is in crisis, the ontological nature of the claim remains the same: a human interpretation of a complex world.

[3] Randall Collins spoke of this tendency as taking micro-situations and then offering macro-conclusions. See Collins, "On the Microfoundations of Macrosociology," *American Journal of Sociology* 86 (1981), 984–1014.

[4] www.nws.noaa.gov/om/hod/pdfs/flash_flood_warning1.pdf.

18

But still, the National Weather Service was applying a label – a warning – that is the result of a human construction. The floodwaters can be real; the urgency is an interpretation, an ascription of meaning that makes a lot of sense, to be sure, but is still a human construction.

There is no better place to see that process in which humans take unformed and ambiguous dynamics and convert them into real, material entities played out with regard to crisis events than in the daily press. By surveying two weeks separated by twenty-four years, we can see how regularly, not to mention inappropriately, crisis is constituted as a real thing.

Two Weeks of Crisis

The week of October 16 through 23, 2017, was not exceptional. There were no major financial collapses or horrific terrorist attacks. No devastating hurricanes made landfall and no major oil leaks despoiled the environment. Businesses started and failed; the Earth continued to warm, the oceans continued to rise, and nations continued to wage wars against each other and with their own inhabitants. Yet, to read the worldwide press was to be confronted with an onslaught of crisis situations. Sure, we recognize that the media is attracted to crisis as a way of claiming audience attention. Even so, scanning that week's papers is a sobering experience.

Three situations dominated the crisis headlines during the week. The first was a confrontation in Spain over secession. Politicians in Catalonia, an autonomous region in the country's northeast, had called for a vote to be held on October 1 to declare or reject independence from Spain. The Spanish government insisted that it would be illegal even to hold the election and assured Catalans it would not recognize the outcome. Yet, more than 2 million Catalans voted *for* independence (92 percent of those who voted).

The secession dispute continued during the week of October 16 to constitute a crisis said to be so dire that relations between Catalonia and Spain had reached a "breaking point." The "very existence of the kingdom of Spain" was threatened.[5] This was crisis raised to the level of existential threat to an entire nation.

---

[5] Matthew Parris, "Catalans Don't Really Want Independence," *The Times* (London) (October 21, 2017), 25. A year later, the parties of Catalonian independence and Spanish unity remained at loggerheads. And yet, the "kingdom of Spain" still carried on. See Raphael Minder, "A Year After Catalonia Secession Vote, New Unrest and Still No Resolution," *New York Times* (October 1, 2018).

The opioid crisis also appeared in the headlines this week. Two years prior, a report issued by Princeton University revealed a shocking reversal of decades of public health progress in the United States: mortality rates were suddenly *rising*, and average lifespan was *declining*. The cause: suicides and opioid drug poisonings.[6] For this week in October 2017, there was speculation that President Donald Trump, then ten months into his term, would declare the opioid epidemic to be a national public health crisis. He didn't. But the crisis remained in the headlines.

The *Dayton* (Ohio) *Daily News* reported on a "powerful prescription drug monitoring system" designed to help fight the "opiate addiction crisis"; the *Tampa Bay Times* found "No Evidence to Prove Medicaid Expansion Is Fuelling the Opioid Crisis"; and the Tribune Content Agency distributed an item headlined, "After Bombshell Story, Senators Discuss Solutions to Opioid Crisis," the "bombshell" referring to a congressional vote weakening the Justice Department's ability to crack down on opioid distribution by pharmaceutical companies.[7]

Tensions on the Korean peninsula remained in the news this week, still constituting a crisis some two months after President Trump warned that the United States would unleash "fire and fury" on North Korea if its leader, Kim Jong-Un, continued to make threats against the United States and its allies. Although fading just a bit in news coverage during the week of October 16, there was still significant concern. "Russia's Putin Calls to Resolve North Korean Crisis via Dialogue" was a reminder of the dangerous situation.[8]

Although these were the most prominent dynamics to attract the crisis label during the week, there were more, many more. A Myanmar "crisis" warranted the attention of the United Nations High Commissioner on Human Rights, seeking to determine if violence against Rohingya Muslims rose to the level of genocide. A Mideast Gulf "crisis" – arising from tensions between Saudi Arabia and Qatar – threatened to undermine coordinated efforts against the Islamic State. Kenya experienced

---

[6] Anne Case and Angus Deaton, "Rising Morbidity and Mortality in Midlife among White Non-Hispanic Americans in the 21st Century," *Proceedings of the National Academy of Sciences of the United States of America* 112 (2015), 15078–15083.

[7] "The Nation is in the midst of an unprecedented opioid epidemic," noted the Health Resource and Services Administration a year later; "116 people a day die from opioid-related drug overdoses." Accessed at www.hrsa.gov/opioids.

[8] Polina Nikolska, "Russia's Putin Calls to Resolve North Korean Crisis via Dialogue," *Reuters* (October 19, 2017). A year later, tensions continued to ebb and flow between the United States and North Korea. The US president explained, "I was really tough and so was he, and we went back and forth. And then we fell in love, OK? No, really, he wrote me beautiful letters, and they're great letters. We fell in love." Quoted in John Bacon, "President Donald Trump on Kim Jong Un: 'We fell in Love' Over 'Beautiful Letters,'" *USA Today* (September 30, 2018).

a "vote crisis" when its presidential election was annulled by the country's Supreme Court. The ongoing "humanitarian crisis" across Europe triggered by mass migration continued to draw attention, as did another "humanitarian crisis" in Puerto Rico three weeks after a devastating hurricane. And Trump's feuds with leading Republican senators were fueling a "crisis" within the Grand Old Party.

Not all the events labeled as crises were quite as troubling as these. A "Toblerone crisis" swept England triggered by candy-maker Cadbury's decision to shrink the size of its iconic chocolate treat by increasing the gaps between the bar's distinctive triangular peaks.[9] The *Times of London* informed readers that "the Irish" were suffering an "identity crisis."[10] And a startling decline in men's sperm count would soon, readers were cautioned, trigger "a male infertility crisis" across Europe, North America, Australia, and New Zealand.[11]

And what of the same week in 1993, twenty-four years earlier? No single crisis dominated the news, although talk of a "trade crisis" was the most widespread. Negotiations being held on the General Agreement on Tariffs and Trade were said to have reached an impasse between the United States and the European Commission over subsidized farm exports. Medical care, or the lack thereof, seemed to have reached "crisis" proportions in Australia, the United Kingdom, and Canada. That crisis was laid to "the continued shortage of doctors prepared to work" for the government when private practice paid so much better. An underfunded court system in the United Kingdom created a "cash crisis in the justice system." Across Canada, declining church membership was predicted to be an omen of a coming religious crisis. France faced an "unemployment crisis" that produced a third day of "chaos and violent clashes" in Paris. A boycott by Yemen's ruling class heralded a "political crisis" there, as did corruption allegations against leading politicians in Brazil. The Palestine Liberation Organization's Yasser Arafat told World Bank officials that the PLO was struggling to maintain existing institutions such as hospitals due to a "financial crisis." London's Royal Ballet faced its own

---

[9] Deirdre Hipwell, "Toblerone 'Crisis' Was Never a Case of Biting off More than You Can Chew," *The Times* (London) (October 21, 2017).

[10] John Walsh, "Ireland Must Get a Grip on Its Identity Crisis," *The Times* (London) (October 21, 2017), 23.

[11] Marcia Inhorn, "A Male Infertility Crisis Is Coming: The Middle East Can Help." *New York Times* (October 21, 2017). "According to scientists at the Hebrew University of Jerusalem, sperm counts among men in the west have more than halved in the past 40 years and are currently falling by an average of 1.4% a year. Humanity could soon become extinct, it was claimed by some commentators." Talk about an existential crisis! See Robin McKie, "The Infertility Crisis Is Beyond Doubt: Now Scientists Must Find a Case," *The Guardian* (July 29, 2017).

financial crisis and was forced to cancel a new Kenneth MacMillan work. And Fox TV announced the cancellation of a late-night show hosted by comedian Chevy Chase after only six weeks on the air. The poor ratings for the show had created, according to a columnist for the *New York Times*, a "crisis for Fox," which now had to find ways to fill the vacated air time.[12]

Crises as Things

The bandwidth of events covered by the term "crisis" – from threats of national secession and potential nuclear war to the design of a candy bar and the cancellation of a dud television show – is so wide and its application so indiscriminate as to defuse the depth charge intended by its deployment.[13] But there is something else happening here. None of these so-called crises were things at all. Rather, they were claims intended to attract attention and assert urgency.

To be sure, there *were* things described in the various claims: a Catalonian vote with a specified outcome, the cancellation of a TV show. But there was no object to point to and say, there it is, there's the thing we're counting as a crisis. And yet we persist in thinking of crises as real things, events that objectively pose real threats. Why do we do that?

Well, to start with, the notion that the universe is composed of things is comforting. The opposite – no-*thing*ness – is simply too troubling, ambiguous, and overwhelming for many people to contemplate. Not for everyone. Jean-Paul Sartre, for instance, accepted the awareness of no-thingness as a liberating opportunity for the exercise of free will and self-determination.[14] But most people seek to overcome the sense of unease and dread by engaging in what Alfred North Whitehead called false concreteness.[15] In that way, we can believe that we are surrounded not by no-things but by things – real, concrete objects. See, the world does have objective meaning!

And even if we put such philosophical musings aside, there's this: people *like* things. And that is probably too mild a statement of the matter. People place value not just on the accumulation of things but also on things themselves.

---

[12] Bill Carter, "Chevy Chase's Show Canceled after 6 Weeks," *New York Times* (October 18, 1993).

[13] I admire that usage of "depth charge" that I found in a book review written by Daphine Merkin in discussing the proliferate use of the word "trauma." See Merkin, "Shaken," *New York Times Book Review* (October 21, 2018), 21.

[14] Sartre, *Being and Nothingness*.

[15] Alfred North Whitehead, *Process and Reality: An Essay in Cosmology* (New York: Free Press, 1929/1978).

Egyptian pharaohs, for instance, insisted on being buried with material objects – furniture, jewelry, carvings, and so on – to accompany them on the journey to the afterlife.[16] Cognitive linguists Giles Fauconnier and Mark Turner insist that "one of the most arresting singularities of human beings is our continual invention and deployment of and attachment to things."[17] Humans make things, carry them, gift them, repair them, collect them, and show them off. Things are, in many ways, our daily bread.

It may well be unconscious, but in our desire for things we imagine real objects even when there are none. To do that, we translate ideas, concepts, abstractions, and beliefs into "material anchors," thus first associating concepts with physical entities and then coming to believe that the concepts and the entities are the same. This is a process known as reification.

Richard Colignon takes as a definition of reification the "error of regarding an abstraction as a real phenomenon."[18] It is a conversion from abstraction into thing – a cognitive *error*, Colignon insists – that occurs in the human mind. That error may not be intended, but it is one that serves a purpose: that of simplifying complex, ambiguous contingencies into concrete, tangible things. Like a crisis.

Once contingencies are reified, they are assigned a special status. They are taken to be objects that exist outside of the human mind, realities of the cosmos rather than imagined products of our own construction.[19] That confusion becomes cemented as reality in our thinking when we forget that we are dealing in simplification.[20]

Rather than treating the world as a dizzying, confusing array of abstract dynamics, people now come to treat those forces as objects. We neglect to take into consideration the abstraction and instead settle for the idea of concreteness. In so doing, we confuse abstractions for the "actual entities" that make up our world.[21]

Sometimes, the act of reification is quite conscious and deliberate. We build temples and cathedrals to serve as the physical manifestation of our

[16] Those elaborate burial rituals were also intended as material symbols of faith. See Jock Agai, "Resurrection Imageries: A Study of the Motives for Extravagant Burial Rituals in Ancient Egypt." *Verbum et Ecclesia* 36 (2015), 1–7.

[17] Giles Fauconnier and Mark Turner, *The Way We Think: Conceptual Blending and the Mind's Hidden Complexity* (New York: Basic Books, 2002), p. 195.

[18] Richard Collignon, "The 'Holistic' and 'Individualistic' Views of Organizations," *Theory and Society* 18 (1989), 83.

[19] Peter Berger and Thomas Luckmann, *The Social Construction of Reality: A Treatise in the Sociology of Knowledge* (New York: Anchor Books, 1966).

[20] Alex Honneth, *Reification: A New Look at an Old Idea* (New York: Oxford University Press, 2008).

[21] Whitehead, *Process and Reality*, 27.

spiritual convictions. Visit a Gothic church to witness just such a majestic manifestation. These High and Late Middle Age structures were intended to be the "place" – real physical locations – where heaven touched earth. And that meaning was not intended in a metaphorical sense alone. There was something in the "stone, wood, glass, lead, and paint used to build Gothic cathedrals" that did more than represent the Divine; these tangible objects made the Divine physically manifest to mortal visitors.[22]

On a less spiritual level, a political leader may insist that a crisis is real as a conscious, deliberate effort to advance a particular agenda. When in January 2019, Donald Trump insisted that "a growing humanitarian and security crisis" existed "at our southern border," he did so in an effort to promote his campaign promise to "build a wall" between Mexico and the United States. Trump transposed abstract notions of the dynamics behind immigration into an actual crisis; a claim of urgency intended to advance a particular set of interests.[23]

Reification does not always involve such purposeful manipulation. Often, the reification process unfolds in less obvious ways, a blending that takes place in our subconscious. Physical materializations of our beliefs find a space in our minds.[24] We construct these material anchors – of unnamed and unknown (and often unknowable) forces – and then take for granted that the material anchor *is* the force. The *thing* and the *dynamic* are construed as one and the same.

Whatever purpose the reification process involves, it is a confusion, a cognitive error. That doesn't mean that the phenomenon of reification isn't useful, even indispensable as we endeavor to make sense of complex, mystifying dynamics. It allows for focus on certain elements of a dynamic while excluding peripheral phenomena. But that advantage is precisely where the caution lies, because reification always involves a human imposition.

When human-authored characterizations are taken to be immutable categories that exist in nature, the cognitive error is compounded. Race is a prime example of the danger of reification. "With the vast expansion of scientific knowledge in this century," proclaimed the executive board of the American Anthropological Association in its 1998 *Statement on Race*,

---

[22] Robert Scott, *The Gothic Enterprise: A Guide to Understanding the Medieval Cathedral* (Berkeley: University of California Press, 2011), pp. 121–122.

[23] He also declared a "national emergency" as a way to institutionalize his construction of a crisis. Deanna Paul, "Trump May Declare a National Emergency in the Border Wall Battle. Here's What That Means," *Washington Post* (January 12, 2019).

[24] Giles Fauconnier, *Mental Spaces: Aspects of Meaning Construction in Natural Language* (Cambridge, MA: MIT Press, 1985).

"it has become clear that human populations are not unambiguous, clearly demarcated, biologically distinct groups."[25] Despite the preponderance of scientific evidence, many people continue to reify race as a real human category. We become blind to the act of human authorship with its attendant opportunities for bias.[26]

It's a blindness that can be troubling. It can support bias precisely because it takes bias to be based on real, natural differences rather than human construction. I am not offering a biased interpretation, the observer may assert. I am just describing what I see in front of me.

Let's return to that *Times of London* story that claimed the Irish were suffering an identity crisis. Taken literally, the statement is risible. Two acts of reification are occurring in that one statement. As should be apparent, there is no such *thing* as "the Irish." The article makes clear that the reference is to the citizens of Ireland, not to people of Irish descent around the world. Still, any attempt to capture a diverse population of nearly five million people *must* be a simplification, not a real thing. It's as much a reification as statements such as "the American people want ..." or "the Chinese believe ..." These notions are all human constructions, existing not as material things but as interpretations typically offered to help prove the author's point or defend the speaker's position on an issue.

There is no such thing as an "identity crisis" either. It is, rather, a human label that has been applied in a wide variety of circumstances to a vast array of conditions, from unfinished ego development in adolescence to widespread social alienation. Of course, the claim's author had some idea in mind: severe self-doubt and naval gazing that had "assumed existential proportions that are unique among developed states." That was the author's intended interpretation.

The diagnosis of identity crisis is problematic when applied to an individual. Even the originator of the psychoanalytic take on identity crisis, Erik Erikson, confessed that the identity crisis designation was a difficult category to specify.[27] When laid on five million people, it is an apparent non-thing, an abstraction.

The author of the newspaper article is, of course, entitled to an interpretation and is free to label that interpretation as an identity crisis. But that claim should never be mistaken for an objective description of a real thing. The application of the construct to an individual is an attempt to

---

[25] www.aaanet.org/stmts/racepp.htm.

[26] Troy Duster, "Race and Reification in Science," *Science* 18 (2005), 1050–1051; Joan Ferrante and Prince Brown Jr., *The Social Construction of Race and Ethnicity in the United States* (New York: Longman, 1998).

[27] Erik Erikson, "Autobiographic Notes on the Identity Crisis," *Daedalus* 99 (1970), 730–759.

capture myriad phenomena under the name of a single thing. It amounts to a reified attachment of concreteness to a human interpretation.

The tendency to reify has been studied largely in relation to religion. Belief in forces that lie beyond full human understanding and comprehension can be turned into an entity, a thing. Natural processes – wind, rain, disease, and so forth – are transformed into gods. Images and other things come to represent these gods and are then worshipped as if they *were* the gods. God evolves from a not-fully-understood dynamic into a "being," one who resides in heaven.[28] Baseball players point to the sky after launching a home run because that is where a very real God resides.[29] The idealization of faith in God as a divine, omnipresent force is converted through the act of reification into a Being who lives overhead.

Other abstractions follow the same pattern. Fear becomes reified as the bogeyman, Christmas's celebratory generosity into Santa Claus, and parental anxieties into razor blades embedded in apples.

Wait. What's this about razor blades? That example – razor blades in apples – refers to an old urban legend that malevolent neighbors were threatening trick-or-treating youngsters on Halloween night. Sociologist Joel Best suggested that a deep-seated sense of threat to children combined with a distrust of strangers contributed to this reification. Abstract anxiety became a thing: a razor blade stuck in an apple.[30] Parents of the baby-boom generation confronted that reified anxiety by urging children (a) not to accept and certainly never to bite into any unwrapped, noncommercial treat, *especially* an apple, and (b) to collect money for UNICEF rather than edible treats.[31]

But here's the thing. There were never any razor blades found in Halloween apples. None ever documented. The few confirmed cases of poisons or drugs mixed into treats came from within the children's own homes, occasionally even the young "victims" themselves seeking attention. Yet the image – a reified manifestation of parental anxiety on a night when their children literally took candy from strangers – retained remarkable staying power.

---

[28] I found Joseph Bracken's analysis of various states of being useful here. See Bracken, "Being: An Entity, an Activity, or Both an Entity and an Activity?" *Journal of Religion* 96 (2016), 77–93.

[29] Lives, and apparently roots for the players' teams. Barry Bonds is credited with popularizing the gesture. It's a striking formulation. "The God that Barry Bonds points to" did not worry "about all the steroid talk – He just digs the long ball." Tom McNichol, "God and Baseball," *Huffington Post* (May 25, 2011).

[30] Joel Best, *Threatened Children: Rhetoric and Concern about Child-Victims* (Chicago: University of Chicago Press, 1990).

[31] Although started earlier by local fundraisers, the official "Trick-or-Treat for UNICEF" campaign began in 1953. See www.unicefusa.org/trick-or-treat.

Take this open letter addressed to readers written by Eppie Lederer in her popular persona as advice columnist Ann Landers:

Dear Readers –
Tonight is Halloween ... Soon it will be dark and your children will be out trick-or-treating. Your doorbell will ring and you will be confronted by children with their hands out. That's the fun part. The dark side of this holiday is that hundreds of children will be injured and some may be killed.
No longer can you allow your youngsters to roam your neighborhood and knock on strangers' doors in search of goodies. The world has changed since you and I went trick-or-treating.
In recent years, there have been reports of people with twisted minds putting razor blades and poison in taffy apples and Halloween candy. It is no longer safe to let your children eat treats that come from strangers.

Parents needed to protect their children from the threat, the advice columnist insisted. "Warn kids not to eat any treats until they have been inspected by a parent or chaperone. Packaged candy is the safest. Inspect the wrapping to make sure it has not been opened."[32] And this letter appeared in 1995, more than four decades after the original push to replace treats with charitable donations and during which time not a single documented case of strangers sticking blades in Halloween treats had occurred. That's the power of reification.

The conversion from concept into thing – in this case, from generalized parental anxiety into a crisis of razor blades embedded in apples – becomes so blended in our thinking that we are barely aware of it. That most arresting aspect of the human mind prompts us to resist arguments that suggest a concept is not a thing. This is a crisis, a real thing, we insist. It is lodged in our mind as a thing. Hundreds of children will be injured, some may be killed, and parents need to be on alert for their malevolent neighbors with their booby-trapped treats.

How did this process by which we assign thingness to the concept of crisis come about? To answer that question, we could probably go back to the beginning of conscious thought. Instead, let's turn to a Greek physician practicing in the Age of Pericles.

Building on Medical Usage

In contemporary discourse on crisis, there is a tendency to seek a metaphoric parallel with medical usage of the term; the argument being that in medical diagnosis, a crisis is a real thing. Sociologist

---

[32] From *St. Louis Post-Dispatch* (October 31, 1995). www.newspapers.com/newspage/ 142419675

Jürgen Habermas pointed to such usage, arguing that, in a medical context, crisis refers to "something objective": the phase of an illness "in which it is decided whether an organism's self-healing powers are sufficient for recovery." That conflation of medical diagnosis with societal analysis leads to an association of crisis with "the idea of an objective force that deprives the subject of some part of his [the patient's] normal sovereignty."[33] There is a disease or condition, there is a human body, and there is an identifiable point at which that body is in crisis.

Paul Shrivastava made an explicit reference to that supposedly objective medical model in his industrial crisis study. A medical crisis, he insisted, "represents the advanced point of a progressively worsening illness, when the illness acquires an objective force against which both patient and doctor are powerless." If doctors were able objectively to identify the phase of an illness "in which the body's self-healing powers became inadequate for recovery, even with external help from life-support systems and medicines," the same should be true of crises "in a social system."[34]

Shrivastava was focusing specifically on the horrific chemical leak in the Indian city of Bhopal. On a December night in 1984, a pesticide-producing subsidiary of US-based Union Carbide leaked the highly toxic methyl isocyanate (MIC) gas into the environment. Half a million residents were exposed. That leak was unquestionably a real thing. More than 2,000 people died immediately and perhaps as many as an addition 20,000 perished from MIC-related diseases. This was an occurrence of staggering scope and tragic consequences. And, naturally, commentators searched for the proper term to characterize what happened. It was a "disaster," a "tragedy," a "horror," even a "massacre."[35] It was for Shrivastava a crisis.

Individuals can determine how legitimate they find any of these labels. There is little doubt, however, that they are just that: labels applied by human observers. What Shrivastava had in mind was something very different. He used crisis not as a label, but, he maintained, as a real thing.

---

[33] Jürgen Habermas, *Legitimation Crisis* (Boston: Beacon Press, 1975), p. 1. Habermas was not endorsing the association of crisis with medicine but observing its usage.

[34] Paul Shrivastava, *Bhopal: Anatomy of a Crisis* (London: Paul Chapman Publishing, 1992), p. 5. The metaphor of an organization as a living organism and crisis as a disease attacking that organism was picked up by Arie de Getus, *The Living Company* (Boston: Harvard Business School, 1997).

[35] Larry Everest, *Behind the Poison Cloud: Union Carbide's Bhopal Massacre* (Chicago: Banner Press, 1985); Sheila Jasanoff, *Leaning from Disaster: Risk Management After Bhopal* (Philadelphia: University of Pennsylvania Press, 1994); Ward Morehouse and M. Arun Subramaniam, *The Bhopal Tragedy: What Really Happened and What It Means for American Workers and Communities at Risk* (New York: Council on International and Public Affairs, 1986).

Crises in social systems, explained Shrivastava, refer to "situations that threaten the existing form and structure of the system." If and when existing social structures are "incapable of resolving economic, social, cultural, and political problems, the system's integration is threatened, and it faces crisis." Industrial crises are always "triggered by a specific event that is identifiable in time and place."[36] This is the crisis-as-event model at its most basic: a specific event triggers a real thing called a crisis.

Shrivastava's use of crisis conformed to a long-standing and well-established linguistic tradition. The *Oxford English Dictionary* finds the first use of the term "crisis" in the English language to be in 1543. The term was framed largely in a medical tradition dating back to the great Greek physician Hippocrates.

In Hippocratic medicine, *kiris* was the point in the progression of disease at which either the illness would begin to triumph and the patient would succumb to death or the opposite would occur and natural processes would make the patient recover.[37] According to Hippocratic doctrine, crises tend to occur on critical days, which were supposed to be a fixed time after the contraction of a disease. "Acute diseases," Hippocrates wrote, "generally come to crisis in fourteen days."[38]

That's a compelling model. Yet, the medical analogy is imperfect, at best. Hippocrates' hoped-for precision over the critical days of a disease's progression has been supplanted, in modern medicine, by a far more constrained certainty. *Mosby's Medical, Nursing, & Allied Health Dictionary* refers to crisis as "a transition for better or worse in the course of a disease, usually indicated by a marked change in the intensity of signs and symptoms."[39] Note the words "transition," " usually indicated" and "marked change." When looking at the definitions of specific types of crises, a more subjective and less reified understanding emerges.

Medical practice continues to strive toward precision in its approach to diagnosis without assuming it can ever arrive at objective precision. Big data is mined to develop algorithms that might be helpful in pinpointing patients "in crisis."[40] Predictive aids can be useful in refining guidelines.

---

[36] Shrivastava, *Bhopal*, 5.

[37] George Hefferman, "The Concept of *Krisis* in Husserl's *The Crisis of the European Sciences and Transcendental Phenomenology*," *Husserl Studies* 33 (2017), 229–257. "The concept [of crisis] probably predates Hippocrates," wrote Roger Cooter, "and may possibly have emerged from observing fever episodes in malaria." See Cooter, "Historical Key Word: Crisis," *The Lancet* 373 (2009), 887.

[38] Quoted from Henry Ducachet, *The Prognosis and Crisis of Hippocrates* (New York: J. Eastburn and Co., 1819), p. 90.

[39] *Mosby's Medical, Nursing, & Allied Health Dictionary* (2001).

[40] Ronald Kessler et al., "Predicting Suicides After Psychiatric Hospitalization in U.S. Army Soldiers: The Army Study to Assess Risk and Resilience in Servicemembers (Army STARRS)," *JAMA Psychiatry* 72 (2015), 49–57.

But physicians are far less willing to ascribe objective, universal under-standing to the term "crisis" than either Hippocrates or Shrivastava.

Andrew Kolodny, co-director of Opioid Policy Research at the Heller School for Social Policy and Management and executive director of Physicians for Responsible Opioid Prescribing, agreed that the term "crisis" has no specific meaning. It is used, rather, "to indicate a worsening problem that requires urgent action."[41] In other words, the term "crisis" refers not to a thing but to a claim of urgency.

The second fundamental flaw in the medical crisis analogy lies in applicability. Even if there were such a thing as a true crisis stage in the interaction between a human body and a disease, can we really apply that insight to a large, complex social unit? Is a crisis in the body's struggle with hypertension, for instance, parallel to a possibility of bankruptcy in a business, the approach of a Category 5 hurricane to a small island, or the urgent need to deal with a gas leak in Bhopal?

Bruno Latour insisted that it was not parallel; society was not a "transparent container" amenable to a detached, focused scientific gaze. Rather, "society" was a human-constructed category, an abstract representation: "In crisis medicine, doctors confront a body that is fixed and finite in its spatial and physical dimensions, and then focus on the decisive moment when this finite body hinges on the brink of life or death. But does society ever admit to such spatial and temporal finitude? What, for example, are the finite boundaries of society?"[42] In truth, no such boundaries exist.

J. B. Shank agreed with Latour. The use of "crisis" as "a rhetorical term of art" can be a "powerful" discursive tool, Shank concluded.[43] However, given that organizations, or for that matter societies, are not entities in the way that a body is, crisis must be considered a metaphor, not a technical, objective thing.

Even during Hippocrates' lifetime, the notion of crisis took on a broader, notably less precise sense. There was an option to think of crises in figurative rather than literal terms.

A More Figurative Approach

Thucydides, an Athenian historian and military leader, appropriated medical language in his writing, relying particularly on the metaphor of

---

[41] Andrew Kolodny, personal correspondence with author (2017).
[42] Bruno Latour, "Postmodern? No, Simply Amodern! Steps toward an Anthropology of Science," *Studies in the History and Philosophy of Science* 21 (1990), 153.
[43] J. B. Shank, "Crisis: A Useful Category of Post-Social Scientific Historical Analysis?" *American Historical Review* 113 (2008), 1098.

disease.[44] In his *History of the Peloponnesian War, kpisis* took on the implication of a turning point.[45] The language may have been medically influenced, but the intended meaning changed from an identifiable, specific, scientifically confirmed state to a figurative, even metaphorical turning point in the state of affairs.

Now, observers of society could call on "crisis" as a conceptual notion of narrative drama. Historians deployed the term, for example, to represent turning points, moments of stress, and years of uncertainty, typically followed by structural changes.[46] The failure of nation-states represents a crisis, as do civil wars, attempts at reconciliation and/or reconstruction, and competing dynamics of a receding feudal status quo and the nascent forces of capitalism.

As can be seen, it is not just the popular press with its need for compelling headlines that over-promotes the concept of "crisis." Crisis situations have become so abundant in the narratives of historians (Table 2.1) that the use of the word has become, in the critique offered by Randolph Starn, overly permissive.[47] Jay Sexton worked to narrow the definition to a shift in "the underlying tectonic plates of historical change," a powerful metaphor to be sure, and one that emphasizes the figurative rather than objective nature of crisis.[48] The deployment of the label "crisis" will always be a human creation, a linguistic flourish intended to emphasize a human interpretation of the world. But even when we recognize that the crisis term is woefully overused, we typically do not question the underlying ontology with which we assign the state of corporeal entity to the concept.

But What about … ? The Threshold Argument

The impact of the 1984 Union Carbide chemical leak in Bhopal was appalling, likely the worst industrial disaster in history. The 1986 explosion of the shuttle Challenger was a catastrophe that rocked NASA and the country. Levee breaks devastated New Orleans in 2005. Rampant gun violence in Chicago posed a daily threat to thousands of young people. The September 11 terrorist attacks on the World Trade Center and the Pentagon killed thousands, as had the bombing raid on Pearl Harbor

---

[44] Lisa Kallet, "The Diseased Body Politic, Athenian Public Finance, and the Massacre at Mykalessos (Thucydides 7.27–29)," *American Journal of Philology* 120 (1999), 223–244.
[45] Shank, "Crisis."
[46] Peter Burke, "The Crisis in the Arts of the Seventeenth Century: A Crisis of Representation?" *Journal of Interdisciplinary History* 40 (2009), 239–261.
[47] Randolph Starn, "Historians and 'Crisis,'" *Past and Present* 52 (1971), 3–22.
[48] Sexton, *A National Forged by Crisis*, 5.

Table 2.1 *Historians find crises everywhere – a sampling*

AUTHOR	WORK TITLE
Robert H. Zieger	"Pinchot and Coolidge: The Politics of the 1923 Anthracite Crisis" (1965)
Jack M. Schick	*The Berlin Crisis, 1958–1962* (1971)
Robert G. Williams	*Export Agriculture and the Crisis in Central America (1986)*
Michael Bernstein	"The Contemporary American Banking Crisis in Historical Perspective" (1994)
K. . Cuordileone	"Politics in an Age of Anxiety: Cold War Political Culture and the Crisis in American Masculinity, 1949–1960" (2000)
Geoffrey Parker	*Global Crisis: War, Climate Change and Catastrophe in the Seventeenth Century* (2002)
Jorge A. Nallim	*Transformations and Crisis of Liberalism in Argentina, 1930–1955* (2012)
Phil Booth	*Crisis of Empire: Doctrine and Dissent at the End of Late Antiquity* (2014)
Daniel J. Tortora	*Carolina in Crisis: Cherokees, Colonists, and Slaves in the American Southeast, 1756–1763* (2015)

three decades earlier. A series of deadly terrorist attacks in France during 2015 marked by bloodshed at the offices of *Charlie Hebdo* and the Bataclan concert hall shook that country. Even though we can concede that the term "crisis" is often inappropriately applied to trivialities, surely these events were of such scope and consequence that they can be deemed – inherently, objectively – to be crises.

This is the *threshold thesis*. It is appealing but wrongheaded. In his insightful historical study of naval incidents in which foreign powers attacked US ships, or non-US vessels carrying American passengers, military historian Douglas Peifer focused on three incidents:[49]

• In 1898, an explosion aboard the USS *Maine* was followed by its sinking into Havana Harbor. The armored cruiser had been stationed in Cuba as that country rebelled against its colonial ties to Spain. Three-quarters of the crew perished. The perpetrators of the explosion were unknown. It was even possible that an internal fire rather than an external attack was responsible. Nonetheless, American newspapers tried to force the issue: "Crisis is at Hand" and "Remember the Maine, To Hell with Spain!" Two months later, the United States declared war on the country thought to be responsible.

---

[49] Douglas Peifer, *Choosing War: Presidential Decisions in the* Maine, Lusitania, *and* Panay *Incidents* (New York: Oxford University Press, 2016).

- The British RMS *Lusitania* was, on May 17, 1915, the largest passenger liner in the world. That was the day that the liner was sunk by a torpedo fired by a German U-boat.[50] At the time, England and Germany were at war. Each country attempted to blockade the other's shipping lanes. Safeguards preventing attacks on passage ships fell by the wayside, especially as the German navy relied more heavily on submarines. In the days before the *Lusitania*'s sailing out of New York City (headed to Liverpool), the Germany Embassy in the United States placed ads in American newspapers reminding potential passengers that "a state of war exists between Germany and her allies and the United Kingdom and her allies" and that "travelers sailing in the war zone on the ships of Great Britain or her allies do so at their own risk." Of the 1,198 *Lusitania* passengers who perished, 128 were Americans.
- In December 1937, the USS *Panay* came under fire from Japanese fighter planes. The small, lightly armed gunboat was anchored on China's Yangtze River. Japan had invaded China several months prior to the attack, and the *Panay* was helping evacuate Americans from Chinese cities under threat. The ship sank, three crewmen plus a reporter died, and several dozen more were injured. The Japanese government apologized and paid a $2 million indemnity to the United States (about $38 million in current dollars), all while insisting that there had been no apparent US markings on the ship (despite the *Panay*'s flying of the US flag).

None of these incidents, noted Peifer, led immediately to war. The United States did go to war with Spain – the alleged culprit in the never-fully-explained explosion of the *Maine*, at least according to the popular press – until two months after the incident. It was almost exactly two years after the sinking of the *Lusitania* that the United States entered the war against Germany and its allies; it took four years – with the added impetus, of course, of Pearl Harbor – to bring about a declaration of war against Japan.

In analyzing these three incidents, Peifer demonstrated persuasively that the manner in which the US presidents at the time – McKinley, Wilson, and Franklin Roosevelt, respectively – responded to the incidents was shaped by the interests of the particular president. Wilson, for instance, was staunchly committed to keeping the country out of a raging war between the British and the Germans. His intention was to remain an "honest" (i.e., neutral) broker in the final peace talks. So, yes, American ships were attacked; American lives were lost. But the attacks

---

[50] U – for underwater – boats were German submarines.

on the *Lusitania* and the *Panay* did not lead to war. American neutrality remained the policy.[51]

Now, Peifer introduced his threshold argument. Each of the three described incidents, he noted, "fell short of the threshold that compels a military response." They failed to reach a threshold point at which the president would have had no choice to go to war. Compare that to Japan's attack on Pearl Harbor and al Qaeda's attacks on New York City and Washington, DC, on September 11. The Pearl Harbor and September 11 attacks, Peifer noted, "killed thousands of American citizens on US. sovereign territory, with little debate as to whether the United States needed to retaliate."[52] Unlike the *Maine*, the *Lusitania*, and the *Panay*, both Pearl Harbor and September 11 crossed some imagined-as-real threshold.

The threshold argument can be thus proposed: some events are, by their nature, crises. That proposition rests on two variables: the *scope* of the event and the *consensus* (or existence of "little debate") on the meaning of the event.

It is true that only one congressperson – Jeannette Rankin from Montana – voted against Roosevelt's demand for a declaration of war the day after Pearl Harbor.[53] So yes, a consensus had formed in the United States that a state of war with Japan already existed. The president and Congress had no choice, Peifer insisted, but to respond with a declaration of war. But the existence of consensus and overwhelming political pressure to respond in a military mode does not alter the ontological construction of a claim.

Claims Are Always Human Constructions.

FDR's famous "date of infamy" speech in response to the Pearl Harbor attack certainly contained many objective and verifiable descriptions:

- "The attack yesterday on the Hawaiian Islands has caused severe damage to American naval and military forces."
- "Very many American lives have been lost."
- "In addition, American ships have been reported torpedoed on the high seas between San Francisco and Honolulu."

---

[51] Although not included in Peifer's study, Michael Beschloss details another example of a president carefully avoiding war despite a direct military attack. In 1807, Thomas Jefferson purposefully maneuvered to avoid war after the British navy attacked the USS *Chesapeake*, killing three and wounding others. Jefferson was convinced that the United States was unprepared for another war with England. See Beschloss, *Presidents of War*.

[52] Peifer, *Choosing War*, 8.   [53] Rankin considered herself an "absolute pacifist."

- "Yesterday the Japanese Government also launched an attack against Malaya. Last night Japanese forces attacked Hong Kong. Last night Japanese forces attacked Guam. Last night Japanese forces attacked the Philippine Islands. Last night the Japanese attacked Midway Island."

These were descriptions, and they were accurate.

"The facts of yesterday," Roosevelt insisted, "speak for themselves." On that point, Roosevelt was wrong. Facts, *never* "speak for themselves." They always await the assignment of meaning. That is what FDR provided with his statement – a subjective statement that ascribed meaning to the events that he would describe – that "yesterday, December 7, 1941" was "a date which will live in infamy."

Rather than speaking for themselves, facts await ascription of meaning. FDR staked his claim to that meaning: a state of war already existed. As it happens, his ascription of meaning was taken as plausible by most Americans and nearly all in Congress. It was deemed to be far more plausible than Congresswoman Rankin's counterclaim that "taking our army and navy across thousands of miles of ocean to fight and die certainly cannot come under the head of protecting our shores."[54] The plausibility or non-plausibility of an ascription of meaning helps shape the legitimacy that is granted that claim. However, even accuracy and plausibility do not transform a claim into an objective thing.

We can and should make judgments about the accuracy and plausibility of any and all claims. Most people believed FDR's claim to be accurate and far more plausible than Rankin's counter-assertion that a state of war between the United States and Japan did not exist. But that consensus does not – cannot – alter the ontological nature of that or any other claim.

Leaders making claims will always have a choice as to how the event that they are referencing will be represented. Likewise, followers will always have the option of making a judgment concerning that claim's legitimacy in comparison to other claims. Jeannette Rankin's counter-assertion that the Pearl Harbor attack was not a hostile act against the United States was not plausible, and her political career imploded over her opposition to declaring war on Japan. But there have been hostile acts against the US military both before and since that have not evoked a militaristic response. The "facts" do not speak for themselves. And no interpretation is built into the nature of the event itself, no matter the scope and certainly no matter the popularity of the claim. There are real facts. They become crises only through the act of asserting a claim.

[54] Quoted in James Lopach and Jean Luckowski, *Jeannette Rankin: A Political Woman* (Boulder: University of Colorado Press, 2005), p. 185.

One group firmly committed to the reification of urgency is composed of crisis management professionals. Operating solidly within the crisis-as-event model, these experts insist that these events – crises – are besetting us at an ever-increasing pace. It behooves leaders – of businesses, communities, and nations – to learn how to manage those events.

3   Advancing the Crisis-as-Event Model

For leaders hoping to learn how to manage a crisis, any crisis, a robust crisis management industry exists offering just that kind of practical, step-by-step advice.[1] As a sampling of such practical titles indicates, the emphasis is on packaging specific formulae to help guide a response to crisis events:

- "7 Critical Steps to Crisis Management."[2]
- "How to Manage in a Crisis: Plan Ahead, Be Well Prepared."[3]
- "Managing Your Business through a Crisis: 6 Steps to Success."[4]
- "4 Steps for Effectively Managing a PR Crisis."[5]

There may be sound advice on offer here. In evaluating the quality of that advice, a critic might endorse some suggestions, question others, and offer alternative courses for action.[6]

A critique is something different, focusing on the assumptions that underlie the core notion of "crisis management." The specific recommendations offered by crisis management experts, as valid and varied as they might be, reside solidly in the crisis-as-event model. It's a model that depicts the dynamics of crisis management unfolding in a clear and predictable sequence. First, an objectively threatening event occurs. Now, a crisis is triggered. Then the leader responds to that event, either effectively or not. By following solid, experience-based advice, leaders can learn to respond better. In that way, the crisis management industry

---

[1] Steve Tobak, "How to Manage a Crisis, Any Crisis." *CNet* (August 23, 2008).
[2] www.inc.com/bruce-condit/7-critical-steps-to-crisis-management.html
[3] www.grovewell.com/global-leadership-training/how-to-manage-in-a-crisis.
[4] www.mlrpc.com/articles/managing-business-crisis-6-steps-success.
[5] www.adweek.com/digital/4-steps-for-effectively-managing-a-pr-crisis.
[6] Working from within complexity theory, Dawn Gilpin and Pricilla Murphy offer a robust criticism to traditional approaches to crisis management. With their emphasis on "overly rigid crisis planning procedures," crisis experts typically pay insufficient attention to "the role of contingency, uncertainty, and happenstance; the unexpected confluence of unrelated events; and the destabilizing influence of rapidly changing circumstances." See Gilpin and Murphy, *Crisis Management in a Complex World* (Oxford: Oxford University Press, 2008), pp. 4–5.

advances one particular crisis model. Before analyzing that dominant approach, let's take a detailed look at one leader whose crisis management response attracted virtually universal condemnation from the experts.

A Bad Day for United Airlines

April 9, 2017, was undoubtedly a bad day for United Airlines. It was a Sunday in Chicago. O'Hare Airport security personnel were called aboard United Flight 3411, scheduled for a 5:40 p.m. takeoff to Louisville, Kentucky. Onboard flight attendants asked security personal for help in dealing with a noncooperating passenger. That individual, Dr. David Dao, was then forcibly dragged down the aisle of the plane as it was preparing to take off.

What triggered this confrontation was a request from the flight crew for volunteers to give up their seat to make room for four airline employees. These employees "needed to get on the flight," according to United, "in order to work another [flight] in Louisville or else that flight would be cancelled."[7]

Airlines routinely overbook flights, selling more seats than the airplane has. The reason is an economic one: to maximize plane utilization. Experience has taught them that there will often be a small number of "no-shows": passengers with reservations who simply fail to appear for their flight. Rather than flying with an unoccupied (although already paid for) seat, the plane can accommodate another paying customer.

It's a well-established practice of the industry, with rules imposed by the Federal Aviation Administration dictating how and when to seek "volunteers" – in exchange for a reward – to give up their seats. For some passengers in no particular rush to arrive at their destination, the exchange can be quite attractive.

On the Sunday afternoon in question, United Flight 3411 crew personnel asked for four volunteers, offering $400 along with an overnight hotel room and a booking on the next flight scheduled to leave in twenty-one hours. On most days and for most flights, this would have gone fine. Not on this day for this flight. With the next Louisville flight not departing until the following day, there were no takers. Following established airline protocol, crew members upped the ante to $800. Still no volunteers. Now what?

---

[7] Quoted from Christina Zdanowicz and Emanuella Grinberg, "Passenger Dragged Off Overbooked United Flight," *CNN.com* (April 10, 2017).

United had rules for bumping passengers in the absence of volunteers. In a typical situation when there were other passengers hoping to get onboard, flight crew would ask for volunteers. If there were none forthcoming, that would be the end of it. Ticketed passengers still waiting at the gate would hold on for the next flight. This situation was different. Rather than other passengers, United was demanding (not requesting) seats for airline employees who "needed" to be on this flight. In that scenario, four already seated passengers would have to deplane.

Protocol now called for four names to be selected randomly for removal. Well, not exactly randomly. First-class passengers were excluded from the pool. So were any passengers who had paid full fare for their coach seats or who were members of United's frequent flier program. Four passengers flying with discounted coach-class reservations were selected, announced, and invited to leave. Three of the selected passengers complied. One did not. Shouting "I have to go home," Dr. Dao insisted that he could not miss his Monday morning clinic hours. That's when things got really messy.

For *this* situation, there was no protocol. Air crew members elected to request assistance from Chicago Department of Aviation (CDA) ground-based security. CDA officers then entered the plane – there was no protocol for them either – and forcibly removed Dao.[8] A passenger recorded the action on a mobile phone.[9]

Mobile phones are ubiquitous these days. Their capacity to record events allows the possibility of anyone and everyone becoming a witness. Social media quickly spreads videos, and soon thousands, even millions, have shared an experience.

At first, the video from Flight 3411 shows very little. Then we hear a passenger, presumably Dao, screaming while another passenger gasps, "Oh my God!" We can see Dao's bloodied face (he would claim his nose was broken in the scuffle), his glasses askew, and his sweater pulled up in a way that exposes part of his torso. Security officers drag Dao by his arms. He may be unconscious at this point; his eyes are closed, and he has stopped screaming. "Good work," another traveler shouts, presumably in sarcasm. "Way to go." An unidentified woman follows quickly behind, likely Dao's flying companion. The video lasts less than one minute.

As those images spread via social media, a spokesperson for United talked with a *New York Times* reporter. "We had asked several times, politely" for Dao to give up his seat. He refused, so "we had to call"

---

[8] One of these officers who was subsequently fired for his actions that day sued CDA, claiming a lack of adequate training in handling escalating situations like this.
[9] The video can be viewed at www.youtube.com/watch?v=VrDWY6C1178.

security officers. All this was done, the spokesperson insisted, to ensure that the other passengers arrived at their destination on time.[10]

Realizing that a more satisfactory answer was needed in response to mounting public outrage stoked by the spread of that video, United CEO Oscar Munoz issued his own statement the next day:

> This is an upsetting event to all of us here at United. I apologize for having to re-accommodate these customers. Our team is moving with a sense of urgency to work with the authorities and conduct our own detailed review of what happened. We are also reaching out to this passenger to talk directly to him and further address and resolve this situation.[11]

Despite Munoz's claim of a "sense of urgency," his statement was widely condemned by commentators with expertise in crisis management. The image of Dao being forcefully dragged from a plane was not discussed but rather lumped under a so-called re-accommodation procedure. Further, Munoz seemed to be apologizing to "all of us here at United" rather than to the passenger who had been dragged off the plane or the others who had witnessed the event.

A second communication followed immediately, not from "Oscar Munoz, CEO" but from "Oscar":

> The truly horrific event that occurred on this flight has elicited many responses from all of us: outrage, anger, disappointment. I share all of those sentiments, and one above all: my deepest apologies for what happened. Like you, I continue to be disturbed by what happened on this flight and I deeply apologize to the customer forcibly removed and to all the customers aboard. No one should ever be mistreated this way.
>
> I want you to know that we take full responsibility and we will work to make it right.
>
> It's never too late to do the right thing. I have committed to our customers and our employees that we are going to fix what's broken, so this never happens again. This will include a thorough review of crew movement, our policies for incentivizing volunteers in these situations, how we handle oversold situations and an examination of how we partner with airport authorities and local law enforcement. We'll communicate the results of our review by April 30th.[12]
>
> I promise you we will do better.
>
> Sincerely,
>
> Oscar[13]

---

[10] Daniel Victor and Matt Stevens, "United Airlines Passenger Is Dragged from an Overbooked Flight," *New York Times* (April 10, 2017).

[11] http://newsroom.united.com/news-releases?item=124753.

[12] A new policy was put into place whereby United would conduct all re-accommodation procedures at least an hour before takeoff. This would, it was hoped, avoid any future onboard flare-ups.

[13] http://newsroom.united.com/news-releases?item=124755.

Despite that apology, customer perception of the airline fell to its lowest level in 10 years.[14]

This was the "mother of all social media crises," said the experts who quickly weighed in.[15] Munoz had failed to shift immediately into "crisis mode" and thus mishandled the situation.[16] His initial statement – "I apologize for having to re-accommodate these customers" – was condemned as "cold." The second "Oscar" communication was considered to be the apology that "should have been made immediately."[17] The delay was inexcusable. Under the headline "United Airlines Shows How to Make a PR Crisis a Total Disaster," a public relations expert insisted: "Had United shown compassion and intent to make things right, they could have come out of this at the very least looking like an airline that cares. Instead they've just made it even worse."[18]

"What's clear is that Mr. Munoz – and presumably those who were advising him – were lost in the fog," wrote a magazine columnist. "They instinctively put United and its staff before the customers who'd witnessed a very unpleasant incident and, much more importantly, before Mr. Dao, whose only crime, it seems, was to be selected for removal."[19]

Ironically, PR Week had named Munoz "Communicator of the Year" just a month before the incident. "Munoz has shown himself to be a smart, dedicated, and excellent leader who understands the value of communications," the magazine enthused, particularly praising his "ability to connect and share with employees his vision for the airline and get them to rally behind it."[20] Clearly, that excellence wasn't enough to help Munoz navigate this particular situation.

The Prevailing Crisis Management Model

In the crisis-as-event model, the forceful expulsion of a passenger combined with the viral spread of the disturbing video created a real crisis at United Airlines. Its leader, CEO Oscar Munoz, responded ineptly, at

---

[14] Ted Marzilli, "United Airlines Hits Lowest Consumer Perception in 10 Years," *YouGovBrandIndex* (April 13, 2017).

[15] Sean Czarnecki, "Timeline of a Crisis," *PR Week* (June 6, 2017).

[16] John Bacon, "What United Airlines Must Do after PR Nightmare to Win Back Customers," *USA Today* (April 12, 2017).

[17] Marzilli, "United Airlines Hits Lowest Consumer Perception in 10 Years."

[18] Alanna Petroff, "United Airlines Shows How to Make a PR Crisis a Total Disaster," *CNN Money* (April 17, 2017).

[19] Andy Coulson, "How United Airlines Should Have Handled This PR Crisis," *GQ* (April 12, 2017).

[20] *PR Week* Staff, "United Airlines CEO Oscar Munoz Named PR Week U.S. Communicator of the Year," *PR Week* (March 9, 2017).

least at first. Much advice followed about how to better manage a crisis situation.

Insisting that crises are objective facts to be managed, experts teach courses, write books, and sell advice on how to navigate through turmoil. Academics and consultants alike agree on one central observation: effective crisis management requires that those "in charge" tend to the core values and critical infrastructure of their units, always mindful of the well-being of members.[21]

A common – and unexamined – assertion of crisis management experts is that there has never been a greater need for effective crisis leadership than "today," whenever that "today" may be. "Man-made and natural disasters have become increasingly prevalent," we are told, leading to "a precipitous growth in the sheer number of major crises."[22] "Ours is a time of crisis," we are assured. Maybe crises were once rare and unusual, not any more. They have become "common parts of the social, psychological, political, economic, and organizational landscape of modern life," an "integral feature of the new information/systems age."[23]

Business crises, in particular, have become "a defining feature of corporate America in the last 10 years" – a claim offered in 2006, before the financial crisis, the retailing apocalypse, widespread data breaches, regular revelations of sexual misconduct at work, and the hijacking of social media by foreign entities attempting to sway US elections.[24] Once thought of as rare and exceptional, crises have become, in this model, "an almost routine event."[25]

Not only are crisis events more frequent than ever before, they are also – and this may be even more troubling – more variable, with more types and causes. The world has become so dire that we may well be living in a state

---

[21] Arjen Boin et al., "Leadership Style, Crisis Response, and Blame Management: The Case of Hurricane Katrina," *Public Administration* 88 (2010), 706–723.

[22] Mitroff, *Why Some Companies Emerge Stronger and Better from a Crisis*, 3.

[23] Ian Mitroff and Gus Anagnos, *Managing Crisis Before They Happen: What Every Executive and Manager Needs to Know about Crisis Management* (New York: AMACON, 2001), p. 3; David Roochnik, *Retrieving Aristotle in an Age of Crisis* (Albany: State University of New York Press, 2013), p. 1; Matthew Seeger et al., *Communication and Organizational Crisis* (Westport: Praeger, 2013), 3. In an unconvincing attempt to provide empirical evidence for their claim that crises had become more prominent than ever before (remember, their book appeared in 2001), Mitroff and Anagnos provided a list of fourteen "events," including "Mad cow disease" and the "Challenger explosion." They conclude, "In short, crises are no longer an aberrant, rare, random, or peripheral feature of today's society. They are built into the very fabric and fiber of modern societies" (p. 4).

[24] Erika James and Lynn Wooten, "Diversity Crises: How Firms Manage Discrimination Lawsuits," *Academy of Management Journal* 49 (2006), 1103.

[25] Clara Kulicha et al., "Solving the Crisis: When Agency Is the Preferred Leadership for Implementing Change," *Leadership Quarterly* 29 (2018), 296.

of *permanent* crisis.[26] And a wide variety of crisis management experts stand at the ready to offer "unique" guidance. But if the variety of experts is wide – consultants, practitioners, researchers, and lawyers – their view of crises is remarkably homogeneous.

Startling Homogeneity

To examine how the crisis management industry adheres to and reinforces the crisis-as-event model, we can start by noting the absence of ontological inquiry into the construct of crisis. Experts, rather, take crisis events as real and objectively urgent. In response to these crisis events, organizations need effective crisis management. It's a self-reinforcing argument on behalf of an underlying model that is never explicitly stated or critically examined.

To avoid the kind of "knee-jerk decisions" that often accompany "intense crisis-induced stress," leaders would be well advised to surround themselves with "trained professionals" when their units are hit with a crisis event. This was the advice of one professional, who explained that the consultants "are experts at what they do and have done it many times before."[27] The advice is packaged to appear unique and uniquely helpful. Experts marshal evidence that their backgrounds and "years of experience" imbue them with the capability to offer "unique approaches" and special expertise. Hire *us*, not *them*.

There may well be competitive advantages held by one individual or firm over another. Trident DMG, for instance, prides itself in providing lawyers, most prominently founder Lanny Davis, to help with the management of "reputational risk and brand damage related to a corporate crisis." In doing so, Trident touts the tactical advantage of hiring a lawyer for the task, ensuring "the benefit of attorney-client privilege."[28] Secrets will be kept.

---

[26] In order, W. Jack Duncan et al., "Surviving Organizational Disasters," *Business Horizons* 54 (2011), 135; Mitroff, *Why Some Companies Emerge Stronger and Better from a Crisis*; Seeger et al., *Communication and Organizational Crisis*, 3; Marie Mikušová and Andrea Čopiková, "What Business Owners Expect from a Crisis Manager? A Competency Model Survey Results from Czech Businesses," *Journal of Contingencies and Crisis Management* 24 (2016), 162; Ronald Heifetz et al., "Leadership in a (Permanent) Crisis," *Harvard Business Review* 87 (2009), 62–70.

[27] Steven Fink quoted in David Ketchen Jr., "How Penn State Turned a Crisis into a Disaster: An Interview with Crisis Management Pioneer Steven Fink," *Business Horizon* 57 (2014), 670.

[28] www.lannyjdavis.com. In 2018, Michael D. Cohen, Donald Trump's former personal lawyer, hired Davis to help him navigate his way through guilty pleas on counts relating to tax fraud, false statements to a bank, and campaign finance violations tied to his work in

However, an analysis of the crisis management "solutions" exposes less the variety that exists across various consultants than the "startling homogeneity" of their assumptions.[29] In their adoption of the crisis-as-event model, experts agree on core principles, and none more fundamental than the position of leaders as the central response mechanism to the event. When times get tough, leaders shift into "crisis mode." And there is much for leaders to learn in preparation for the onset of an inevitable crisis.

Learning to Prepare and Respond

In their effort to apply leading-edge knowledge to the solution of real-world problems, universities around the world have organized crisis management programs aimed at preparing leaders. Harvard University's John F. Kennedy School of Government has set as its mission the bringing together of "students, scholars and practitioners" who will be taught how to "combine thought and action to make the world a better place." Part of the fulfillment of its mission involves a "Program on Crisis Leadership" that seeks "to improve society's capacity to deal with natural disasters; infrastructure, technology, and systems failures; emergent infectious disease; and terrorism."[30]

Course conveners promise a "comprehensive perspective, looking at risk-reduction strategies, emergency preparedness and response, and disaster recovery."[31] These are the shared assumptions of the crisis-as-event model: an event elicits a response that, when handled properly, will lead to recovery.

The Kennedy School's program is rather typical of high-level university-affiliated programs. The University of Michigan's Ross School of Business offers a course that "prepares you to lead in high-pressure, high-stakes environments."[32] MIT presents a class specifically designed to deal with crises within business organizations. Crises are categorized by their objective characteristics: "cyber security and data breach," "supply-chain management," "terrorism," and "operations disruptions," for

---

the 2016 presidential campaign. See Manuel Roig-Franzia, "Lanny Davis, the Ultimate Clinton Loyalist, Is Now Michael Cohen's Lawyer. But Don't Call It Revenge," *Washington Post* (August 23, 2018). Davis has his own five rules. See Lanny J. Davis, *Crisis Tales: Five Rules for Coping with Crisis in Business, Politics, and Life* (New York: Threshold, 2013).

[29] This rich phrase is from Paul DiMaggio and Walter Powell, "The Iron Cage Revisited: Collective Rationality and Institutional Isomorphism in Organizational Fields," *American Sociological Review* 48 (1983), 147–160.

[30] www.hks.harvard.edu/more/about-us.

[31] www.hks.harvard.edu/centers/research-initiatives/crisisleadership.

[32] https://michiganross.umich.edu/sanger/crisis-challenge.

instance.[33] Specific responses can be tailored to these different crisis types.

When it comes to teaching crisis management, there is plenty of competition, although all of it from within the startlingly homogenous crisis-as-event model. Consulting companies often compete directly with universities for executive education programs. Major consulting firms boast of special departments devoted exclusively to crisis management. Under the heading "Unforeseen Advantage – Crisis Management," Deloitte's Center for Crisis Management warns, "the next crisis that could threaten your company may already be taking shape."[34] Learning to prepare for and respond to "a major crisis" event will allow Deloitte's clients to emerge stronger than ever. Adhering to the pattern suggested by the crisis-as-event model, Deloitte categorizes crises by their supposedly objective characteristics: regulatory, cyber, and strategic crises with special attention to risks in the financial services industry, the site of the global collapse of 2008.

Deloitte refers to a neat delineation between "human-made" and "natural" disasters. That's a common feature of the crisis-as-event model. The rendering of crises as things allows for the construction of either/or classifications. Was this event human-made *or* natural, internal *or* external, planned-for *or* unpredictable?[35] Those characteristics are held to be objective and indisputable, not subject to interpretation and, perhaps, manipulation.

However the nature of the event is characterized, it is maintained that the "greatest damage to an organization" caused by a crisis "is often the result of poor management of the crisis rather than the crisis itself." So, let Deloitte help with "crises simulations" and lessons on "crisis communications." And because crises may occur on the individual level, there are experts for that eventuality as well.

Clients in Bet-You-Life Predicaments

Crisis management consultants focus, for the most part, on organizations and other social units threatened by crisis events. There is a subset, however, who specialize in helping out individuals in jeopardy. This specialization is typically referred to as "reputation management." Take Sitrick and Company.

---

[33] http://professional.mit.edu/programs/short-programs/crisis-management.
[34] www2.deloitte.com/global/en/pages/risk/topics/center-for-crisis-management.html.
[35] Pierre Bourdieu wrote about the fallacy of epistemological couples, of which this is an example. Couples are conceptualized in opposition to each other: human-made versus natural crises, for example. See Bourdieu, "What Makes a Social Class?"

Since its founding in 1989, Sitrick has focused on "high profile . . . bet-your-life situations."[36] Clients ranging from convicted sex offenders, celebrities who find themselves in trouble, and notable lawbreakers built Sitrick's reputation. That, likely, was the reason that Hollywood producer Harvey Weinstein turned to Sitrick in the fall of 2017 after firing his original crisis management team.

In 2017–2018, much of the entertainment industry underwent a searing evaluation of attitudes and behaviors ranging from abuse, to assault, and to rape directed by powerful men toward women and men of considerably less power. The #MeToo movement "shattered the silence and pushed sexual harassment and the lived experiences of so many women to the forefront of the national conversation."[37] Sexual assault centers found themselves overwhelmed.[38] Although sexist and assaultive behavior was hardly a new phenomenon, the prominence of the involved figures from the entertainment industry invited rapt attention. And the trigger was the cascade of accusations against Harvey Weinstein.

A producer of high-quality films and a maker of movie stars, most notably Gwyneth Paltrow, Weinstein built first Miramax and then The Weinstein Company into major Hollywood players. In doing so, he acquired a reputation as a bully, a sexist, even a predator. As early as 1995 – this was twenty-two years before a *New York Times* front-page story detailed multiple allegations of sexual abuse and rape – Brad Pitt "threatened to beat up" Weinstein after Gwyneth Paltrow "told him that the movie mogul had sexually harassed her."[39] Major 2017 stories in the *Times* and the *New Yorker* finally brought Weinstein's ugly history into the open.

In response to those exposés, the producer quickly issued a statement apologizing for past behaviors while vowing to become a "better person." The press exposure amounted to a "wake-up call," even though his past behavior, he insisted, reflected the culture of the 1960s and 1970s, "when all the rules about behavior and workplaces were different." He was claiming to have been, at least in part, a carrier of a prevailing macho culture.

Although emphatically denying charges of assault, rape, or any non-consensual sex, Weinstein explained that he intended to "channel the anger" into charitable efforts, including gun control and scholarships for young "women directors."[40] The following day, his lawyer issued

---

[36] http://sitrick.com/about.   [37] www.pbs.org/program/metoo-now-what.

[38] Molly Redden, "Calls to Anti-Sexual Assault Helpline Up by 21% after Harvey Weinstein Allegations," *The Guardian* (October 25, 2017).

[39] Mike Miller, "How Brad Pitt Threatened Harvey Weinstein After He Allegedly Harassed Gwyneth Paltrow," *People* (October 10, 2017).

[40] Harvey Weinstein, "Statement," *The Cut* (October 5, 2017).

a considerably less contrite follow-up statement labelling the *Times*'s story as defamatory and threatening to sue. It was an empty threat.

In the crisis-as-event model, the multiple claims levelled against Weinstein constituted a reputational crisis. Experts lined up to denounce the statements made by Weinstein and his lawyers as among "the worst" ever. "This is not a strategy that makes the future easy for him," commented one professional. "His narcissism, coupled with his self-serving refuge in a culture of the past and pledge to donate money to good causes combined with his accompanying threats of lawsuits, made the crisis worse."[41] Here was yet another example of a bungled response.

Reputation is a special judgment regarding the relative standing and desirability of an individual or organization, and it is directly linked to power and influence available to individuals and organizations.[42] Weinstein, remember, was also the co-founder of The Weinstein Company. The company's reputation suffered as a result of the accusations. Board members resigned in the immediate aftermath, employees owned up to their own complicity, and the company – already in financial difficulties before the story broke – eventually declared bankruptcy and sold its assets to a private equity firm.

Weinstein's decision to retain Sitrick was hardly a surprise. Firm founder Michael Sitrick leveraged his background as a journalist to aid clients in "trying to get accurate information in the public domain."[43] Both the Los Angeles Roman Catholic Archdiocese and the Church of Scientology retained Sitrick to devise reputation-enhancing strategies during damaging investigations. Representing Harvey Weinstein, however, proved to an altogether different challenge for Sitrick.

After turning to Sitrick, Weinstein adopted a new approach. His Sitrick handler defined her task not as creating a new public image for Weinstein, but rather "to make sure the facts are as accurately and fairly reported as possible."[44] Sitrick's strategy promised that, at a minimum, the underlying facts would not be wished away, at least not entirely. Rather, Weinstein would show contrition without admitting to any specific criminal act. That

---

[41] Gene Maddaus, "Harvey Weinstein's Crisis Response 'One of the Worst' Experts Have Seen," *Variety* (October 11, 2017).

[42] Alex Bitektine, "Toward a Theory of Social Judgments of Organizations: The Case of Legitimacy, Reputation, and Status," *Academy of Management Review* 36 (2011), 151–179; Daniel Carpenter, *Reputation and Power: Organizational Image and Pharmaceutical Regulation at the FDA* (Princeton: Princeton University Press, 2010); David Deephouse and Suzanne Carter, "An Examination of Differences between Organizational Legitimacy and Organizational Reputation," *Journal of Management Studies* 42 (2005), 329–360.

[43] This quote and background from Sitrick are from Abby Aguirre, "He Fixes the Worst PR Crises Imaginable," *New York Times* (June 1, 2018).

[44] Kaitlin Menza, "Can This Woman Save Weinstein?" *The Cut* (November 10, 2017).

response seemed to bet on a public willingness to forgive and move on: "Mr. Weinstein has begun counseling, has listened to the community and is pursuing a better path" in hopes that "if we make enough progress, he will be given a second chance."[45] That was the statement released by his Sitrick team. It was not a viable strategy. The crisis-as-event model misled Sitrick experts into conceiving of Weinstein as the victim of an urgent situation. In that view, the crisis event resided outside of their client and his actions. They got that wrong: Weinstein *was* the urgency.

In May 2016 a New York City grand jury indicted Weinstein on multiple counts of rape and criminal sexual assault (three additional criminal assault charges were added in the summer of 2018). At that point, Sitrick and Weinstein parted company.[46] The notion of positioning Weinstein as the one in need of crisis advice to restore his reputation proved untenable. Weinstein has yet to be convicted of a single criminal act. Yet, more than eighty women came forward with accusations, many of which were corroborated by contemporaneous testimony. For those women, the crisis was being perpetuated *by* Weinstein, not *to* Weinstein.

Attacks on women are real. Weinstein was a self-admitted macho bully who stood accused of multiple criminal attacks, and who had been led off in handcuffs. Those were the brute facts. The notion that it was Weinstein who had suffered a reputation crisis was a self-serving construction that ultimately collapsed under its own weight.

Companies can and often do suffer when the reputation of their founders is shaken: Martha Stewart's Omnimedia, Dov Charney's American Apparel, and Travis Kalanick's Uber, for instance. Business organizations face myriad circumstances beyond the reputation of the founder that can be labeled as a crisis. When crisis consultants turn their attention to offering aid to these organizations, their focus tends toward the top of the unit, toward the leader.

The Measure of a Leader

Once urgency has been reified as an objective crisis, leaders are expected to enter into crisis mode.[47] "The measure of a leader," readers of the

---

[45] Aguirre, "He Fixes the Worst PR Crises Imaginable."

[46] The reasons for the breakup of the relationship were not made public, although Sitrick subsequently filed for arbitration claiming that Weinstein had failed to pay his bills. See Aguirre, "He Fixes the Worst PR Crises Imaginable." Weinstein then hired Herald PR, which promotes itself as a "NYC-based full service public relations, digital marketing, social media management, and website development firm." See http://heraldpr.com/about.

[47] The idea of leading in a crisis mode is a popular concept in both academic studies and popular commentary. For an example of each, see Epaminondas Koronis and

Harvard Business Review were told in an article entitled "How a Good Leader Reacts to a Crisis," is "often tested during a crisis." Engage directly, demonstrate control, respond promptly but not hurriedly, and maintain composure; these are the hallmarks of "good" crisis leadership.[48]

Fundamental to the crisis-as-event model is agreement on "the criticality and centrality of crisis leadership."[49] The Australian Institute of Management cautioned, "as a leader, a crisis will test your competency on many levels."[50] By creating the image of an organization "under siege" due to the crisis situation, proponents of the crisis-as-event model advocate for "strong" leadership that involves "force of will, influence, personal charisma, experience, and decisiveness, to name just a few."[51] The expectation for leaders in the crisis-as-event model is high.

The supposed relationship between strong leaders and effective crisis response is not complicated: "People experience crisis as episodes of threat and uncertainty, a grave predicament requiring urgent action." A "natural inclination" directs people to "look to leaders" to reduce stress and return the organization to "normality." Effective crisis response transforms individuals into "true leaders" and leaders into "statesmen."[52]

Even though experts define crisis as an unexpected or unthinkable event, leaders need to be prepared. That preparation requires that they be capable of reading their environment.[53] A common theme of leadership literature evokes special skills at anticipating events and interpreting

---

Stavros Ponis, "Better Than Before: The Resilient Organization in Crisis Mode," *Journal of Business Strategy* 39 (2018), 32–42 and Kara Swisher and Walter Isaacson, "Uber in a Crisis Mode," *CNBC* (March 27, 2017).

[48] John Baldoni, "How a Good Leader Reacts to a Crisis," *Harvard Business Review Web* (January 4, 2011), 2.

[49] Mercela Lucero et al., "Crisis Leadership: When Should the CEO Step Up?" *Corporate Communications: An International Journal* 14 (2009), 234.

[50] www.aim.com.au/blog/crisis-management-%E2%80%93-lessons-leadership.

[51] Grant and Mack, "Healthy Leadership during Organizational Crisis."

[52] Boin and 't Hart, "Public Leadership in Times of Crisis," 544. For other evocations of the need for "strong" leadership during crises, see Tony Jacques, "Crisis Leadership: A View from the Executive Suite," *Journal of Public Affairs* 12 (2012), 366–372; Rosabeth Moss Kanter, "Leadership and the Psychology of Turnarounds," *Harvard Business Review* 81 (2003), 3–11; and Robin Kielkowski, "Leadership during Crisis," *Journal of Leadership Studies* 7 (2013), 62–65.

[53] These definitions of crises are from Benjamin Baran and Marisa Adelman, "Preparing for the Unthinkable: Leadership Development for Organizational Crisis," *Industrial and Organizational Psychology* 3 (2010), 45–47, and Joel Brockner and Erika James, "Toward an Understanding of When Executives See Crisis as Opportunity," *Journal of Applied Behavioral Science* 44 (2008), 94–115.

complex dynamics.[54] And given the increasing complexity and dynamism of the world, today's leaders need help figuring out the best way to do that.

Environmental scanning, it is argued, with an emphasis on "monitoring and maintaining external relationships" will improve the capacity of leaders to anticipate crises. Reliance on a team will help ensure that leadership has timely access to matters that may be threatening "separate and distinct organizational elements."[55]

In viewing leadership as "essential during a crisis," experts counsel leaders to restore "people's confidence in themselves and one another."[56] To help leaders rise to the challenge, the University of Michigan Ross School of Business teaches "the leadership skills you'll practice," including the capacity to "navigate ambiguity," the skill to "perform under pressure," and the capacity to "exercise good judgment."[57] MIT's Crisis Management and Business Continuity program offers a class on "Emergency Preparedness and the Dimensions of Meta-Leadership."[58] The emphasis is on decisiveness and effective communications.

Communicating to Manage the Damage

Effective leadership in a crisis mode amounts to a series of concrete steps that executives should take in response to the threatening event. Special emphasis is placed on the communications responsibilities of leaders during a crisis.[59] "If there was a cardinal rule in crisis communication, it must certainly be the criticality and centrality of crisis leadership," wrote Mercela Lucero and colleagues.[60] Crisis communication, as it is conceptualized within the crisis-as-event model, represents a "struggle for control." How will the crisis event be understood? Because "the

---

[54] H. Igor Ansoff, "Conceptual Underpinnings of Systemic Strategic Management," *European Journal of Operational Research* 19 (1985), 2–19.

[55] Quotes from Seeger et al., *Communication and Organizational Crisis*, 67; Littlejohn, *Crisis Management*, 13.

[56] Kanter, "Leadership and the Psychology of Turnarounds," 3; Kielkowski, "Leadership during Crisis," 62.

[57] https://michiganross.umich.edu/sanger/crisis-challenge.

[58] http://professional.mit.edu/programs/short-programs/crisis-management.

[59] Argenti, "Crisis Communication"; Kathleen Fearn-Banks, *Crisis Communications: A Casebook Approach* (New York: Routledge, 2011); Alain Guilbert, "Crisis Communications," *Ivey Business Journal* 64 (1999), 78–89; Simon Taylor, *Defending Your Reputation: A Practical Guide to Crisis Communications* (London: Thorogood, 2001); Alan Zaremba, *Crisis Communication: Theory and Practice* (Armonk, NY: M. E. Sharpe, 2010).

[60] Lucero et al., "Crisis Leadership," 234.

responsibility for the crisis, its magnitude, and its duration are contestable," crisis managers will need to proceed thoughtfully in constructing their message, both during and after the event.[61] Effective communication will allow for the "creation and retention of meaningful interpretations among organizational participants."[62]

Crisis communication does not just target internal constituents. When in the crisis mode, leaders are urged to be sure to "make contact with all important segments of your public" and "tell them what you can."[63] Cover-ups, which can involve silence, denial, and/or outright lying, are bound to be perceived by the public as 'being worse than the 'crime.'"

That's an unfortunate cliché of the crisis management industry, that the cover-up is always worse than the crime. No it isn't. That sentiment conveniently places its emphasis on crisis management while trivializing the antecedent criminal act. But the assertion of the cliché leads to the articulated goal of crisis communication: "to minimize the damage – not to escape it."[64] Communication consists as much of listening as it does of talking.

Making Plans to Respond

"Most business disasters occur because executives are caught out by foreseeable events," noted Abraham Carmeli and John Schaubroeck.[65] The crisis management industry intends to help organizations minimize disruption through planning. After all, "all organizations will experience a crisis at some point in time." Therefore, leaders always need a plan to help "respond to the crisis well."[66] Leaders "must have a well-thought-out approach" to deal with crisis, noted a former corporate general counsel. Executives, we are told, typically avoid this stage because they are "preoccupied with the market pressures of the present quarter." That's no excuse, wrote a former aerospace executive reflecting on the Challenger disaster.[67] "We must make plans for

---

[61] Robert Heath and Dan Millar, *Responding to Crisis: A Rhetorical Approach to Crisis Communication* (New York: Routledge, 2003), p. 5.

[62] Seeger et al., *Communication and Organizational Crisis*, 19.

[63] Meyers and Holusha, *When It Hits the Fan*, 234.

[64] Adubato, *What Were They Thinking?* 79, 184.

[65] Abraham Carmeli and John Schaubroeck, "Organizational Crisis-Preparedness: The Importance of Learning from Failures," *Long-Range Planning* 41 (2008), 178.

[66] Melissa Bowers et al., "Organizational Culture and Leadership Style: The Missing Combination for Selecting the Right Leaders for Effective Crisis Management," *Business Horizons* 60 (2017), 563.

[67] In 1986 the US space shuttle *Challenger* exploded less than two minutes into its flight, killing all seven crew members.

dealing with crises; action plans, communication plans, fire drills, essential relationships"; and, he emphasized, "practice counts."[68]

Looking at the businesses that were so devastated by the September 11 attack – employees killed and traumatized, offices destroyed, communication channels clogged, and neighborhoods demolished – a corporate communications professor acknowledged that even the best thought-out plan may not be fully up to the task of such a monumental catastrophe. Still, having a contingency plan – alternative work sites, communication channels, crisis command centers, and strong communication expertise – would allow leaders "to improvise as needed, think on their feet, make quick decisions," but to do so with a "strong foundation."[69] As always in the crisis management industry, it is the event that triggers and the leader who responds. That is the core of the crisis-as-event model.

The Implicit Model of Crisis Management: Crisis-as-Event

The crisis-as-event model spans many sources of expertise, universities as well as consultants. It is an approach that can be helpful in guiding future responses to urgency. There may well be advantageous distinctions among the offerings, but the approaches are remarkably homogeneous. They all rest on a shared ontological assumption: crises are things.

When a mode of analysis – in this case, of how best to manage a crisis event – morphs into a profession, an inevitable outcome will be an agreement on "the definition and promulgation of normative rules."[70] There will, of course, be different specific suggestions, but crisis professionals adhere to that theoretical model (summarized in Table 3.1).

The crisis management industry rests firmly on the reification of urgency as an objective event. In that way, the industry fits neatly and uncritically into the crisis-as-event model. The positivist ontology of the model is never made explicit. Rather, it resides in the taken-for-granted assumption that crises are real occurrences – elemental, self-sufficient material particulars that carry an inherent threat.[71]

Positivism asserts not only that reality exists independently of human consciousness but also that humans are capable of acquiring truth.

---

[68] Norman Augustine, "Managing the Crisis You Tried to Prevent," *Harvard Business Review* 73 (1995), 150–151.
[69] Argenti, "Crisis Communication," 105.
[70] DiMaggio and Powell, "The Iron Cage Revisited," 152.
[71] David Weissman credits the notion of a "self-sufficient material particular" to Aristotle. See Weissman, *A Social Ontology* (New Haven: Yale University Press, 2000).

Table 3.1 *Crisis-as-event assumptions built into crisis management*

ASSERTION	FOR EXAMPLE
Crisis as things	• Horrific events, disasters, infrastructure failures, disease, terrorist attacks, etc.
Crises becoming more frequent	• Growth in the sheer numbers, becoming common feature, the norm, state of permanent crisis, etc.
Central role of leaders	• Leaders are tested, forged in crisis, etc.
High value on top-down communication from leader	• Connect with employees and other stakeholders, create meaningful and shared understanding of events, etc.
Leaders need advice	• Turn to experts to avoid knee-jerk reactions, etc.
Leaders need to scan and plan	• Environmental scanning to avoid being surprised by foreseeable events, make plans, practice response, etc.

Through the application of observation and scientific reasoning, the truth is "out there," ready and capable of being obtained. The application of a rigorous and disciplined process will render the immutable laws of the universe apparent. Knowledge and truth will become paired. The world can and does yield its nature to us, or at least to those of us who possess the capacity to read that world. That belief in the capacity to read the world objectively is precisely why the industry emphasizes its role in helping crisis leaders get it right: "own the crisis" – assuming that crisis is a thing to be possessed – "or it will own you."[72]

Academic inquiry regularly echoes that same ontological approach and, in doing so, reinforces the crisis-as-event model. Typically, the opening paragraphs of an article on crisis rely on implicitly positivist definitions. "Organizational crises are acute, public, arduous threats to an organization and its stakeholders," starts one such study, "that can be elicited, for instance, by financial fraud, employee discrimination, or revelations of life-threatening product safety problems."[73] They are real, and they need to be recognized as such.

Perhaps the most commonly cited definition comes from Christine Pearson and Judith Clair's 1988 *Academy of Management Review* piece, in which they propose, "*An organizational crisis is a low-probability, high-impact event that threatens the viability of the organization and is characterized*

---

[72] Lauren Leader-Chivée "CEOs: Own the Crisis Or It Will Own You," *Harvard Business Review Web* (March 26, 2014).

[73] Andreas König et al., "A Blessing and a Curse: How CEOs Trait Empathy Affects Their Management of Organizational Crises." *Academy of Management Review* (2018).

by ambiguity of cause, effect, and means of resolution, as well as by a belief that decisions must be made swiftly."[74] This definition has become the de facto go-to construction of crisis as an event.[75] Even without that particular citation, definitions tend to coalesce on the crisis-as-event model. A crisis is an "extreme event," one that is "emotionally charged" and "shocks" or "jolts" an organization.[76]

There have certainly been efforts that focus on the perceptions of the leaders rather than on the event itself.[77] But even in these cases, the authors either explicitly embrace the crisis-as-event model (Karl Weick, for example, who calls on Pearson and Clair's definition of crisis as "a

---

[74] Christine Pearson and Judith Clair, "Reframing Crisis Management." *Academy of Management Review* 23 (1998), 60. Emphasis in the original. Their definition, in turn, builds on these eight prior works: Donna Aguilera, *Crisis Intervention: Theory and Methodology* (St. Louis: Mosby, 1986); Dutton, "The Processing of Crisis and Non-Crisis Strategic Issues"; Charles Hermann, "Some Consequences of Crisis Which Limit the Viability of Organizations," *Administrative Science Quarterly* 8 (1963), 61–82; Susan Jackson and Jane Dutton, "Discerning Threats and Opportunities," *Administrative Science Quarterly* 33 (1988), 370–387; Enrico Quarantelli, "Disaster Crisis Management: A Summary of Research Findings," *Journal of Management Studies* 25 (1988), 373–385; Paul Shrivastava, "Crisis Theory and Practice: Towards a Sustainable Future," *Industrial and Environmental Crisis Quarterly* 7 (1993), 23–42; Paul Shrivastava et al., "Understanding Industrial Crises," *Journal of Management Studies* 25 (1988), 285–303; and Karl Slaikeu, *Crisis Intervention: A Handbook for Practice and Research* (Upper Saddle River, NJ: Pearson, 1986). Together, then, these nine works can be taken as the modern foundation of the academic field of crisis management.

[75] See, for example, William Kahn et al., "Organizational Crises and the Disturbance of Relational Systems," *Academy of Management Review* 38 (2013), 377–396. Juan Madera and D. Brent Smith, "The Effects of Leader Negative Emotions on Evaluations of Leadership in a Crisis Situation: The Role of Anger and Sadness," *Leadership Quarterly* 20 (2009), 103–114; Eric J. McNulty et al., "Integrating Brain Science into Crisis Leadership Development," *Journal of Leadership Studies* 11 (2018), 7-20; Yu Tieying et al., "Misery Loves Company: The Spread of Negative Impacts Resulting from an Organizational Crisis," *Academy of Management Review* 33 (2008), 452–472; and Ethlyn Williams et al., "Crisis, Charisma, Values, and Voting Behavior in the 2004 Presidential Election," *Leadership Quarterly* 20 (2009), 70–86.

[76] Vinit Desai, "Mass Media and Massive Failures: Determining Organizational Efforts to Defend Field Legitimacy During Crisis," *Academy of Management Journal* 54 (2011), 264; Alfred Marcus and Robert Goodman, "Victims and Shareholders: The Dilemmas of Presenting Corporate Policy during a Crisis," *Academy of Management Journal* 34 (1991), 284.

[77] Achilles Armenakis et al., "Symbolic Actions Used by Business Turnaround Change Agents," *Academy of Management Journal* 38 (1994), 229–233; Richard Daft and Karl Weick, "Toward a Model of Organizations as Interpretation Systems," *Academy of Management Review* 9 (1984), 284–295; Richard Johnson, "Defending Ways of Life: The (Anti-)terrorist Rhetorics of Bush and Blair," *Theory, Culture and Society* 19 (2002), 211–231; Thomas Milburn et al., "Organizational Crisis. Part II: Strategies and Responses," *Human Relations* 36 (1983), 1161–1180; Dean Tjosvold, "Effects of Crisis Orientation on Managers' Approach to Controversy in Decision Making," *Academy of Management Journal* 27 (1984), 130–138; Sylvia Walby, *Crisis* (Malden, MA: Polity, 2015); Karl Weick, "Enacted Sensemaking in Crisis Situations," *Journal of Management Studies* 25 (1998), 305–317.

low probability/high consequence event that threatens the most fundamental goals of an organization") or do not explicitly offer a definition of
crisis.[78]

With the crisis firmly established as a thing – possessing extreme and
threatening characteristics – academics working within the crisis-as-event
model pose research questions that tease out subtleties of crises and their
relationship to organizations, among them such questions as the
following:

- What are the strategies employed by organizations to maintain their
  legitimacy in the face of existential threats?[79]
- What are the varieties of ethical considerations that can be applied to
  leader response in a crisis situation?[80]
- What are the variations of leadership development programs that might
  best be employed to prepare leaders to respond to a crisis?[81]
- What characteristics – behavioral and personality traits – influence the
  manner in which CEOs respond to crises?[82]

The choice of analytic unit for the crisis-as-event model is always the
event itself.

That choice, once made, allows for a process of categorization:

- Is the event internal – say, a product failure resulting from a flawed
  development process – or external – say, an environmental disturbance – to the unit?[83]
- If the event is external, is its source political, social, economic, or
  natural?[84]
- Does the event pose a threat, an opportunity, or some combination of
  the two?[85]

---

[78] Weick, "Enacted Sensemaking in Crisis Situations," 305.
[79] Myria Allen and Rachel Caillouet, "Legitimation Endeavors: Impression Management
Strategies Used by an Organization in Crisis," *Communication Monographs* 61 (1994),
45–62.
[80] David Bauman, "Evaluating Ethical Approaches to Crisis Leadership: Insights from
Unintentional Harm Research," *Journal of Business Ethics* 98 (2011), 281–295.
[81] Baran and Adelman, "Preparing for the Unthinkable."
[82] Grant and Mack, "Healthy Leadership during Organizational Crisis"; König et al., "A
Blessing and a Curse."
[83] Achilles Armenakis and William Fredenberger, "Organizational Change Readiness
Practices of Business Turnaround Change Agents," *Knowledge and Process Management*
4 (1997), 143–152.
[84] Brockner and James, "Toward an Understanding of When Executives See Crisis as
Opportunity"; Falkheimer and Heide, "Crisis Communicators in Charge."
[85] Jackson and Dutton, "Discerning Threats and Opportunities"; Thomas Milburn et al.,
"Organizational Crisis. Part I: Definition and Conceptualization," *Human Relations* 36
(1983), 1141–1160.

- Was the event "sudden" – say, a tsunami or terrorist attack – or "smoldering – brought on, perhaps, by a macho culture that long condoned sexual harassment?[86]
- Was the event an incident, an accident, a conflict, or a physical disruption?[87]
- Was the event a "normal" outcome of a complex system in constant interaction or an unanticipated and unforeseeable surprise?[88]

Once these, or other, classification systems are codified, typologies can be derived to help develop theories of the situational/contextual effectiveness of various strategies for response.[89]

Defining a crisis as an event also invites the imposition of temporal boundaries. Scholars can focus on what is taken to be the antecedent event that triggered the crisis.[90] Attention is also focused on the post-crisis or crisis termination period and how governing structures work to rebuild viability and legitimacy. In all cases, the underlying reified assumption – that a crisis is a thing that occurs to a firm – remains unexamined.[91] The crisis-as-claim model questions these assumptions.

We can start altering our assumptions by noting that the classifications offered by the crisis-as-event model are less about labeling the event than about sorting the claims made by leaders. When the incident aboard United Flight 3411 first became public, spokespeople for the airline characterized the event as triggered by an external force: an uncooperative passenger who refused to give up his seat after being "asked several times, politely." The CEO added that the company and its crew were simply doing what they "had" to do to "re-accommodate" customers.

By shifting focus from the event to the claim, an entirely separate analysis emerges. We note, for example, the lack of acknowledgment that airline employees – and airport security forces – were poorly trained for dealing with such an escalating situation, no mention of industry-wide policies allowing for the removal of paid passengers, and no mention of

---

[86] Erika James and Lynn Wooten, "Leadership as (Un)Usual: How to Display Competence in Times of Crisis," *Organizational Dynamics* 34 (2005), 141–152.

[87] Pauchant and Mitroff, *Transforming the Crisis-Prone Organization*.

[88] Perrow, *Normal Accidents*; Pauchant and Mitroff, *Transforming the Crisis-Prone Organization*; Seeger et al. *Communication and Organizational Crisis*.

[89] For example, William Benoit, *Accounts, Excuses, and Apologies: A Theory of Image Restoration Strategies* (Albany: State University of New York Press, 1995), and Coombs, *Ongoing Crisis Communication*.

[90] Lynn Isabella, "Managing the Challenges of Trigger Events: The Mindsets Governing Adaptation to Change," *Business Horizons* 35 (1992), 59–66.

[91] In an insightful piece by Paul 't Hart and Arjen Boin, the ambiguity of and long tail associated with crisis termination is analyzed. See 't Hart and Boin, "Between Crisis and Normalcy: The Long Shadow of Post-Crisis Politics," in *Managing Crisis: Threats, Dilemmas, Opportunities* (Springfield, IL: Charles C. Thomas, 2001), pp. 28–46.

the limited pool of passengers from which the "volunteers" were randomly selected.

Now, rather than criticizing Munoz for the way he responded to the event, we can pose a different set of questions:

- What prompted CEO Oscar Munoz, a widely respected communicator with an ability "to connect and share with employees his vision for the airline and get them to rally behind it," to respond in the way he did? To what extent was he exercising power and advancing a set of interests?
- How and why was the "event" framed as an incident that unfolded completely within the hermetically sealed confines of that particular flight on that particular day? That was the domain of the viral video, of course. But wasn't there more to the story? How and why, for instance, has the airline industry adopted policies that encourage overbooking and allow for bumping of passengers with confirmed reservations? And what about the training afforded airline personnel and the Chicago Department of Aviation ground officers?
- Was there really a crisis here at all here? Was Munoz's handling of the situation as clumsy as the experts insisted? Sure, there were some uneasy moments and the airline's image took a short-term hit. But how can we evaluate Munoz's actions – his claim of "outrage, anger, and disappointment" – beyond expert assertions that he had turned "a PR crisis" into a "total disaster"?

In the crisis-as-claim model, the claim as well as the behaviors of the claims maker become the central focus.

To recalibrate our understanding of crises and to formulate a new model, we need a robust theoretical foundation. That process of building the underlying theory of the crisis-as-claim model begins in the following chapter.

4   Problems, Crises, and Contextual Constructionism

The literature emerging from within the crisis-as-event model intends to be imminently practical and extremely useful. Based on the best available evidence and on an analysis of past approaches to crisis management, these experts tell us, here is what leaders should do and what they must avoid.

But while offering actionable advice, the crisis-as-event model underplays theory. To be sure, there *is* an underlying theory to the model: a positivist approach that holds that crises are real, material things and leaders respond in an effort to "own" that crisis to save/redeem/revitalize the threatened entity. So it isn't that the crisis-as-event literature is atheoretical, exactly. It's just that the theorizing is tacit rather than explicit, unspoken rather than acknowledged. That's a problem. By failing to articulate the governing theory of the model, proponents obscure the possibility of critical analysis of that theory.

What is called for is a new model of crisis with its own distinct underlying theory. The purpose of this chapter is to build that theory and articulate it explicitly. Many fields help in this endeavor to create a new model of crisis and to articulate the underlying theory: psychology, history, philosophy, and so on. Because my model builds mainly on sociological theory of knowledge, it is worth asking: why sociology?

By making a choice to lean heavily on sociological theory, I seek to address what I consider to be the two major shortcomings of the crisis-as-event model. First, the dominant literature fails to ask questions concerning the ontological construction of the notion of a crisis. How do we know that some dynamics are worthy of and likely to attract the crisis label and others less so?

We can't really believe that dynamics constitute a threat just because someone in a position of power claims it is a crisis. But what is the alternative? Because crisis management experts take the objective structure of a crisis event as a given, they do not address such ontological inquiries. Sociologists, however, for nearly half a century have been building theory concerning the social construction of knowledge. It is this body of theorizing that offers a counterbalance to the reification of urgency by the crisis management industry.

Second, the crisis-as-event model avoids any critical engagement with matters of interests and power. When leaders say their units are facing a crisis, they are inherently and unavoidably advancing interests and asserting power. That observation does not suggest that all claims are inherently illegitimate because they advance interests and assert power. Not at all. It does suggest – really, it *demands* – that interests and power be considered and analyzed. Yet, crisis management moves right to the seven essential lessons for surviving disaster and for crisis proofing an organization without engaging in a dialogue with manifestations of interests and power.

Sociological theory again offers an important theoretical counterbalance. Claims-making theory demands a full consideration of the advancement of interests and the assertion of power by the claims maker. Any and every time a claim is constructed, we are told, remain alert to underlying assertions of power. Before moving to construct a theory of crisis-as-claim, let's consider some of the competing claims of urgency that emerged from the 2016 US presidential election, and one that did not.

There's a Crisis in Here Somewhere

Many times during the 2016 presidential campaign Republican candidate Donald Trump asserted an urgent claim regarding threats to the integrity of the electoral process. "The election is absolutely being rigged by the dishonest and distorted media pushing Crooked Hillary," he tweeted, referring to his Democratic opponent Hillary Clinton, "but also at many polling places – SAD."[1] Forces were organizing to deprive Trump and his supporters of victory by committing, he insisted, massive "voter fraud."

At an October 10 rally in Ambridge, Pennsylvania, the candidate urged his supporters to monitor polls as a precaution, and not just their own polling places. "Watch other communities," he urged, "because we don't want this election stolen from us." A week later, Trump expanded his warning of widespread fraud by providing details: "People that have died 10 years ago are still voting." He was citing a Pew Charitable Trust report as evidence: "The following information comes straight from Pew Research, quote, 'Approximately 24 million people – one out of every eight – voter registrations in the United States are no longer valid or [are]

---

[1] https://twitter.com/realDonaldTrump/status/787699930718695425.

significantly inaccurate.'"[2] The line of reasoning ran directly from a flawed registration system containing numerous clerical errors to fraudulently cast votes.

The information Trump provided came directly from the report. At least his quote did. But he misrepresented the report's content. The Pew Charitable Trust was not suggesting voter fraud at all. The problem it was addressing, rather, resided in sloppy, inefficient registration processes. That one-in-eight estimate did not reflect dead people voting. "Dead voters," the report said explicitly, were "rare." There was *no* hint of any voter fraud, organized or otherwise.

Regardless, Trump continued to rely on the report to bolster his warning:

One in eight. More than 1.8 million deceased individuals, right now, are listed as voters. Oh, that's wonderful. Well, if they're going to vote for me, we'll think about it, right? But I have a feeling they're not going to vote for me. Of the 1.8 million, 1.8 million is voting for someone else.[3]

Trump claimed that the integrity of the election was at stake.

Shortly after his inauguration in January 2017, Trump acted on that claim. "I will be asking for a major investigation into VOTER FRAUD, including those registered to vote in two states, those who are illegal and," the president tweeted, "even those registered to vote who are dead (and many for a long time). Depending on results, we will strengthen up voting procedures!"[4]

The newly created Presidential Advisory Commission on Election Integrity took on the mission of promoting "honest and fair Federal elections." The enabling executive order defined the mandate and, in so doing, the scope and limits of the commission quite specifically: "The term 'improper voter registration' means any situation where an individual who does not possess the legal right to vote in a jurisdiction is included as an eligible voter on that jurisdiction's voter list, regardless of the state of mind or intent of such individual."[5]

The commission quickly descended into disarray before being dissolved by another executive order eight months later. "Despite

---

[2] Quote from Robert Farley, "Trump's Bogus Voter Fraud Claims," *FactCheck.org* (October 19, 2016). The report itself, "Inaccurate, Costly, and Inefficient: Evidence That America's Voter Registration System Needs an Upgrade," was released in 2012. www.pewtrusts.org/~/media/legacy/uploadedfiles/pcs_assets/2012/pewupgradingvoterre gistrationpdf.pdf.

[3] Ibid.

[4] Quoted in Daniella Silva, "President Trump Says He'll Ask for 'Major Investigation' into Unsubstantiated Allegations of Voter Fraud," *NBCNews.com* (January 25, 2017).

[5] *Presidential Advisory Commission on Election Integrity* (July 13, 2017).

substantial evidence of voter fraud," Trump asserted without benefit of any evidence, "many states have refused to provide the Presidential Advisory Commission on Election Integrity with basic information relevant to its inquiry."[6]

The definition of voter impropriety as contained in the commission's founding document made no mention of attempts by states or localities to suppress votes. Yet claims of voter suppression were also raised before and after the election. "Voter *suppression* is the problem, not voter fraud," a union leader insisted. I've emphasized the word "suppression" in that statement to highlight the very different label being used.

Efforts to prevent voter fraud, it was asserted, had a negative impact on voter participation. The greatest impact was among marginalized, non-white groups:

At best, the efforts to stop so-called voter fraud are misguided and unnecessary. At worst, they are textbook "dog-whistles," with roots in some of our nation's ugliest periods of discrimination designed to deny citizens the right to vote … the curtailing of early vote hours, illegal voter purges, the restriction of absentee voting and other disenfranchising practices have all been used to limit eligible voters from exercising their Constitutional right to vote.[7]

Although there may have been many explanatory reasons, the decline of African American and Hispanic participation in the 2016 election was blamed in part on explicit attempts to prevent them from voting.

No evidence surfaced supporting claims of widespread voter fraud, and the extent to which voter suppression impacted the outcome of the election was unclear. Additional talk about Russian interference, along with the last-minute insertion of the FBI and the many faults of the Democrats' campaign clouded any easy conclusion. But another factor was not just influential but decisive in determining who took the oath of office in January 2017. Although that factor was discussed after the election, it was never labeled a crisis, not by either party. Perhaps that lack of urgency was due to the fact that the relevant event occurred more than two centuries earlier.

Despite all the other factors, one objective reality remains. Hillary Clinton beat Donald Trump by 2.8 million votes. So, why wasn't *she* president? It was because of the fifty-five men who attended the Constitutional Convention in Philadelphia in the spring and summer of

---

[6] *Statement by the Press Secretary on the Presidential Advisory Commission on Election Integrity* (January 3, 2018).

[7] Tefere Gerbre, "Voter Suppression Is the Problem, Not Voter Fraud," *HuffingtonPost.com* (May 24, 2017). For a study of voter suppression aimed at minority voters, see Carol Anderson, *One Person, No Vote: Suppression Is Destroying Our Democracy* (New York: Bloomsbury, 2018).

1787. The founders of the Republic adopted as their official goal the formation "of a more perfect Union." Perfection may have been their shared ideal, but it was an intention profoundly shaped by compromise. Delegates remained fiercely committed to the advancement of their economic, regional, racial, and patriarchal interests.[8] The most contentious debates focused on the matter of slavery.

Compromises were reached concerning how and if the population of enslaved African Americans would be counted to determine the number of a state's representatives in the House of Representatives (the three-fifths compromise allowed 60 percent of slaves to be counted though not to vote), and whether Congress should have the right to ban foreign slave trade (yes, but only after 1808).[9] That three-fifths compromise also figured into another contentious matter: how to elect the chief executive. The outcome of *that* debate determined who was inaugurated in January 2017.

Popular or direct voting for the president was a generation away from the Philadelphia gathering. Among the delegates, there was considerable suspicion of the capacity of poorly educated citizens to make an informed choice concerning this newly created position (there was no executive branch in the previous governmental compact, the Articles of Confederation) that carried with it considerable power. James Madison, the "Father of the Constitution," endorsed an Electoral College as a way not just to avoid a popular vote but also to enhance the power of slave-holding states to influence the outcome. Madison was a slave owner himself. His home state of Virginia claimed the largest enslaved community in the new United States.[10] As a result, the state benefited greatly from the three-fifths rule in terms of representation in the House.

The Electoral College was set up so that the number of electoral votes cast for president from each state would equal the number of senators plus the number of representatives. Every state was allocated two senators, so clout could be gained only by having a greater number of representatives. Once again, slave-holding states would benefit without, considering enslaved African Americans as potential voters. Madison's

---

[8] All of these interests were contested except for patriarchy, which represented a shared bias of the participants. See F. Feeley, "The New Republican Man and the Role of Women in the New Republic," in *Comparative Patriarchy and American Institutions: The Language, Culture, and Politics of Liberalism* (Newcastle upon Tyne: Cambridge Scholars Publishing, 2010), pp. 10–38.

[9] The House of Representatives was granted sole authority to initiate tax laws, still a sore point from the days of British colonial rule. So the matter of representation in that chamber received serious attention.

[10] Sonia Yaco and Beatriz Betancourt Hardy, "Historians, Archivists, and Social Activism," *Archival Science* 13 (2013), 253–272.

home state was the biggest winner in the Electoral College structure, becoming the single most influential voting bloc in the presidential election. Thus, the Electoral College was put into place in 1787 and remains in force to this day.

Popular (i.e., white male) voting became the norm after 1824. Now, the possibility existed for a divergence between the popular and the Electoral College vote.[11] That happened once in 1876 but then seemed to fade as a possibility.[12] It was the 2000 election that returned the issue to the public's attention.

Democrat Al Gore won the popular vote against Republican George Bush by the slimmest of margins, about 500,000 votes out of the more than 100 million cast. Yet Bush won the Electoral College vote, 271 to 266. Sixteen years later, another Republican won the presidency by losing the popular vote but winning in the Electoral College. Without the Electoral College, a mechanism established in 1787, at least in part to benefit slave states, neither George Bush nor Donald Trump would have been president.

There was discussion about the mechanism for selecting the president after both the 2000 and 2016 elections. Yet, very few people labeled it a crisis. *New York Times* columnist Michelle Goldberg did call the Constitution a "suicide pact" for allowing someone who had not won the popular vote to become president.[13] Mostly, however, there was no urgency attached to solving the problem.[14] "I prefer direct national election of our president," suggested a constitutional law professor in an exceedingly measured tone. The College "is a feature of the kind of government we have chosen from the beginning in which the states are

---

[11] Paul Finkelman, "Voters and Voices: Reevaluations in the Aftermath of the 2000 Presidential Election: The Proslavery Origins of the Electoral College," *Cardozo Law Review* 23 (2002), 1145–1157. The right of all male US citizens to vote regardless of "race, color, or previous condition of servitude" was added to the Constitution as the Fifteenth Amendment in 1870. Women's right to vote was recognized in the Nineteenth Amendment ratified fifty years later.

[12] Two other American presidents were elected without a majority vote, but in both cases – Lincoln in 1860 and Wilson in 1912 – they won a plurality of the popular vote and a majority of the Electoral College running against more than one additional candidate. In these instances, the Electoral College arguably helped ensure a smooth transition.

[13] Quoted in Eddie Scarry, "Trump's Election Shows the Constitution May Be a 'Suicide Pact,'" *Washington Post* (September 25, 2017).

[14] In response to the 2016 election outcome, a number of state legislatures and the District of Columbia agreed to the National Popular Vote Interstate Compact. How electoral votes are allocated by a state is left to the discretion of the state legislature. Under the compact, states would allocate all of their electoral votes to the winner of the national popular vote. The twelve states that had signed the compact by November 2018 (accounting for 172 electoral votes) agreed to enact the new procedure if and when signees represented an absolute majority (270) of the Electoral College. See www .nationalpopularvote.com.

important subsidiary (in some instances, primary) units of government," intoned another.[15]

No presidential commission was established to ensure honesty and fairness. The Electoral College is simply a rule of the game, a taken-for-granted mechanism that twice in sixteen years deprived the winner of the popular vote of a victory. No crisis here.

How We Know What We Know

Who gets to determine whether a unit faces a crisis? Is the Electoral College a two-century-old rule of the game or an ongoing usurpation of direct democracy? And who gets to name the crisis? Voter fraud or voter suppression? Voter fraud, if and when it occurs, is illegal. Voter suppression occurs largely through legal means: photo ID laws, limitations on voting hours, and the like. And the Electoral College is foundational to US constitutional governance.

We are drawn, inevitably, to assertions of urgency: impending massive fraud, restrictions placed on voting of marginalized groups. When no such assertion is forthcoming – there was no claim that a cabal of slave-holders had, two centuries earlier, "rigged" the 2016 election – there is diminished interest in responding. But how do we think about those assertions?

In the crisis-as-event model, crises are real, and their meaning is objective and self-evident. The crisis-as-claim model rejects those assumptions. Rather, it places the nature of the claim and the interests of the claims maker under the microscope. What was one person's interest in warning of voter fraud and another's interest in calling attention to voter suppression? To undertake such an analysis, a new interpretation is required, one that starts with a theory of socially constructed knowledge.

What We "Know" to Be Real Is Not, *Except in Its Consequences*

How do we know that there is an effort to "rig" the election, either through fraud or suppression? Or that the Electoral College provides a mechanism for constraining the popular voice and was created in part to do just that in a presidential election? How, indeed, do we *know* anything? Knowing, it turns out, is a far-from-simple matter.

In a 1973 lecture, "On Constructing a Reality," delivered to the International Conference on Environmental Design Research, philosopher/

---

[15] Akhil Reed Amar and Charles Fried as quoted in "Room for Debate: Should the Electoral College Be Abolished?" *New York Times* (November 16, 2016).

physicist Heinz von Foerster asserted that the *"environment as we perceive it is our invention."*[16] It's not the environment that is our invention; it is the way it is perceived – that is, created by the observer. Knowledge of the world is something separate from the world itself. What we know is, in fact, what we *think* we know.

Von Foerster was proposing the basis for constructionism, an approach that takes the process of perceiving meaning as central to the generation of all human knowledge. His point was that knowledge does not present objective reality to people. Rather, knowledge offers a "symbolic universe," one that is filtered through human observation. That term, "symbolic universe," comes not from von Foerster but rather from Peter Berger and Thomas Luckmann's seminal study on the sociology of knowledge that appeared seven years prior to the Environmental Design lecture.

Von Foerster was not concerned with the process by which reality came to be perceived. He spoke only of the need to draw a distinction between "constructed" and "objective" reality. Berger and Luckmann's 1966 *Social Construction of Reality* agreed with that distinction while focusing on the process by which knowledge came to be and the embeddedness of that construction process within a social system. Thus, their core assertion: knowledge is socially constructed.

There is an actual world, a reality that Berger and Luckmann defined as "a quality appertaining to phenomena that we recognize as having a being independent of our own volition (we cannot 'wish them away')."[17] Those corporal phenomena, however, are not the same as knowledge; nor are they perfectly captured by knowledge. Rather, knowledge resides in an interpretive process by which people come to believe that what they think to be real and true is, in fact, real and true.

Knowledge, then, is not reality; it is our interpretation of reality. That's a vital distinction, insisting as it does that we do not, cannot, know anything independently of human intervention. Our "knowing" of reality involves the creation of "provinces of meaning" that are circumscribed knowledge "enclaves." Some aspects of reality are selectively invited into our provinces; others are filtered out. Berger and Luckmann employed the metaphor of a curtain being raised and lowered between the person as "knower" and the external world as "reality."

People believe that what they know is real, that they are experiencing directly and understanding fully reality as it is in its true state. What

---

[16] Heinz von Foerster, "On Constructing a Reality," in *Observing Systems* (Seaside, CA: Intersystems, 1973), 228. Emphasis in original.
[17] Berger and Luckmann, *Social Construction of Reality*, 1.

people think to be real becomes real to them and forms the basis for future decisions and actions. This is similar to the famous Thomas Theorem that states that what people think to be real becomes real in its consequences.[18]

Berger and Luckmann were sociologists, not physicists like von Foerster. When people "knew" the world to be flat, say, von Foerster would insist as a physicist that they were wrong in their knowledge. But that scientifically based assertion of wrongness was not what Berger and Luckmann were focused on. It was the knowledge itself, the absolute belief in the flatness of the world, say, that attracted their attention.

The sociology of knowledge should not focus on objective reality, those phenomena that reside independently of human volition. *That* is not knowledge. Berger and Luckmann insisted that attention be paid to the subjective interpretation that emerged from social interaction and then became embedded in our minds as knowledge. It was, after all, knowledge rather than any scientific "truth" that impacted people's decisions and actions. *I believe that the Earth is flat; therefore, I will avoid signing up for any long ocean voyages!*

Of course, I'm being a bit frivolous with this example. We know that by the time of Columbus's travels, any educated European would have accepted that the Earth was not flat, and Columbus would not "fall" off. But the point is, believing something to be true makes it true in its consequences.

Berger and Luckmann's social constructionism mounted a dizzying assault on the traditional scientific, positivist views of the real world. By offering a "radical theoretical shift," constructionists "invite us to be critical of the idea that our observations of the world unproblematically yield its nature to us," wrote Vivian Burr. They "challenge the view that conventional knowledge is based upon objective, unbiased observation of the world."[19] In raising that challenge, constructionists offer a perspective sharply divergent from "hard science" epistemological positions that can be labeled "positivism" and "empiricism." Constructionism demands caution about declaring what is real and suspicion about any and all assertions of truth.

At its most exacting expression – a position labeled "strict constructionism" – constructionists insist that there is no such thing as an objective fact. What we think to be true, believe with certainty to be true, is not

---

[18] That theorem, dating to the 1920s, was the product of William Isaac Thomas and Dorothy Swaine Thomas.

[19] Vivian Burr, *Social Constructionism* (London: Routledge, 2015), p. 2. The "radical theoretical shift" quote is from Kallie Pihlaimen, *The Work of History: Constructivism and the Politics of the Past* (New York: Routledge, 2017), p. i.

a direct reflection of anything other than human interpretation. That interpretation is itself a by-product of human interactions and choices.

Even without such a strict view, it is possible to accept the assertion that human knowledge is not based on objective, unbiased observations of the world. The labels we attach to our conceptions of objective reality – "fraud" or "suppression," for instance – are interpretations, nothing more or less. A field of sociological study, social problems, emerged to focus on what were labeled as threats to the prevailing values and norms of a community.

Is not the act of attaching the label *problem* to one element of the environment but not another simply another example of our construction of knowledge? Malcom Spector and John Kituse insisted that this is exactly what a social problem was: a label attached to a definition of reality that was no more or less real than any other label.

When Is a Problem a Problem?

Starting in the 1920s and flowing initially from the Sociology Department at the University of Chicago, an approach to social problems emerged that emphasized the context of human behavior. The underlying ontological construction of problems as real things was assumed. There *was* behavior that was objectively deviant and that manifests itself in crime, juvenile delinquency, drug addiction, prostitution, suicide, and so on. These behaviors inherently constituted a "social problem." But there was also a context for that behavior, a "social structure and culture" that generated these distinctive behavioral patterns.

"The problems current in a society," wrote Robert Merton and Robert Nisbet, "register the social costs of a particular organization of social life."[20] It was the forces of a "disorganized" social life – fragmented families, community conditions, poverty – that shaped patterns of deviant behavior.[21] Writing in 1925, L. K. Frank asserted that "one of the first questions raised by the subject of social problems is, what are the conditions which generate these difficulties." C. Wright Mills continued the campaign to place social problems analysis within a broader framework, in his case, of corporate capitalism and its enabling institutions.[22] The objective reality of the threat was assumed.

---

[20] Robert Merton and Robert Nisbet, "Preface," in *Contemporary Social Problems* (New York: Harcourt Brace, 1961), p. ix.

[21] Bernard Harcourt et al., "Seeing Crime and Punishment through a Sociological Lens: Contributions, Practices, and the Future," *University of Chicago Law School Legal Forum* 2005 (2005), 289–323.

[22] L. K. Frank, "Social Problems," *American Journal of Sociology* 30 (1925), 463; C. Wright Mills, "The Professional Ideology of Social Pathologists," *American Journal of Sociology* 49 (1943), 165–180.

Not so fast, cautioned Émile Durkheim. Pathologies are organic to any and all social systems.[23] What is normal is a precursor to what is trouble. In a 1977 *Social Problems* article, Robert Emerson and Sheldon Messinger agreed with Durkheim, insisting that "any social setting generates a number of evanescent, ambiguous difficulties that may ultimately be – but are not immediately – identified as 'deviant.'"[24] It is only when those difficulties are recognized, defined, and targeted for remedy do they become social problems. That identification process, with its implications of power and influence, could now be more fully interrogated. That's just what Joseph Gusfield did.

The infusion of social constructionism into the social problems literature preceded Gusfield. Howard Becker cautioned against an uncritical application of the label "deviant," and Herbert Blumer criticized "traditional" social problems theory, with its insistence that social problems represented objective conditions, as a "gross misunderstanding of the nature of social problems."[25] It was Gusfield who asked the question: who gets to decide what a social problem is and what it isn't? Furthermore, what shall we call a potential problem? Who gets to decide these matters?

Labels are tools people call upon to construct their world, to apply meaning to its confounding contingencies. *This* is a problem, but *that* isn't. It's a kind of shortcut in assigning meaning, and it's a powerful one. And there will always be options for constructing and applying labels, choices to be made among a "plurality of possible realities."[26] His 1981 *Culture of Public Problems* found in campaigns against drunk driving an illustrative instance of how a problem is constructed, enabling an analysis of the consequences of that construction.

There is a reality that cannot simply be wished away. People drive carelessly when intoxicated and people are killed by car crashes. Okay, but *what* is the problem? How do we understand it? Label it? Respond to it? Is it, "drunk drivers cause accidents that kill people"? Sure, that's one way to frame the matter. It is only one among several, however.

In the competition for control over how problems will be defined, the victors get to impose not just their characterization but also their controlling vocabulary and their roadmap to potential solutions. When

[23] Émile Durkheim, *The Rules of Sociological Method* (New York: Free Press, 1966).

[24] Robert Emerson and Sheldon Messinger, "The Micro-Politics of Trouble," *Social Problems* 25 (1977), 121.

[25] Howard Becker, "Whose Side Are We On?" *Social Problems* 14 (1967), 239–247; Herbert Blumer, "Social Problems as Collective Behavior," *Social Problems* 18 (1971), 298.

[26] Joseph Gusfield, *The Culture of Public Programs: Drinking-Driving and the Symbolic Order* (Chicago: University of Chicago Press, 1981), p. 3.

individuals and groups assume ownership over a problem – say, the International Drunk Driving Prevention Association or Mothers Against Drunk Driving, not to mention anti-drunk-driving campaigns sponsored by various brewers and automobile manufacturers – the problem of drunk driving gets attention. But it also comes to be defined in a particular way. It is understood as careless, reckless, and otherwise foolish *individual* behavior. And now the "solution" becomes apparent (if difficult to achieve) as well: prevent irresponsible individuals from driving while drunk.

Preventing drunk individuals from driving may sound like a perfectly reasonable and effective solution. Perhaps it is. Constructing the problem in that way lends itself to a specific set of responses: responsible driving campaigns, designated driver arrangements, warnings, penalties, loss of driver's license, and even incarceration. But when a problem is thus defined – in this case, driving while drunk – alternatives may be rejected as beside the point or inconvenient. Other approaches may not even be considered.

What about the responsibility of the auto industry to design a car based on the assumption that individuals will occasionally behave foolishly, even recklessly? Or the lack of mass transportation, especially late in the evening? Couldn't roads be designed in ways that might substantially reduce the impact of driving under the influence? In his analysis, Gusfield does not suggest that any one of these approaches would "solve" the problem, just that the framing of a problem directs attention toward some approaches and simultaneously away from others.

It was Spector and Kituse's 1973 "Social Problems: A Reformulation" and the 1987 publication of *Constructing Social Problems* that marked the full integration of social constructionism in the theory of social problems.[27] Their work upended the prevailing ontology of the field by refuting a belief in the "objective nature" of a social problem. The study of social problems, in their view, must focus not on conditions but rather on *"activities of groups making assertions of grievances and claims to organizations, agencies, and institutions about some putative conditions."*[28] Just as Berger and Luckmann turned the sociology of knowledge away from a consideration of the objective universe, Spector and Kituse navigated social problems away from objective conditions and toward claims of grievance.

---

[27] Joseph Schneider, "Social Problems Theory: The Constructionist View," *Annual Review of Sociology* 11 (1985), 209–229.

[28] Malcolm Spector and John Kitsuse, "Social Problems: A Reformulation," *Social Problems* 21 (1973), 146. Emphasis in the original.

There are individuals and groups who advocate for both attention to and solutions for particular social problems: let's solve drunk driving, end gang violence, cure juvenile delinquency. It was true, of course, that these claims makers – that was Spector and Kituse's term for advocates of a particular problem definition and a specific solution – *asserted* truth. Their claims insisted that the referent problems were real; they were conditions that were inherently problematic, and their definitions of those problems were fully objective. But Spector and Kituse were not distracted by such self-assured contentions.[29] Berger and Luckmann had already acknowledged that the construction of knowledge led holders of that knowledge to believe they possessed objective truth. That was a delusion. Spector and Kituse agreed.

The central "problem" for Spector and Kituse was not the condition that formed the subject matter of the assertion, not the reality of crime or poverty. The debate over whether voter fraud and voter suppression were *real* problems, for instance, would not have interested them. What they focused on, instead, was the process by which (a) the claim emerged and (b) the audience for the claim responded.

Social problems scholars should not judge the *content* of the assertion of the social problem: was it true or not? They should pay attention instead to the underlying *dynamics* that explain why some claims are made and others not, and why some claims are responded to and others are not. Problems did not exist aside from their construction. Someone claims that a problem is real. What are the consequences of the claim of voter fraud or voter suppression, or the lack of a claim concerning the impact of the Electoral College? To the extent that a claim becomes believed, it is real in its consequences.

Spector and Kituse recognized that not all claims have an equal chance in a contest for acceptance. The power of a claim to attract adherents, however, did not reside in alignment of the claim with the objective world. Endorsement arose, instead, out of the process through which claimants transformed their claims into a shared sense of reality, a process dependent on factors such as resources and consistency of perspective. Accuracy, for them, was not part of the equation. Some groups were simply better able than others to define problems and achieve responsiveness.

After Spector and Kituse, scholars could analyze the nature and process of the claim of a problem. Issues of power and control came to light

---

[29] Darin Weinberg, "On the Social Construction of Social Problems and Social Problems Theory: A Contribution to the Legacy of John Kitsuse," *American Sociologist* 40 (2009), 61–78.

when questions were raised such as why, for example, witches were held to be a social problem by the political and social elite of seventeenth-century New England, but not witch hunts.[30] Why and how did cocaine abuse come to be labeled as a "scourge" – President George H. W. Bush's language – with the evolution of crack cocaine and its alleged prominence in minority communities?[31] Why wasn't equal outrage applied to the twin – and more damaging – "scourges" of alcohol and tobacco? And why did illegal immigration into the United States attract so much attention and worry at a time when it was abating?[32]

Given that crime was typically identified as a pressing social problem, it is not surprising that the field of criminology also absorbed the ontological perspective of constructionism.

The New Criminology and the Role of Power

Criminology – broadly defined as the "study of crimes, criminals, and society's response" – had its origins in classical theory. Cesure Baccaria produced an early essay, in 1804, in which he insisted that criminal laws and proper mechanisms for the creation and maintenance of civil society were necessary. The implicit ontological assumption being made here was that crimes were taken to be real. They were concrete facts of nature: objective attacks on the social order that could inherently be considered crimes. With that understanding, a solution also presented itself: crimes needed to be controlled by proper laws, adequate enforcement, and appropriate punishment.

A century after Baccaria, theologian Frederick Wines heralded a "new criminology" with its emphasis on humanizing trends in prison and sentencing reform as a way to wed "modern science" to social progress.[33] That perspective on crime as objectively threatening to proper social order (itself a human invention) remained largely unchallenged

---

[30] Thomas Szasz, *The Manufacture of Madness* (New York: Delta Books, 1970).

[31] Peter Lyons and Barbara Rittner, "The Construction of the Crack Babies Phenomenon as a Social Problem," *American Journal of Orthopsychiatry* 68 (1998), 313–320; David Mustow, "Evolution of American Attitudes toward Substance Abuse," *Annals of the New York Academy of Science* 562 (1988), 3–7. The *New York Times* would, much later, report on its own culpability in spreading the "crack baby" myth with headlines such as "Crack Babies Turn 5, and Schools Brace." "The myth of the 'crack baby' – crafted from equal parts bad science and racist stereotypes – was debunked by the turn of the 2000's. But by then, the discredited notion that cocaine was uniquely and permanently damaging to the unborn had been written into social policies and the legal code." Editors, "Slandering the Unborn," *New York Times* (December 28, 2018).

[32] "Border Crossings Have Been Declining for Years, Despite Claims of a 'Crisis of Illegal Immigration,'" *New York Times* (June 20, 2018).

[33] Frederick Wines, *The New Criminology* (New York: James Kempster, 1904), p. 3.

until the 1970 publication of Richard Quinney's groundbreaking *The Social Reality of Crime*.

Quinney adopted a strict social constructionist posture toward crime in the same way that Spector and Kituse would with social problems. Crime, to Quinney, was a constructed, not an objective, reality. "I adopt a nominalistic position contrary to that of the positivists," he wrote. There was no such thing as a natural or objective crime: "I can accept no universal essences ... we have no reason to believe in the objective existence of anything."[34] Constructing a situation as a problem or a crime (or affixing any other label) was an attribution of meaning rather than a description of objective truth.

Quinney insisted on inserting the dynamic of *power* into the process of claiming a problem or, particularly, of labeling a behavior as a crime. What should or should not be called a crime? Were voter ID laws a crime or a proper enforcement mechanism? There will always be conflicting views over such questions. How about marijuana use? Drinking? Selling merchandise on Sunday? After all, interracial marriage, homosexuality, even public celebrations of Christmas were all labeled as criminal acts at some time and in some communities in the United States. The question of deciding what a crime will be gets resolved through a process of intergroup conflict. And at the heart of that process lies the power of groups to impose (or resist the imposition of) the criminal label to specific behaviors.

So what, exactly, is "crime." It is a nothing more than a label, a claim made on human conduct "*that is created by authorized agents in a politically organized society.*"[35] There is no crime without a definition imposed by particular elements of a society. "Bad acts" by individuals were labeled crimes because they threated the "order" of the state. "Bad acts" by the state were not labeled as crimes when they were seen as supportive of social order. Just because an act was labeled as a crime did not make that act inherently criminal. "Instead, we now had to see how every aspect of crime," wrote Francis Cullen, "was intimately affected by how it was conceptualized or defined."[36] And Quinney went even further.

Why is it that the state designates particular behaviors to be criminal? How can failure to pay a debt be classified as a crime, but adding hidden, undiscernible fees to a loan be legal? The answer, for Quinney, resided in the matter of interests. State actors *always* have an interest in determining

---

[34] Richard Quinney, *The Social Reality of Crime* (Boston: Little, Brown, 1970), p. 4.

[35] Ibid., 15. Emphasis in the original.

[36] Cullen quoted in John Wozniak, "Richard Quinney's *The Social Reality of Crime*: A Marked Departure from and Reinterpretation of Traditional Criminology," *Social Justice* 41 (2015), 199.

what is or is not a crime. The act of constructing an understanding of reality by attaching a label was *always* an expression of interests. The attachment of a label can be thought of as making a claim. Therefore, the study of claims making adds a final element to a constructionist theory of crisis as a claim of urgency.

A Tournament of Claims

A horrific event occurred. The world witnessed the deadly aftermath on television. Law enforcement investigators worked frantically to piece together a story. They knew the end, but little else. It was the night of October 21, 2017. Approximately 22,000 country music fans amassed on the Las Vegas Strip to enjoy the closing performance of the Route 91 Harvest festival. At 10:05, Stephen Paddock opened fire from his thirty-second-floor room at the nearby Mandalay Hotel. Ten minutes and well over 1,000 rounds later, 58 people lay dead with another 546 injured. Paddock then stopped – he had plenty of ammunition left and law enforcement would not gain access to his room for another hour – and shot and killed himself.

This was the deadliest mass shooting by an individual in US history. Paddock had availed himself of a legally purchased "bump stock" that he affixed to his legally purchased semiautomatic rifle, allowing him to fire off legally purchased rounds of bullets at a rate comparable to a fully automatic weapon.[37]

The Vegas shooting was an incident, a one-off occurrence. But it may also be constructed as "an *instance* of a larger problem."[38] Placing an incident within the framework of an instance of something bigger involves claims making. And almost immediately after the shooting, there were claims made as to what, exactly, the event meant, how it should be constructed, what should be done in response:

- For Kentucky Governor Matt Bevin, the incident was an instance of evil. "To all those political opportunists who are seizing on the tragedy in Las Vegas to call for more gun regs," he tweeted, "you can't regulate evil."[39]
- For Hilary Clinton, the 2016 Democratic presidential candidate, the incident was an instance of the uncontrolled power of the National Rifle

---

[37] Bump stocks were made illegal by executive order in December 2018.

[38] Joel Best, "The Social Construction of a Mass Shooting Epidemic," *Reason: Free Minds and Free Market* (July 16, 2013). Emphasis in original.

[39] Quoted in Todd Frankel, "Why Gun Violence Research Has Been Shut Down for 20 Years," *Washington Post* (October 4, 2017).

Association (NRA) and overly malleable Republican allies to block gun control legislation: "Our grief isn't enough. We can and must put politics aside, stand up to the NRA, and work together to try to stop this from happening again."[40]

- For the UK's *Guardian*, the incident was an instance of what happens when gun ownership permeates a society: "No other developed nation comes close to the rate of gun violence in America. Americans own an estimated 265 million guns, more than one gun for every adult."[41]
- For the NRA, the incident was an instance of the dangers that arise when "law-abiding Americans" lack adequate weaponry to defend themselves: "In an increasingly dangerous world, the NRA remains focused on our mission: strengthening Americans' Second Amendment freedom to defend themselves, their families and their communities."[42]
- For the editors of the *Journal of the American Medical Association*, the incident was an instance of a public health failure: "The key to reducing firearm deaths in the United States is to understand and reduce exposure to the cause, just like in any epidemic, and in this case, that is guns."[43]

There was general agreement on facts, but conflicting claims about their meaning:

- Too much "evil."
- Too many guns with no willingness to control their types and numbers.
- Too few guns, preventing self-defense.
- Failure to treat gun violence as a public health issue.

What we see in these responses is a multiplicity of competing claims.

Spector and Kituse quoted sociologist Robert Nisbet: "A social problem cannot be said to exist until it is defined as one."[44] That act of "being said" constituted, for Spector and Kituse, a claim. Specifically, a claim was an "activity" that took the form of calling attention to situations that the claims maker found to be "repugnant" with the intention of mobilizing social forces "to do something about" that situation.[45]

For Spector and Kituse, claims making was a form of interaction in which one party makes a demand on another party that something be

---

[40] Michael Gryboski, "7 Reactions to the Las Vegas Shooting Massacre," *Christian Post* (October 3, 2017).

[41] www.theguardian.com/us-news/ng-interactive/2017/oct/02/america-mass-shootings-gun-violence.

[42] https://home.nra.org/joint-statement.

[43] Howard Bauchner et al., "Death by Gun Violence – A Public Health Crisis," *The JAMA Network* (November 14, 2017).

[44] Spector and Kitsuse, *Constructing Social Problems*, 5.   [45] Ibid., 78.

done about a problematic condition. There was always, in this interaction, a claims maker and an intended audience. Spector and Kituse made no grand representations about claims, focusing instead on demands, complaints, gripes, and requests, typically from individuals or groups asserting their "right at least to be heard."[46]

A claim *always* reflects the perception of the claims maker, *always* constitutes an evaluation: too many guns, too few guns. That was the appeal of Nisbet's insistence that a "social problem cannot be said to exist until it is defined as one." Conditions do not objectively present themselves as problems, but rather "remain undifferentiated until they are perceived, defined, and evaluated."[47]

Problems are not objective, independent conditions; rather, they are subjects of claims.[48] And those claims can no more be classified as "real" than as "spurious." There is no objective reality at all to a claim of a social problem, Spector and Krause insisted.

There is disadvantage and suffering, but these conditions can be said to be "problems" only under two conditions. First, some individual or group states a claim that evaluates a condition as a problem; and second, others are persuaded by the claim. The reality of the problem is located not in conditions but in the claim itself and in its perception by others.[49] "Too many guns" is no more, or less, a social problem than "too few guns." These are competing claims made in an effort to interpret and label reality.

By focusing on the claim rather than on the conditions to which the claim made reference, sociologists could further explore questions about interests and power. "All types of claims making have one thing in common," wrote Patrick Archer, "[t]he interests of certain people or groups."[50]

An *interest* is defined as any stake in achieving a particular outcome. That stake can be financial, of course, but needs to be understood much more broadly:

- A *power* interest in maintaining or upending the status quo of influence distribution.
- A *self-serving* interest in attributing positive judgments to oneself and negative judgments to forces external to oneself.

---

[46] Ibid.   [47] Ibid., 128.
[48] Patrick Archer, "Towards a Theory of Interest Claims in Constructing Social Problems," *Quantitative Sociology Review* 11 (2015), 46–60.
[49] Gale Miller and James Holstein, "Reconsidering Social Constructionism," in *Reconsidering Social Constructionism: Debates in Social Problems Theory* (New York: Aldine de Gruyter, 1993), pp. 5–24.
[50] Ibid., 48.

- An *ideological* interest in advancing a particular perspective.
- A *social* interest in maintaining or changing status distribution.
- An *identity* interest in advancing self- or group image.
- A *professional* interest in advancing the goals of a group.
- An *altruistic* interest in seeking improvements in society.

These interests shape how dynamics are constructed, and then are advanced by claims of urgency.

Claims are not offered in a vacuum. Individuals and groups will assert a claim based on what is deemed to be *"advantageous or beneficial"* to them.[51] That is to say, claims are asserted for a reason, and that reason can be located in the claims maker. We can draw a direct line between the interests of the NRA and its claim concerning the meaning of the Las Vegas massacre, just as we can connect a label of a gun death "epidemic" with the American Medical Association. So, what was the role, if any, of "objective reality"?

By denying any role for objective reality, strict constructionists invited criticism for engaging in uncritical relativism. It was possible, surely, to accept the basic premise of human knowledge as being socially constructed without ceding any possibility of making judgments among various claims. Writing in the wake of Richard Quinney's work, British criminologists Ian Taylor and colleagues asserted a need to move beyond the relativist, uncritical subjectivism inherent in the work of strict social constructionists.[52] A number of constructionists found value in making some judgment about the legitimacy of a claim.

Inquiring about Reasoning and Evidence

Strict constructionists such as Spector and Kituse seemed to block off any avenue for the consideration of a claim's legitimacy. What they intended to investigate only was the process by which the claim was asserted and taken on as "knowledge" by others.[53] For some, even those who accepted the social construction of knowledge while also insisting that a world existed that could not be "wished away," that was not satisfactory.

Contextual constructionists insisted on a capacity to judge claims in the context of a can't-be-wished-away world. People could and should "always inquire about the reasoning and evidence upon which claims are based," Joel Best argued, "and we can evaluate some claims as being

[51] Ibid. Emphasis in original.
[52] Ian Taylor et al., *The New Criminology: For a Social Theory of Deviance* (New York: Harper & Row, 1973).
[53] Miller and Holstein, "Reconsidering Social Constructionism."

more persuasive than others."[54] It is "neither possible nor desirable to ignore the context of claims."[55] That was the position of contextual constructionism.

Contextual constructionists advocated the study of claims making "within its context of culture and social structure." That approach allowed for the matter of how much evidence there is behind any claim "to demand equal attention with attention to the process of why some claims are successful and others are not."[56]

To pass judgment on a claim, philosopher John Searle suggested distinguishing between the objective facts and subjective features of that claim. Yes, Niels Bohr, there is a moon, even when no one is looking at it. These are what Searle called "brute facts."[57] Any and all attempts to project meaning on those objective, brute facts require a subjective assignment of meaning by the observer to the facts. Brute facts became social facts through a subjective, wholly human undertaking.

In the contextual constructionist framework, social problems have both an objective and a subjective element.[58] What evidence does the claims maker marshal for the claim's objective statement of non-constructed reality, of brute facts? And what line of reasoning is followed within the claim that arrives at its representation of meaning? "All human knowledge is socially constructed," Best concluded, "but that does not mean that we are incapable of judging among claims."[59]

That is the theoretical position from which I build the crisis-as-claim model.

A Contextual Constructionist Model of Crisis-as-Claim

Given a goal of building a crisis-as-claim model, many, and highly diverse, conceptions of knowledge, problems, and claims can be called upon. What I have attempted to do instead is to seek patterns and themes in some of the more prominent literature that can be forged into a contextual constructionist crisis-as-claim model (see Table 4.1).

The crisis-as-claim model starts with the view that the world is not observed in an objective, unbiased way. The model rejects the

[54] Joel Best, personal correspondence with author (2017).
[55] Joel Best, "Constructionism in Context," in *Images of Issues: Typifying Contemporary Social Problems* (New York: Aldine de Gruyter, 1995), p. 346.
[56] Joel Best, "But Seriously Folks: The Limitations of the Strict Constructionist Interpretation of Social Problems," in *Reconsidering Social Constructionism*, 129–147.
[57] John Searle, *The Construction of Social Reality* (New York: Free Press, 1995), p. 9.
[58] Brian Jones et al., "Toward a Unified Model for Social Problems Theory," *Journal for the Theory of Social Behavior* 19 (1989), 339.
[59] Joel Best, personal correspondence with author (2017). Quoted with permission.

Table 4.1 *Major theoretical contributions*

KEY POINTS	CORE IMPLICATIONS FOR THE CRISES-AS-CLAIM MODEL
SOCIAL CONSTRUCTION OF KNOWLEDGE *Main Work: Berger & Luckmann (1966)* • Knowledge is not reality; it is a belief or an interpretation of reality that grows out of a process of social interaction. • People create provinces of meaning that imperfectly approximate reality but that constitute reality for them.	"Crisis" is a province for meaning constructed by people; it is not real in and of itself.
SOCIAL REALITY OF CRIME *Main Work: Quinney (1970)* • Crime is a label, a claim imposed on human conduct by authorized agents of the state. • Competing claims on what behaviors should be labeled as criminal will be resolved through a process of conflict. • At the heart of that process lies the power of groups to impose (or resist the imposition of) a criminal label of specific behaviors. • Labels are asserted as a means of advancing interests.	Any analysis of claims-making activity needs to heed the dynamics of power and appreciate the underlying statement of interests by the claims maker.
CONSTRUCTING SOCIAL PROBLEMS *Main Work: Spector & Kituse (1973)* • Problems do not exist aside from their construction. • Competing claims will likely be made in defining problems and demanding attention. • A claim always reflects the perception of the claims marker. • The success of one claim in comparison to another is based on the power and other characteristics of the claims makers.	Study the claims maker, the claim, and the process by which the claim emerges.
MICRO-POLITICS OF TROUBLE *Main Work: Emerson & Messinger (1977)* • Any social setting generates a number of evanescent, ambiguous difficulties. • They may or not get labeled as problems to be remedied.	All units constantly face potential threats that do not become crises unless and until they are labeled as such.

Table 4.1 *(cont.)*

KEY POINTS	CORE IMPLICATIONS FOR THE CRISES-AS-CLAIM MODEL
CULTURE OF PUBLIC PROBLEMS *Main Work: Gusfield (1981, 1996)*	
• Social problems have no objective, single definition. • The way that social problems are defined is a result of choices made by the claims maker and, in turn, impacts how the issue is addressed	Pay attention to conflicting definitions of a problem and the responses that are offered or refuted.
CONSTRUCTION OF REALITY *Main Work: Searle (1995)*	
• "Brute" facts combine with subjective attribution of meaning to constitute reality for people.	Claims need to be evaluated on both their objective treatment of brute facts and on their subjective attribution of meaning.
CONTEXTUAL CONSTRUCTIONISM *Main Work: Best (1993, 1995)*	
• Labeling a problem as a claim should not be taken as an inherent act of delegitimization. • All human knowledge is socially constructed, but it is neither possible nor desirable to ignore the context of claims.	Analysis of claims can and should offer an approach to evaluating claims that takes into account the context of the claims-making process

position assumed in the crisis-as-event model that crises are real, objective things. Claims are never based on an unbiased understanding of objective facts; rather, they are labels applied to dynamics. Therefore, the contentions of truth embedded in a claim must always be treated critically.

From Emerson and Messinger (1977), the crisis-as-claim model accepts the existence of ever-present complex dynamics that can be seen as threats to a social unit. The mere existence of complex dynamics is not sufficient to generate a claim of urgency. It is not even necessary. It is up to the unit's leader to determine what dynamics merit a claim of urgency. Then and only then will there be a crisis.

Gusfield adds another important element to the crisis-as-claim model. The act of asserting that a contingency is a problem involves a process of construction. That is, the act of labeling and explaining the crisis directs attention toward some responses and away from others. The model looks at the discursive elements of a claim of urgency for insight into what interpretations are being advanced, and what interpretations are being blocked by the way "problems" are constructed.

There can always be multiple claims relating to the same contingencies, noted Spector and Kituse. Claims of urgency may offer different, even competing interpretations of what the crisis is and what/who caused it. Likewise, situations that are claimed to be crises by some can be claimed to be non-crises by others. The requirement to evaluate claims can help sort and classify such different, competing interpretations.

The "winning" claim in a tournament of competing claims – that is, the claim that imposes a dominant definition of the meaning of an event on a social unit – will be determined by a number of factors, most particularly the power of the competing claims makers. And that power will always be asserted – not sometimes or mostly but *always* – on behalf of the interests of the claims maker.

Even while insisting that all claims are assertions of interests, the crisis-as-claim model does not insist that all claims of urgency be delegitimized. Rather, there must be a critical stance taken in regard to any and all claims. Based on both the evidence and reasoning contained in a claim of urgency, it is possible and desirable to evaluate the claim. What evidence does the claim maker marshal for an objective statement of non-constructed reality? And what line of reasoning is followed within the claim that arrives at its ascription of meaning?

The crisis-as-claim model argues that claims consist of both objective description and subjective ascription. Therefore, it should be possible to devise a classification system that sorts claims along these lines. In the next chapter, I offer a scheme for doing just that.

5 An Objective Description and a Subjective Uh-Oh!

The crisis-as-claim model assumes that all claims are exercises in power and assertions of interests. Furthermore, the model urges that the intended audience for a claim retain a critical posture. We can and should question the legitimacy of all claims. But questioning, even doubting, is *not* the same as disparaging or dismissing. We need to find an approach to distinguish legitimacy in a claim. What, exactly, does it mean to say this claim is (or is not) legitimate?

Consider first this straightforward claim issued by meteorologist Eric Holthaus as a Category 5 hurricane approached Puerto Rico in September 2017: "Hurricane Maria is now less than 24 hours from Cat 5 landfall in Puerto Rico. I can't emphasize this enough: This is a catastrophic storm."[1] That's about as terse and yet complete a claim of urgency as you're likely to come across. The island of Puerto Rico, and its three-and-a-half million inhabitants, faced imminent and considerable threat. Residents should take appropriate actions. ASAP.

In hindsight, we know of the devastation and calamity the hurricane visited on the island. But even absent such hindsight, it should be possible to develop a system for classifying claims. Was Holthaus's claim legitimate? A classification system will give us a way to analyze this and any other claim of urgency. Before offering that classification system, let's examine a claim far more elaborate than the one issued by the meteorologist: the claim by a CEO that his company had no choice but to respond to a crisis.

"We Don't Have a Choice"

It was the occasion of a Japanese motor show in October 1999 that Carlos Ghosn offered his public appraisal of the urgent situation facing Nissan

---

[1] http://grist.org/article/hurricane-maria-poses-a-catastrophic-threat-to-the-caribbean.
Hurricanes are classified according to the Saffir–Simpson hurricane wind scale (SSHWS). The categories reflect the intensity of the storm's sustained winds. With sustained winds of 157 miles per hour or more, a Category 5 represents the most intense storm.

Motors. Ghosn, who had just been named the company's chief operating officer, knew that Nissan was in deep trouble.[2] Upon arriving in Japan, he found a "lack of a sense of urgency" among Nissan executives. They did not seem overly concerned with the company's abysmal financial performance. But that was about to change. The steps needed to bring the once-mighty automaker back to profitability would involve "sacrifice" and "pain," of that Ghosn was sure. However, he added, "believe me, we don't have a choice."[3] Ghosn turned up the heat.

A number of management missteps kicked off a two-decade-long decline at Nissan starting in the 1980s. Executives changed the company's brand name in the United States from the well-known Datsun to the completely unfamiliar Nissan. Then they allowed their popular Z-car to drift with little infusion of innovative technology. Less obvious but even more troubling was Nissan's inability to achieve flexibility in its relationship with suppliers. Its cost of parts ranged from 15 to 20 percent above domestic competitors, principally Toyota and Honda. Aggressive competition from those same Japanese companies in the United States forced Nissan to take a $1,000 discount on its cars in that huge market.

Sales declined, but costs did not. Despite several announced restructuring plans, Nissan achieved little real cost improvement. After the company borrowed money from the government-owned Japan Development Bank to stay afloat, executives decided to court potential partners. Talks with both Daimler Chrysler and Ford proved fruitless. Then, France-based Renault agreed to an alliance. As a precondition of the partnership, Nissan executives consented to have Renault's second-in-command, Carlos Ghosn, installed as Nissan's COO under CEO Yoshikazu Hanawa. The agreement was announced on April 15, 1999, and the Ghosn era at Nissan began. It would span nearly two decades.

Upon his arrival, Ghosn announced that his goal was "to do everything in my power to bring Nissan back to profitability at the earliest date possible and revive it as a highly attractive company." Between April and late June 1999, Ghosn toured Nissan plants, subsidiaries, and dealerships in Japan, the United States, Europe, and Taiwan. Performance numbers told him a great deal about Nissan, but not the underlying causes of the problems.

By early July, Ghosn reached some conclusions. Perhaps the most surprising was the lack of urgency among Nissan executives: "For a company that has been losing money for seven years out of eight,

[2] Carlos Ghosn, "We Don't Have a Choice," *Automotive News* (November 8, 1999).
[3] Bert Spector, *Implementing Organizational Change: Theory Into Practice* (Upper Saddle River, NJ: Pearson, 2013).

there is not enough of a sense of urgency. People should be banging their heads on the walls everywhere." Increasing a sense of urgency was on his mind when he announced his diagnosis to the press and, more importantly, to employees within the company. "As promised," he said, "I am here to communicate to you the Nissan revival plan."

At the motor show in October, Ghosn piled on details:

The key facts and figures about Nissan point to a reality: Nissan is in bad shape.... Nissan has been losing global market share continuously since 1991.... Today, we are at 4.9 percent world market share. We lost 1.7 points of world market share since 1991. Our production has dropped by more than 600,000 cars over the same period of time.... Nissan has been struggling with its profitability since 1991. Seven of the last eight years, including our forecast for 1999, show a loss.... Nissan has been, and still is, a highly indebted company.... We estimate our net debt level today, after the capital injection from Renault, to be at 1.4 trillion yen, or $12.6 billion.

After that sobering report, Ghosn offered his diagnosis of underlying reasons for Nissan's poor performance:

- "Lack of a clear profit orientation."
- "Insufficient focus on customers and too much focus on chasing competitors."
- "Lack of cross-functional, cross-border, intra-hierarchical lines of work in the company."
- "No shared vision or common long-term plan."

And then came his by now standard observation: "No sense of urgency."

Finally, Ghosn unfolded a plan for recovery based on a simple principle: "No sacred cows, no taboos, no constraints." A detailed list of interventions followed, including slashing debt by nearly $7 billion, closing five factories, and eliminating 21,000 jobs. Ghosn concluded by saying,

We all share a dream: a dream of a reconstructed and revived company, a dream of a thoughtful and bold Nissan on track to perform profitable growth in a balanced alliance with Renault to create a major global player in the world car industry. This dream becomes today a vision with the Nissan revival plan. This vision will become a reality as long as every single Nissan employee will share it with us.

Nissan achieved the results promised in Ghosn's revival plan a full year ahead of time.

A Typology as a Way of Classifying Claims of Urgency

What criterion can be applied to Holthaus's claim to determine how it should be classified? And what about the claims made by Carlos Ghosn?

We know that Hurricane Maria proved devastating to Puerto Rico. And what about Ghosn's performance at Nissan? A judgment on that is far more complex.

Certainly, Ghosn oversaw a remarkable turnaround. The troubled company returned to profitability while regaining lost market share. Ghosn became something of a business leader-hero throughout Asia and literally a manga comic book hero and best-selling author in Japan. And yet . . .

In the decade after the turnaround, with Ghosn dividing his time among Nissan, Renault, and the joint alliance (which expanded to include Mitsubishi in 2017), cracks began to show in Nissan's performance. The company acknowledged that it had used unqualified personnel to conduct postproduction inspections, leading to a major recall in 2017. There were also reports of falsified emission tests emerging from some Japan-based factories. Questions were raised about the sustainability of performance improvements under Ghosn.[4]

Then, in a crushing denouncement to Ghosn's meteoric ascent, Nissan's board fired the man who had led the turnaround. The Japanese government moved to arrest Ghosn on charges of underreporting income and other "significant acts of misconduct." The auto company's CEO – by then, Ghosn was serving as the board chair – suggested that the dynamics of Ghosn's leadership, particularly the long-term concentration of power in a single person, had stifled the flow of information and opinion to and from Ghosn. "Beyond being sorry," lamented Nissan CEO Hiroto Saikawa, "I feel big disappointment and frustration and despair and indignation and resentment."[5] Ghosn maintained that he had been "wrongly accused and unfairly detained based on meritless and unsubstantiated accusations."[6] Meanwhile, an internal investigation conducted at Nissan revealed "evidence of significant underreporting of compensation, as well as misuse of company assets for personal purposes."[7] Soon thereafter, Ghosn was removed from leadership positions at Mitsubishi and Renault.

---

[4] Masamichi Hoshi, "Carlos Ghosn's Short-Term Mindset Puts Nissan in a Fix," *Nikkei Asian Review* (February 19, 2018).

[5] Ghosn was suspected of underreporting his income by about $44 million, a violation of Japan's Financial Instruments and Exchange Act with potential penalties of prison time and/or fines. Nissan CEO Hiroto Saikawa is quoted in Simon Denyer, "Nissan Says Chairman Carlos Ghosn Arrested for Financial Misconduct," *Washington Post* (November 19, 2018).

[6] Motoko Rich, "Carlos Ghosn Emerges to Say He Was 'Wrongly Accused and Unfairly Detained,'" *New York Times* (January 7, 2019).

[7] Amelia Lucas, "Nissan Probe Reportedly Finds Ousted Chairman Ghosn Failed to Disclose $80 Million in Deferred Pay," *CNBC* (November 29, 2018).

Post facto assessments may speak to the character of key players and, most certainly in the case of Carlos Ghosn, offer insight into the disturbing dynamics of heroic leadership. Such assessments say nothing, however, about the nature of the claims of urgency themselves. Ghosn's asserted claim of urgency no less than Eric Holthaus's dire warnings to the residents of Puerto Rico can and should be examined and classified based on some generalizable system of analysis.

To pursue the classification challenge, my primary tool is a *typology*, which is a kind of classification system that identifies types based on multiple dimensions. A typology creates classifications within a specified phenomenal space, in this case, within the space of all claims of urgency.[8] Classification involves the assignment of "labels to a set of instances in such a way that instances with the same label share some common properties and logically belong to the same class."[9] Classification is foundational to all knowledge because it enables pattern recognition. The process of sorting "entities into groups or classes on the basis of their similarity" helps us understand complex phenomena. Once phenomena are sorted by some classification system, generalizations can be drawn about members of that classification.[10] Creating a classification framework enables comprehension, understanding, explanation, attribution, extrapolation, and prediction.[11]

How we classify a phenomenon has a real impact on how we behave. We know, for instance, that decision making is guided by the classifications we use.[12] If a phenomenon is classified as this rather than that, we make different decisions. In his study of criminal classification systems, Lee Sechrest noted the degree to which offenders in prison were treated differently based on their assignment to a classification system. Were inmates antisocial? Did they present with physiological problems? Were they compulsive? Whatever classification system was employed, the

---

[8] Kenneth Bailey, *Typologies and Taxonomies: An Introduction to Classification Techniques* (Thousand Oaks, CA: Sage, 1994).

[9] Sanghamitra Bandyopadhyay and Sriparna Saha, *Unsupervised Classification: Similarity Measures, Classical and Metaheuristic Approaches and Applications* (Heidelberg: Springer, 2013), p. 1.

[10] Ernst Mayr, "Biological Classification: Toward a Synthesis of Opposing Methodologies," *Science* 214 (1981), 510–516.

[11] Bailey, *Typologies and Taxonomies*, 1; Daniel Parrochia and Pierre Neuville, *Towards a General Theory of Classifications* (Basel: Springer, 2013); William Starbuck and Frances Milliken, "Executives Perceptual Filters: What They Notice and How They Make Sense," in *The Executive Effect: Concepts and Methods for Studying Top Managers* (Greenwich, CT: JAI Press, 1988), pp. 35–65.

[12] L. B. Sechrest, "Research on Quality Assurance," *Professional Psychology: Research and Practice* 18 (1987), 113–116.

placement of individuals within a classification mattered; it influenced treatment.

In a business setting, the manner in which a company's competitive strategy is classified – by markets, costs, differentiation, and so on – will shape decisions by executives.[13] Once a business unit is classified as a "cash cow," for instance, it will receive far less investment than a unit said to be a "star."[14] There is often intense internal debate about at what point a star business has slipped into the cash cow category. A star classification attracts investment; a cash cow rides out its market position without much additional investment. It's a debate intensified by the knowledge that classifications matter.

Devising a typology capable of classifying claims of urgency says nothing about whether such claims will be believed. I address the matter of believability in the next chapter. For now, I am offering a typology that classifies claims along two dimensions concurrently: accuracy and plausibility.

Typologies are excellent classification tools, but it is useful to understand more precisely what typologies are and are not. As a method of classification, typologies are conceptual, not empirical. That is to say, a typology classifies ideas, not data. As such, it offers an approach to rendering significant abstract phenomena comprehensible and for directing ongoing discourse. A typology builds its specific classifications based on propositional logic, not on data sets and measurements.[15] The phenomenon being studied is defined, and then a process of logical extrapolation leads to sorting along multiple dimensions.

For a typology to function properly as a type of classification system, all of the phenomenon being considered – in this case, all claims of urgency – must fit into that structure. A typology is meant to be both comprehensive (all examples of the focal phenomenon can be classified somewhere in the typology) and mutually exclusive (all examples of the focal phenomenon must be sorted into only one specific classification).[16]

Typology construction depends on a process of applying propositional logic. It starts with a definition and then moves logically from one proposal to the next. My starting point, thus, is the definition of a crisis as

---

[13] James Chrisman et al., "Toward a System for Classifying Business Strategies," *Academy of Management Review* 13 (1988), 413–428.

[14] This is the Boston Consulting Group's famous typology for categorizing businesses on the basis of market share and market growth. See www.bcgmatrix.org.

[15] Taxonomies, a term that is often mistakenly used interchangeably with typologies, is a classification that does derive from empirical data. See Bailey, *Typologies and Taxonomies*.

[16] Charles Snow and David Ketchen Jr., "Typology-Driven Theorizing: A Response to Delbridge and Fiss," *Academy of Management Review* (2013), 231–233.

Table 5.1 *Components of a claim of urgency*

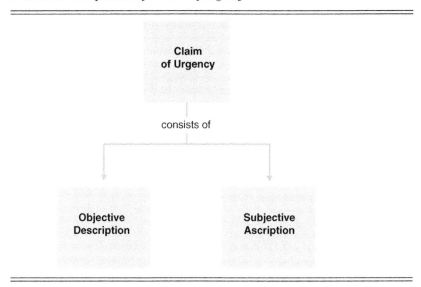

a claim of urgency. And I propose that all claims of urgency contain two elements: an objective description and a subjective ascription (Table 5.1). All claims of crisis can be slotted into one subgroup – known as a cell – of the typology.

A Near-infinite Variety with Two Core Elements

Claims of urgency come in a near-infinite array: international tensions, financial setbacks, social upheavals, natural disasters, system breakdowns, technological displacement. Every era comes with its own set of urgent dynamics. The crisis label gets bandied about rather indiscriminately to situations both grand and trivial. Still, a classification system should cover them all. That is possible because all of the claims include the same two foundational elements, the elements that will serve as the dimensions of my typology.

The first element is an objective description, pointing to particular exigencies upon which the assertion of threat will be based. These are the "brute facts" that cannot be wished away. The second element is a subjective ascription of meaning to what is being described. This is the element that seeks to define the import and meaning of those brute facts.

Table 5.2 *Description and ascription from Carlos Ghosn*

OBJECTIVE DESCRIPTION	SUBJECTIVE ASCRIPTION
"Nissan has been losing global market share continuously since 1991."	"The key facts and figures about Nissan point to a reality: Nissan is in bad shape."
"Seven of the last eight years, including our forecast for 1999, show a loss."	"Lack of a clear profit orientation."
"Today, we are at 4.9 percent world market share. We lost 1.7 points of world market share since 1991."	"No sense of urgency."

Parsing Holthaus's claim is as simple as his claim is straightforward: "Hurricane Maria is now less than 24 hours from Cat 5 landfall in Puerto Rico." That is the objective description. The rest – "I can't emphasize this enough: This is a catastrophic storm" – is subjective ascription. The descriptive element is objective because it refers to a thing that resides outside of Holthaus's mind: a storm brewing in the Atlantic Ocean.

Note, I did not say it was *true*, just that it was descriptive of an objective thing: an observable weather pattern. Objective elements are capable of being verified or discredited. Was there really such a weather pattern? The ascriptive element of a claim, conversely, does not contain an objective thing. The words "This is a catastrophic storm" – represent Holthanus's ascription. It is the "uh-oh" contention that big trouble is coming.

If a claim were *just* descriptive, it would have no larger meaning. Yeah, so there's a storm forming somewhere in the Atlantic. So what? On the other hand, if a claim contained only ascription of big trouble, it would be an empty threat, an unspecified risk with no known object. A well-known and frequently used icon depicts crisis with a singular image: a newspaper with a banner headline blaring the phrase: UH-OH! The joke is, there is no source of the threat, no objective description of anything that might impose a sense of urgency. Just an uh-oh.

Although separating the objective description from the subjective ascription in Holthaus's claim is easy, the same process can be applied to any and all claims. Go back and look at Ghosn's claim of urgency at Nissan. It is relatively easy to separate objective description from subjective attribution of meaning (Table 5.2).

Now we see the opportunity in the crisis-as-claim model to parse the objective and subjective elements of any and all claims of urgency. The next logical step takes us closer to the construction of a typology. We can evaluate each element by the application of an appropriate criterion.

Accuracy and Plausibility

Description of real-world things and brute facts can be evaluated. So can ascription of meaning. It's just that the criteria for evaluation need to be different. I propose *accuracy* as the appropriate criterion for analyzing the descriptive element of a claim, and *plausibility* as the appropriate criterion for sorting ascription of meaning. Accuracy is a much simpler concept to understand, so let's start there.

Objective Accuracy   Accuracy reflects the extent to which the descriptive elements of a claim adhere to cold, hard facts.[17] A well-known quote, typically attributed to Daniel Patrick Moynihan – "You are entitled to your own opinion, but you're not entitled to your own facts" – suggests that accuracy is not a matter of interpretive whim. There is a real, material world against which description can and should be measured. This assumption – fundamental to contextual constructionism – is basic to the proposed typology.

Remember the story of Albert Einstein and Niels Bohr debating if the moon existed when no one was looking at it? In my typology, that debate is dispensed with. The existence of the moon is a brute fact. It cannot be denied or wished away. To claim that it reflects the light of the sun is accurate. To insist that it is made of green cheese is inaccurate. And the claim that the moon does not exist if no one is looking at it amounts to an absurd denial of a brute fact.

Sure, our understanding of cold, hard facts can and does change. Science once held that the sun revolved around the Earth, then "proved" that the sun was at the center of the universe, and subsequently discovered that the sun is not at the precise center of the solar system at all. Science once maintained that matter existed in three states: solid, liquid, or gas. Then came the laboratory creation of a new material state: the time crystal.[18]

So yes, knowledge of the real world evolves. Nonetheless, it is still possible, using the best tools we have available, to validate the accuracy of the descriptive element of a claim with reference to things that exist outside of the claims-makers' mind and beyond their interpretation. We

---

[17] John Miles Foley, *Oral Tradition and the Internet: Pathways of the Mind* (Urbana: University of Illinois Press, 2012).
[18] Piers Coleman, "Quantum Physics: Time Crystals," *Nature* 493 (2013), 166.

know that claims makers can and do lie in their descriptions in order to manipulate meaning and attract support. "Cigarette smoking is no more 'addictive' than coffee, tea or Twinkies," insisted the CEO of RJR Nabisco in 1994. "In spite of the wildly speculative and false stories of arms for hostages and alleged ransom payments, we did not, repeat, did not, trade weapons or anything else for hostages. Nor will we," insisted Ronald Reagan in 1986. Champion bicyclist Lance Armstrong repeatedly avowed, "I have never doped."[19] Lies all.

When the facts are on your side, use them. When the facts are against you, pound the table and make stuff up. That paraphrase of sage legal advice suggests the degree to which "fake news," "big lies," and "alternative facts" can be marshaled to promote what is politely referred to as a "strategic narrative"; a story that advances the interests of the claims maker while discrediting opponents.[20]

To be sure, determining accuracy is not always easy. Cold, hard facts may be difficult to ascertain. Take these claims asserted by a *New York Times* columnist depicting the devastation on Puerto Rico a month after the island was struck by the storm that meteorologist Eric Holthaus warned about in September 2017:

- More than 80 percent: the portion of the island's electric grid that is not functioning.
- 28 percent: the share of Puerto Rican residents who lack running water.
- 72 percent: the share of residents who have running water and thus are subject to the health department recommendation that people boil or disinfect their water before drinking it.
- 100 percent: the share who are in one of the two previous categories.
- 40 percent: the share of residents who lack a cellphone signal.
- 20 out of 51: the number of sewage treatment plants not functioning.
- 5 out of 18: the number of toxic waste sites that have not been inspected by the Environmental Protection Agency since the hurricane.
- Close to half: the portion of hospitals without electricity.
- 48: the official death toll, although health experts believe – and media reports suggest – the real number to be higher.[21]

---

[19] These three quotes can be found, in order, at www.c-span.org/video/?c3336890/1994-ceos-testify, www.nytimes.com/1986/11/14/us/transcript-of-remarks-by-reagan-about-iran.html, and www.theguardian.com/sport/2013/jan/18/lance-armstrong-doping-denials-quotes.

[20] Irma Khaldarova and Mervi Pantti, "Fake News," *Journalism Practice* 19 (2016), 891–901.

[21] David Leonhardt, "Puerto Rico's Crisis by the Numbers," *New York Times* (October 17, 2017).

This is objective description. But just how accurate is it? How closely does the description conform to cold, hard facts?

The claim, for instance, describes "media reports" that "suggest" the death toll to be higher than forty-eight. That is easily confirmed. The online version of the column contains a handy hyperlink that demonstrates that there were, indeed, such reports. A subsequent assessment provided by the Milken Institute School of Public Health at George Washington University tallied a staggering 2,975 "excess deaths in Puerto Rico after Hurricane Maria and its devastation across Puerto Rico."[22] So yes indeed, the "real number" of deaths was higher than forty-eight.

Other objective elements of the claim are not so easily verifiable. Was 28 percent really the share of Puerto Rican residents who lacked running water at the time of the claim? Are these descriptions accurate? Because they are descriptive statements referencing real things, they are verifiable, allowing for a judgment of accuracy – but not easily. The matter of *source credibility* – an issue I deal with in the following chapter – becomes especially salient in shaping believability when accuracy is difficult to determine.

Subjective Ascription   Accuracy may be difficult to ascertain, but the concept is clear. The concept of accuracy cannot be applied to ascription, however. The *Times* article on the devastation in Puerto Rico appeared under the headline: "The Humanitarian Crisis in Puerto Rico, by the Numbers." This is the uh-oh element of the claim: a "humanitarian crisis." And yet, we can't determine that the label "humanitarian crisis" is accurate. Nor can we conclude that it is inaccurate. We need a different criterion of judgment.

Was the aftermath of Hurricane Maria "truly" a humanitarian disaster? That is the wrong question. The label reflects a subjective judgment. So, if the ascriptive element of a claim is not either accurate or inaccurate, what dimension can be applied? When it comes to evaluating ascription, we should think in terms not of accuracy but of plausibility. Is the uh-oh claim of a humanitarian crisis plausible?

---

[22] Lynn Goldman, "We Calculated the Deaths from Maria. Politics Played No Role," *Washington Post* (September 15, 2018). That figure became a matter of controversy when, in September 2018 as a hurricane approached the US coastline, President Trump tweeted that "they had anywhere from 6 to 18 deaths" when he visited Puerto Rico two weeks after the hurricane. "Then, a long time later, they started to report really large numbers," which Trump attributed to political motives. Quoted in John Wagner and Joel Achenbach, "Trump Is Rebuked after Questioning Number of Deaths Attributed to Hurricane Maria," *Washington Post* (September 13, 2018).

Given what we know about the force of a Category 5 hurricane, the depiction of damage contained in the "humanitarian crisis" claim is, indeed, plausible. The National Hurricane Center has provided a definition, one that anyone can access: a storm with sustained winds of at least 157 miles per hour. And there's more: "A high percentage of framed homes will be destroyed, with total roof failure and wall collapse. Fallen trees and power poles will isolate rural areas. Power outages will last for weeks to possibly months. Most of the area will be uninhabitable for weeks or months."[23] Now we can see why Holthaus's subjective ascription of "a catastrophic storm" attached to a rapidly approaching Category 5 hurricane or the news report of a "humanitarian crisis" in its aftermath are both plausible.

We can undertake the same evaluation of Ghosn's speech. There were certainly objective descriptions – financial and performance outcomes – that could be confirmed or refuted by referencing public documents. In the reporting that accompanied that speech, and it was extensive, there were no suggestions that his description of bad performance was inaccurate. But what about his subjective ascription? The statement that "we didn't have a choice" can't be judged on the basis of accuracy. It is neither true nor false. It represented, after all, nothing more (or less) than Ghosn's judgment. This is where plausibility comes in to play.

Plausibility is a far trickier concept than accuracy to define. To use it as a dimension of a typology, we need to be more specific than the typical understanding of plausibility as the "quality of being believed." It is an argument that is "potentially" believable.[24] These are useful starting points, but they do not help much in determining just what that quality is, or how to operationalize it in the service of classification. What is plausibility or implausibility? Fortunately, the concept can be imbued with a formal character prior to being applied to the subjective element of a claim.

Plausibility is an inference drawn on the basis of well-defined reasoning. In his *Critique of Pure Reason*, Kant referenced the need for "discursive clarity," by which he meant clear, logical argument.[25] Plausibility insists that reliable principles and methods of reasoning are utilized in a transparent process that moves the formation of an ascription in a coherent, logical progression. Plausibility requires a claim to be

---

[23] www.nhc.noaa.gov/aboutsshws.php.
[24] Doug Lombardi et al., "Plausibility Judgments in Conceptual Change and Epistemic Cognition," *Educational Psychologist* 51 (2016), 35–56; Elizabeth Wagar, "Credibility," *Archives of Pathology & Laboratory Medicine* 138 (2014), 873.
[25] Immanuel Kant, *Critique of Pure Reason* (New York: St. Martin's Press, 1781/1998), p. 103.

structured in such a way that it offers a logical path of compatible propositions.[26]

We wonder as we evaluate the plausibility of a claim, has there been intellectual rigor and honesty brought to bear as the claims maker moves from *A* to *B*? When these criteria are met, we can judge the ascriptive element to be plausible. We may or may not fully *believe* it; we may or may not *agree* with it. We may agree with the objective description of Puerto Rico after the hurricane but think that the resulting destruction does not rise to the level of a humanitarian crisis. Even so, we can *accept* the claim of humanitarian crisis as a plausible label. In Holthaus's warning, his reasoning took him from "Hurricane Maria is now a Category 5 storm approaching the island of Puerto Rico" to "catastrophic." Given the logical progression from Category 5 to catastrophe, that element of Holthaus's claim is plausible.

How about Ghosn's progression from "our production has dropped by more than 600,000 cars" to "we don't have a choice"? Have alternative, competing representations been taken into account in a transparent and honest way?[27] Do the descriptive facts of Ghosn's case lead logically to his ascription? I am not asking whether Holthaus and Ghosn were right. Nor am I denying that other ascriptions might have also been plausible. I am suggesting only that in the crisis-as-claim model, we interrogate the subjective, ascriptive elements of claims in a way that allows us the opportunity to judge plausibility. To deal with the classification of claims, I propose the typology depicted in Table 5.3. Each quadrant is named on what I consider to be its dominant characteristic.[28]

Reading the Typology

The two dimensions that can be applied to the classification of a claim are accuracy and plausibility. Accuracy applies to the objective, descriptive element of a claim, and plausibility to the subjective, ascriptive element that attributes meaning to the claim. A claim that is both accurate and plausible such as "Hurricane Maria is now less than 24 hours from Cat 5 landfall in Puerto Rico. I can't emphasize this enough: This is

---

[26] Evandro Agazzi, "Consistency, Truth, and Ontology," *Studia Logica: An International Journal for Symbolic Logic* 97 (2011), 7–29; Sarah Von der Mühlen et al., "Judging the Plausibility of Arguments in Scientific Texts: A Student–Scientist Comparison," *Thinking & Reasoning* 22 (2016), 221–249.

[27] Francisco Rosillo, *Determination of Value: Guidance on Developing and Supporting Credible Opinions* (Hoboken, NJ: Wiley, 2008).

[28] This follows Mayr's view of naming classification taxa after a single characteristic or a dominant subset of characteristics (Mayr, "Biological Classification").

Table 5.3 *A typology of claims of urgency*

	Implausible	Plausible
Accurate	Deceptive	Legitimate
Inaccurate	Bogus	Reckless

a catastrophic storm" is thus classified as a *legitimate* claim. So is Ghosn's "we don't have a choice" claim.

Labeling a claim as legitimate is not equivalent to asserting that it is true. The typology is not a tool for settling arguments, not designed to separate right from wrong. Nor can it predict how claims will be taken or what impact they will have. Legitimacy will influence but not determine whether people believe a claim.

And what about the possibilities of non-legitimate claims? A claim that is accurate in its description but implausible in terms of its subjective ascription is labeled a *deceptive* claim. Consider Donald Trump's claim at the 2016 Republican Presidential convention that this was "a moment of crisis for our nation."[29] It was that claim that fueled his run for the nomination in 2016 and served as the centerpiece of his July acceptance speech. Over the next seventy-five minutes, the candidate provided the details of his claim:

- "The attacks on our police and the terrorism in our cities threaten our very way of life."
- "Americans watching this address tonight have seen the recent images of violence in our streets and chaos in our communities."
- "Nearly 180,000 illegal immigrants with criminal records, ordered deported from our country, are tonight roaming free to threaten peaceful citizens."

---

[29] Donald Trump, "2016 RNC Draft Speech Transcript," *Politico* (July 21, 2016).

- "Our roads and bridges are falling apart, our airports are in Third World condition, and forty-three million Americans are on food stamps."
- "America is far less safe – and the world is far less stable – than when [Barack] Obama made the decision to put Hillary Clinton in charge of America's foreign policy [as Secretary of State]."

The clear intent was to claim urgency; to make the case that the country faced a crisis.

We know that US presidential candidates, especially those seeking to oust an incumbent party, frequently declare the country to be facing a crisis that their election will solve. Warren Harding did it in 1920 with his call for a return to "normalcy"; so did John Kennedy in 1960 with assertions of a mythical "missile gap" between the United States and its Cold War foe, the Soviet Union.[30]

Once the election is over, the winners often strike a conciliatory note. Abraham Lincoln's used his second inaugural address, delivered while civil war was still raging, to set a tone of reconciliation and unification: "With malice toward none, with charity for all." After his electoral victory, Trump offered no such reconciliation. After condemning "a small group in our nation's capital," in his inaugural speech, he returned to his picture of chaos and crisis:

Mothers and children trapped in poverty in our inner cities, rusted out factories scattered like tombstones across the landscape of our nation, an education system flush with cash but which leaves our young and beautiful students deprived of all knowledge, and the crime, the gangs, and the drugs that have stolen too many lives and robbed our country of so much unrealized potential. This American carnage stops right here and stops right now.[31]

"American carnage" neatly captured his claim of crisis and set the posture of his new administration.

As with any claim of urgency, it is possible to differentiate objective description from subjective ascription in Trump's "American carnage" imagery (Table 5.4). Let's just evaluate one specific claim, the statement that "nearly 180,000 illegal immigrants with criminal records, ordered deported from our country, are tonight roaming free to threaten peaceful citizens."

---

[30] Michael Haydock, "The Dark Side of Normalcy: The United States under President Warren Harding," *American History* 34 (1999), 16–25; Jonathan Renshon, "Assessing Capabilities in International Politics: Biased Overestimation and the Case of the Imaginary 'Missile Gap,'" *Journal of Strategic Studies* 32 (2009), 115–147.

[31] Donald Trump, "Inauguration Speech," *Politico* (2017).

Table 5.4 *Description and ascription from the "American carnage" claim*

OBJECTIVE DESCRIPTION	SUBJECTIVE ASCRIPTION
"Attacks on our police and the terrorism in our cities . . . "	" . . . threaten our very way of life."
"Recent image of violence in our streets . . . "	" . . . and chaos in our communities."
"Nearly 180,000 illegal immigrants with criminal records, ordered deported from our country . . . "	" . . . are tonight roaming free to threaten peaceful citizens."
" . . . and forty-three million Americans are on food stamps."	"America is far less safe – and the world is far less stable – than when Obama made the decision to put Hillary Clinton in charge of America's foreign policy."

The descriptive element of the claim – "nearly 180,000 illegal immigrants with criminal records, ordered deported from our country" – was, indeed, accurate. "We found that number to be basically correct," noted fact-checking site *Politifact*.[32] How about the progression from that description to the ascription of meaning: that these people "are tonight roaming free to threaten peaceful citizens"?

What is expected from plausibility is that alternative, competing ascriptions have been taken into account in a transparent and honest way.[33] If, and only if, we interrogate the subjective, ascriptive elements of claims in this way can we come to a judgment concerning plausibility. Where was the logical progression from that raw number to "roaming free" and threatening "peaceful citizens"? It was a progression that depended not on logic but on biases and stereotypes. This particular claim, then, failed the test of plausibility and can thus be labeled as deceptive.

The label *bogus* is applied to claims that are both inaccurate and implausible. A famous example would be the 1938 radio broadcast of H. G. Wells's "War of the Worlds." Produced by Orson Welles in a semi-documentary style for his *Mercury Theater on the Air*, the claim of a Martian invasion that was embedded in his production was neither accurate nor plausible. It was, after all, just a radio drama, broadcast on the eve of Halloween.

---

[32] "According to numbers ultimately from the Senate Judiciary committee, there are 925,000 immigrants ordered deported who are still present in the country, and about twenty percent of them have a criminal record." See Allison Graves and Neelesh Moorthy, "Fact-Checking Donald Trump on the Final Night of the Republican Convention," *Politifact* (July 21, 2016).

[33] Rosillo, *Determination of Value*.

The broadcast opened with a standard radio announcement: "The Columbia Broadcasting System and its affiliated stations present Orson Welles and 'The Mercury Theatre on the Air' in *The War of the Worlds* by H. G. Wells." The first half of the drama then proceeded, constructed entirely around "news bulletins" that interrupted what seemed to be a mundane radio broadcast of "the musical stylings" of "Ramon Raquello and his orchestra." Then came this: "Ladies and Gentlemen, we interrupt our program of dance music to bring you a special bulletin from the Intercontinental Radio News." That broadcast break-in was a faithful reproduction of the kind of bulletins that regularly reported on the rise of Nazi Germany throughout the decade. In this case, however, it was a report not of escalating tensions in Europe but of "several explosions" on Mars.[34]

Back and forth the broadcast went, alternating between Raquello's "musical stylings" purposefully rendered slightly off-key by the studio orchestra and increasingly alarming reports concerning an object spotted landing in the town of Grover's Mill, New Jersey. Listeners heard first a sound emanating from the object, then a hatch opening while local "police" cautioned gawkers to stand back from "the thing." Finally, the intrepid radio news reporter on the scene, "Carl Phillips" (portrayed by actor Frank Readick) described a "creature" emerging from the object with black eyes that gleamed "like a serpent," a V-shaped mouth dripping with saliva, and "rimless lips that seem to quiver and pulsate." Within seven minutes, listeners were told, the alien invaders had wiped out the entire New Jersey State Militia.

Forty minutes into the broadcast, a station break interrupted the building tension, followed by the announcement, "You are listening to the 'Mercury Theater' broadcast of *War of the Worlds*." Now the drama assumed a more traditional format. The claim of the first forty minutes was, of course, bogus. The broadcast was not intended to be anything else. There was no widespread panic as some newspapers reported at the time.[35] But some had believed the bogus claim of a Martian attack, at least until the station break.

A far more serious bogus claim circulated in the heat of the 2016 presidential campaign. A right-wing talk-show host posted a video on YouTube, commenting:

---

[34] All quotes are from Brad Schwartz, *Broadcast Hysteria: Orson Welles' War of the Worlds and the Art of Fake News* (New York: Hill and Wang, 2015).

[35] Schwartz, *Broadcast Hysteria*. The author debunked the popular notion that there was "widespread" panic. Welles certainly intended to scare listeners. Whether he intended for his broadcast to be mistaken for "real" remains ambiguous.

When I think about all the children Hillary Clinton has personally murdered and chopped up and raped, I have zero fear standing up against her. Yeah, you heard me right. Hillary Clinton has personally murdered children. I just can't hold back the truth anymore.[36]

Further rumors spread on the Internet. Clinton campaign chair, John Podesta, was holding children in secret chambers at the Comet Ping Pong, a DC neighborhood pizza joint. This was all part of a sex ring directed by the candidate herself.

Edgar Welch, a former fire fighter and would-be actor, apparently believed the claim. On a cold weekend day, he drove from North Carolina to the nation's capital and then entered the restaurant armed with a Colt AR-15 assault rifle, a .38-caliber Colt revolver, and a folding knife. En route, he texted a friend, saying, "Raiding a pedo [pedophile] ring, possibly sacraficing [sic] the lives of a few for the lives of many. Standing up against a corrupt system that kidnaps, tortures and rapes babies and children in our own backyard." When he arrived at the Comet Ping Pong, he fired several shots and then darted around the premises searching for the imprisoned children. Welch remained inside for forty-five minutes before surrendering to police. There was no accuracy to the claim, of course, and no plausibility that such a thing might even occur under Hillary Clinton's direction. Yet, there he was: an armed rescuer, responding to a bogus claim.

A claim that is inaccurate but plausible – a *reckless* claim – is perhaps the most nefarious category of the typology. These kinds of claims are so dangerous precisely because they *are* plausible. Reckless claims can and have led to war. Let's visit President Lyndon Johnson's 1964 Gulf of Tonkin speech in which he made a reckless claim: alleging an attack on the USS *Maddox* somewhere off the coast of North Vietnam that most likely never happened.

Vietnam, a Southeast Asian country that abuts China, Laos, and Cambodia, had been an independent republic since the tenth century. For a thousand years prior to that, the land had been ruled by China. In the late nineteenth century, French imperialists established colonial rule, imposing Western and Catholic institutions on what was called French Indochina.

In the early years of World War II, as the French succumbed to the Germans, Japan occupied Vietnam. During that occupation, a nationalist-oriented communist liberation movement led by Ho Chi Minh opened a guerrilla war against its occupiers (with at least some quiet

---

[36] This quote and details of the story are from Marc Fisher et al., "Pizzagate: From Rumor to Hashtag to Gunfire in D.C.," *Washington Post* (December 6, 2016).

support from the United States). With the 1945 defeat of Japan, Ho declared an independent Democratic Republic of Vietnam. The French, however, had every intention of reclaiming the territory as its own. France's wartime allies – the United States, the United Kingdom, and China – agreed to help it do so. With the support of the USSR and Mao Zedong's newly established Communist China, Ho turned his attention to liberating Vietnam from French rule. The United States sent naval carriers into the Gulf of Tonkin in support of what proved to be a doomed French effort.

The French collapse climaxed with the 1954 battle of Diem Bien Phu. France agreed to a ceasefire, and Vietnam was "temporarily" partitioned (intended for 300 days) along the 17th parallel. Ho Chi Minh would control the North, while a non-Communist government under the protection of the United States (and to a lesser degree the United Kingdom) took root in the South with its capital in Saigon.

The United States was firmly committed to keeping the Communist North from gaining a foothold below that no-longer-temporary dividing line. In defense of America's support for South Vietnam against the North, President Dwight Eisenhower proposed a "domino" theory. A takeover of South Vietnam by the Communist forces of Ho Chi Minh, he asserted, would have a domino effect on the remainder of Southeast Asia, threatening Laos, Cambodia, Thailand, India, Japan, and the Philippines.[37] Given that these years represented a "hot" phase of the Cold War (a real war in Korea had just ended in a virtual stalemate), US leaders from both parties accepted the argument that the "Red Tide" needed to be stopped at the 17th parallel. Ho Chi Minh keep up the fight for independence.

Resistance to Western rule within Vietnam became more pronounced when, in 1960, the forces of the North aligned with an insurgent rebellion in the South under the banner of the National Liberation Front (NLF). Now, it was President John Kennedy's turn to side with the South by sending military "advisors." The American military oversaw a program to relocate rural Vietnamese to buffer them from the influence, often imposed through terrorist tactics, of the NLF. That awful situation became significantly worse when the inept performance of the South's army and government led to the assassination of the South's

---

[37] For readers not familiar with dominos, it is a game played with small, rectangular tiles. They can be stood end-to-end in long, single-file lines. Toppling the lead domino backward into the line causes a cascade of falling tiles. This was the basis of Eisenhower's metaphor. It was, in fact, a quite powerful metaphor in that it made his rationale concrete and easy to understand, even though there was little to support its accuracy or plausibility.

president and protests emanating from the South's Buddhist community (including the self-emulation of monks). Johnson assumed the presidency following Kennedy's 1963 assassination, facing serious deterioration of the South's and the US position. He was determined to chart a new, more aggressive path. That's where the Gulf of Tonkin incident came into play.

"The best historical evidence available now" – this was historian David Anderson writing about the August 1964 Gulf of Tonkin incident for Columbia University's *Guide to the Vietnam War* in 2002 – "is that there was no attack on US ships on August 4."[38] *No* attack. There *was*, apparently, confusion among Pentagon officials about just what had transpired 8,000 miles away in the rough weather and heavy seas off the coast of what was then North Vietnam. The *Maddox* commander wasn't sure himself. There may have been false or "ghost" images on the ship's radar providing erroneous data on an attack that never took place. He went so far as to urge a follow-up investigation before any response be undertaken.

Those doubts reached the White House within an hour of the original communiqué. Secretary of Defense Robert McNamara acknowledged in a meeting of the Joint Chiefs of Staff that he lacked "a clear and convincing showing that an attack" on the *Maddox* had, in fact, occurred.[39] Johnson was well aware of these uncertainties. "For all I know, our Navy was shooting at whales out there," he admitted privately.[40] But he wanted to escalate the war, so he did not convey that sense of uncertainty when he spoke to the American public.

Addressing the nation just before midnight, and with full awareness of the dubious nature of the reports of the attack, Johnson first offered his construction of what had transpired in the Gulf:

The performance of commanders and crew in this engagement is in the highest tradition of the United States Navy.[41] But repeated acts of violence against the Armed Forces of the United States must be met not only with alert defense, but with positive reply. That reply is being given as I speak to you tonight. Air action is now in execution against gunboats and certain supporting facilities in North Vietnam which have been used in these hostile actions. . . .

He then insisted on his "solemn responsibility" to respond:

---

[38] David Anderson, *The Columbia Guide to the Vietnam War* (New York: Columbia University Press, 2002), 45.
[39] Quoted from the National Security Archive accessed at https://nsarchive2.gwu.edu//NS AEBB/NSAEBB132/tapes.htm.
[40] Quoted in Ken Burns and Lynn Novick, *The Vietnam War*, produced by Florentine Films and WETA (2017).
[41] It's hard to know for sure what Johnson meant by this. We do know that the commander explicitly urged caution and further investigation before formulating a response.

It is a solemn responsibility to have to order even limited military action by forces whose overall strength is as vast and as awesome as those of the United States of America. But it is my considered conviction, shared throughout your Government, that firmness in the right is indispensable today for peace; that firmness will always be measured. Its mission is peace.[42]

And it was a construction that proved compelling. On August 7, a joint Gulf of Tonkin resolution passed Congress with only two dissenting votes – Wayne Morse (D-Ore.) and Ernest Gruening (D-Alaska) – authorizing the president "to take all necessary steps, including the use of armed force, to assist any member or protocol state of the Southeast Asia Collective Defense Treaty requesting assistance in defense of its freedom."[43]

Johnson repeatedly cited the Gulf of Tonkin resolution as his constitutional authority to mount an ever-widening and deadly war. Ten years and 1.4 million deaths later, the United States withdrew its forces and the North consolidated control of all of Vietnam.[44] Saigon was renamed Ho Chi Minh City; by the 1990s, the United States and a united Vietnam became cautious allies.

US commitment to supporting the military actions of South Vietnam predated Johnson's Gulf of Tonkin speech by a decade. It is possible, even likely, that the president would have pursued his policy of escalation absent the resulting congressional resolution. But it is also the case that, as a long-standing senator and Senate leader, Johnson valued the congressional institution and sought its approval. Might a rigorous and open debate on the claimed attack in the Gulf have had an impact on his subsequent actions? Impossible to say.

What is clear is that the claim of urgency that Johnson made late in the night of August 4, 1964, was based on an incident that he knew at the time might not have happened and which historians now believe never occurred. Was the claim plausible? Of course. North and South Vietnam had been at war for nearly a decade, and the United States was providing military aid to the South. That's what made it so enticing and

---

[42] Lyndon Johnson, *Report on the Gulf of Tonkin Incident* (August 4, 1964).

[43] Gruening did not suspect Johnson was lying. Rather, he saw the incident as a minor skirmish that was the "inevitable development of the US steady escalation of our own military activities." The resolution was repealed in 1971 following congressional investigations determining that the *Maddox* had been on a secret intelligence mission and that the attack had most likely not occurred. Gruening quoted in Robert David Johnson, "Ernest Gruening and the Tonkin Gulf Resolution: Continuities in American Dissent," *Journal of American – East Asian Relations* 2 (1993), 133.

[44] This estimate of total casualties from 1965 to 1975 is from Guenter Lewy, *America in Vietnam* (New York: Oxford University Press, 1978).

dangerous. But was it accurate? Most likely not. It would be classified, therefore, as a reckless claim.

Move On, Folks – There's Nothing to See Here

The proposed typology can be applied equally to claims of non-crisis. One such nothing-to-see here claim came in June 2008 when Borders Books CEO George Jones sat down for an interview on CNBC. Retailing was in a slump brought on by the early onset of a global recession. Borders Books, second in size only to Barnes & Noble among book retailers, was certainly feeling the crunch. That much Jones owned up to in speaking with the interviewer: "It's a tough economic climate out there right now, and it's affecting just about all retailers. And it certainly has affected us. I think everyone's affected by the increase in gas prices to record levels. And food prices are high. It affects consumer spending. So, yes, it's affected us."

Jones did not, however, express great worry:

Well, sales are slightly down. In our first quarter results, we were down about 4% in same store sales, in our super stores, and down only 0.8% in our mall specialty stores. Frankly, we were cruising along with some nice increases before that. . . . So, we've adjusted our plans. We're planning real conservatively right now.

It was innovation – new concept stores that would invite customers to experience actual books while also accessing Internet services – that would allow Borders Books to thrive:

One of the key things that we're doing is introducing an intermingling of the Internet and the digital world with the bricks-and-mortar stores to a greater degree than what's been happening in the industry. We're seeing great results with these stores. We have 9 of them open so far. We're really pleased. Customer reaction has been very, very strong.

No question was asked about potential competition from online book retailers, specifically Amazon.

By the time Borders built its own online platform for selling books in June 2008, the die was cast. At the end of that year – remember, this was the same year of Jones's cautiously optimistic interview – the company's stock plummeted, its profitability disappeared (for good, as it turns out), and assets were sold to raise cash. Jones himself would be fired in January 2009. Further asset sales and layoffs failed to revive the doomed company. Traffic may have been up in concept stores; sales, however, were down. Borders filed for bankruptcy in early 2011.

For Jones, his "there's nothing to see here" construct suggested extreme naivety concerning the future of his industry and company.

Customers still wanted to buy books (although not CDs or DVDs, largely replaced by streaming technology), just not from bricks-and-mortar stores. The claim of denial was accurate in its particulars but implausible in insisting that the company's future would thrive on bricks-and-mortar stores. It was a deceptive claim of denial.

Not all statements of "there's nothing to see here" are expressions of naivety. Some are intended expressly to deceive. Elaine Frantz Parsons, historian of the Ku Klux Klan, noted a robust strain of Klan denialism among politicians and the popular press, even at the height of its racist terrorism in Southern states after the Civil War. No one denied the eruption of violence. Despite the disguise of the white hoods, Klan members were widely known in their communities and some openly confessed to – perhaps "bragged" about – their crimes.

Twisting plausibility to deny the existence of a white-hooded terror group, congressional Democrats insisted that the real perpetrators of violence were actually Southern blacks and their Republican allies. Leaders opposing the Republican-led Reconstruction project – an effort that amounted to a "large-scale experiment in interracial democracy" – insisted that reports of the secret resistance force were simply not true.[45] The claims of denial in this case were bogus, neither accurate nor plausible.

Whenever individuals assert claims, they are simultaneously asserting interests. The same holds for claims of denial. The bogus Klan-denialism of post–Civil War Democrats advanced their partisan interest in repudiating the Reconstruction policies of the Republican Party enabling the Klan in its murderous resistance. When BorderBooks' George Jones offered his deceptive claim of denial, he had an interest in asserting his own competence. Leaders can also deny urgency with explicitly illegal intent. Enron CEO Ken Lay is a perfect example.

In an August 16, 2001, speech that became an important building block in the indictment for securities fraud brought against him and his company, Lay assured employees that the value of their stock options would be restored: "I think we've got a lot of great stuff going on. We don't get much credit for it in the market place, for damned sure. But we will. . . . I'm excited, and I think the next few months, the next few years are going to be great for Enron, and great for Enron's employees."[46] Not only would there not be another few great years for Enron, there would be

---

[45] Elaine Frantz Parsons, *Ku-Klux: The Birth of the Klan during Reconstruction* (Chapel Hill: University of North Carolina Press, 2015). The characterization of Reconstruction is from History.com Editors, "Reconstruction," *History* (2009).
[46] Ken Lay, "Speaking to Enron All-Employees Meeting," *YouTube* (August 16, 2001).

no "next year" at all. Lay was offering a reckless claim of denial: plausible but inaccurate.

The stunning rise and even more astounding fall of this Houston-based energy trading company would become the stuff of legend, books, plays, and made-for-TV movies.[47] *Fortune* crowned Enron the most innovative company in America five years in a row. Under the guidance of Lay and his CEO Jeffrey Skilling, the stock price soared into the $90s, an impressive figure in the later years of the twentieth century. But all was not well.

Much of Enron's appearance of prosperity and growth was an outcome of balance-sheet manipulation, particularly the use of off-balance-sheet entities bearing Hollywood sci-fi names like Raptor, Obi 1, Condor, and Merlin. Although listed as separate organizations, they were in fact partnerships run by a small number of top Enron executives and intended to obfuscate the true performance of the company.

Possibly aware of impending collapse, Skilling abruptly resigned in August 2001.[48] Nervous investors sent Enron's stock price plummeting. The off-balance-book arrangements collapsed, losses and debt piled up, and the company imploded. Stock price quickly tumbled into the $30s. Enron board members and executives, including Lay and Skilling, had already undertaken a massive sell-off of their personal stock, adding well over $1 billion to their personal wealth. Employees, by and large, held on to their increasingly devalued options.

"Our core businesses are extremely strong," Lay assured employees at the public meeting, "Our new businesses are doing great." Two months later, Enron's quarterly report revealed deeply troubling performance, losses and write-downs that drove the stock price even lower. When that price fell below a dollar a share, the company declared bankruptcy. Top executives were arrested and eventually sentenced to prison time, while Enron's accounting firm, Arthur Andersen, collapsed due to obstruction of justice charges and scandal.

The phrase "move on, folks – there's nothing to see here" is typically attributed to police in their attempt to disperse gawkers from a crime scene. The *Urban Dictionary* ascribes deeper, even sarcastic meaning to the phrase, suggesting that the denial of anything to see is employed as a deception.[49] That deceptive attribution could certainly be ascribed to Lay's denial of a crisis at Enron. It was inaccurate but plausible.

Politicians issue bogus nothing-to-see-here denials with some regularity:

---

[47] Bert Spector, "HRM at Enron: The Unindicted Co-conspirator," *Organizational Dynamics* 32 (2003), 207–220.
[48] He cited "personal reasons" and quickly began selling off his Enron stock.
[49] www.urbandictionary.com/define.php?term=nothing%20to%20see%20her.

- In the midst of Watergate investigations into his involvement in the break-in of Democratic National Committee headquarters and the subsequent White House–directed cover-up, President Richard Nixon declared publicly that "people have got to know whether or not their President is a crook. Well, I'm not a crook." Extensive hearings and the airing of secretly recorded Oval Office tapes revealed the extent of his knowledge and guilt, forcing Nixon to resign just ahead of an impeachment vote.
- During inquiries into allegations that President Bill Clinton had conducted a sexual relationship with a White House intern, he insisted, "I did not have sexual relations with that woman, Miss Lewinsky." Then, when confronted with irrefutable evidence to the contrary, he admitted that he had conducted a relationship "with Miss Lewinsky that was not appropriate. In fact, it was wrong."
- Donald Trump denied any knowledge of hush-money payments to a performer in pornographic movies on his behalf; a claim soon refuted by his own lawyers.

The there's-nothing-to-see-here claim can – like counterclaims that yes, there is something to see here – can be held to the same evaluative criteria of accuracy and plausibility.

It is certainly possible to issue a legitimate claim of denial. President Barack Obama's 2011 decision to produce a copy of his Hawaiian birth certificate amounted to a legitimate denial of the racist "birther" stories suggesting that he was not born in the United States and therefore not eligible to serve as president. Determining legitimacy, or lack of legitimacy, helps explain which claims will be believed. But it is far from the whole story.

Leaders who stake a claim will, for the most part, want those claims to be believed. The legitimacy of a claim will certainly influence belief, but it is not determinate. Belief formation, in turns out, is a complex process.

6   Believing Claims of Urgency – Or Not

It's an iconic moment from a classic fifties-era Broadway musical. The Music Man, con artist "Professor" Harold Hill, is about to arrive in the fictional town of River City, Iowa. His goal is to sell the locals something they neither want nor need: marching band instruments and uniforms. Now, he had no intention of delivering those goods. He *is* a con man, after all. The plan, instead, is to take the money and run. But Harold Hill has this nagging problem to solve first: how to create demand where there is none.

Not to worry. The professor has a scheme, one that has worked well in the past. He will create a moral panic in town and offer the opportunity for a wholesome marching band to restore proper order.[1] And he pounces on an opportunity presented by the news that the local billiards parlor has just installed a brand-new pool table.

Billiards is a table game played with two white balls, a red ball, and no pockets. Pool tables have pockets, a cue ball, and fifteen numbered balls. At quick glance, there seems to be nothing to differentiate the two games on moral grounds. The Music Man, however, needs to convince everyone otherwise, to scare folks into believing that there is trouble in River City. So he constructs his claim with a song:

> Ya got trouble, my friend, right here,
> I say, trouble right here in River City.[2]

The song builds on the objective description of a pool table before making a case – a subjective ascription – for the dangers posed by pool in contrast to billiards.

Do the good and gullible citizens of River City believe the Music Man's claim? Well, let's just say that by the end of the play, love has blossomed, everyone is a bit wiser, while a fully uniformed and well-equipped marching band parades down Main Street blaring "Seventy-Six Trombones."

---

[1] "Moral panics" – the identification of hidden perils in superficially harmless things and events, say, the installation of a pool table – have received serious academic attention. See, for example, Stanley Cohen, *Folk Devils and Moral Panics* (London: Routledge, 2011).

[2] Words by Meredith Wilson.

This is all great fun, but it does point to an important point: legitimacy and belief are not the same. Simply because a claim of urgency is legitimate does not mean it will be believed. Likewise, non-legitimate claims – reckless, bogus, or, as in the Music Man's case, deceptive – may well be believed. Assigning a label of legitimacy to a claim is separate from the determination of belief. And the process of belief formation is complex, imperfect, even messy.

To initiate an inquiry into the belief formation process – defining *belief* as "holding a cognitive pro-attitude"[3] – we can leave the world of Broadway fantasy and examine one non-legitimate claim – a reckless claim based on plausible logic but inaccurate description that was widely believed and led to war.

Irrefutable and Wrong

In March 2003, the United States and a "coalition of the willing" (mainly the United Kingdom and Australia) mounted a military invasion into Iraq. The ensuing war cost the United States $1.7 trillion, not including the potential benefits owed to veterans that could add an additional $6 trillion. There were 4,424 military deaths, with an additional 31,952 wounded in action. The number of Iraqi civilian casualties has been counted at 134,000.[4] And all this despite the fact that there was no Pearl Harbor, no direct attack at all. President George W. Bush and his advisors needed to construct a clear-and-present danger that people believed was tantamount to an actual attack. To do that, they required a compelling claims maker. They got one in Colin Powell.

In selecting Powell – a retired four-star general who was now secretary of state – Bush passed over his own UN ambassador, John Negroponte. It was Powell, the president reasoned, not Negroponte, who "had high credibility" with the general public.[5] When Powell spoke, Bush thought, he would be believed. On that score, the president was correct. Powell's task was to address the UN Security Council and convince his immediate audience (and the world) that the situation was urgent, even in the absence of an actual attack.

The ascriptive element of the Bush-Powell claim was simple: Iraq's weapons of mass destruction posed a real and immediate danger to the

---

[3] Definition of belief from Wesley Buckwalter et al., "Belief through Thick and Thin," *Noûs* 49 (2015), 748–775; G. H. Langley, "Belief," *Philosophy* 8 (1933), 66–76.

[4] Figures from http://watson.brown.edu/costsofwar/costs/economic, www.defense.gov/casualty.pdf, and www.iraqbodycount.org. Also, there were 197 British and 2 Australian troops killed.

[5] George Bush, *Decision Points* (New York: Crown, 2010), 244–245.

world. Preemptive action was required. The overall story line was a bit more complex than that, but still compelling.

The administration's claim, wrote David Zarefsky, was "that Iraq either was rapidly developing or already had weapons of mass destruction, in violation of sanctions imposed after the 1991 Persian Gulf War." The threat resided in the "widely shared assumption that a rogue state such as Iraq would freely make them available to terrorist organizations who would not hesitate to use them against Western powers."[6] It was just that "widely shared assumption" that made Powell's ascription – that it was simply too dangerous and the stakes were too high to wait – seem plausible.

In his speech, Powell first offered objective description, "proof" of the fact of weapons of mass destruction in Iraq. After amassing details – pictures, transcriptions from intercepted messages – said to provide objective evidence of his claim, Powell turned to subjective ascription, telling his Security Council audience:

[O]ver three months ago, this Council recognized that Iraq continued to pose a threat to international peace and security, and that Iraq had been and remained in material breach of its disarmament obligations. Today, Iraq still poses a threat and Iraq still remains in material breach. Indeed, by its failure to seize on its one last opportunity to come clean and disarm, Iraq has put itself in deeper material breach and closer to the day when it will face serious consequences for its continued defiance of the Council.

"We must not shrink from whatever is ahead of us," he concluded dramatically, "We must not fail in our duty and our responsibility to the citizens of the countries that are represented by this body."[7]

Not everyone accepted the accuracy of Powell's claim. Hans Blix, the United Nation's own head of Monitoring, Verification and Inspection, warned the Security Council that what little evidence had been found in more than 700 inspections was highly inconclusive. Behind the scenes, senior US government officials, including those with access to top-secret intelligence, doubted any increasing threat posed by Saddam Hussein. Occasional news reports, most persistently emanating from the Knight Ridder Newspapers' Washington, DC, bureau, pushed on the same "lack of hard evidence" as a caution against any rush to judgment.[8]

---

[6] David Zarefsky, "Making the Case for War: Colin Powell at the United Nations," *Rhetoric & Public Affairs* 10 (2007), 276.

[7] A complete transcript of this speech is available at www.washingtonpost.com/wp-srv/nation/transcripts/powelltext_020503.html.

[8] Max Follmer, "The Reporting Team That Got Iraq Right," *Huffington Post* (May 25, 2011).

Iraq, it became clear as the war progressed, did *not* possess weapons of mass destruction. The asserted weapons development program was non-existent. Much of the evidence presented by Powell was, in fact, inaccurate, as were the peripheral claims made to bolster the sense of immediate threat. Iraq's President Hussein, for instance, had nothing to do with al Qaeda, the terrorist organization behind the September 11 attacks.[9] Powell would later acknowledge the pervasive inaccuracies of his claim, referring to the speech as a "great intelligence failure" and a "blot" on his record.[10]

The image of Saddam Hussein as a tyrannical, perhaps unstable, strongman associated with acts of butchery against internal dissidents helped make Powell's ascription plausible. A previous war against Hussein turned him into an ideal villain. And Powell fluently presented the case against him.

A *New York Times* editorial enthused over Powell's "powerful" claim:

Secretary of State Colin Powell presented the United Nations and a global television audience yesterday with the most powerful case to date that Saddam Hussein stands in defiance of Security Council resolutions and has no intention of revealing or surrendering whatever unconventional weapons he may have. In doing so, with the help of spy satellite photos and communications intercepts, Mr. Powell placed squarely before the Security Council the fateful question of how it should respond.

Although falling short of endorsing military action (urging that the United Nations instead "continue to let diplomacy work"), the *Times*'s editorial writers *believed* Powell.[11]

The *Washington Post* joined the chorus of believers. Powell's speech was "irrefutable," so much so that "it is hard to imagine how anyone could doubt that Iraq possesses weapons of mass destruction."[12] Remember, Iraq did *not* possess weapons of mass destruction. Nonetheless, Powell's

---

[9] Studies of the language employed by the administration in justifying the Iraq War have noted the recurring rhetorical device of connecting that conflict to the earlier attacks of September 11. See Sue Lockett John et al., "Going Public, Crisis after Crisis: The Bush Administration and the Press from September 11 to Saddam," *Rhetoric and Public Affairs* 10 (2007), 195–219, and Justin Rex, "The President's War Agenda: A Rhetorical View," *Presidential Studies Quarterly* 41 (2011), 93–118.

[10] Jason Breslow, "Speech 'Was a Great Intelligence Failure,'" *PBS Frontline* (May 17, 2016); Steven Weisman, "Powell Calls His UN Speech a Lasting Blot on His Record," *New York Times* (September 9, 2005). George Bush eventually admitted that he was "sick" when he learned that the intelligence had been "off-base." He continued to justify the invasion, however, on the grounds that Iraq and the world were "better off" without Hussein. See Peter Baker, "Unlike His Brother, George W. Bush Stands by His Call to Invade Iraq," *New York Times* (May 15, 2015).

[11] Editors, "Case Against Iraq," *New York Times* (September 6, 2003).

[12] "Editors, "Irrefutable," *Washington Post* (February 6, 2003).

claim was widely believed.[13] With the leadership of the United States and the strong support of the United Kingdom, war ensued.

Purposeful Believing

Beliefs are "*enduring, unquestioned ontological representations of the world* and comprise *primary convictions about events, causes, agency, and objects.*"[14] Because beliefs are held to be true, they guide people's understanding of the world and motivate their behaviors. In fact, that is *why* we form beliefs: to guide our actions.[15]

The content of a claim of urgency – its objective description and subjective ascription – influences audience belief in its validity. As people evaluate a claim, they mostly value truth and the avoidance of error – mostly, but not entirely. Additional powerful forces shape our beliefs. Belief formation occurs only after predictable mental processes mediate the content (Table 6.1).

What else besides truth and the avoidance of error do people value? Well, we value cognitive comfort, which involves the maintenance rather than the disruption of our own assumptions and biases, those we bring to bear as we decide whether or not to believe new claims. We also value credibility on the part of the claims maker. And we value membership in a community of like-minded thinkers. That belief formation process impacts us – all of us – in a systematic way. And claims makers, for the most part, *want* to be believed.

Leaders Seeking Believability

It makes perfect sense that claims makers typically hope their audience believes that their claims are legitimate: both objectively accurate and subjectively plausible. In that way, they seek to attract belief. I say "typically" rather than "always" because there is an alternative approach.

---

[13] The Security Council, the immediate audience for Powell's speech, did not endorse military action against Iraq. UN Secretary General Kofi Annan declared that the war "was not in conformity with the UN charter," adding, "From our point of view and from the charter point of view, it was illegal." See Ewen MacAskill and Julian Borger, "Iran War Illegal and Breached UN Charter, Says Annan," *The Guardian* (September 15, 2004).

[14] Michael Connors and Peter Halligan, "A Cognitive Account of Belief: A Tentative Roadmap," *Frontiers of Psychology* 5 (2014), 2. Emphasis in the original.

[15] Peter Halligan, "Belief and Illness," *Psychologist* 20 (2007), 358–361, and Steven Sloman and Phillip Fernbach, *The Knowledge Illusion: Why We Never Think Alone* (New York: Riverhead Books, 2017).

Table 6.1 *A belief formation process*

Claim
filtered through
Belief mediators
Claims-maker credibility
Like-minded group influence
Desire for cognitive comfort
Claim content
Audience belief

Leaders may not care if the audience believes their claims as long as they possess the power to compel obedience.

Achieving obedience, it turns out, is a remarkably simple process. Ever since the Milgram experiments of the late 1950s–early 1960s in which subjects, all male, administered what they were tricked into believing were painful, even potentially fatal, electric shocks when told to do so by a technician dressed in a white lab coat, we have been unable to deny the power of authority to command obedience.

When claims makers are leaders operating from a position of hierarchical authority, they have the option to ignore believability altogether. Why exert effort to convince people of the legitimacy of your claim when leaders possess the power of enforcement? They could simply tell people: you *will* seek shelter from the approaching storm; the country *will* go to war against Iraq. Compliant behavior will be rewarded; noncompliance will be punished. In a framework of compliance, believably becomes irrelevant.

There may be times and circumstances when straightforward mandates and the expectation of obedience are appropriate – in the midst of a military battle, perhaps. Even so, there is an answer to the "why bother" question, a compelling one. Any attempt to shape a response to a claim of urgency based entirely on top-down mandates and obedience can be highly problematic.

The most obvious drawback to demanding obedience is that leaders can be wrong in their assessment of the situation and / or their belief in the requirement for an urgent response. Those with less hierarchical power may have different, even better-informed notions of how to interpret the environment and shape a response. The impact of top-down demands for compliance will be to drive out alternative views and encourage silence rather than discussion.

Obedient as opposed to committed behavior can harm the unit in other ways as well. Time and effort will need to be expended on achieving and enforcing compliance. Compliant individuals expect to be incentivized to engage in behaviors that align with the goals of the unit or punished for noncompliant behavior. Furthermore, compliance is likely to drive out creativity. Innovative paths to dealing with the urgent situation contained in a claim will give way to satisficing, meeting the bare minimum standards of behaviors contained in the claim. Motivation, effort above and beyond base requirements, and the application of ingenuity in shaping the urgent response grow out of committed behavior based on belief, not from compliant behavior based on obedience.[16]

So, yes, there is a lot riding on the question of whether a leader's claim will be believed. For a politician, belief can translate to votes and support in opinion polls. For a business leader, belief will impact the amount of discretionary effort and creativity exerted by employees. There is a benefit for non-leaders as well, because, as it turns out, people *want* to believe.

Overcoming Doubt and Connecting Dots

Think of belief as an act of filling a gap. There is, after all, always some room for doubt in any claim. Is there really a Category 5 hurricane forming in the Atlantic? Will it actually strike us? And will it do as much damage as the experts claim it will? This list can go on:

- Will our business *really* go bankrupt unless we dramatically restructure?
- Will arming schoolteachers *really* make students safer?
- Does Iraq *really* possess weapons of mass destruction?
- Or, for that matter, will pool tables *really* make River City immoral?

---

[16] The literature on the performance advantages of committed rather than compliant behavior is extensive. Reviews can be found in John Meyer, *Handbook of Employee Commitment* (Cheltenham: Edward Elgar, 2016), and Richard Mowday et al., *Employee-Organization Linkages: The Psychology of Commitment, Absenteeism, and Turnover* (New York: Atlantic Press, 1982).

Certitude does not come easily. Beliefs can be formed in the absence of absolute proof; in reality, they always are. Beliefs help span that void by alleviating doubt.[17] And, as it turns out, not only do we want to believe, we believe what we want to believe. That is because all believing is purposeful.

Believing starts with pattern recognition. We notice patterns, or at least think we do. *A* typically precedes *B*, which leads to *C*. We then look for further instances of that same pattern and intuit a rule of thumb, a heuristic.[18] By forming a pattern, we render a decidedly nonlinear, ambiguous, complex, and ever-changing world suddenly comprehendible. We all partake in this hunt for patterns.

Of course, people look at the same world and "see" different patterns. Some folks look at the universe, for instance, and find conclusive evidence of intentional design created by someone or something divine. Others see the intricacy of scientific order. Some people find patterns that provide evidence of free will, others of determinism.

Just because we recognize patterns, however, doesn't mean that the pattern is real. Rather, the perception of a pattern is formed in our minds. From the complex intake of sensory data, the brain seeks simpler patterns and then infuses those patterns with meaning.[19] Humans "can't help it," wrote Michael Shermer, "Our brains evolved to connect the dots in meaningful patterns that explain why things happen."[20] It's just the way our brains work.

Perceived patterns become beliefs.[21] We develop our own hypotheses based on those perceived patterns. This is how the world works. These are the reasons things happen the way they do. Then we seek "truth" within our preferred model, verification that our models represent the world accurately.

Even though we are all pattern seekers, there are differences in how we process stimuli from our environment and integrate those stimuli into our pattern perceptions. The most significant distinction, cognitive scientists tell us, resides in the complexity of individual cognition.[22] Based on some

[17] Michael Shermer, *The Believing Brain: From Ghosts and Gods to Politics and Conspiracies – How We Construct Beliefs and Reinforce Them as Truths* (New York: Times Books, 2011).
[18] Leonidas Spiliopoulos, "Pattern Recognition and Subjective Belief Learning in a Repeated Constant-Sum Game," *Games and Economic Behavior* 75 (2012), 921–935.
[19] Dan Ariely, *Predictably Irrational: The Hidden Forces That Shape Our Decisions* (New York: HarperCollins, 2008).
[20] Shermer, *The Believing Brain*, 5.
[21] James Borhek and Richard Curtis, *A Sociology of Belief* (New York: John Wiley & Sons, 1975).
[22] Lars Larson and Kendrith Rowland, "Leadership Style and Cognitive Complexity," *Academy of Management Journal* 17 (1974), 37–45, and Stellan Ohlsson, *Deep Learning: How the Mind Overrides Experience* (Cambridge: Cambridge University Press, 2011).

combination of experience and biology, some individuals are more competent than others at formulating and maintaining complex pattern recognition. These are folks who are comfortable with, even welcoming to, paradoxes and contradictions.

Individuals with low cognitive complexity, on the other hand, cling to clear categorical distinctions. These are folks who are made uneasy by ambiguity and tend to follow their own preestablished heuristics rigidly. High cognitive complexity allows for the assimilation of cues that contradict comfortable mental images. Low cognitive complexity filters out evidence of contradictions.

The capacity for cognitive complexity is different from, even unrelated to, any of the traditional measures we use to gauge intelligence.[23] People with high IQs are no more or less likely to be comfortable with complexity than people with low IQs. We all undertake the mental work of engaging complexity; we simply go about it differently. And we all want to believe, perhaps even *need* to believe, that patterns exist. The possibility of spending one's life in a world that lacks any coherence or meaning is overwhelming. We all believe *some*thing. But that doesn't mean people believe *any*thing. We make active decisions as we consider claims – believing some, rejecting others.

The topology of claims offered in Chapter 5 focused solely on the content of the claim. Is it objectively accurate? Is it subjectively plausible? An epistemological rationalist would like to think that our belief formation process stops there. What else do we need? But it isn't that simple. When we examine the process of belief formation, we can see that forces beyond the legitimacy of the claim are brought to bear. We have to take into account the audience for that claim. It is the audience, after all, that grants or withholds a judgment of believability.

The matter of how we think our way to a belief in a claim is complex. We know that the neuroscience of the brain allows people to make a quick judgment about truth often based on intuition. People do apply reason, but as a second, delayed step. Not delayed for long, but rather after an initial response. That reasoning is active, conscious, and requires some mental exertion. And it leads us to belief.

I made the statement earlier that we believe what we want to believe. In that way, belief is purposeful, helping us achieve desired goals. Neuroscientists refer to this process as "motivated cognition."[24] Most people are not motivated to believe that their company is failing, even

[23] Robert Hooijberg et al., "Leadership Complexity and Development of the Leaderplex Model," *Journal of Management* 23 (1997), 375–408.
[24] Brent Hughes and Jamil Zaki, "The Neuroscience of Motivated Cognition," *Science and Society* 19 (2015), 62–64.

less that their own past behaviors may have contributed in some way to the current urgency. Yet, many people want to believe – are motivated to believe – that their organization will survive the current tumult. That may be a motive based on instrumental economics (*I'd like to hold onto my well-paid job*), a broader commitment to the organization (*I would really like to see everything work out*) or, most likely, some combination of the two. These drives combine to create a motivation to believe, say, Carlos Ghosn's claim of urgency regarding Nissan or Colin Powell's claim concerning the immediate threat posed by Iraq. By accepting their claims and adopting their solutions as our own, we have hope for the future.

Claims-Maker Credibility

When we evaluate a claim of urgency – the company needs to make a drastic break from the past if it is to survive, the country needs to go to war even though it has not been attacked, and so on – we all bring into play our acquired habits of understanding. We have learned certain meanings that can be applied either directly or indirectly to the claim. A large part of that learning derives from absorbing and accepting what previous authority figures – parents, teachers, religious and community leaders – have asserted to be true. We may not remember the precise moment at which we accepted something as true. Think of the debates that followed the 2017 Las Vegas mass shootings (or every other mass shooting in America).

The Second Amendment to the US Constitution reads: "A well regulated militia being necessary to the security of a free state, the rights of the people to keep and bear arms shall not be infringed." Who taught some of us that these words guarantee individual citizens a fundamental, even sacred right "to keep and bear arms"? Who taught some others of us that the Second Amendment recognized the right, even the need, for the nation to have a "well regulated Militia"? We may not know for sure. The whole process may have been subconscious. Yet we freely, naturally, almost unconsciously evoke those beliefs when evaluating competing claims. What we can say with certainty is this: whoever that early authority figure was, it was someone we found to be credible – that is, someone to whom we ascribed the quality of believability.

When George Bush dispatched Colin Powell to the United Nations in the spring of 2003, there was no war in Iraq. If there was to be a war, the United States had to start one.[25] Now, consider this counter–factual.

---

[25] The Iraq War was what Richard Haass called a "war of choice." See Haass, *War of Necessity, War of Choice: A Memoir of Two Iraq Wars* (New York: Simon & Schuster, 2009).

What if the US ambassador to the United Nations, John Negroponte – a career diplomat without military credentials or much of a public profile – had made the pitch for war rather than Powell?[26] Would he have been believed to the same extent that Powell was? There is no real answer to that, of course. Negroponte didn't deliver the speech. That's what makes it a *counter*factual. But even to consider the question raises the importance of the credibility of the claims maker.

Economists talk about the "high costs" associated with acquiring knowledge on our own.[27] There are times when the cost of knowledge acquisition would be so high as to become prohibitive. We have experienced many claims in *Constructing Crisis* that could not be easily verified or denied: that Enron's top brass had great ideas in the pipeline that would allow the company, and its stock, to rebound, or that Iraq possessed weapons of mass destruction. The Iraq and Enron claims we now know to have been inaccurate.

In these cases – Ken Lay hoping that Enron employees would not sell their stock no less than George Bush on the verge of starting a war against Iraq – the leaders wanted, even perhaps needed, their claims to be believed. In each case, they were counting on what they hoped would be the credibility of the messenger. Let's refer to that as claims-maker credibility, an attribution one person makes to another involving an assumption that the other is trustworthy and reliable.

Powell's description, as we now know, was *in*accurate. But he was persuasive in part because his audience largely found him credible. Americans "hold military figures in high regard," wrote Pete Vernon in the *Columbia Journalism Review*. Vernon was not writing about Powell specifically. Yet he noted how "a four-star general was given the benefit of the doubt in a way that civilian politicians wouldn't have received."[28]

A generation of Americans who experienced the dissembling of generals during the Vietnam War – General William Westmorland and his continuous lies to both the public and his own command staff about the progress of the war, most prominently – may not be quite as ready to grant

---

[26] Powell insisted that the speech could not have been delivered by Negroponte because it was "a little above that pay grade." But there have been instances of a president allowing his UN ambassador to handle vital Security Council communications tasks, such as John Kennedy's Ambassador Adlai Stevenson during the Cuban missile crisis. Powell quote is from Breslow, "Speech 'Was a Great Intelligence Failure.'"

[27] Russell Hardin, "The Economics of Religious Belief," *Journal of Institutional and Theoretical Economics* 153 (1997), 259–278.

[28] Pete Vernon, "The Media Today: The John Kelly Narrative Takes Hold," *Columbia Journalism Review* (August 3, 2017).

such easy credibility to a military general.[29] However, when people's experience with a leader – a general, a CEO, a politician, and so on – has been positive, there is likely to be a grant of credibility. Ken Lay relied on his credibility to assure employees that the value of their stock options would soon be restored. It wasn't, of course, and employees soon found their retirement savings wiped out.

Lay had every reason to know at the time of his speech to employees that Enron was unlikely ever to recover (he and other Enron corporate officers had already sold off much of their own stock). Yet, employees *believed* him. How do we know? To start, they greeted Lay the day of his all-employee address with a standing ovation that surprised even him ("Boy, I didn't expect that!"). But perhaps more telling was the fact that they held onto their stock. As the company tumbled into disarray, employees kept believing in a delusional future.[30]

Lay was a credible source right up to the end, when he was eventually found guilty of conspiracy and fraud. No longer credible, Lay died while awaiting sentencing. He was a revered figure within Enron, the founder who had driven the company to unexpected heights and made employees unimaginably wealthy, at least on paper and until that paper became worthless. For those employees, Lay possessed credibility. He would make Enron better and make them financially whole again.

Part of what gives claims makers credibility is their fluency at persuasion. The *New York Times* gushed over Colin Powell's use of "spy satellite photos and communications intercepts." The paper's editorial writers associated his fluency with source credibility. "Mr. Powell's presentation was all the more convincing," they wrote, "because he dispensed with apocalyptic invocations of a struggle of good and evil and focused on shaping a sober, factual case against Mr. Hussein's regime."[31] It's a compelling association between fluency and credibility, but one that can have dangerous consequences.

There is no better example of the distorting, even harmful impact of fluency than the debate over competing claims concerning the safety and efficacy of vaccines: "Less than 20 years ago, health experts thought it was only a matter of time before measles was completely eradicated in the United States." This is from an article published by *Health Day* in 2017:

---

[29] On Westmorland's record, see Andrew Krepinevich Jr., *The Army and Vietnam* (Baltimore: Johns Hopkins University Press, 1988).

[30] There was a period when selling stock by employees was frozen due to a change in pension plan administration, but the pattern of holding on to their Enron portfolio characterized their behavior both before and after the freeze. See Spector, "HRM at Enron."

[31] Editors, "Case Against Iraq," *New York Times* (September 6, 2003).

"But over the past 15 years, the disease has gained a new foothold in the United States, likely due to parents choosing not to vaccinate their children."[32] Choosing not to vaccinate their children? Why would a parent make that decision?

The vast majority of Americans believe in both the efficacy and safety of vaccinations, rating the benefits high and the risks low. But that leaves a lot of doubters. Seventeen percent of Americans oppose mandatory vaccination for children, 10 percent insist that the risks of vaccination outweighs the benefits, and 27 percent opt out of mandatory vaccinations for nonmedical (i.e., other than a life-threatening allergy to a component of the vaccine) reasons.[33]

The beliefs of those who refuse to vaccinate their children has a damaging impact: "Overall, measles incidence doubled, from 0.28 per million in 2001 to 0.56 per million in 2015. Infants and young children were hit hardest, and most cases were among the unvaccinated"[34] The disease is still rare, but the impact is notable. A 2015 measles outbreak associated with non-vaccinated visitors to Disneyland spread beyond Southern California, constituting a "large, multi-state outbreak," according to the CDC.[35] Another outbreak in Washington State in 2019 led the governor to declare a state of emergency, noting that the "existence of 26 confirmed cases in the state of Washington creates an extreme public health risk that may quickly spread to other counties."[36]

The question of beliefs in vaccines was a matter with serious consequences. Although highly unlikely, it is still possible for vaccinated children to catch the measles.[37] The greater threat, however, lies in pockets of non-vaccinated kids. Infants, who are not even eligible for vaccination until they reach the age of six months, are especially vulnerable.[38]

---

[32] Steven Reinberg, "Measles Making a Comeback in the United States," *Heath Day* (October 3, 2017).

[33] Carl Funk et al., "Vast Majority of Americans Say Benefits of Childhood Vaccines Outweigh Risks," *Pew Research Center* (February 2, 2017). Most states allow for nonmedical exemptions based on parents' religious, philosophical, or personal beliefs. The American Medical Association passed a resolution in 2015 calling for the elimination of all such nonmedical exemptions (www.wire.ama-assn.org).

[34] Reinberg, "Measles Making a Comeback in the United States."

[35] Accessed at www.cdc.gov/measles/cases-outbreaks.html.

[36] www.governor.wa.gov/news-media/inslee-declares-local-public-health-emergency-after -identifying-outbreak-measles

[37] Ninety-three percent of children develop an effective immunity after their first vaccination shot, and 97 percent after their second. See James Steckelberg, "Measles Vaccine: Can I Get the Measles if I've Already Been Vaccinated?" *Mayo Clinic* (no date).

[38] wwwnc.cdc.gov/travel/yellowbook/2018/international-travel-with-infants-children/vac cine-recommendations-for-infants-and-children.

The percentage of non-vaccinated young children in the United States quadrupled between 2001 and 2018.[39] A study in 2017 found lingering pockets of skepticism. Parents in rural communities were more likely to opt out of immunization for their children, although some urban areas – Seattle, Spokane, and Tacoma, Washington, prominent among them – were also considered "hot spots" where the risk of a measles outbreak was high.[40] The World Health Organization declared "vaccine hesitancy" to be one of the top ten global health threats of 2019.[41] And there had been an earlier claim suggesting the vaccine was unsafe, one that seemed highly credible.

In 1998, British gastroenterologist Andrew Wakefield sounded that alarm. The measles-mumps-rubella (MMR) vaccination, commonly administered to children, was dangerous, he warned.[42] "Onset of behavioral symptoms was associated, according to the parents, with measles, mumps, and rubella vaccination in eight of the 12 children," Wakefield and thirteen co-authors claimed. Eight out of 12! The article continued: "We saw several children who, after a period of apparent normality, lost acquired skills, including communication." It did offer a slight caution: "We did not prove an association between measles, mumps, and rubella vaccine and the syndrome described."[43] But the claim had been made. The "syndrome," although not named explicitly, was clearly autism. And this was coming from a highly credible, well-respected, peer-reviewed medical journal.

It should never have been published. The claim was bogus, neither accurate nor plausible. Wakefield's study was based on a tiny number of patients, had no control group that would weed out coincidental associations, relied entirely on parental reporting, and offered no plausible biological mechanism for connecting the vaccine to the claimed outcomes. The journal was forced to retract the article, the co-authors denounced Wakefield, and follow-up research failed to replicate his findings. The MMR vaccine, determined *all* other studies, was both

---

[39] Lena Sun, "Percentage of Young US Children Who Don't Receive Any Vaccines Has Quadrupled Since 2001" *Washington Post* (October 11, 2018).

[40] Jacqueline Olive et al., "The State of the Antivaccine Movement in the United States: A Focused Examination of Nonmedical Exemptions in States and Counties," *PLOS Medicine* (June 12, 2018).

[41] www.who.int/emergencies/ten-threats-to-global-health-in-2019?smid=nytcore-ios-share

[42] MMR vaccine is delivered in two doses, the first between ages 12 and 15 months, and the second at 4 through 6 years (www.cdc.gov/vaccines/vpd/mmr/public/index.html).

[43] A. J. Wakefield et al., "Ileal-Lymphoid-Nodular Hyperplasia, Non-Specific Colitis, and Pervasive Developmental Disorder in Children," *Lancet* 351 (1998), 637, 641.

safe and effective.[44] But the claim was there, in a highly respected journal, no less.

Some prominent individuals continued to ignore the science and contribute to the raising of doubts. Robert F. Kennedy Jr. became a proponent of the position that the MMR vaccine caused autism. He even offered to chair a commission on vaccines under the auspices of newly elected President Donald Trump, who himself once tweeted, "My friend's son, immediate #autism after #vaccines 10 yrs ago. So sad. Keep up good work[.] Nay-sayers will understand soon."[45] However, perhaps the most influential claims maker insisting that vaccines caused autism was not the president; it was television personality Jenny McCarthy.

Before listening to McCarthy's claim that the MMR vaccine caused autism in her son Evan, let's allow a respected, infectious disease specialist to speak first. Citing a mass of scientific data refuting any claim of association between the vaccine and autism, Dr. Tanja Popovic of the CDC told a television interviewer, "Based on what we know right now, we don't think that there is any association." The interviewer was not satisfied with Popovic's seemingly equivocal assertion: "But that's not saying with 100 percent certainty there isn't one." Taking one more stab at being believed, Popovic simply repeated her position, only this time more emphatically: "That *is* saying that, based on the evidence that we have right now, we don't think that there is one."[46] Her insistence may have been emphatic, yet she continued to frame her assertion in the cautious, equivocal language of science.

Now to Jenny McCarthy. In her television appearances, McCarthy would grab papers presumably containing results of scientific studies and say, "It's bullshit." The cause and effect was clear in her mind: "They vaccinated our baby, and something happened. That's it." Facing a non-challenging interviewer in Oprah Winfrey, who nodded empathetically in response to her claims, McCarthy touted her insightfulness ("Mommy instinct") and her research chops ("the University of Google is where I got my degree from"). She refuted all of the scientific studies. "My science is named Evan," McCarthy insisted, referring to her

---

[44] Jeffrey Gerber and Paul Offit, "Vaccines and Autism: A Tale of Shifting Hypotheses," *Clinical Infectious Diseases* 48 (2009), 456–461. The *British Medical Journal* concluded that Wakefield was not just a sloppy scientist. He engaged in fraud motivated by financial gain. See Fiona Goldee, "The Fraud Behind the MMR Scare," *British Medical Journal* (2011).

[45] Abbey Phillip and Lena Sun, "Vaccine Skeptic Robert Kennedy Jr. Says Trump Asked Him to Lead Commission on 'Vaccine Safety,'" *Washington Post* (January 10, 2017). Trump tweet accessed at www.trumptwitterarchive.com/highlights/vaccines.

[46] "Vaccines: An Unhealthy Skepticism," *Times Video* (February 2, 2015).

son, "He's at home. That's my science."[47] Her claim touted science illiteracy as a virtue.

We know from decades of research that speaker fluency influences believability. "Nonfluencies" – which include awkward vocal patterns, superfluous repetition, and constant corrections – reduce believability.[48] We saw how powerfully Colin Powell's fluency influenced newspaper editorial writers. Now look at the delivery of the claims by Popovic and McCarthy.

McCarthy used a simple but powerful voice to state her claim. It was her son who was under threat, and by extension, the children of all audience members. The claim – "They vaccinated our baby, and something happened. That's it" – was straightforward and understandable – a pattern that was easy to follow. There was no hesitancy, no equivocation. One event followed another sequentially – first the vaccination and then the developmental disorder – thus creating the assumption of cause and effect.

How accurate were the descriptive elements of McCarthy's claim? Most of McCarthy's audience had no way of verifying her descriptions. The only real way they could respond to questions about descriptive accuracy was by posing another question: why would she lie? The sympathetic, non-challenging climate created by her questioner – Winfrey herself possessed an extraordinarily high attribution of source credibility – added to the sense that, at the very least, McCarthy was not lying.[49]

The scientist, conversely, stumbled. Never knowing anything with "100 percent certainty," experts, especially scientists, often assert their claims in the equivocal language of "based on what we know right now." Not all listeners will be comfortable with the scientific uncertainty and ambiguity of that message. While experts insist that *most* children will be safe, parents wonder: sure, but will *my* child be safe?[50] As I noted earlier, some people have difficulty with and a high intolerance for ambiguity. For them, ambiguity and uncertainty breed discomfort and stress. Rather than recognizing complexity, they seek certainty.[51]

[47] Quoted in Seth Mnookin, *The Panic Virus: A True Story of Medicine, Science, and Fear* (New York: Simon & Schuster, 2011), pp. 253–254.
[48] This research is reviewed in Daniel O'Keefe, *Persuasion: Theory and Research* (Thousand Oaks, CA: Sage, 2002).
[49] Oprah Winfrey is regularly rated among the most trusted people in the United States. http://news.gallup.com/poll/224672/barack-obama-hillary-clinton-retain-admired-titles.aspx
[50] Laura Senier, "'It's Your Most Precious Thing': Worst-Case Thinking, Trust, and Parental Decision Making about Vaccines," *Sociological Inquiry* 78 (2008), 207–229.
[51] Charles Smock, "The Influence of Psychological Stress on the 'Intolerance of Ambiguity,'" *Journal of Abnormal Psychology* 50 (1955), 177–182.

Jenny McCarthy gave that certainty to them when she spoke in non-ambiguous terms. Her child – a specific individual named Evan – was not safe, she insisted. Colin Powell spoke with certitude as well. There was to be no doubt that Iraq possessed weapons of mass destruction. Yet, Tanja Popovic did not. The attribution of source credibility may hinge on matters completely superfluous to any evaluation of the legitimacy of the claim itself. We are more likely to believe a claim of urgency when we attribute credibility to the source of that claim.

We Don't Believe Alone

The name Bernie Madoff means just one thing to most people. He was the greatest con artist in US history, but not the lovable kind depicted in *The Music Man*. His Wall Street investment firm, Bernard L. Madoff Investment Securities LLC, evolved from a penny stock trader to a gigantic Ponzi scheme, bilking investors out of more than $64 billion. Yes, that's *billion*. As the whole world learned, most painfully his investors, his get-rich-with-me claims were bogus.

A Ponzi scheme is not a sound investment strategy; it can't be. Rather, it was, as Madoff reportedly confessed to his son, "One big lie." So, the objective basis for his promise to clients was inaccurate. Furthermore, his investments did not, could not, *always* outperform the market and other investors. That just wasn't plausible. As early as 1999, forensic accounting investigator Harry Markopolos warned anyone who would listen – financial analysts, the Security and Exchange Commission, and so on – that Madoff's numbers made no sense.[52] There was no way that Madoff could deliver the returns he was claiming, not legally, not mathematically; it simply was not possible. It *couldn't* be either accurate or plausible.

Madoff's claim may have been bogus, but it was believed. Wealthy and famous people, banks, family foundations, and charitable organizations continued to pour money down the hole. Why? The simple truth of the matter is that people do not believe alone. We look at others and take cues from them. Madoff's family and friends apparently trusted him; they had invested their own money. He was a well-known philanthropist, and many of the benefiting organizations – Hadassah, the Zuckerman Charitable Remainder Trust, and the United Jewish Endowment Fund among them – returned the favor by investing with him. The Royal Bank of Scotland put money into Bernard L. Madoff Investment Securities. So

---

[52] Harry Markopolos, *No One Would Listen: A True Financial Thriller* (Hoboken, NJ: John Wiley & Sons, 2010).

did France's Société Générale.[53] All of these cues misled people into believing Madoff. His claims must be right. Banks believed him, so did charities; why shouldn't I?

We all pay attention to social cues, but we do not pay attention randomly. We are quite selective in how we define our social group: determining who is in, who is not. And those we invite in tend to be *like* us in some significant way. This is the notion of "homophily," the human preference that motivates us to seek out "similar others."[54] That basic human preference then gets reinforced through the process of socialization in which our selected social group supports us in our beliefs, attitudes, and behaviors.[55] Both forces – homophily and socialization – reinforce a cognitive process in which individuals' beliefs are shaped and reinforced by like-minded others.[56] The process is not always conscious or deliberate, but it is powerful.

We may think alone. Belief formation, however, is not a solo undertaking. Reasoning occurs, and conclusions are drawn within a social structure. The interdependence of our thought process is seamless, often invisible to us: "It is so hard to reject an opinion shared by our peers that too often we don't even try to evaluate claims based on their merits. We let our group do our thinking for us." And mostly we form communities with groups of like-minded people and then make a concerted effort to fit in with that community.[57]

It was the winter of 1972 when renowned *New Yorker* film critic Pauline Kael addressed the Modern Language Association. A contentious presidential election had just ended in a landslide victory for the incumbent, Richard Nixon. His Democratic opponent, George McGovern, carried only one state: Massachusetts. "I live in a rather special world," Kael admitted to the Modern Language scholars, "I only know one person who voted for Nixon." Only one! What about the vast majority of voters who went for Nixon? "Where they are I don't know. They're outside my ken."[58] In Kael's community, it was McGovern by a landslide.

---

[53] Li Huang and J. Keith Murnighan, "Why Everybody Trusted Madoff," *Forbes* (December 22, 2010).

[54] Daniel Haun and Harriet Over, "Like Me: A Homophily-Based Account of Human Culture," in *Epistemological Dimensions of Evolutionary Psychology* (New York: Springer, 2015), p. 118.

[55] Also called "social contagion." See, for example, Gregory Bovasso, "A Network Analysis of Social Contagion Processes in an Organizational Intervention," *Human Relations* 49 (1996), 419–435.

[56] Dennis Gioia and Henry Sims, "Introduction: Social Cognition in Organizations," in *The Thinking Organization* (San Francisco: Jossey-Bass, 1986), pp. 1–19.

[57] Sloman and Fernbach, *The Knowledge Illusion*, 4.

[58] Quoted in James Wolcott, "The Fraudulent Factoid That Refuses to Die," *Vanity Fair* (October 23, 2012). What rendered the story "fraudulent," according to Wolcott, was

The admission by Kael that she lived among a cluster of like-minded individuals who voted for McGovern reflects the reality of how we form communities. We are attracted to like-minded individuals. The principle that we seek to associate with like-minded individuals and distance ourselves from other-minded people is fundamental to the creation and maintenance of social networks of all types.[59] The bond among similar others and the distance inserted between dissimilar others becomes even greater when there is a moral component associated with community membership, when there is a prevailing belief that *our* community adheres to superior values in contrast to *their* community.[60] Simone de Beauvoir insisted that otherness is a fundamental category of human thought: "Man never thinks of himself without thinking about the Other."[61] Constructing the One requires labeling the Other. These Others come to be seen as "outsiders" whose thoughts and actions can be used to define deviance from a social norm.[62]

Any outsider designation carries symbolic meaning. One group considers another to be the Other, outsiders who are in some way deviant and potentially threatening. When claims are made against outsider groups, members who believe themselves to stand not just apart but morally above will grant greater believability to that claim. The Other can now safely be delegitimized. Use of nonhuman language – animal metaphors in particular, which exclude the Others from the rest of humanity – enables the kind of belittlement that can be used to justify punitive and repressive actions by the state representing the interests of the insider group.[63]

That Other dynamic is precisely what British supporters of a referendum on leaving the European Union leaned on in their 2016 campaign. "Britain is a great country," Brexit supporters insisted, claiming, "we will be even greater if we take back control of our own democracy."[64] *Our* superior community is being threatened by *their* Other, decidedly inferior values. But who were they, those threatening

---

the assumption often communicated that Kael was unaware of her isolation. Not so, insisted Wolcott. The quote itself is accepted as accurate.

[59] Miller McPherson et al., "Birds of a Feather: Homophily in Social Networks," *Annual Review of Sociology* 27 (2001), 415–444.

[60] Morteza Dehghani et al., "Purity Homophily in Social Networks," *Journal of Experimental Psychology* 145 (2016), 366–375.

[61] Simone de Beauvoir, *The Second Sex* (New York: Knopf, 1952), p. 69.

[62] Becker, *Outsiders*.

[63] Luca Andrighetto et al., "Excluded from All Humanity: Animal Metaphors Exacerbate the Consequences of Social Exclusion," *Journal of Language and Social Psychology* 35 (2016), 628–644.

[64] Gisela Stuart et al., "Vote Leave for a Fairer Britain," Voteleavetakecontrol.org (June 22, 2016).

Others? As the nation prepared to vote in a referendum on whether to stay in or leave, that outsider group was depicted as a combination of the European Commission and Muslim immigrants.

The main criticism of the European Commission (EC), the European Union's executive branch, focused on allegedly overpaid, unresponsive bureaucrats imposing frustrating regulations on British commerce. As far as the twin threat said to be posed by Muslim immigrants, that suspicion became especially salient following 9/11 and the 7/7 London metro attack. With Muslim immigrants labeled as outsiders *and* terrorists, it became easier for native community members – not all, of course, but a significant number – to believe their presence constituted a crisis, a threat to national identity.

With a threatening Other consisting of a blend of Muslim immigrants and EC regulators firmly implanted in their minds, 52 percent of voters believed there was a crisis. The United Kingdom elected to leave the European project.

There was much silliness at play in the Leave campaign: bogus claims that double-decker buses would be banned and the European Commission would soon outlaw "British toasters and kettles."[65] Yet, we shouldn't be surprised by that fierce desire to protect the self against the other. The observation that "people love those who are like themselves" dates back to Aristotle.

Certainly, the contemporary connectivity that the Internet provides offers a far-reaching technology that allows for the creation of virtual communities that reside beyond physical neighborhoods and local villages. A fractious, partisan media enabled by another technology – cable television and the triumph of niche-focused narrow-casting over wide-audience broadcasting – provides spins on the news that both reflect and help reinforce like-minded communities.

It has become common to hear diagnoses of the increased tribalism into which much of the world has sunk. Common purpose and shared commitment has, in this presentist telling, given way to fierce, narrow loyalties based on race, gender, education, and world view.[66] The tendency, however, has been both strong and persistent throughout time.

Like-minded communities not only guide adherents in belief formation; they also reinforce beliefs once formed through socialization. In that way, our social group enhances both belief formation and belief

---

[65] Remi Banet, "Brexit and E.U. Bans on Bananas," *Yahoo* (May 22, 2016).
[66] Amy Chua, *Political Tribes: Group Instinct and the Fate of Nations* (New York: Penguin, 2018).

persistence. Arguments that may be implausible from a purely rational view – Jenny McCarthy's insistence that the "University of Google" gives her greater credibility than the vast body of scientific data, or Brexit arguments that the European Commission was about to ban double-decker buses and British toasters – can be taken as plausible by members of a particular community.[67] In that way, communities create and then reinforce their own "perceived realism": we *do* need to start a war in Iraq, Ken Lay *will* save our stock-based pensions, vaccines *are* more dangerous than beneficial, and so on. A shared sense of what is plausible and non-plausible comes to be an attribute, even an advantage of belonging.[68]

It turns out that like-minded communities do not just form around social and political issues, or even around ethnicity and race. Business organizations typically evolve their own form of like-minded groups, mainly within functional units. In their classic study of the dynamics of complex organizations, Paul Lawrence and Jay Lorsch noted how "sub-environments" – that was their term – evolved with their own "cognitive and affective orientation."[69] Business functions – marketing, accounting, research and development, production, and so on – became their own like-minded communities, manifesting different ways of thinking, behaving, and interacting.

Other networks develop within organizations. Researchers have found patterns of homophilic clusters formed on the basis of gender and racial identification, for instance.[70] There is much to be said for that process. Individuals can find social support, comfort, and enhanced opportunities for development, at least up to a point.

For Lawrence and Lorsch, group differentiation was adaptive. It was efficient for marketing types to look outside of the organization, to customers and competitors, while production personnel focused more on formal schedules and internally consistent processes. Employees involved in research and development were future oriented, hoping to see long-term investments in future innovations. Accountants were past

---

[67] Hugo Mercier and Dan Sperber, *The Enigma of Reason* (Cambridge, MA: Harvard University Press, 2017).

[68] Melanie Green, "Transportation into Narrative Worlds: The Role of Prior Knowledge and Perceived Realism," *Discourse Processes* 38 (2004), 247–266; Adam Hahs and Milan Colic, "Truth-Making in a World Made Up of Stories," *Explorations: An E-Journal of Narrative Practice* 1 (2010), 72–77.

[69] Paul Lawrence and Jay Lorsch, "Differentiation and Integration in Complex Organizations," *Administrative Science Quarterly* 12 (1967), 7.

[70] Herminia Ibarra, "Homophily and Differential Returns: Sex Differences in Network Structure and Access in an Advertising Firm," *Administrative Science Quarterly* 37 (1992), 422–447, and Kelly Mollica et al., "Racial Homophily and Its Persistence in Newcomers' Social Networks," *Organization Science* 14 (2003), 123–136.

oriented, tasked with ensuring compliance with the rules of accounting practice.

But that adaptation also presented a challenge: how, where, and when would these differentiated groups become integrated into a coherent whole working to achieve a common purpose? Like-minded functional communities create significantly different readings of the environment from other like-minded functional communities. Each group develops a common language, and similar orientation, and a readiness to affix greater credibility to fellow members than to nonmembers.[71] As *intra*group bonds strengthen, *inter*group ties fray.

To individuals who have spent their careers within a single function, the cause as well as the cure to a claimed crisis is likely to seem quite different. A marketer might believe the path to recovery lies in greater customer responsiveness to build market share. Production personnel will hope to see greater discipline and cost consciousness applied to internal processes. Financial types want interventions that will reassure investors by decisively reviving the stock price. And so on. When crisis leaders speak their language, both literally and figuratively, they are more likely to assign belief to their claims. Because belief formation unfolds in a social context, we are more likely to believe a claim of urgency to be legitimate when other members of our like-minded community believe the claim to be legitimate.

Personal Paradigms

People "do not approach any problem with a wholly naïve or virgin mind," philosopher John Dewey noted. Rather, they tackle problems "with certain acquired habitual modes of understanding, with a certain store of previously evolved meanings, or at least of experiences from which meanings may be educed."[72] As the venerable retailer Sears slid toward bankruptcy, its CEO displayed the limitations of approaching a problem with just such a habitual mode of understanding.

In 2004, Kmart purchased Sears for $11 billion. Given the sorry financial state to which both of these old retailers – Kmart could trace its roots back to the 1899 foundation of the S. S. Kresge Company and Sears, even further, to the original 1886 R. W. Sears Watch Company – had deteriorated, it was an iffy proposition at best to suggest that the two would be made stronger by partnership. And yet, Kmart chairman

---

[71] Elizabeth Sillence, "Seeking Out Very Likeminded Others: Exploring Trust and Advice Issues in an Online Health Support Group," *International Journal of Web Based Communities* 6 (2010), 376–394.

[72] John Dewey, *How We Think* (Lexington, MA: D.C. Heath, 1910), p. 106.

Edward Lampert flowed with optimism when he assumed the chairmanship of the resulting Sears Holding conglomerate. A new "great culture" would be forged that would "make the stores more competitive while staying focused on the customer."[73] The odds were never in Lampert's favor, and his approach to the problem – not with an open mind but with a paradigm formed by "previously evolved meanings" – didn't help. The chairman knew just what was needed for a dramatic turnaround. Lampert had a philosophy, an acquired habitual mode of understanding the world. He adhered to a form of "rugged individualism" derived from his intellectual hero, writer Ayn Rand.

Through novels and essays, Rand extolled the virtues of men of "unborrowed vision," extraordinary super-men who lived by the judgment of their own minds and were willing to stand alone against tradition and popular opinion. As a "passionate individualist," Rand insisted that self-interest was superior, both morally and practically, to altruism and collectivism.[74] Rational self-interest was the philosophy that Lambert adopted as his own and through which he viewed the challenge at Sears.

While touting "integrated retail" as a major strategic initiative – those were the words in his strategy documents – Lambert moved in the opposite direction, one reflective of Rand's passionate, even brutal individualism. The appropriate response to Sears's urgent decline, with hundreds of millions of dollars lost every quarter, would be to pit one division against another. This was not an unintended consequence of actions taken by Lampert. It was the goal of what came to be called the "warring divisions model."[75]

Lambert was operating through the lens of a guiding personal belief paradigm. He took on the Sears challenge with a preexisting belief system and then interpreted the situation he found through that lens. The decline at Sears was due to the lack of passionate, self-interested managers; he was sure of that. Likewise, the solution would be found by enacting his belief paradigm, creating a culture of intense competition. As loses continued to pile up, Lambert bet on more of the same. That was just the way the world worked, even when it didn't. In late 2018, Sears Holding declared bankruptcy.[76]

---

[73] Quoted in Parija Bhatnagar, "The Kmart-Sears Deal," *CNN Money* (November 14, 2004).

[74] Rand quotes from The Atlas Society available at https://atlassociety.org/objectivism/atlas-university/introduction-to-ayn-rand-s-ideas.

[75] Mina Kimes, "At Sears, Eddie Lampert's Warring Divisions Model Adds to Trouble," *Bloomberg Business Week* (July 11, 2013).

[76] The chain remained operational as Lambert purchased Sears Holding through bankruptcy court for $5.2 billion.

Thomas Kuhn defined a paradigm as a comprehensive body of shared assumptions concerning "what the world is like."[77] In offering an intellectual history of major innovations in scientific thought, Kuhn noted that a paradigm offered a useful guide to knowledge generation, helping to determine what questions will be asked, what evidence will be considered, and what solutions will be proposed. "Normal science" operated within just that kind of "conceptual box" defined by the reigning paradigm. For ancient Greeks, a geocentric astronomical paradigm placed the Earth at the center of the universe. It was a paradigm eventually upended by Copernican heliocentrism.

Paradigms are useful. But they are also constricting. Nothing truly novel or "necessarily subversive" could arise within the box imposed by a paradigm. Thinking "out of the box," a metaphor that became a cliché in the 1970s, was something that Lampert simply wasn't able to do.

Like Kuhn's scientific paradigms, personal belief systems box in our thinking. We don't doubt Edward Lambert's sincerity in seeking a "true" and effective solution to the failures at Sears. He invested millions in the project. But as he considered both the problems and potential solutions, his inquiry into what was undoubtedly an urgent situation narrowed. He saw evidence, proof really, that he – and Ayn Rand – had been right all along. Sears would recover only through emphasis on individual competition. When performance continued to deteriorate, he blamed recalcitrant and resistant subordinates for not getting on board. He found himself in an ever-deepening hole and kept digging.

What we can conclude is that we are more likely to believe a claim of urgency when the content of that claim confirms our previously formed beliefs. This leaves one troubling matter to confront. Is it possible to support a claim without believing that the claim itself is either accurate or plausible? Belief, remember, is defined as a cognitive pro-attitude, one that is formed in the absence of absolute certainty. Granted that all believing is purposeful. But can and will people purposefully believe in a claim even knowing that it is not legitimate? Yes, they can and yes, occasionally, they will. Analyzing that phenomenon requires delving into what has become known as a post-truth moment.

Post-Truth as an Act of Nullification

• "Muslim migrant beats up Dutch boy on crutches!"
• "Muslim destroys a statue of Virgin Mary!"

[77] Kuhn, *Scientific Revolutions*, 5.

- "Islamist mob pushes teenage boy off roof and beats him to death!"

Videos with these three explosive titles first appeared on the website of the UK-based "Britain First." That organization promoted itself as a "patriotic political party and street movement that opposes and fights the many injustices that are *routinely* inflicted on the British people." In assuming anti-Muslim, anti-immigrant positions, Britain First pledged to "take our country back" by defending "our people, our nation, our heritage and culture."[78] The three videos were posted with the intention of serving that mission.

The legitimacy of the videos was immediately questioned. The subjective ascription was implicit rather than explicit: Muslims generally and Muslim immigrants in particularly presented a clear-and-present social danger. The videos were not staged, but they were deployed on behalf of a bogus claim. None of the incidents involved immigrants. The perpetrator of the attack on the Dutch boy had been identified. He was neither a Muslim nor an immigrant. Nonetheless, less than a year into his tenure as president, Donald Trump re-tweeted all three.[79]

The president offered no comments about his posting. Press Secretary Sarah Sanders did, however. "Whether it's a real video," Sanders insisted, "the threat is real." And "that's what the President is talking about, the need for national security, the need for military spending. Those are very real things. There's nothing fake about them."[80] Maybe these were not "real videos," but they spoke to "real things" that people could believe in.

This was a bold defense of misrepresentation. The objective accuracy of the videos was unimportant, the president's spokeswoman insisted. Her appeal for support was based on some higher-order "realness" that overrode any need for specific claim legitimacy. The intended audience for the claim did not have to believe that the videos were accurate to believe in what they represented. So what if they were lies? That didn't matter! Viewers could believe in the underlying anti-Muslim / anti-immigrant message communicated by those videos.

Reporters at the press conference were nonplussed. One wondered, "So, it doesn't matter if the video is fake?" A second jumped in. "Even if it's a *fake* video?" Was Sanders really defending lying? "Look," Sanders retorted, "I'm not talking about the nature of the video. I think you're focusing on the wrong thing." The "wrong thing," in this case, was the

---

[78] www.britainfirst.org/mission-statement. Emphasis in the original.
[79] Ashley Parker and John Warner, "Trump Retweets Inflammatory and Unverified Anti-Muslim Videos," *Washington Post* (November 29, 2017).
[80] Quotes from Christina Wilkie, "White House: It Doesn't Matter if Anti-Muslim Videos Are Real Because the 'Threat Is Real,'" *CNBC* (November 29, 2017).

accuracy of the claims communicated by the videos. By deflecting focus away from the specific content of the claim, the "nature of the video," Sanders sought to create a post-truth moment. She was not lying in her defense. Rather, she was defending a lie. She insisted that the legitimacy of the videos was irrelevant, the "wrong thing."

On behalf of achieving what was held to be a superior end – restricting Muslim immigration to deal with a "real threat" – the administration defended spreading non-legitimate claims.[81] Accuracy, in fact, was beside the point. Consideration of the specific content of a claim was now nullified, not just subordinated but eliminated from the belief formation process.

An Imperfect Search for Legitimacy

When presented with a claim of urgency, we typically make a decision about belief. Do we believe the content of the claim? A belief formation process takes into account, whether or not consciously, all four factors: claim content, claims-maker credibility, the desire to fit in with a like-minded group, and the goal of achieving cognitive comfort. Then we support the claim *because* we believe it. We want to think that what we believe is legitimate, both accurate and plausible. There is no distance between belief and believing in: we do both simultaneously.

We know, of course, how imperfect the belief formation process is, often misleading us into believing something is legitimate when it isn't. In that case, people get fooled. They are duped. We refer to "falling" for a non-legitimate claim. The editorial writers at the *New York Times* and the *Washington Post*, we can say, "fell" for Colin Powell's reckless claim (inaccurate/plausible) that Iraq possessed weapons of mass destruction. They were duped in large part by the claims-maker's credibility. The *Times* editorial staff retrospectively apologized for its "questionable" coverage, admitting, "We wish we had been more aggressive in re-examining the claims as new evidence emerged – or failed to emerge."[82] Falling for non-legitimate claims, as the *Times* did, is thought to be a deficiency and most definitely not a point of pride.

"Falling for" is construed in the negative, something to be avoided if possible. What leads us astray from a clinically rational assessment of

---

[81] From the earliest days of his presidential campaign, Trump had made clear his support "for a total and complete shutdown of Muslims entering the United States until our country's representatives can figure out what the hell is going on." Quoted in Jenna Johnson, "Trump Calls for 'Total and Complete Shutdown of Muslims Entering the United States,'" *Washington Post* (December 7, 2015).

[82] Editors, "From the Editors: The *Times* and Iraq," *New York Times* (May 26, 2004).

a claim's content is the power of the other three factors on the belief formation map: the credibility of the claims maker, the beliefs of our peers, and our own personal belief paradigms.

Leaders may lie, of course. In his sixteenth-century treatise *The Prince*, Machiavelli noted that it was necessary for the prince to be "a great pretender and dissembler" to deceive a man "who will allow himself to be deceived." Enron was not on the road to recovery when Ken Lay claimed that it was. Certainly, there was grave doubt that the USS *Maddox* had been attacked by North Vietnamese gunships in the Gulf of Tonkin. Lyndon Johnson knew that and committed a lie of omission. Lies are told by leaders in the hope of deceiving by generating a false belief. At least, that's how we typically conceive of lying.

Let's return to that "falling" metaphor. When we fall for a claim, we arrive at a faulty conclusion. We have been fooled. But there is another possibility, one requiring a different metaphor. What if, rather than falling, some folks leap, eyes wide open, fully aware that they are being asked to support a claim that everyone – claims maker and audience – acknowledges is inaccurate?

A post-truth claim builds on a lie, a purposeful misrepresentation of objective description (Table 6.2). But it involves more than making a bogus or reckless claim; there is an active, willing bargain struck between claims maker and intended audience.

People in that audience are being lied to. What makes it a post-truth claim is that they *know* they are being lied to, and they believe in the claim anyway. The claims maker and the intended audience have entered into a perverse compact in which the content of the claim has been nullified as a matter of concern. Audience members accept the lie. They may even admire the wily skills and audaciousness of the liar. That is what is meant by a "post-truth" moment.

Post-Truth Claims Making

Professional wrestling in the United States is a post-truth sport. As a competition, it is a lie. Everything about it is fake. However, it is a lie told for a higher purpose: entertainment. Observing American wrestling in the 1950s, French literary theorist Roland Barthes saw a theatrical spectacle. Of course, the matches were "rigged," but who cared? Fans abandoned themselves "to the primary virtue of the spectacle, which is to abolish all motives and consequences." Wrestlers were not trying to win. Rather, their passion was directed entirely to the performance, to playing a role, and to embodying a "sort of mythological fight between Good and

Table 6.2 *The territory of a post-truth claim*

	Implausible	Plausible
Accurate	Deceptive	Legitimate
Inaccurate	Bogus	Reckless

Evil." What mattered to the wrestling audience "was not what it thinks but what it sees."[83]

It was Vince McMahon's World Wrestling Federation that fully embraced the mythological spectacle of wrestling events. Forty-four years after Barthes's insightful essay, he changed the name of his World Wrestling Federation to the World Wrestling *Entertainment*. McMahon's intent was to avoid any confusion as to what wrestling was meant to be. Fans were being treated not to a sports competition but to "sports entertainment," blending "soap opera, action-adventure, rock show, talk show, comedy, and all that stuff."[84] The rules of the game were made explicitly clear. Join us, he invited fans, in pretending that this is a real competition. Why? Because we're good at entertaining you and you like to be entertained. The goal of McMahon's rebranding was to render the claim of professional wrestling accurate. Yet, in the immediacy of the fake contests, the sham was intense. Wrestlers groaned and bled. Fans cheered and bet on the outcomes of matches.[85] The wrestlers adhered

[83] Roland Barthes, *Mythologies* (New York: Noonday Press, 1957/1972), 15, 23.
[84] McMahon quoted in Thomas Mannarelli, *The World Wrestling Federation* (Fontainebleau, France: INSEAD, 2000), 4.
[85] Barthes insisted that no wrestling fan would bet on the outcome of a match precisely because they know the results are not "true" or "logical." That doesn't seem to be quite the case anymore. Vice.com reports brisk wagering every year leading up to and including the climatic Wrestle Mania event. Given the knowledge that someone has access to the scripted outcome of every match, such wagering doesn't make much sense. But there it is. See Art Tavana, "People Are Making Tons of Money Betting on (Fake) Pro Wrestling," *Vice.com* (January 31, 2014).

strictly to a rule known as Kayfabe in which the fakery is never publicly acknowledged.

It's possible, despite McMahon's openness, that some rabid fans believed they were watching a real contest. But for the most part, followers of professional wrestling understood that they were being tricked. "Of course I know it's fake," said a fan, "But does that make it any less entertaining? No." Fans enjoyed the trickery: "Wrestling is entertainment at its very best."[86]

Fans are not just in on the trick; they are part of it, co-creating the fakery with the wrestlers and organizers. Their cheering for and against combatants – Virgil the Kentucky Butcher, Randy "Macho Man" Savage, Sensational Sherri, and so on – becomes part of the show. When Donald Trump entered the wrestling ring in 2007 during WrestleMania XXIII to body-slam and shave the head of Vince McMahon, he became a fellow trickster, participating in the sham.[87]

When the trickster is an organizational leader making an obviously inaccurate claim, the audience may know it is being tricked but still lend support to the trickster. They don't believe, but they do believe in. We have now entered a post-truth moment.

Post-truth involves lying – a reliance on inaccurate description – but it treats lying in a particular way. Lying is typically engaged in as a tool of deception. Post-truth claims openly embrace the act of lying on behalf of a larger purpose. They serve as wish fulfillments. Those who believe that Muslim immigrants are dangerous embrace inflammatory videos not as accurate but as real representations of their deeply held fears.[88] Again, we should admit that some people will believe the lie, will fall for it in the traditional sense. They may have accepted the three anti-Muslim videos as literal examples of the social dangers posed by Muslim immigrants. For some others, including the president's press secretary, the videos spoke not to deceptions but to "real things."

The intent of the post-truth claims makers, with the participation of an enthusiastic audience, is to negate any concern for the legitimacy of the

---

[86] Chris Mueller, "Why Do People Watch the WWE if They Know It's Fake?" *Bleacher Report* (January 25, 2010).

[87] Trump, a frequent sponsor and occasional participant in staged matches, was himself inducted into the World Wrestling Entertainment Hall of Fame in 2013. "Long before he stepped into the Oval Office," WWE's webpage declares, "Trump was helping to shape the future of the squared circle" (www.wwe.com/superstars/donald-trump).

[88] The notion of hoaxes as wish fulfillment is from Kevin Young, *Bunk: The Rise of Hoaxes, Humbug, Plagiarists, Phonies, Post-Facts, and Fake News* (Minneapolis: Graywolf Press, 2018).

claim. Professional wrestling fans accept that logic and truth are irrelevant in influencing the outcome of scripted matches.[89] Sarah Sanders appealed to that same willingness to enter into a world of spectacle. The accuracy and plausibility of particular claims asserted by the videos – do they legitimately depict the dangers of Muslim immigrants? – is irrelevant and beside the point. It is nullified.

In 2016, the *Oxford Dictionary* made post-truth its "word of the year," pointing to a 2,000 percent spike in the use of the term over the previous twelve months. Post-truth had journeyed from "a peripheral term to being a mainstay in political commentary, now often being used by major publications without the need for clarification or definition in their headlines."[90] There is no mystery as to why that sudden attention: the 2016 Brexit vote in the United Kingdom and election of Donald Trump in the United States.

There is nothing novel in the observation that politicians lie when they make claims, some consciously, regularly, and outrageously. It would be difficult to think of a US president who did not lie.[91] But the concept of post-truth implies a dynamic beyond simply lying, even lying often and boldly. When Bill Clinton denied the accuracy of claims that he had a sexual relationship with "that woman, Miss Lewinsky," he was lying with an intention to protect himself from embarrassment and to deceive others.[92]

What seemed to be unusual in a post-truth moment was the willingness to openly, explicitly, even proudly abandon accuracy entirely. Leaders could invite followers to look past the "claim content" element of the belief formation process. Followers were asked to base their support on

---

[89] Barthes insisted that no wrestling fan would bet on the outcome of a match precisely because they know the results are not "true" or "logical." That doesn't seem to be quite the case anymore. Vice.com reports brisk wagering every year leading up to and including the climatic Wrestle Mania event. Given the knowledge that someone has access to the scripted outcome of every match, such wagering doesn't make much sense. But there it is. See Art Tavana, "People Are Making Tons of Money Betting on (Fake) Pro Wrestling," *Vice.com* (January 31, 2014).

[90] Neil Midgley, "Word of the Year 2016 Is . . . " *Oxford Dictionary* (2016). The origin of the term in its current meaning comes from a 1992 essay in *The Nation*. Playwright Steve Tesich worried that "'we, as a free people, have freely decided that we want to live in some post-truth world." See Tesich, "A Government of Lies," *The Nation* (January 1992).

[91] Perhaps Gerald Ford and Jimmy Carter. Ford couldn't get elected, and Carter couldn't get re-elected.

[92] "I can only tell you I was motivated by many factors. First, by a desire to protect myself from the embarrassment of my own conduct. I was also very concerned about protecting my family." August 17, 1998, speech transcript.

"alternative facts."[93] When "truth isn't truth," one story is as good – as worthy of endorsement – as any other.[94]

The *Oxford Dictionary*'s definition of post-truth – "relating to or denoting circumstances in which objective facts are less influential in shaping public opinion than appeals to emotion or personal belief" – noted that the content of the claim had simply ceased to matter. People were leaping to support claims either knowing they were inaccurate or not caring. In that way, the role of claim content in the belief formation process was nullified (Table 6.3).

In a post-truth moment, political leaders assume the role of an entertaining trickster. "In a treacherous world," noted Emily Ogden, "you need a treacherous ally."[95] The trickster and the tricked enter into a mutual pact, one forged by the identification of a mutual enemy.[96] Sure, it may be a lie, but it's a lie being told on behalf of my (perceived) interests as a way to attack those who hold (perceived) antithetical interests. It is a lie intended not to deceive but to invite a shared embrace of a common foe.

At first glance, it is an entertaining thought. The trickster gains strength from the audience precisely because a kind of fraud is taken for granted. In fact, charges of fraud only enhance the entertainment value. We know, of course, that magicians don't saw their assistants in half and then figure out a way of piecing them back together. But we still gasp at the trick and wonder: how did they do that? How did they make the illusion seem so real? Tricksters are frauds and swindlers, making patently bogus claims. But they do so in the name of a higher value. For professional wrestlers and magicians, that value is entertainment. For purveyors of and the audience for those anti-Muslim videos, that higher value lies in some toxic brew of insecurity, anxiety, and bias.[97]

---

[93] White House senior advisor Kellyanne Conway famously defended lies by saying they were "alternative facts." See Eric Bradner, "Conway: Trump White House Offered 'Alternative Facts' on Crowd Size," *CNN* (January 23, 2017).

[94] The "truth isn't truth" quote is from Rudolph Giuliani, Donald Trump's personal lawyer. See Melissa Gomez, "Giuliani Says 'Truth Isn't Truth' in Defense of Trump's Legal Strategy," *New York Times* (August 19, 2018). I don't want to suggest that "truth" is an uncomplicated construct. Defining truth is a challenge that has plagued philosophers forever. See, for example, Volker Halbach and Leon Horsten, *Principles of Truth* (Frankfurt: Ontos Verlag, 2004).

[95] Emily Ogden, "Donald Trump, Mesmerist," *New York Times* (August 4, 2018).

[96] Ogden's insights are derived from her cultural history of mesmerism in the United States. See *Credulity: A Cultural History of U.S. Mesmerism* (Chicago: University of Chicago Press, 2018)

[97] It's probably not a coincidence that the 2018 *Oxford Dictionary* word of the year was "toxic." See https://en.oxforddictionaries.com/word-of-the-year/word-of-the-year -2018.

Table 6.3 *Nullifying content in a post-truth claim*

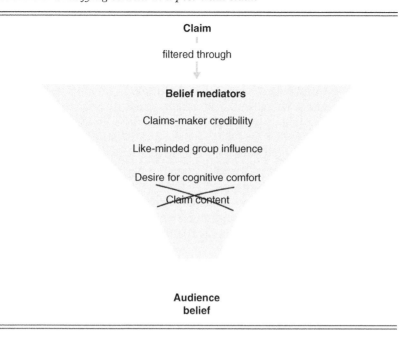

Claim

filtered through

Belief mediators

Claims-maker credibility

Like-minded group influence

Desire for cognitive comfort

~~Claim content~~

Audience belief

In the hands of powerful claims makers, entertainment may still be valued. Donald Trump had been a reality-TV star and a professional wrestling performer before entering politics. But there are more ominous dynamics at play in post-truth moments. In analyzing the twentieth-century rise of mad, authoritarian dictatorships, philosopher–political theorist Hannah Arendt noted a tendency among prominent tyrants to engage in a similar ploy.[98] Like other tricksters, these leaders made absurd claims in the conviction that their audience "did not particularly object to being deceived."[99]

As leader of the Italian Fascist Congress, Benito Mussolini spoke openly of the need to build an Italian myth of past greatness that had little if anything to do with facts. Mussolini admitted such, openly and proudly. "We have built our myth," he lectured followers, "The myth is a faith, a passion. It is not necessary for it to be a reality." The task of the fascist

---

[98] Hannah Arendt distinguished between authoritarians and totalitarians in terms of scope of their ambition. See Arendt, *The Origins of Totalitarianism* (New York: Harcourt, Brace, 1958).

[99] Ibid., 382.

leader was to "translate" the myth into a "total reality," a task to which all else would be subordinated.[100] Join in the trick, leaders invited followers. When post-truth claims nullify claim content, the claims maker aspires to create a belief *in* by relying on the other three elements of the belief formation process. Post-truth claims appeal to personal paradigms by supporting audience members' biases. The specific claim – again, think of the anti-Muslim videos – may not be accurate. But it *could* be because it aligns with our own personal paradigm. Now, the falsehood can be supported.[101] Social psychologist Daniel Effron noted, "Falsehoods that feel close to reality may be perceived as less dishonest when people imagine how they could have been true in alternative circumstances."[102]

There is a potentially powerful draw for post-truth claims. Hannah Arendt noted that in countries with a deep and pervasive history of anti-Semitism, "the audience was ready at all times to believe the worst."[103] Absurd claims that played on that anti-Semitic theme could be believed in based on that bias. When common enemies were targeted, claims could be believed in without paying attention to the specific content.

Peer pressure is also called into play by post-truth claims makers. Audience members are welcomed into a like-minded community. Arendt referenced the "mob" as a compliant and gullible mass of individuals who seek to become part of a community of like-minded individuals. Post-truth claims makers often rely on large, boisterous rallies that help tighten the bonds among like-minded individuals. It becomes easier to accept a falsehood as "it could be true" when it is enthusiastically endorsed by fellow like-minded celebrants.

Post-truth claims makers place heavy emphasis on source credibility. You can believe in me and therefore believe in what I say. "Just remember," Trump told supporters at a rally, "what you are seeing and what you are reading is not what's happening. Just stick with us."[104] As followers project credibility onto the claims maker, they are more likely to believe in the claim without evaluating its specific content. In that way, post-truth claims reinforce collusion between claims maker and audience.

---

[100] Quoted in Jason Stanley, *How Fascism Works: The Politics of Us and Them* (New York: Random House, 2018), p. 5.

[101] Daniel Effron, "It Could Have Been True: How Counterfactual Thoughts Reduce Condemnation of Falsehoods and Increase Political Polarization," *Personality and Social Psychology Bulletin* 44 (2017), 729–745.

[102] Daniel Effron and Kathy Brewis, "Politicians' Lies and the Power of Imagination," *London Business School* (May 2, 2018).

[103] Ibid.

[104] Rob Tornoe, "Trump to Veterans: Don't Believe What You're Reading or Seeing," *Philadelphia Inquirer* (July 24, 2018).

In post-truth moments, claims maker and supporters enter into a self-sealing pact. The claims maker lies by asserting non-legitimate claims, while the intended audience puts aside that acknowledged non-legitimacy in support of a belief in some shared goal. It is, to be sure, an asymmetrical pact. The claims maker retains and builds power by developing a kind of cognitive dependency from supporters. Abandon your own reasoning, allow me to lie, and then believe in the purpose to which I am deploying the lie.

A willingness to bend away from accuracy in support of a credible claims maker constitutes a dependent interaction in which individuals look to stronger leaders "for nurturance, guidance, protection, and support, even in situations where autonomous functioning is possible."[105] That is a tendency that sprouts, modern psychologists tell us, from a sense of personal powerlessness and ineffectiveness. Lacking a "will to truth," dependent individuals are thus motivated to attach themselves and delegate their thinking to a powerful individual directing understanding and inviting belief *in*.[106]

Whatever the intent of the claims maker, all share a common trait. All claims makers are storytellers.

---

[105] Robert Bornstein, "An Interactionist Perspective on Interpersonal Dependency," *Current Directions of Psychological Science* 20 (2011), 124.

[106] The term "will to truth" is from Friedrich Nietzsche. See Scott Jenkins, "Nietzsche's Questions Concerning the Will to Truth," *Journal of the History of Philosophy* 50 (2012), 265–289.

7   The Power of a Good (Crisis) Narrative

When Colin Powell appeared before the UN Security Council to stake his reckless claim (plausible but inaccurate) that Iraq's Saddam Hussein was amassing weapons of mass destruction, he brought with him a credibility built up over years of service to the US government and its military. It was precisely that credibility that President Bush intended to leverage into public, even global support for his war of choice against Iraq. But there was something else in play when Powell made his claim.

Powell told a good story, one with a compelling narrative, a frightening villain, and a heroic posse ready to charge in to save the day. Jenny McCarthy told a forceful story as well, one with evil, uncaring scientists relying on "bullshit" research to pose a threat to the children of America. There is nothing like a compelling narrative to help convey a claim to its intended audience.

The crisis-as-event model takes crisis to be an objective thing, and the story that leaders tell becomes a way to help others appreciate the urgency that those leaders have discerned. Now, when we shift analysis to the claim, we pay attention to the mechanics employed in the crisis assertion. And we note that the claim of urgency is embedded within an overarching narrative structure (Table 7.1). That's an element of claims making that is often overlooked.[1] It shouldn't be.

Narratives – typically defined as oral or written accounts of connected events – add polish to an asserted claim. A story helps make the claim more appealing, more compelling, and more believable. It is a way to shape the perceptions of the claims-maker's audience. Rather than simply hoping that the intended audience for a claim sees the same patterns and reaches the same conclusions as the leader, claims makers call on narrative structure as a way of inviting followers into a shared understanding of patterns, of how A influences B and then shapes C. That invitation comes

---

[1] For two important exceptions, see George Baca, *Conjuring Crisis: Racism and Civil Rights in a Southern Military City* (New Brunswick, NJ: Rutgers University Press, 2010) and Matthew Seeger and Timothy Sellnow, *Narratives of Crisis: Telling Stories of Ruin and Renewal* (Stanford: Stanford University Press, 2016).

Table 7.1 *Two levels of claim construction*

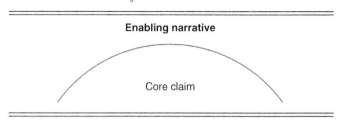

in the form of a compelling story that acts as a carrier of the core claim, the objective descriptions and subjective ascriptions contained in the claim.

"For better or worse," wrote Jerome Bruner, narrative "is our preferred, even our obligatory medium for expressing human aspirations and their vicissitudes, our own and those of others."[2] Crisis narratives are thus called on as a way of providing a richness of context, symbols, and images. Now, claims makers can marshal those narrative elements in a way intended to communicate what, precisely, is under threat. Here, the narrative's author/claims maker constructs a story in a way intended to make clear what is at stake in this urgent situation: our business, our community, our country, perhaps even civilization itself.

Then, through the deployment of the traditional artifice of drama – plot lines, protagonists and antagonists, conflict and tension, and the desire for release and the hope of resolution – the narrative construction seeks to transport its audience. It appeals to listeners on both logical and emotional levels. Narrative, in other words, is a powerful tool for making "the best possible case" for the embedded claim.[3]

But keep in mind that it is an artifice. All narratives are human constructions through which the narrative author manipulates the ambiguously complex dynamics of the world into a clear sequence of well-defined events, an unambiguous delineation of protagonists and antagonists, and a self-assured assertion of cause and effect.

It should be stressed that the fact of human construction doesn't render the narrative deployed on behalf of the claim to be inherently illegitimate. Not at all. The content of the core claim – the objective description and subjective ascription carried by the narrative structure – can and should be judged on its merits: accuracy and plausibility. But we can always be

---

[2] Jerome Bruner, *Making Stories: Law, Literature, Life* (New York: Farrar, Straus & Giroux, 2002), p. 89.
[3] Walter Fisher, *Human Communication as Narration: Toward a Philosophy of Reason, Value, and Action* (Columbia: University of South Carolina Press, 1987), p. 116.

cognizant about how the power of crisis narratives is deployed for legitimate and non-legitimate claims (deceptive, reckless, and bogus) alike.

The narrative, thus, becomes an artifice built on top of a human intervention, demanding critical appraisal both on its own and in interaction with the claim. To examine the construction of that narrative artifice and consider its implications, I start with a legitimate claim. Then, I can note how this claim, no less than any other, makes use of narrative structure.

Revealing Skeletons

"The business has failed to change."

When a newly appointed board chair opens an address to employees with that blunt assessment, the audience is likely to sit up and pay attention. This was Marks & Spencer's Archie Norman speaking to employees in November 2017. The legendary British retailer has been selling clothing, home goods, and food items from its London base and, eventually, around the globe since its nineteenth-century founding. After a performance peak in 1998 – in that year, Marks & Spencer (M&S) became the first British retailer to surpass £1 billion in profitability – sales eroded steadily.

While M&S retained its classic (some would say stodgy) styling, competitors focused on trendy youthful consumers in smaller, specialty shops. Those rivals enjoyed dramatically lower costs than M&S, a situation exacerbated by the retailer's reluctance to engage in overseas sourcing. M&S focused on a specific definition of quality – "*Clothing fit and comfort of the highest standard*" as determined by "*the U.K.'s most comprehensive survey of customer measurement*" – that spoke to a small segment of the clothing-buying public while virtually writing off the youthful, trendy market.[4] Clothing displays within its stores were organized by categories of the cloth used in the merchandise – knits, wool, suede, easy wear – rather than by style. The business remained so tradition bound that it did not start accepting bank credit cards until 2001. Process innovations that allowed clothing retailers including Primark, Zara, and H&M to offer fashionable items at reduced prices simply eluded the British icon.

M&S's post-1998 decline was a wake-up call, but one that failed to evoke an adequate response. What followed, instead, were fifteen years of rolling catch-up efforts in which one initiative after another failed to

---

[4] Quoted from the 1998 *Annual Report* in Michael Piche et al., *Marks & Spencer and Zara: Process Competition in the Textile Apparel Industry* (Fontainebleau, France: INSEAD, 2002), p. 2. Emphasis in original.

resuscitate M&S: revitalized store designs, dramatic price cuts, separate food emporiums, a "real clothes for real women" marketing campaign, the drawing back of the company's international expansion, corporate restructuring, discontinuation of the cherished St. Michael's clothing brand, frequent store "cullings," elimination of consumer electronics sales, and a "Look Behind the Label" campaign intended to emphasize the business's social responsibility. All of these efforts disappointed investors and customers alike.

In September 2017, the M&S board announced the appointment of Archie Norman as its chair.[5] Norman "has a breadth of experience with an extensive track record in retail and brands," read the official announcement, "He was instrumental in transforming a number of major British businesses including Kingfisher, ASDA and Energis."[6] M&S's stock price soared on the announcement. Norman, after all, had compiled an impressive track record of successful turnarounds.

As was his pattern as the leader of troubled companies in the past, most particularly the ASDA grocery chain, Norman immediately undertook a tour of stores.[7] He preferred to meet with employees personally and experience the retail space directly rather than attempting to learn about the business through layers of management and official reports. The new board chair quickly concluded that far too much of M&S's offerings were aimed at "over-55" shoppers. The store's famed food courts were laid out in a confusing, unappealing manner, clothing buying cycles were too long, and M&S's information and data systems were "dated."[8] And this was all before making his first statement on the interim performance of M&S two months after accepting the position.

Now, Norman took the opportunity to present his story. M&S, he insisted, had "failed to change in line with customers and as fast as competition." Norman embedded his claim in a crisis narrative that reached beyond description and ascription to appeal to his audience. In a torrent of metaphors, Norman vowed that cupboards would be opened, skeletons revealed, carpets pulled up to see what was underneath, and a "few sacred cows" slaughtered to reverse M&S's decline. He continued:

> That failure isn't to do with the strategy or the intellectual approach nearly as much as it is to do with the organization, the culture and the capability.
> So the really important thing about today is that the genesis of any turnaround of this scale starts with the recognition of the unvarnished truth, the

---

[5] In the United Kingdom., the positions of CEO and board chair are separated.
[6] https://corporate.marksandspencer.com/aboutus/our-leadership-team/archie-norman.
[7] I detailed Norman's experience at ASDA in Spector, *Implementing Organizational Change*.
[8] Zoe Wood, "Not Just for Over-55s! M&S Chairman Says Chain Needs Younger Clothing," *The Guardian* (November 5, 2017).

ability of the leadership team to talk openly and frankly in an unsparing way about what the business is today and what the challenges are that we face, and to be so critical and invite the whole organization to be part of our journey of transformation. That is what you'll see from Steve [Rowe, M&S CEO], and that is why this is really an important day for us. That unvarnished truth will bring the wellspring of energy from everybody, from store colleague, to store manager, to buyer, to marketer.

Then, Norman offered his conclusion in the form of an invitation "to be part of our program of change and transformation. We know that this business is a really, really special business. It's just our job to make it special again."[9] Norman's past record suggested that progress was likely to be forthcoming, although he had never taken on a century-old national landmark, with quite the same level of entrenched tradition. He moved forward on multiple fronts, closing underperforming stores and adding a food delivery service. And he did so within the context of a forceful narrative.

Considering the Narrative

The crisis-as-claim model requires a critical analysis of the structure of a claim's construction. So, let's open that analysis with a recognition that if there is any universal facet of human communication, it lies in the desire, perhaps even the need, to tell a story. Narratives are constructed representations in which human or human-like characters participate in an event or a series of events, traveling from beginning to middle to end.[10] Embedding a claim within a narrative is meant to add sparkle to a claim and aid the claims maker in persuading their audience.

Archie Norman hoped to be convincing. The author of a crisis narrative – the human hand behind the narrative's construction – is always sending a message to the audience.[11] Here is how I would *like* you to understand the urgency that I am asserting. Hierarchical headers are imbued with formal authority, so their intention goes further. Here is how I *expect* you to understand the urgency that I am asserting.

---

[9] https://seekingalpha.com/article/4122231-marks-spencer-groups-maksy-ceo-steve-rowe-q3-2017-results-earnings-call-transcript

[10] This definition is based on H. Porter Abbott, *The Cambridge Introduction to Narrative* (Cambridge: Cambridge University Press, 2008), and Jaber Gubrium and James Holstein, *Analyzing Narrative Reality* (Thousand Oaks, CA: Sage, 2009).

[11] For an analysis of the narrative author, see Abbott, *The Cambridge Introduction to Narrative* and Molly Patterson and Kristen Monroe, "Narrative in Political Science," *Annual Review of Political Science* 1 (1998), 315–331. Shaul Shenhav et al., "Story Coalitions: Applying Narrative Theory to the Study of Coalition Formation," *Political Psychology* 35 (2014), 661–678.

Because there is a beginning, middle, and end, there is neatness to a narrative, a circumscribed flow of events from one to the other. That neatness – first A happened, then B, followed by C – doesn't exist in a chaotic, confusing, and ambiguous world. Wait a minute, we might think. Don't the roots of B go back much further than A? And didn't an awful lot of dynamics unfold between B and C that your story leaves out? Narratives can elide these concerns by means of a neat construction of the world, one that replaces confusion and ambiguity with an imposed clarity in which the noise of a chaotic world is eliminated, and events are sequenced in order to declare cause and effect.[12] The narrative author makes choices about what to leave in and what to leave out. In that way, the narrative guides its audience.

There will always be human agency behind a narrative. Through the act of constructing a story, the claims maker determines sequencing and, in doing so, asserts cause and effect. The goal is clear: to make a case for a particular point of view regarding urgency and how to respond. We paid too much attention to one market niche at the expense of others, Norman insisted, our design decisions got sloppy, and we started losing money: A to B to C. These may all be perfectly legitimate assertions. It is vital, nonetheless, to remember that they are assertions, human concoctions intended to convince listeners that *this* is the right story rather than *that* one.

Of course, narratives often come in more complex forms: multiple points of view (the 1950 Japanese film *Rashomon* tells the story of a crime from different perspectives), unreliable narrators (the 2012 best-seller *Gone Girl*), and ambiguous endings (much of French cinema). However, when deploying narrative as a persuasive instrument, claims makers seek to ascribe cause and effect through a straightforward structure.

Think of Jenny McCarthy and her claim that the MMR vaccination caused her son's autism. The claim itself was bogus, but the narrative was compelling: "They vaccinated our baby and something happened. That's it." The claims-maker's story left no room for complexity or ambiguity. McCarthy offered not a detached claim about the dangers of vaccination. Rather, it was an emotional tale about her baby under threat. There is no explicit statement of cause and effect: no my baby got autism *because* of the vaccination. There's really no need. The assertion of causation is inescapable, located in two narrative choices: how the

---

[12] Abbott, *The Cambridge Introduction to Narrative*; Gubrium and Holstein, *Analyzing Narrative Reality*.

events are sequenced and what is not included in the story. First the vaccination shot, then the onset of autism. Any other possible mediating factors are eliminated. In McCarthy's narrative, nothing else matters. There was the vaccination, and then the "something" happened. "That's it."

The implicit, albeit flawed, reasoning is clear: *post hoc ergo propter hoc*; that is, *after* this, therefore *because* of this. That's a classic logical fallacy. Yet, there's no denying that McCarthy presented a simple, not to say simplified, narrative that gained power through that structure. Therein lies the potential for dangerous consequences of embedding claims in compelling stories. From within the crisis-as-claim model, we can observe that McCarthy's claim was bogus: neither accurate nor plausible. Colin Powell's claim concerning weapons of mass destruction in Iraq was reckless: plausible but inaccurate. To the extent that their claims gained power through a compelling narrative structure, people were misled into believing what was not real.

There's no argument that everyone or even most people believe a claim simply because it comes wrapped in a powerful narrative. The belief formation process is multifaceted and complex. McCarthy's narrative for convincing people that the vaccination caused autism was not convincing enough to sway the vast majority of parents.

The point is not that a good story will always be convincing to everyone. Of course not. What a good story can do is enhance the appeal of a claim and thus render it more believable than had it been a simple statement of description and ascription. That's why we need to appreciate just what constitutes a "good" – that is, appealing – crisis narrative and appreciate the power to convince and mislead. For that inquiry, we can turn to the field of narrative theory.

Crisis Narratives as Textual Performance

Narrative theorists most typically focus on stories set in an explicitly imagined world, one that unfolds through children's stories, screenplays, folktales, novels, and so on.[13] These studies are foundational to the development of narrative theory. Issues of accuracy and plausibility are

---

[13] For example, Michael Cadden, *Telling Children's Stories: Narrative Theory and Children's Literature* (Lincoln: University of Nebraska Press, 2011); Vladimir Propp, *Morphology of the Folktale* (Austin: University of Texas Press, 1968); George Varotsis, *Screenplay and Narrative Theory: The Screenplectics Model of Complex Narrative Systems* (Lanham: Lexington Books, 2015); Richard Walsh, *The Rhetoric of Fictionality; Narrative Theory and the Idea of Fiction* (Columbus: Ohio State University Press, 2007).

replaced by an appreciation of the mechanics upon which a narrative is built and the ways in which narratives attract and appeal.[14] When real-world crisis claims are embedded in a narrative, the author's intent is different than make-believe. Now, the claims maker is seeking to communicate what is taken to be an actual event, not a fairy tale. Under that circumstance, accuracy and plausibility must be considered. Was it accurate for Archie Norman to assert that M&S's offerings were targeting "over-55" shoppers? Was it plausible to insist that the company's buying cycles – the time required to decide, purchase, acquire, deliver to stores, and sell – were too long? I judge that these and other claims made by Norman were both accurate and plausible.[15] Was he *right*; that is, do you agree with his conclusion? That's a different question. His claims were legitimate. Yet, his narrative, like any narrative, is a fiction, a product of human construction rather than an objectively given thing that is determined by nature with scientific precision.

Think of crisis narratives as attempts to create "real fiction." In such cases, the construction of a story – even while relying on fictional devises of plot, threat, protagonists, and antagonists – is meant to be taken as true.[16] If we examine the description and ascription embedded in the narrative, we can judge Norman's claim to be legitimate. Through the same process, we can evaluate Jenny McCarthy's claim to be bogus. Carlos Ghosn's claim at Nissan was legitimate, so was George Bush's claim in response to September 11. The claims of Lyndon Johnson regarding the Gulf of Tonkin and Colin Powell's concerning Iraq's weaponry were reckless. And yet, in all of these cases, legitimate or otherwise, the narratives were purposeful constructs in which interests were being asserted and power was being exercised through the deployment of narrative structure.

Lyndon Johnson wanted an escalation of the war in Vietnam and George W. Bush, Colin Powell's commander in chief, wanted regime change in Iraq.[17] They also wanted approval for their chosen course of

---

[14] I am not suggesting that plausibility is irrelevant to a fictional narrative. Animals may talk and trees may befriend young children. But there can still be a logic operating within the patently constructed universe of a fictional story. Real-world narratives, however, require a plausibility that adheres to the known logic of the universe in which they are told.

[15] I'm judging accuracy based on other work on M&S. See Judi Bevan, *The Rise and Fall of Marks and Spencer* (London: Profile Books, 2007), and Piche et al., *Marks & Spencer and Zara*.

[16] That's a term from Fisher, *Human Communication as Narration.*

[17] Bush reportedly first brought up his desire for an overthrow of Hussein with the UK's Tony Blair just nine days after the 9/11 attacks. See David Rose, "Bush and Blair Made Secret Pact for Iraq War," *The Guardian* (April 4, 2004). The article, I think, overstates any notion of an actual "pact." Nonetheless, there was clearly an early and mutual statement of interest in regime change in Iraq.

action. Their narratives relied on reckless claims of urgency (plausible / inaccurate) to make their best case and win support. Norman wanted employees to get on board the revamp that he and his CEO believed would return M&S to peak performance, so his narrative was constructed to achieve that goal.

Regardless of the underlying legitimacy of the claim, in other words, *all* crisis narratives should be appreciated as textual performances. The author builds them with care, purpose, and a clear focus on the audience. Narrative structure provides the tool by which claims of urgency can attract an audience and influence reasoning.

In addressing employers, investors, and perhaps even consumers, Norman chose his words carefully to build a narrative. So did Lyndon Johnson when he spoke to the nation about the Gulf of Tonkin. The North Vietnamese launched an unprovoked attack on an American ship, my duty as president is to protect national interests; therefore, I have ordered bombing attacks: *A* to *B* to *C*. The US Senate overwhelmingly believed the story, and the war escalated with congressional approval.

In their reliance on a narrative, claims makers take a position both on what the world should look like and how that idealization will be achieved. In that way, the narrative seeks to shape perceptions of such elusive constructs of "good" and "evil," "truth" and "reality," "cause" and "effect."[18] Through the performance of storytelling, the claims maker seeks to make clear what might otherwise remain murky and uncertain. By remaining alert to the building blocks necessary to construct a narrative, we as the narrative audience can and should be watchful for the influence and perhaps even the manipulation by the claims maker that underpins that construction.

Drama thrives on tension; it is what keeps people interested in the story.[19] To build drama, claims makers go beyond a clinical statement of description and ascription and construct a story. As a way of inviting a compelling emotional response for the audience, the claims maker tells of a breach, some reversal of fortunes in which something important is placed in jeopardy. That's the source of urgency.

That threat is what attracts the emotional investment of the narrative's intended audience. It's what Aristotle recognized as *peripeteia*, or reversal of circumstances. "Something goes awry," Bruner notes, "Otherwise

---

[18] Scott Allison and George Goethals, *Heroes: What They Do and Why We Need Them* (Oxford: Oxford University Press, 2011); Kent Puckett, *Narrative Theory: A Critical Introduction* (Cambridge: Cambridge University Press, 2016); Paul Ricoeur, *Time and Narrative* (Chicago: University of Chicago Press, 1984); Gabriela Spector-Merseel, "Narrative Research: Time for a Paradigm," *Narrative Inquiry* 20 (2010), 204–224.

[19] http://blogs.yis.ac.jp/15whitinga/2011/10/15/the-elements-tension-drama-journal

there is nothing to tell about."[20] That *peripeteia* is what makes the narrative form so well suited for claims of urgency – the dramatization of communal threat. And it is also what gives crisis narratives their common form, their master narrative.

Constructing a Master Crisis Narrative

Through the examination of claims of urgency, it is possible to recognize a master narrative: a global organizing story line under which more specific, localized narratives will fit.[21] Once the master is established, smaller, more specific, localized narratives can be offered to provide greater understanding.

We can examine how different master narratives can be brought to bear on the same set of urgent circumstances, in this case, the French Revolution. Let's start with a master narrative that can be called the "Great Man." This is a view of the world authored by nineteenth-century Scottish social philosopher Thomas Carlyle, who insisted that "Universal History, the history of what man has accomplished in this world, is at bottom the History of the Great Men who have worked here."[22]

Carlyle was an historian of the French Revolution, having produced a massive three-volume tome that is said to have served as a source for Charles Dickens's *A Tale of Two Cities*.[23] In his application of that Great Man master narrative to the 1789 uprising, the French Revolution became an instance of the failure of the *Ancien Régime* to replace its inept head, Louis XVI, with an "Able-Man."[24] That is a master narrative – Great Men or lack of Great Men determining history – with a specific example played out in the telling of the French Revolution. There was no Great Man, the regime collapsed; thus, the Great Man master narrative is upheld.

There are, of course, other master narratives that, when applied to the same French Revolution, produce a significantly different spin. Marxist

---

[20] Bruner, *Making Stories*, 17.
[21] Master narrative theory comes from Frances Smith and Debbie Dougherty, "Revealing a Master Narrative: Discourses of Retirement throughout the Working Life," *Management Communication Quarterly* 26 (2012), 453–478, and Deborah Tannen, "'We've Never Been Close, We're Very Different': Three Narrative Types in System Discourse," *Narrative Inquiry* 18 (2008), 206–222.
[22] I've had the opportunity to spend some quality time with Carlyle's work. See Spector, "Carlyle, Freud, and the Great Man Theory More Fully Considered."
[23] David Marcus, "The Carlylean Vision of *A Tale of Two Cities*," *Studies in the Novel* 8 (1976), 56–68.
[24] Thomas Carlyle, *On Heroes, Hero-worship, and the Heroic in History* (New Haven: Yale University Press, 1841/2013), p. 162.

scholars, for instance, hew to a master narrative that sees world history as determined by class conflict. When the French Revolution is constructed from a Marxist perspective, the incompetence of Louis XVI no longer occupies center stage. The Marxist narrative of the revolution now insists on class struggle in which rural peasants aligned with urban rebels as the core dynamic. In this telling, the decline of feudalism invited French bourgeois capitalists to usurp property from rural citizens, who then formed common ground with anti-capitalist urban revolutionaries. Applying a different master narrative to the same contingencies leads to a completely different understanding. The lack of a Great Man has been replaced by the tensions arising from class struggle.

And one more example. A Freudian master narrative will point to the forces of family dysfunction with particular emphasis on father-son conflict. In this case, the revolution represents not the failure of an individual leader or the inevitability of class friction, but an eruption of intra-family tensions. The "collective, unconscious images" of family disorder in the country rather than class tensions or the lack of a Great Man emerge as the source of the "revolutionary politics" behind the events of 1789.[25]

The variety of interpretations is dizzying – Rashomon-like in complexity, all reflecting different master narratives. In recognizing that these different narratives are exploring the same phenomenon, the French Revolution, we can appreciate the power of the master narrative selected by the various authors. Like any claim, we can judge the accuracy and plausibility of arguments presented from the Carlyle, Marx, or Freud perspective. We cannot determine, however, that one master narrative is "right" and another "wrong."

Crisis claims makers work within their own master narrative: the *once-glorious-kingdom-under-threat* narrative. That master crisis narrative is an archetype that can be applied in a wide variety of settings. We can consider that master narrative first in the context of fiction. Here, there is no attempt by the author to be true or real, just entertaining.

Disney's popular 2013 animated film *Frozen* tells the story of a princess, a handsome iceman, and a rather goofy snowman in their search for the princess' sister. The plot, loosely based on a Hans Christian Andersen tale, is triggered when the apparently idyllic kingdom of Arendelle is transformed into a sad, frozen enclave.[26] It is a story built

---

[25] The Marxist narrative is from Georges Lefebvre and the Freudian narrative and quote are from Lynn Hunt. See Hunt, *The Family Romance of the French Revolution* (Berkeley: University of California Press, 1992), p. xiii, and Lefebvre, *The Coming of the French Revolution, 1789* (Princeton: Princeton University Press, 1947).

[26] The story and screenplay are credited to Jennifer Lee, Chris Buck, and Shane Morris. See www.imdb.com/title/tt2294629/?ref_=nv_sr_1.

on the foundation of the master crisis narrative: the once-glorious-kingdom-under-threat.

I use the example of an animated film not to trivialize the concept of the master crisis narrative, but rather to expose and explore its mechanics. We can clearly hear that same master narrative in Archie Norman's call to make M&S "special again." There were no scandals or revelations of terrible misdeeds. But there was an urgent situation. We were once special, our specialness has been tarnished, and we need to make us special again. This is the master narrative in claims of urgency. The master crisis narrative gets played out regularly in the world of politics. Crises present the opportunity for new policies, new leaders, and often calls for both. In his 1980 presidential campaign, Ronald Reagan adopted the slogan, "Let's Make America Great Again," as a way of connecting to that master narrative.

Implicit in any once-glorious-kingdom-under-threat crisis narrative are two assumptions: the kingdom *was* once glorious, and the leader is the protagonist who will confront that threat and return the kingdom to its glory. Reagan's campaign narrative touched on both. In his 1980 speech accepting the Republican Party's nomination, he painted a verbal image of grave threat. "Never before in our history," Reagan insisted, "have Americans been called upon to face three grave threats to our very existence, any one of which could destroy us." *Never before in history*! These three existential threats to the country came from "a disintegrating economy, a weakened defense, and an energy policy based on the sharing of scarcity."[27] This was a grave, even unprecedented threat.

A campaign poster depicting a smiling candidate superimposed on a waving flag with the White House in the background and the promise "Let's Make America Great Again" was clear about both what was threatened – the country symbolized by the flag – and the promise of the narrative. Put Reagan in the White House and the glory will be restored. "For those who have abandoned hope," he promised, "we'll restore hope and we'll welcome them into a great national crusade to make America great again!"[28] Variations on the "Make America Great Again" slogan have been echoed in several presidential campaigns since Reagan's: Bill Clinton in 1992 in a small way and Donald Trump in 2016 as a major theme. It always represents a call to return the kingdom to its former exceptionalism.

---

[27] Ronald Reagan, "Address Accepting the Presidential Nomination at the Republican National Convention in Detroit," *The American Presidency Project* (July 17, 1980).
[28] Ibid.

Reagan was nothing if not consistent in adhering to that master narrative. In his 1989 farewell address, Reagan insisted on writing a satisfying ending to his chosen narrative. The glory that was once America had indeed been fully restored. To help make that point, he borrowed a metaphor from John Winthrop: the "city upon the hill."

Winthrop, an English Puritan lawyer and a key founder of the Massachusetts Bay Colony, introduced the "city upon the hill" construct in a sermon composed prior to his arrival in the New World. The colony would engage in a special covenant with God to serve as a holy model – a city on a hill – for other English colonies to emulate.[29] It was an image Reagan had used before as a metaphor for American exceptionalism, and it now served as a neat wrap-up to his master narrative, the final act for his self-constructed drama.

The "shining city" was Reagan's take on what was to be understood as good and true. It was a "tall proud city built on rocks stronger than oceans, windswept, God blessed, and teeming with people of all kinds living in harmony and peace."[30] And it was a city where, "if there had to be city walls, the walls had doors, and the doors were open to anyone with the will and the heart to get here."[31] That city, Reagan insisted, had been disrupted, tarnished severely in the 1970s under the leadership of Democrats and even moderate Republicans. Under his stewardship, the crisis of the late 1970s had given way to redemption. "How stands the city?" he asked rhetorically. There was little suspense and no surprise in his answer:

More prosperous, more secure and happier than it was eight years ago. But more than that: after 200 years, two centuries, she still stands strong and true on the granite ridge, and her glow has held steady no matter what storm. And she's still a beacon, still a magnet for all who must have freedom, for all the Pilgrims from all the lost places who are hurtling through the darkness, toward home.

The exceptional kingdom had been returned to glory.

Reagan's elaboration in his Farewell Address represents a final act for the story imposed by the narrative author and offered as truth. It was

---

[29] Godfrey Hodgson, *The Myth of American Exceptionalism* (New Haven: Yale University Press, 2009).

[30] That image of a "God blessed" America has echoes of Woody Guthrie's angry musical retort to Irving Berlin's smug, dirge-like "God Bless America." Guthrie's response took the form of "This Land Is Your Land." See Joe Klein, *Woody Guthrie: A Life* (New York: Knopf, 1980).

[31] Ronald Reagan, "Transcript of Reagan's Farewell Address to American People," *New York Times* (1989). In 2016, the Republican Party embarked on a major departure from Reagan's vision of a nation "open to anyone with the will and the heart to get here."

a construction intended to advance a particular point of view. All narratives are, of course, acts of human invention in which the author makes a self-interested case. And all presidents construct a self-enhancing triumphant story.[32]

In the case of Reagan's presidency, other authors offered competing narratives suggesting the damage caused by and under his presidency: a rollback in civil rights progress, his ignoring of the spreading AIDS epidemic, regressive tax policies that encouraged increasing income inequality, his running up of massive federal debt, and his tendency to lie about his own experiences.[33] Like all presidents, Reagan had a purpose in constructing the narrative as he did. He was able to decide what to include and what to omit. The same can be said of all narrative authors. All claims of urgency are assertions of interests embedded within a compelling story.

Small-n Explications of the Crisis Narrative

A direct physical attack on the kingdom does not require much elaboration. Leaders can apply the crisis narrative in its purest form. The kingdom is under attack by enemies. George Bush addressed Congress in the aftermath of the September 11 attacks with just that master narrative, "Enemies of freedom" had "committed an act of war against our country."

That essential crisis narrative – the kingdom under direct attack – is paralleled by FDR's address to Congress following Pearl Harbor: "Yesterday, December 7, 1941 – a date which will live in infamy – the United States of America was suddenly and deliberately attacked by naval and air forces of the Empire of Japan." The kingdom had been "at peace with that Nation." No longer.

In the absence of a "Pearl Harbor" moment, a claim of urgency needs to be augmented by more specific, "small-n" narratives.[34] The plot is offered in more detail; the urgency further elaborated. For most crisis narratives, there are two main small-n narratives employed to give shape and detail to the master narrative.

---

[32] Even Richard Nixon, upon resigning from the presidency in disgrace, managed to tout his "time of achievement in which we can all be proud, achievements that represent the shared efforts of the Administration, the Congress, and the people." See www.pbs.org /newshour/spc/character/links/nixon_speech.html.

[33] For an assessment of Reagan's complex legacy, see James Ceaser, "The Social Construction of Ronald Reagan," in *The Enduring Ronald Reagan* (Lexington: University Press of Kentucky, 2009), pp. 37–50.

[34] Tannen, "'We've Never Been Close, We're Very Different.'"

The A-Few-Bad-Apples Narrative

Disney is useful again in examining a prototypical small-n crisis narrative within a fictional setting. In *Lion King*, a benevolent and wise king, with his son, Simba, as heir apparent, rules the utopian animal kingdom of the Pride Lands. Crisis erupts from within, however, when the king's jealous younger brother, Scar, plots to murder the king and convince Simba to flee. It is a rather simple narrative, one that presents a classic version of the kingdom upended by a few bad apples, in this case, Scar and his hyena cohorts.

Lion King is an example from a fictional world. A version of the few-bad-apples narrative appears with some regularity in the real world as well. Take Jim Stumpf's claim concerning an unfolding scandal at Wells Fargo Bank. The story he offers carries the same few-bad-apples small-n narrative as *Lion King*. "Before we start or as we start, I want to tell you, your audience and our customers," Stumpf told CNBC's Jim Cramer, "that we are sorry." As part of his popular *Mad Money* show, Cramer had long championed Wells Fargo Bank, of which Stumpf was the current CEO. This was a financial institution viewed by Cramer as "one of the best run banks in the world and a stock we own for my charitable trust."[35] Not any more.

Emerging from the Gold Rush heyday of mid-nineteenth-century San Francisco, Wells Fargo – the joint creation of Henry Wells and William Fargo – combined stagecoach deliveries with banking operations to service first Western prospectors and then the entire nation.[36] The company built an immense private mail delivery system that was put out of business in a single stroke in 1918 when the government, as part of its war effort, nationalized the postal system. With only one bank in San Francisco, Wells Fargo was forced to undertake a massive rebuilding project.[37] It was a successful effort, as it turned out. By the 1980s, the bank had expanded across California to become a regional powerhouse and the seventh-largest bank in the country.[38]

Wells Fargo's reputation for sound management, cautious and incremental innovation, and integrity had once attracted Jim Cramer. Now he had serious doubts. Here's why. Five days prior to the interview, this was September 2016, the Consumer Financial Protection Bureau, the Los

---

[35] All quotes from www.cnbc.com/2016/09/18/wells-fargo-ceo-john-stumpf-talks-with-cnbcs-cramer-im-accountable.html.

[36] History of Wells Fargo is found at www.wellsfargo.com/about/corporate/history.

[37] Wells Fargo managed to survive the 1906 San Francisco earthquake and fire, with bank president I. W. Hellman telegraphing, "Building Destroyed, Vault Intact, Credit Unaffected."

[38] Interstate banking was prohibited by federal law until the mid-1980s.

Angeles City Attorney, and the Office of the Comptroller of the Currency levied a $185 million fine against Wells Fargo, charging that more than 2 million bank accounts or credit cards were opened or applied for on behalf of customers without their knowledge. That was "stunning news," said Cramer, which "raised lots of questions."

In the immediate aftermath of the revelation, 5,300 employees were fired. The Consumer Financial Protection Bureau found that these employees had been creating fake accounts for real customers dating back to 2011. The Los Angeles City Attorney's office added helpful details of the misdeeds:

In the practice known at Wells Fargo as "pinning," a Wells Fargo banker obtains a debit card number, and personally sets the PIN, often to 0000, without customer authorization. "Pinning" permits a banker to enroll a customer in online banking, for which the banker would receive a solution (sales credit). To bypass computer prompts requiring customer contact information, bankers impersonate the customer online, and input false generic email addresses.[39]

In that way, an unauthorized account was opened without the knowledge or – obviously – the consent of the customer.

The bank's aggressive sales incentive program was implicated in the motivation of employees to create unwanted accounts as a means of inflating sales numbers. Again, the LA City Attorney's office provided illuminating details:

Wells Fargo has strict quotas regulating the number of daily "solutions" that its bankers must reach; these "solutions" include the opening of all new banking and credit card accounts. Managers constantly hound, berate, demean and threaten employees to meet these unreachable quotas. Managers often tell employees to do whatever it takes to reach their quotas. Employees who do not reach their quotas are often required to work hours beyond their typical work schedule without being compensated for that extra work time, and/or are threatened with termination.[40]

The FBI opened investigations, while Congress held hearings in which the bank and its officers were castigated in an unusually bipartisan manner. Bank customers filed class action lawsuits. The bank's board "clawed back" millions in bonus money paid to Stumpf. A month after the scandal broke, that same board fired Stumpf.

By any measure, Stumpf's televised narrative tale of the crisis at Wells Fargo was spectacularly ineffective. He failed to save his job, and the bank

---

[39] Quoted in Matt Levine, "Wells Fargo Opened a Couple Million Fake Accounts," *Bloomberg Opinion* (September 9, 2016).
[40] Ibid.

continued to reel from the repercussions of the scandal.[41] So, what, in addition to "we are sorry," did Stumpf include in the story he told that day?

Stumpf spun a narrative in which a glorious bank was betrayed by a few bad apples:

We deeply regret any situation where a customer got a product they did not request. That has never – there is nothing in our culture, nothing in our vision and values that would support that. It's just the opposite. Our goal is to make it right by a customer every time, 100%. And we don't do that, we feel accountable.

There were a lot of employees at the bank, Stumpf explained. Some were bound to be bad, to violate the company's culture, vision, and values:

Let me tell you a little bit about our business. We have at any one time 100,000 team members in our branch and retail bank network. And we hire people and people turn over, of those 100,000 the vast majority do the right thing, they come to work. Their life's work and mission is to help people. And I love these people. Every year, on average for the last five years 1,000 did not do the right thing.[42]

Cramer was not satisfied with that answer. Stumpf's narrative simply did not seem to mesh with the facts revealed by the multiple investigations.

Was this really a case of a few bad apples? Wasn't there *something* bigger and more profoundly corrupt lodged in the culture of the bank that prompted unethical, illegal behavior on such a scale? Five thousand is a significant number of employees, after all. Perhaps rather than a few bad apples violating Wells Fargo's culture, these 5,300 employees were simply doing what they believed was expected of them. Here, Stumpf began to stammer, sticking doggedly to his few-bad-apples narrative:

Th – th – this – no, no. We have had – we know, running a business, that not everyone can do everything right every minute of every day. That's why you build compliance programs. That's why you do training. That's why you do coaching.

---

[41] The firing of Stumpf did little to repair the bank's standing. In early 2018, the Federal Reserve found that the bank had failed to correct its problems and would, as a result, be barred from future growth unless and until the Fed was satisfied that effective corrective steps had been taken. In May of that year, the bank launched a new ad campaign promising "a complete recommitment to you, fixing what went wrong, making things right, and ending product-sales goals for branch bankers so we can focus on your satisfaction." This was a new day for the bank, the ad went on. "We're holding ourselves accountable to find and fix issues proactively, because earning back your trust is our greatest priority." See James Peltz, "Wells Fargo Launches Ad Campaign to Leave Accounts Scandal Behind. Not Everyone Is Buying It," *Los Angeles Times* (May 9, 2018).

[42] That statement is a bit slippery. An average of 1,000 for 5 years *is* 5,000 people.

And unfortunately, 1,000 – 1% of – of these 100,000 who are in a seat at any one time in the year, you know – they didn't get it right.

The soon-to-be-unemployed CEO concluded, "I—I – I have to say we've got the vast majority do the right thing every day."[43]

The few-bad-apples narrative is a way to claim that the kingdom has suffered a crisis, but it nonetheless remains fundamentally strong and solid. It is a crisis narrative constructed to reinforce rather than upend the existing power structure. "The best thing I can do," Stumpf insisted, "is stay on as CEO, make sure the small number of bad actors are removed, and continue reinforcing the banks culture of making it right by a customer every time, 100%." His board, apparently, did not agree.

The few-bad-apples small-n narrative is a "reflexive defense" to charges of misconduct, noted linguistic specialist Geoff Nunberg, "It's an ancient bit of counsel, whether it's said of bad apples or rotten ones, or of bushels, barrels, baskets or bins. Benjamin Franklin had it as 'the rotten apple spoils his companion,' which goes back to Shakespeare's time."[44] Given that Nunberg's observation came five years before Stumpf's stammering tale of a few bad apples tarnishing Wells Fargo's reputation by violating its culture, the ongoing appeal of the small-n narrative is apparent, not terribly effective, but apparent.

The Forces-Beyond-Our-Control Narrative

In the *Genesis* narrative of Noah's Ark, it is literally an act of God – a great flood – that creates chaos on Earth while allowing for the possibility of human redemption. In the classic 1939 film *The Wizard of Oz*, a Kansas tornado propels the protagonist into a magical world "over the rainbow." And in the animated movie *Land Before Time*, a massive drought forces dinosaurs to seek refuge in the Great Valley.

These stories and other similar narratives offer another small-n variant of the master: a claim that the crisis has been brought about by forces-beyond-our-control. These forces may be acts of nature (or of God directing nature) or actions by bad players outside the kingdom wreaking havoc. In either case, the narrative allows the claims maker to admit urgency while pointing a finger of blame *away* from the kingdom. This is a crisis all right, but it's a crisis whose origins reside outside of the unit that I am leading.

---

[43] I'm quoting here directly from the transcript as published by CNBC. The stammering is from that transcript.
[44] Geoff Nunberg, "Bad Apple Proverbs: There's One in Every Bunch," *National Public Radio* (May 5, 2011).

For a dramatic forces-beyond-our-control story, it's hard to beat a magnitude 9.0 earthquake and a resulting forty-foot tsunami. That's what happened off the coast of Japan in March 2011. The quake itself was gargantuan, a "rare and complex double quake giving a severe duration of about 3 minutes."[45] Japan moved several meters and the local coastline subsided noticeably. Sixteen thousand people died in the resulting seismic sea wave that towered more than forty feet.[46]

One of the many horrifying stories to emerge from this disaster unfolded at a nuclear power plant. The tsunami's force disabled the power supply and cooling mechanisms of three of Japan's Fukushima Daiichi nuclear reactors. The plant, operated by Tokyo Electric and Power Company (TEPCO), was overwhelmed. "All three cores," noted the World Nuclear Association, "largely melted away in the first three days."[47]

To reduce internal pressure and prevent the discharge of radioactive coolant water into the sea, TEPCO management decided to release radioactive isotopes into the air. Continued fires and explosions led to the release of even more radiation, requiring the evacuation of 50,000 Fukushima families.[48] TEPCO didn't act in isolation. Government overseers were involved in the decision-making process. But as later probes discovered, consultation between on-the-scene plant operators, the upper management of TEPCO, and government officials was confused and haphazard. So, who was to blame?

No one, insisted the plant's operators. To support their assertion, TEPCO managers constructed a small-n crisis narrative that laid responsibility on forces beyond their control. It was nature, the largest fault slip ever recorded, they noted. *That's* what caused the radiation leakage. It was the earthquake and tsunami, resulting in an "accident" at the plant and contaminating the surrounding environment: A to B to C.

By using the term "accident" to characterize the resulting catastrophe, TEPCO officials constructed a scenario in which the catastrophe wasn't their fault. An internal investigation undertaken by TEPCO agreed: the earthquake and tsunami were beyond all expectations and could not reasonably have been foreseen. The accident was an act of nature. So was the resulting disruption to the surrounding community.[49]

[45] www.world-nuclear.org/information-library/safety-and-security/safety-of-plants/fukush ima-accident.aspx

[46] www.livescience.com/39110-japan-2011-earthquake-tsunami-facts.html   [47] Ibid.

[48] Regulators rated the reactor disaster as a "7," the highest rating on a scale created by the Atomic Energy Agency and comparable only to the 1986 Chernobyl incident in the Soviet Union.

[49] Hiroshi Hiyama, "Fukushima Was 'Man-Made' Disaster: Japanese Probe." Phys.Org (July 4, 2012).

Dissatisfied with the company's own conclusion that it bore no responsibility, the Japanese Parliament authorized a separate probe. And that investigation offered a very different narrative. Sure, there was a natural occurrence for which no one could be blamed. But what followed – the core meltdown, the release of radiation, and the need to evacuate tens of thousands of residents – *that* was the result of human failure. There was, the review concluded, "collusion between the government, the regulators and (plant operator) ... and the lack of governance by said parties. They effectively betrayed the nation's right to be safe from nuclear accidents." Particularly troubling were postponements of tsunami protection measures – a plan to construct a seawall was scraped as unnecessary – that left the plant "vulnerable." Therefore, the report concluded, "the disaster was clearly man-made."[50]

The Japanese courts concurred with the conclusions of the parliamentary inquiry. Rather than accepting the forces-beyond-our-control crisis narrative, they pointed the blame finger back *at* the plant's operators, as well as government regulators. True enough, no one caused the earthquake and resultant tsunami. But company and government overseers had been "negligent" in not preventing meltdowns. The disaster – everything that happened after the tsunami – had been under TEPCO's control. After the ruling, the company "sincerely" apologized for "the accident that occurred at our Fukushima power plant."[51] But it was still, in the company's narrative, an accident.

The interplay between acts of nature and organizational response is, admittedly, complex. It is precisely that complexity that offers the opportunity for multiple, even competing crisis narratives in which complexity is replaced by clarity of plot and certainty of cause and effect.

Combining Small-n Narratives to Tell the Master Crisis Story

Let's consider the 2005 hurricane and subsequent flooding of New Orleans not as a crisis event but as a cascade of ever-evolving claims. What we see is how both small-n narratives – the few-bad-apples and the forces-beyond-our control narratives – were brought to bear in service of the master crisis narrative.

In late August of that year, Hurricane Katrina struck the Louisiana coast, missing a direct hit on the city. Still, 80 percent of New Orleans flooded, chaos spread, non-evacuated citizens huddled at the

---

[50] Ibid.
[51] Motoko Rich, "Japan and Utility Are Found Negligent Again in Fukushima Meltdowns," *New York Times* (October 10, 2012).

Superdome, and people died, a *lot* of people died.[52] So, what's the small-n narrative advanced by various claims? Was the "glorious kingdom" of New Orleans threated by a few bad apples, by forces beyond our control, or some combination of the two?

By focusing on the claims, we can spot a shift in the two small-n narratives. The master narrative of the once-glorious-kingdom-under-threat remained, but the more specific narrative morphed from a forces-beyond-our-control story into a-few-bad-apples saga:

August 26 – Katrina gains strength as it approaches the Gulf Coast.	Forces-beyond-our-control
August 28 – Katrina becomes a Category 5 hurricane as it moves closer.	*Forces-beyond-our-control*
August 29 – a levee is breached in the Lower Ninth Ward, and more breaks are reported in the Industrial Canal and 17th Street Canal. Water begins pouring into eastern New Orleans, the Lower Ninth Ward, and St. Bernard Parish.	*Forces-beyond-our-control*
August 30 – Eighty percent of New Orleans is covered in water as high as 20 feet; looting begins, officers are redirected from rescue operations to stop violence.	*Forces-beyond-our-control* and *a-few-bad-apples*
September 1 – Mayor Ray Nagin sends out an SOS for more help and buses to get out people stuck in the convention center; FEMA Director Michael Brown says he has finally learned about the evacuees stuck in the convention center.	*A-few-bad-apples*
September 4–5 New Orleans police officers shoot six unarmed residents on Danziger Bridge in the city. Two are killed.[a]	*A-few-bad-apples*

[a] Five of the involved police officers were later convicted of federal crimes related to the shootings.

The deployment of these narratives is apparent. What may be less obvious but no less significant is precisely how the notion of an event – any crisis event, from the flooding of New Orleans to the scandal at Wells Fargo – gets constructed.

The crisis-as-event model never critically considers the notion of an event. That's a mistake. Critical questions can and should be asked. Why construct the "event" of New Orleans's catastrophic flooding as starting

---

[52] There is no definitive number of Katrina-related deaths in New Orleans. The National Oceanic and Atmospheric Administration placed the number at 1,200. See Carl Bialik, "We Still Don't Know How Many People Died Because of Katrina," *FiveThirtyEight* (August 26, 2015).

when the hurricane made landfall? Why not dig deeper, go back further? To ask those questions squarely confronts the power exercised by the narrative author, the claims maker of the crisis.

The Power of the Crisis Narrative Author

The crisis-as-claim model acknowledges that any crisis narrative is a human construction. We should therefore expect there to be competing constructions. Recall the multiple analyses of the French Revolution: same contingencies but radically different versions of the story. In the same way, crisis leaders as authors of claims of urgency, always make choices about how to define the contours of the event they are describing. In making that decision, they are exercising the power of a narrative author to circumscribe the event.

Let's keep that in mind: the exercise of power built into the process of constructing a claim and embedding it in a narrative. That act of construction is intended to de-contest the meaning of a crisis by fixing the understanding of the narrative. When a particular narrative becomes nonnegotiable, it intends to assert itself as the controlling frame for any and all subsequent discussions and responses.

Authors of crisis narratives seek to define the event that is said to be triggering the urgency. There will always be a "once-upon-a-time" element that defines the onset of the crisis. This once-upon-a-time device is known in narrative theory as the "initiating event."[53] And it is as arbitrary as every other element of a story.

The major event in the Katrina story was the flooding and subsequent fatal chaos of the city. But was it the *initiating* event? Yes, but only in one telling of the story. There is an option, one that reshapes our comprehension in a powerful way by insisting that the storm wasn't the initiating event at all. In *The Great Deluge* (2006), historian Douglas Brinkley constructs a startlingly different narrative by reaching back decades. The Great Mississippi Flood of 1927 demonstrated the folly of construction projects that left New Orleans vulnerable to hurricane flooding. City officials prepared an emergency evacuation plan in 2000 that was, by their own reckoning, woefully inadequate. The city's mayor, the same Ray Nagin who called for additional help two days after Katrina's landfall, "seemed to ignore" the need for further work.[54] New Orleans had been wracked for years by an astronomical crime rate – often the number two

---

[53] William Labov, "Where Should I Begin?" in *Telling Stories: Language, Narrative, and Social Life* (Washington, DC: Georgetown University Press, 2010), pp. 7–22.

[54] Douglas Brinkley, *The Great Deluge: Hurricane Katrina, New Orleans, and the Mississippi Gulf Coast* (New York: Harper, 2007), p. 19.

murder capital of the country – along with corrupt, poorly trained police. These factors would all come into violent interplay in the days immediately after the hurricane.

In rejecting the landfall of Katrina as the initiating event in his narrative, Brinkley added considerable nuance to the image of a once-glorious-kingdom-under-threat. Mayor Ray Nagin no long longer came across as a put-upon victim but as a contributor to the city's inept preparation.[55] The city's luminous jazz tradition may have attracted tourists but had done little to erect economic or social structures capable of creating a resilient community. The same could be said about regulations that allowed for the open-carry of alcoholic beverages in the city's French Quarter. It attracted a certain type of tourist but did little to build New Orleans into a functioning community.

Within Brinkley's narrative, social, cultural, and economic forces are at play that are missing from the forces-of-nature story of New Orleans's crisis. The city had a disproportionately high percentage of citizens living beneath the poverty line. City hospitals were unprepared for large-scale emergencies. The poorly engineered construction of levees, combined with a lack of regular maintenance by the Army Corps of Engineers, left the city vulnerable, a disaster waiting to happen. Even though the hurricane missed a direct hit on New Orleans, there were still hundreds of deaths. Two-thirds of those could be attributed to the flooding caused by construction failures. And many of the areas hardest hit by that flooding, including the Lower Ninth Ward, were predominately poor and black, a result of decades of racial discrimination.

Backing away from the narrative that takes the arrival of the storm as the imitating event, a fundamentally different story emerges. Was the breakdown in order and care the result of an uncontrollable act of nature or the outcome of widespread failures, venal corruption, and long-festering incompetence? And were the deaths the result of forces of nature or decades of oblivious, systematic neglect? The power of the narrative author resides in the capacity to answer those questions through their own stories.

Stories gain their power over listeners by virtue of their construction: the characters, language, description, plot, and so forth. The Greek storyteller Aesop was a master at narrative construction. He created fables that

---

[55] In the immediate aftermath of the flooding, with New Orleans full of private contractors looking for rebuilding work, Nagin took cash bribes. In 2014, he was sentenced to ten years on federal corruption charges. See Allen Johnson Jr. and Campbell Robertson, "10-Year Term on Graft Charges for C. Ray Nagin, Former Mayor of New Orleans," *New York Times* (July 9, 2014).

appealed to both adults and children, typically teaching a lesson about, say, the dangers of "crying wolf":

> There was once a young Shepherd Boy who tended his sheep at the foot of a mountain near a dark forest.
>
> It was rather lonely for him all day, so he thought upon a plan by which he could get a little company and some excitement.
>
> He rushed down towards the village calling out *"Wolf, Wolf,"* and the villagers came out to meet him, and some of them stopped with him for a considerable time.
>
> This pleased the boy so much that a few days afterwards he tried the same trick, and again the villagers came to his help.
>
> But shortly after this a Wolf actually did come out from the forest, and began to worry the sheep, and the boy of course cried out *"Wolf, Wolf,"* still louder than before.
>
> But this time the villagers, who had been fooled twice before, thought the boy was again deceiving them, and nobody stirred to come to his help.

So the Wolf made a good meal off the boy's flock, and when the boy complained, the wise man of the village said:

"A liar will not be believed, even when he speaks the truth." [56]

This is a story that is smart on many levels. It can be taken as a meta-narrative: a crisis narrative about crisis narratives. The cry of "wolf" amounted to a reckless claim of urgency, offering a narrative of a peaceful "kingdom" of shepherd and flock supposedly under attack by an external predator. It is both perfectly plausible and completely inaccurate. At least at first.

The fable suggests that the authors of reckless claims gain their credibility precisely because the narrative is plausible. But it also insists that reckless claims will, over time, drain credibility from the author when the objective description inherent in the claim – in this case, that a wolf is attacking the boy's flock – comes to be revealed as inaccurate. It's at least a hopeful prospect.

There Is an Alternative Crisis Narrative

The master crisis narrative takes for granted that the social unit under threat is worth preserving. That's why crisis is represented as a *threat*: a "low-probability, high-impact event that threatens the viability of the

---

[56] From www.taleswithmorals.com/aesop-fable-the-sheperds-boy.htm.

organization."[57] It is that sense of a unit under threat of rupture – M&S since 1998 for instance – that impels leaders to claim urgency. Of course these kingdoms are worth saving. In the master crisis narrative, response is focused on recovery.

In the crisis-as-event model, that focus is taken for granted. Did the company's stock price recover from the event? Did the country's economy and pride rebound? But there is another possibility. There are always other possibilities in narration. In particular, there is a possibility of an alternative master narrative that will undermine some basic assumptions. Perhaps the social unit – the business, community, country, and so on – is not so exceptional that it is worthy of preservation. Maybe it needs to be fundamentally upended. Furthermore, it is possible that the leaders are the source of the problem rather than the solution. In that case, crisis is not a dynamic to be prevented and avoided. It may be just what is needed to ensure progress toward a goal far more fundamental than institutional preservation.

[57] Pearson and Clair, "Reframing Crisis Management," 60.

8 To Create Such a Crisis, to Foster Such a Tension

In the once-glorious-kingdom-under-threat master narrative, crisis is problematized as a "bad" situation. The crisis event is taken to be a threat, an attack, a disturbance, a storm, a panic, a failure, a loss, a disaster, some higher-order trouble, a horrific occurrence, a grave predicament, an existential danger, something unthinkable. All things to be avoided if possible and dealt with when necessary. If not managed effectively, after all, the potential outcomes are instability and damage, placing at risk the very existence of the unit. The leader's job is to navigate the unit through the turmoil unleashed by the crisis and preserve the status quo. This is the dominating view of the crisis-as-event model.[1]

There is, however, an alternative narrative, one that welcomes and embraces the opportunities offered by disruption. When an armed rebellion of farmers in western Massachusetts broke out in the late summer of 1786, Thomas Jefferson offered just such a narrative. "What signify a few lives lost in a century or two?" he asked, "The tree of liberty must from time to time be refreshed with the blood of patriots and tyrants."[2] Jefferson, principal author of the Declaration of Independence and then ambassador to France, was celebrating the possibility, even the necessity, of disruption as an enabler of progress.

---

[1] Allen and Caillouet, "Legitimation Endeavors"; Armenakis and Fredenberger, "Organizational Change Readiness"; Baran and Adelman, "Preparing for the Unthinkable"; Benoit, *Accounts, Excuses, and Apologies*; Carmeli and Schaubroeck, "Organizational Crisis-Preparedness"; Duncan et al., "Surviving Organizational Disasters"; W. G. Egelhoff and F. Sen, "An Information-Processing Model of Crisis Management," *Management Communication Quarterly* 5 (1992), 443–484; Karen Fowler et al., "Organizational Preparedness for Coping with a Major Disaster," *Business & Society* 46 (2007), 88–103; Erika Hayes James et al., "Crisis Management: Informing a New Leadership Research Agenda," *Academy of Management Annals* 5 (2011), 455–493; Nancy Koehn, *Forged in Crisis: The Power of Courageous Leadership in Turbulent Times* (New York: Scribner, 2017); Robert Littlefield and Andrea Quenette, "Crisis Leadership and Hurricane Katrina: The Portrayal of Authority by the Media in Natural Disasters," *Journal of Applied Communication Research* 35 (2007), 26–47; Lucero et al., "Crisis Leadership"; Pauchant and Mitroff, *Transforming the Crisis-Prone Organization*; Pearson and Clair, "Reframing Crisis Management"; Shrivastava, *Bhopal*.

[2] Richard Bernstein, *Thomas Jefferson* (New York: Oxford University Press, 2003), p. 70.

That is a powerful reframing of dynamics, from bloody defiance to refreshing the tree of liberty. In this instance, Jefferson was responding to occurrences over which he had no control or influence. It was, in that sense, an armchair defense of rebellion. There have been more directly insurgent leaders who did more than defend disruption. They *caused* disruption. Let's take a look at one who did just that, so much so that he could be considered an apostle of crisis.

"You've *Got* to Have a Crisis"

Reflecting on the nonviolent but confrontational tactics employed by Martin Luther King Jr. during his 1963 campaign to desegregate Birmingham, Alabama, journalist Reese Cleghorn applied the label "apostle of crisis" to the civil rights leader. It was an appropriate label, although, in this case, not one that was offered as a compliment. Cleghorn, a frequent contributor to the *Saturday Evening Post*, deplored King's tactics.

King had brought "racial violence" to "the most rigidly segregated city in America," asserted Cleghorn, a self-proclaimed Southern moderate. He argued that two powerful and opposing forces had been purposefully and recklessly engaged: "The first represented by Bull Connor [Birmingham's commissioner of public safety], vigorously enforcing laws that preserve the status quo." The second force was what King brought into play by his typically illegal marches intended to make "a carefully planned assault on those laws and that discrimination."

From a distance of many decades, we can see where Cleghorn's sympathies lay, and that was not with the civil rights movement. The writer's biases were revealed in the language he used to describe the "noisy Negro crowd" amassed by King: "unruly, drunken Negroes" who were "bellowing, laughing and jeering" while throwing rocks at "Connor's blue-clad policemen." Cleghorn betrayed his preference for Connor and the police as defenders of Birmingham's status quo.

What flowed inevitably from the clash of these oppositional forces was a crisis, one of King's initiation. "King got his crisis" – note Cleghorn's attribution of *his* crisis – "in a hymn-singing, rock-throwing crescendo of peaceful marches and violent strife that sent more than 2,400 Negroes to jail, most of them for such offenses as parading without a permit." It was a confrontation that could have been, *should* have been, avoided in favor of negotiation and gradualism.[3]

---

[3] The position of Southern gradualists held that following the 1954 Supreme Court *Brown v. Board of Education* decision, legal segregation would eventually be eroded. Marching

Cleghorn was correct at one level. The immediate crisis – the eruption of violence in Birmingham – *was* of King's doing. It was his intention to assault "those laws and that discrimination." Sure, Cleghorn was over-emphasizing King's singular role. There were others, both in Birmingham and throughout the South, who were equally ready to confront the status quo of racial segregation.[4] And they agreed with his tactical approach: provoke crisis as a means to a deeper end. "We've got to have a crisis to bargain with," explained King associate Wyatt Tee Walker, "To take a moderate approach hoping to get white help doesn't work. . . . You've *got* to have a crisis."[5]

What was unacknowledged by Cleghorn was that an urgent situation already existed in Birmingham, one that had been allowed to fester for the greater part of 100 years. The city, a major production center for iron and steel in the Southern United States was profoundly and purposefully segregated. As described by King biographer David Lewis:

In the midst of industrial plenty, nonwhites were rigidly restricted to menial and domestic jobs. Segregation was total, and the slightest betrayal of discontent with the racial order was severely, often capitally, punished. Police brutality to blacks was the custom rather than the exception, and the Commissioner of Public Safety, Eugene "Bull" Connor, was notoriously vigilant and cruel.[6]

Public parks were segregated, with drinking fountains labeled "White" and "Colored." Jim Crow laws, established with the blessing of the Supreme Court's 1896 *Plessy* v. *Ferguson* "separate-but-equal" ruling, remained in full force in 1963. Hope that legal segregation would recede following the 1954 Supreme Court *Brown* v. *Board of Education* decision that ruled legal segregation to be unconstitutional were dashed. That was the explosive tinderbox into which King and his supporters marched.

Aligned with some but by no means all of the community's black leadership, King sought to negotiate with Birmingham's white business elite. Deals were struck – "Colored Only" signs were to be removed, for instance – but then ignored. Now, King and his team planned Project C (for Confrontation). "We shall march nonviolently," King told black community members. He knew that their actions would provoke police

---

and demonstrating were thought to be counterproductive in that they would repel rather than engage "moderates" (like Cleghorn) and thus delay rather than hasten the end of Jim Cow.

[4] Without undercutting King's pivotal role in the civil rights movement, Taylor Branch pays full heed to the rich array of individuals who help shape the response to segregation. See Branch, *Parting the Waters: America in the King Years, 1954 – 63* (New York: Simon & Schuster, 1988).

[5] Quoted in "America's Gandhi," *Time* (January 3, 1964).

[6] David Lewis, *King: A Biography* (Urbana: University of Illinois Press, 2013), p. 172.

response, arrests, and violent resistance. It was precisely that response that would "force this nation, this city, this world, to face its own conscience." The confrontation was not among races but between "good and evil."[7] That was his hope, his belief, and his plan. King would, indeed, be an apostle of crisis.

It was no surprise to anyone that Bull Connor proved to be a spectacularly tough and vigilant protector of the segregated status quo. Fully intending for that segregation to be preserved, Connor ordered attack dogs and high-pressure water hoses turned on the marchers. Local organizer James Bevel paraded thousands of children through downtown streets – the "children's crusade." Nearly 1,000 were arrested, and King soon found himself in jail as well.

It was in a jail cell that King learned of a public letter written by local clergy denouncing his tactics as "unwise and untimely." Under the headline, "An Appeal for Law and Order and Common Sense," eight white Alabama ministers offered a bland assurance that every member of the community "is created in the image of God and is entitled to respect as a fellow human being with all basic rights, privileges, and responsibilities which belong to humanity." Then they made their claim.

Improvements were being made in Birmingham, the white ministers insisted, and would continue. Demonstrations, which threatened "defiance, anarchy and subversion," simply made matters worse. Although all forms of hatred and violence were deplorable, so too were "such actions as to incite hatred and violence, however technically peaceful those actions may be."[8] It was these actions that threatened the community with increased violence.

It was that equivalence – between the city's Jim Crow law and order and King's intended "technically peaceful" disruption – and the fact that it was an equivalence drawn by fellow clergy that so outraged King in his jail cell. He first scribbled thoughts on an available newspaper. After being provided with a writing pad, he penned what is now known simply as the "Letter from a Birmingham Jail."[9] One remarkable aspect of the letter is how little time King devoted to delineating the urgency of the immediate situation. He acknowledged it, describing Birmingham as a racially segregated community. He also noted that nearly a decade after the Supreme Court had shot down the concept of "separate but equal," "colored only"

---

[7] Ibid., 180.

[8] The text of the letter is available at https://genius.com/Alabama-clergymen-an-appeal-for-law-and-order-and-common-sense-annotated. "Technically peaceful" was a snide reference to King's nonviolent tactics.

[9] The full text of King's letter can be found in Alton Hornsby Jr., "Martin Luther King, Jr. – Letter from a Birmingham Jail," *Journal of Negro History* 71 (1986), 38–44.

signs still flourished, while the city's commissioner of public safety openly endorsed and promised to enforce racial separation.

There was little dispute that King's description was accurate. In truth, no one bothered to deny it. Connor openly embraced keeping "the whites and the blacks separate."[10] Subjectively, ascriptions such as "injustice is here" perpetuated by the "white power structure" were plausible. His demand for rupture and embrace of provocation was legitimate. But make no mistake, it was also disruptive, purposefully so.

The Birmingham crisis to which the clergy (and before them, Reese Cleghorn) referred had been unleashed by the demonstrators marching in the streets. The real crisis, the underlying condition demanding urgency, was the injustice that permeated Birmingham long before King set foot in the community. Bull Connor and the white power structure of Birmingham were not responding to an urgent situation; they *were* the urgency. By missing that crucial point, King believed, the clergy were lending their support to the system of segregation.

For that support, King took his fellow clergy to task:

You deplore the present demonstrations that are presently taking place in Birmingham. But I am sorry that your statement did not present a similar concern for the conditions that brought the demonstrations into being. I am sure that each of you would want to go beyond the superficial social analyst who looks merely at effects and does not grapple with underlying causes.

It was because of that misdirected attention that the crisis sparked by the demonstrations was profoundly necessary and potentially redemptive.

Speaking directly to ministers, King continued:

You may well ask: "Why direct action? Why sit-ins, marches and so forth? Isn't negotiation a better path?" You are quite right in calling for negotiation. Indeed, this is the very purpose of direct action. Nonviolent direct action seeks to create such a crisis and foster such a tension that a community which has constantly refused to negotiate is forced to confront the issue.

The crisis that he was admittedly provoking was intended to "dramatize" the issue of racial injustice, thus claiming urgency not for the civil unrest and "breakdown" in law and order but for the underlying cause. It was for that purpose that King sought to create tension:

My citing the creation of tension as part of the work of the nonviolent resister may sound rather shocking. But I must confess that I am not afraid of the word "tension." I have earnestly opposed violent tension, but there is a type of constructive, nonviolent tension which is necessary for growth. Just as Socrates felt that it was necessary to create a tension in the mind so that individuals could rise

---

[10] www.youtube.com/watch?v=j9kT1yO4MGg

from the bondage of myths and half-truths to the unfettered realm of creative analysis and objective appraisal, so must we see the need for nonviolent gadflies to create the kind of tension in society that will help men rise from the dark depths of prejudice and racism to the majestic heights of understanding and brotherhood.

So yes, *crisis* was the desired outcome: "The purpose of our direct-action program is to create a situation so crisis-packed that it will inevitably open the door to negotiation." The violent response of Connor and his police force wasn't an unintended consequence and was certainly no surprise. It was the point. King welcomed, even courted crisis to allow progress. He rejected the master narrative of the once-glorious-kingdom-under-threat. With its Jim Crow laws and vicious police enforcement, the "kingdom" of Birmingham needed to be upended.

Apostles of Crisis

By refocusing attention away from the event and toward the claim and the intent of the claims maker, the crisis-as-claim model allows the opportunity for an alternative frame. *You* may understand the dynamics in an entirely negative light, a leader may say. *I* insist, however, that the very same dynamics that are so disturbing to you – an armed rebellion, say, or defiant marches down your streets – offer the opportunity of progress.

Crisis leadership now takes on a radically new meaning. Rather than working to ameliorate the worse impact of a crisis, leaders may seek to embellish the opportunities inherent in disruption. They might even *cause* the disruption. For those insurgent leaders, the explicit intent is not to avoid a rupture in the unit but to create one.

Crisis leaders often accept the need for some disruption in the status quo. But it is a circumscribed disruption, temporary disorder in the service of preservation. Mistakes have been made, the leader will acknowledge, so we need to get better at, say, responding to the youth market or building cars with more appealing designs. It won't be easy, but we will protect, preserve, and in doing so prosper. The status quo ante crisis will be reestablished.

Think of the instances we've come across in which claims of urgency were intended to *preserve*:

- Archie Norman (Marks & Spencer) – "We know that this business is a really, really special business. It's just our job to make it special again."
- Jim Stumpf (Wells Fargo Bank) – "There is nothing in our culture, nothing in our vision and values that would support that. It's just the opposite. Our goal is to make it right by a customer every time, 100%."

- Ronald Reagan (presidential candidate) – "Let's make America great again."

When built into a crisis response, disruption of the unit is framed as an intervention intended ultimately to preserve it. Shaking things up is a tactic employed to restore continuity: of M&S's lofty heritage, of Wells Fargo's customer-centric culture, and of American exceptionalism.

Apostles of crisis make no such assumption. They lean away from preservation, embracing not disruption but rupture. They are not crisis managers; they are crisis *instigators*. Their goal is to stake a claim that a discontinuous break with the status quo is required in response to a deeper urgency. In their claim, it is the break from the status quo that is the point.

It is exactly that welcoming of disruption that so infuriates defenders of the status quo. The Birmingham clergy, for instance, appealed to the "common sense" of "law and order." Their unease is understandable. The act of provoking a crisis does seem like a commonsense violation of a basic need for order and stability in any social unit.

US politicians have been making pleas for "law and order" since the first days of the Republic. In more recent times, "law and order" has been a tool of politicians, offered as a shorthand rebuke of what is taken to be a wasteful and permissive liberal welfare state that tolerated, even advocated civil disobedience and seemingly challenged police authority.[11] King was consciously confronting law and order while strategically inserting tension and confrontation, perhaps even law breaking, into the community.

As illustrated in Table 8.1, insurgent leaders frame disruption in a way that demands attention for underlying urgency. Traditional crisis leaders respond to an immediate threat to their unit. For leaders with an alternative narrative, an immediate threat to the status quo is created. That status quo, their narrative insists, is constituted and led in a way that denies fairness, openness, care, safety, and other first principles to some of its members. These insurgent leaders claim that those underlying dynamics are threatening not the status quo but something far more important. These leaders then instigate an immediate threat, a rupture, to refocus attention on underlying causes.

The hope is that unit leaders will come to reflect upon more profound underlying matters as they respond to the immediacy of the crisis imposed by the rupture. It's a risky approach, certainly, particularly because traditional crisis leaders have access to formal levers of power. These leaders

---

[11] Michael Flamm, *Law and Order: Street Crime, Civil Unrest, and the Crisis of Liberalism in the 1960s* (New York: Columbia University Press, 2007).

Table 8.1 *The dynamics of traditional and mutinous crisis leaders*

Alternative crisis leaders	**Conventional crisis leaders**
respond to	respond to
by creating	
Underlying urgency	**Immediate urgency**
while ignoring	

will respond initially in a way that preserves. That, after all, is what they have been hired or elected to do. The status quo may win out. It often does. But the insertion of urgency by alternative crisis leaders can be a way to address power asymmetries, perhaps the only way.

The dynamics of crisis instigation operate in a separate "dialogical space" from the master narrative.[12] Most particularly, the normative stance of the traditional claim of urgency – that the unit should be restored to its previous status quo – is reconstituted. Normatively, these alternative leaders insist, the unit should not be preserved. The explicit goal, rather, is to breach the status quo in some fundamental way. The crisis threat is embraced rather than problematized, initiated rather than avoided, heightened rather than managed. Now, urgency is a dynamic created purposefully and explicitly to achieve a rupture in the very status quo that claims makers typically work to preserve. Insurgent leaders are, in a very real and immediate way, inciting mutiny.

Mutiny as Voice in Extremis

Now, there's a concept that seldom conjures up anything positive. Perhaps it should. Mutiny is an insurrection, an organized effort to upend, overthrow, and even destroy "proper authority." We typically use the term in a military context, often sailors overthrowing a ship's

---

[12] The phrase "dialogical space" is from Alexandre Adame and Roger Knudson, "Beyond the Counter-Narrative: Exploring Alternative Narratives of Recovery from the Psychiatric Survivor Movement," *Narrative Inquiry* 17 (2007), 171.

captain. Take the September 1797 uprising on the thirty-two-gun British frigate *Hermione*, considered to be the bloodiest mutiny in the history of England's navy.

During the course of that uprising – triggered by brutal punishments ordered by Commander Hugh Pigot on crewmen and junior officers alike – the commander was run through with a bayonet and tossed into the ocean. Most of the senior officers were also killed. Adding insult to fatal injury, the mutineers handed the ship to England's enemy, Spain. The perpetrators – denounced as "pirates and murderers" at home – were hunted by the Royal Navy, and a number of those captured were eventually executed.[13]

Although unsurpassed in British sea history in terms of violence, the *Hermione* mutiny is far less renowned than the one that unfolded eight years earlier on the *Bounty*. Even before the mutiny on the *Bounty*, explorer Henry Hudson found himself, his son, and small number of loyalists abandoned in a small boat. In 1611, the crew of the *Discovery* rebelled against Hudson's continuous, fruitless, and dangerous hunt for the mythical Northeast Passage.

In 1963 Birmingham, Alabama, no one was advocating running bayonets through civic leaders. Quite the opposite. King and his movement were fiercely nonviolent. Thomas Jefferson was not so nonviolent, urging that "the tree of liberty" be from "time to time . . . refreshed with the blood of patriots and tyrants." Either way, nonviolently or otherwise, the idea of mutiny is being positioned in a new dialogical space. Mutiny is now taken to be a principled, passionate although undeniably desperate act of crisis provocation designed to oppose and upend the existing order. That alterative interpretation of mutiny is offered by Patrick Murphy and Ray Coye in their 2013 book *Mutiny and Its Bounty*.

Mutiny, in Murphy and Coye's view, amounts to "an organized movement by members in an organization; based on perceived injustice, marked by coordinated extra-role behavior directed upward despite barriers, and intended to subvert the existing order by usurping or overriding legitimate authority."[14] In situations of extreme urgency, mutiny represents a "potentially ameliorative force,"[15] extreme, sure, but also perhaps positive. It is a view of mutiny as an expression of voice *in extremis*.

---

[13] A. Roger Ekirch, *American Sanctuary: Mutiny, Martyrdom, and National Identity in the Age of Revolution* (New York: Pantheon, 2017), p. 65.

[14] Ray Coye et al., "Using Historic Mutinies to Understand Defiance in Modern Organizations," *Journal of Management History* 16 (2010), 271.

[15] Patrick Murphy and Ray Coye, *Mutiny and Its Bounty: Leadership Lessons from the Age of Discovery* (New Haven: Yale University Press, 2013), p. 2.

Mutinies derive from an underlying claim of urgency. As is true of all claims, calls for mutiny rely on both objective description and subjective ascription. Objectively, the ship's captain is said to be behaving in certain ways. Subjectively, it is claimed that the behavior is inappropriate and/or dangerous. Mutinies, of course, go beyond making a claim; that's what makes them mutinies. They involve forced confrontation and open rebellion against authority. Mutinies morph from claims making to open rebellion when the aggrieved believe they have been stripped of their capacity to voice their grievances. In those special circumstances, mutiny becomes a necessary and compelling rupture, a crisis invited to address underlying urgency.

The demand for voice, for the capacity to speak up as a way of accessing improvement, represents the opportunity for members of a unit "to make an attempt at changing the practices, policies, and outputs of the firm." This notion of voice comes from the work of economist Albert Hirschman. The goal of voice is to provide members with the capacity to address and alter "an objectionable state of affairs" through either individual or collective action. However it manifests itself, voice is a "political action," an articulation of interests, values, or beliefs.[16]

Voice is exercised by members of a social unit who intend to continue their affiliation with that unit. They intend to stay and improve. There is an option to voice: exit.[17] If you are unhappy with the state of affairs in a unit and have been unable to make your voice heard, then leave, exit. This is not an insignificant option. The history of the United States, observed Hirschman, "owes its very existence and growth to millions of decisions favoring exit over voice."[18] Of course, exit is often not a feasible option. When exit is blocked and voice is simultaneously shut down, then mutiny becomes a less startling choice.

Let's get back to the sailors on the *Bounty*, the *Discovery*, and the *Hermione*. For them, voluntary exit was a virtual impossibility. Avenues to voice were blocked by the rigidity of naval protocol and/or the intractability of the ship's commander. What was left was either acquiescence or rebellion in the form of mutiny. When the unit – that is, the domain of the ship and its power structure – is taken to be the source of the threat, the object of crisis instigation is not preservation but upheaval. Because voice

---

[16] Albert Hirschman, *Exit, Voice, and Loyalty: Responses to Decline in Firms, Organizations, and States* (Cambridge, MA: Harvard University Press, 1970), p. 30. Hirschman applied the framework to the interaction between citizens and nation-states in "Exit, Voice, and the State," *World Politics* 31 (1978), 90–107.

[17] Loyalty is Hirschman's third option. Unlike voice and exit, however, loyalty involves acceptance and embrace of the status quo. It may manifest itself in patriotic attachment to the state and brand support to the company.

[18] Hirschman, *Exit, Voice, and Loyalty*, 106.

is denied and exit is unrealistic, mutiny becomes an alternative – extreme, perhaps, and violent often, but an alternative nonetheless.

It isn't too much to conceptualize what King was attempting in Birmingham as a nonviolent mutiny. After nearly a century of being stripped of voice – even, most fundamentally, the right to vote – the African American community of Birmingham took to the streets and provoked confrontation.[19] After all, mutiny is much more than simple dissent, as powerful as dissent may be.

Think of mutiny, Murphy and Coye suggest, "as a small but nimble venture, lacking many resources and having its own boundaries, subsumed by a larger organization that is fundamentally opposed to it," an upward, internal coordinating force."[20] In his "Letter," King constructed an alternative narrative that extolled the benefits of a virtual mutiny in Birmingham to disrupt the status quo. And what about exit as an option? King did not "have" to be in Birmingham, many of the city's civic leaders – defenders of law and order – argued. That fact alone got him denounced as an "outside agitator." If he didn't like what was happening here, why not just go somewhere else? He wasn't *from* Birmingham, after all.

Such reasoning was specious, King insisted. Exit was not a viable option, not for him and certainly not for the African American citizens of the city. His home, King insisted, was the United States, and the community impacted by segregation extended far beyond any single city. "I am cognizant of the interrelatedness of all communities and states," King lectured the gradualists, "Injustice anywhere is a threat to justice everywhere. We are caught in an inescapable network of mutuality, tied in a single garment of destiny." By redefining community, King asserted a rightful interest in redemption of and for his home.

King was revoking the legitimacy of exit as a strategy not just for Birmingham's black community but also for any American citizen. Voice would be asserted in the face of injustice. So, when negotiation failed, as it did in Birmingham prior to the demonstrations, mutiny would become an option, really the only option. King led, but not away from crisis. Apostles of crises lead, rather, *to* a state of tension. The intention of mutinous leaders is to eventuate a shift, if not a radical cleavage in the existing order.[21] Apostles of crisis may be social activists like King, but

---

[19] For a comprehensive history of voting rights violations in the years spanning the 1870 passage of the Fifteenth Amendment to the US Constitution and the passage of the Voting Rights Act of 1965, see Gary May, *Bending Toward Justice: The Voting Rights Act and the Transformation of American Democracy* (Durham, NC: Duke University Press, 2014).

[20] Murphy and Coye, *Mutiny and Its Bounty*, 4.

[21] Michael Foucault, *The History of Sexuality* (New York: Vintage, 1980).

they may also be thinkers who intend through their words to upend ruling orthodoxies and break free of prevailing intellectual paradigms.

Mutineers of the Mind

Claims of urgency arise when one order is challenged by another, when the normal is disrupted by the exceptional.[22] It shouldn't be surprising, then, that urgency is often provoked by thought leaders. Essays and books have been written about crises in legitimacy, modernity, Islamic and Western civilizations, capitalist democracies, authority, and constitutionalism.[23] In these and other cases, one thought order has been pitted against another: Enlightenment against "revealed" truth, democracy against fascism, tribalism against the nation-state, the veneration of rationality against the acceptance of falsehoods.[24] There is a rich history of mutinies led not by activists but intellectuals daring to challenge prevailing thought status quo. The seventeenth-century writings of René Descartes, Benedict de (Baruch) Spinoza, and Galileo Galilei provoked one of most turbulent and significant upheavals in the history of Western thought. They were mutineers of the mind.

European thought in the Middle Ages was dominated by the omnipotent authority of God. "Truth" was unknowable because God was unknowable. Instead, it was "revealed," a process that drove straight through the institution of the Church as articulated by its human agents. Theology dominated thought in Western Christendom. Descartes, Spinoza, and Galileo actively and purposefully sought to provoke a crisis in that intellectual and institutional hegemony to first rupture and then supplant.

In a remarkable confluence of rebellious work, Galileo's *Dialogue Concerning Two Chief World Systems* (1622), Descartes's *Meditations on*

---

[22] Jamie Priestly, "A Paradoxical Approach to Crisis," in *Discourse and Crisis*, 465–475.

[23] David Brooks, "The Crisis of Western Civ," *New York Times* (April 21, 2017); Hilary Rodham Clinton, "American Democracy Is in Crisis," *The Atlantic* (September 16, 2018); Paul Douglass, *The Crisis in Modernism: Bergson and the Vitalist Controversy* (Cambridge: Cambridge University Press, 2010); James Freedman, *Crisis and Legitimacy: The Administrative Process and American Government* (Cambridge: Cambridge University Press, 1978); Nancy Luxon, *Crisis in Authority: Politics, Trust, and Truth-Telling in Freud and Foucault* (Cambridge: Cambridge University Press, 2015); Benjamin Straumann, *Crisis and Constitutionalism: Roman Political Thought from the Fall of the Republic to the Age of Revolution* (New York: Oxford University Press, 2016); J. Donald Walters, *Crisis in Modern Thought* (Nevada City: Chrystal Clarity Publishers, 1987).

[24] Madeline Albright, *Fascism: A Warning* (New York: HarperCollins, 2018); Steven Levitsky and Daniel Ziblatt, *How Democracies Die* (New York: Penguin, 2018); Robert Reich, "The New Tribalism and the Decline of the Nation State," *Huffington Post* (March 24, 2014); David Roberts, "America Is Facing an Epistemic Crisis," *Vox* (November 2, 2017); Stanley, *How Fascism Works*.

First Philosophy (1641), and Spinoza's *Ethics* (1677) staked a claim for intellectual mutiny. "The highest activity a human being can attain is learning for understanding," insisted Spinoza, "because to understand is to be free." Galileo defended independent reasoning by insisting that "the authority of a thousand is not worth the humble reasoning of a single individual." And, perhaps the most directly mutinous of all, Descartes insisted *cogito, ergo sum*, "I think" – not, I *accept*, or I *obey*, but I *think* – "therefore I am." All three, rebellious advocates of human rationality, openly and explicitly disturbed the peace. This new philosophy with its insistence that truth was knowable rather than revealed definitely did that.

In his history of "the making of modernity," Jonathan Israel noted that the abrasion of the two orders created a profoundly disquieting tension. You can't push against the status quo without expecting defenders of the status quo to push back. There was, in fact, an aggressively mounted "counter-offensive at all levels of society" to the "godless" works by Spinoza and his ilk.[25] These mutineers were seen as attempting to overthrow accepted values and beliefs. And overturning accepted values and beliefs was precisely what Enlightenment thinkers had in mind. This was taken to be a crisis.

Defenders of the status quo believed that their kingdom was under threat. They were right to think that way. The challenge from the rationalist philosophers amounted to subversion: an "odious and dangerous" argument that was "little better than atheism."[26] Rallies were held, bonfires were lit, and godless books were burned. Galileo, who advocated Copernican heliocentrism in a direct challenge to geocentrism, fared the worst of the three. He was tried by the Roman Inquisition, forced to recant, and placed under lifetime house arrest.

The mutiny of the seventeenth-century philosopher-scientists came to fruition a century later in the full bloom of the Age of Enlightenment. Leading Enlightenment thinkers – John Locke, Jean-Jacques Rousseau, Voltaire, and Adam Smith among them – demanded that reasoning rather than faith be accepted as the portal between the human mind and the world. Human reason provided the only route to absolute certainty and complete knowledge of the world.

The status quo, so rigorously and righteously defended by the Church, did violence to the rightful position of "man" and debased the "rights of man." To Enlightenment philosophers, religion generally and Christianity specifically served as a "dark power," always "dragging

---

[25] Jonathan Israel, *A Revolution of the Mind: Radical Enlightenment and the Intellectual Origins of Modern Democracy* (Princeton: Princeton University Press, 2010).

[26] Ibid., 24–25.

back the human spirit on its path toward progress and happiness."[27]
Revelation was offered in obedience to the pronouncements of the
Church. Enlightenment, conversely, came about through the autonomous application of observation and experimentation, and the process
of learning.[28] Only by creating such a crisis and fostering such a tension
would these mutinous intellectuals force Church hegemony to lose
ground to free thinking.

The Enlightenment mutiny of the mind found fertile soil in the
American democratic project. It was three years after the conclusion of
the Revolution and with a government – under the Articles of
Confederation – featuring a weak central Congress. It was at that point
that Thomas Jefferson, a prominent Enlightenment thinker-turned-
statesman, made his pronouncements concerning the farmer-led rebellion in the west: "No country should be so long without" revolution.[29]
For Jefferson, a regular uprising was a cause of celebration, a sign of
a system capable of self-correction.

The 1786 rebellion arose from farmers, many of whom had fought in
the Revolution, who found themselves squeezed by heavy individual debt
as well as high taxes – higher than under the British – imposed for the state
to pay off its own considerable war debt. Under the direction of a former
Continental Army captain, Daniel Shays, farmers tried and failed to
negotiate a settlement with the state legislature located in Boston.[30]
When that failed, Shays's farmers seized the state's arsenal in
Springfield and shut down the court system.

This was no small brushup. Nearly a quarter of all New England men
old enough to bear arms participated. Additional uprisings spread as far
south as Virginia, where a temporarily retired George Washington
became convinced of the need for a stronger central government capable
of containing such uprisings. It eventually took a force of 4,000 state
militia to quell Shays' rebellion.

Jefferson's response – admittedly offered from the safe remove of his
Paris home on the Champs-Élysées – reflected his faith that enlightened
individuals were capable of correcting flaws in civic institutions. "The
spirit of resistance to government is so valuable on certain occasions, that

---

[27] This assessment is from Christopher Dawson, *Progress and Religion: An Historical Inquiry*
(Washington, DC: Catholic University Press 2001), p. 21.

[28] Linda Mitchell, "The Enlightenment," in *Events That Changed the World in the Eighteenth
Century* (Connecticut: Greenwood Press, 1998), pp. 77–96.

[29] Bernstein, *Thomas Jefferson*, 70.

[30] Shays' leadership role was probably somewhat symbolic and exaggerated in the stories of
the time and since. Nonetheless, it was his name that became attached to the rebellion.
See Leonard Richards, *Shays' Rebellion: The American Revolution's Final Battle*
(Philadelphia: University of Pennsylvania Press, 2003).

I wish it to be always kept alive," he wrote. "It will often be exercised when wrong, but better so than not to be exercised at all. I like a little rebellion now and then." Mutinies were, in his redolent metaphor, a "natural manure," the fertile soil from which progress would grow.[31] Crisis could be called upon to create a new and, given his Enlightenment faith in the perfectibility of humans, an inevitably better order from the old.

By replacing the will of God with the independent human mind, one freed from the authoritarianism of the Church, Enlightenment thinkers welcomed a crisis that upended prevailing thoughts and attitudes. Certainly, many of America's Enlightenment thinkers were flawed in important ways, most significantly, their tolerance for and participation in slavery and their eagerness to usurp the land and disrupt the civilization of indigenous people in the name of expansion. Yet, the country's founding document – the Declaration of Independence, not the Constitution – enshrined Enlightenment principles as the aspirational goal of the country: "We hold these truths to be self-evident, that all men are created equal, that they are endowed by their Creator with certain unalienable Rights, that among these are Life, Liberty and the pursuit of Happiness, that to secure these rights, Governments are instituted among Men, deriving their just powers from the consent of the governed." Flawed as subsistent execution might have been, it was a document that embraced Enlightenment values into a national creed.

Martin Luther King positioned himself within that Declaration of Independence–sanctioned Enlightenment tradition. He had purposefully upended law and order. Enlightenment thinkers assaulted the reigning order of a divinely revealed, Church-mediated truth. All of these provocations sought to generate a friction-ridden interplay between an old order and an upstart challenger. The radical proposition of the Enlightenment can serve to remind us that it is not just social activists like King who are provocateurs. Never underestimate the potential for revolutionary ideas and those who generate those ideas to challenge the status quo.

Welcoming Tension, Inviting Discomfort

What is striking about King was his capacity to combine social activism with thought leadership. Believing that progress was never a matter of chance, he insisted on combing the two strands of mutiny. King often paraphrased the nineteenth-century Unitarian minister Theodore Parker, who insisted, "things refuse to be mismanaged long." The "arc" of

---

[31] Bernstein, *Thomas Jefferson*, 70.

progress, added Parker, is long and slow, "but from what I see, bends towards justice."[32] King agreed but insisted that the bending did *not* occur independently of human intervention. "Ere long all America will tremble," said Parker, writing less than a decade before the Civil War about the fundamental immorality and non-sustainability of slavery.[33] King's provocation of a crisis in Birmingham was fully intended to make the existing city power structure, ere long, tremble.

There's a solid line connecting King's idea of progress to the eighteenth-century German philosopher Immanuel Kant. Reason and intellect must be brought to bear on human development if human immaturity, imposed and nurtured by the twin institutions of church and state, was to be addressed. By upending norms, creating a crisis, fostering tension, King would demand reflection and response. The outcome would be wisdom.

Not for everyone, of course. King was hardly naive. He placed no stock in the futile hope that his instigated crisis would lead to reconsideration and wisdom on the part of Bull Connor and his White Citizens Council supporters.[34] The disruption was intended, rather, to move the community's more "moderate" elements, those willing to condemn segregation but eager to avoid confrontation. Community members who were "more committed to 'order' than to justice" had constantly failed to negotiate with civil rights advocates.[35] Now, they would be forced to confront the issue of justice as the only path to restore order. That, at least, was the hope and expectation. Would it happen? Kant and Jefferson placed their bets on reason. Parker and King added faith in a just God. In any crisis that juxtaposed "good and evil," King was sure, "good will win."[36] They all understood crisis as a necessary and appropriate prod for progress.

King was a man of thought who added direct action to the mix, provoking crisis to demand reflection and action. That was the same belief that led two professional football players to "take a knee" to welcome tension and invite discomfort within the most profitable professional sports league in the world.

---

[32] Theodore Parker, *Ten Sermons on Religion* (London: Trübner & Co., 1853), p. 78.

[33] Ibid.

[34] Connor died in 1973 without providing any public evidence of growth on racial matters. Wisdom, or at least apology, is possible, however. George Wallace was the governor of Alabama who proclaimed in his 1963 inaugural message, "Segregation now, segregation tomorrow, segregation forever." Years later, he acknowledged his past bigotry, assumed responsibility for the resulting harm, and asked for forgiveness from civil rights leader John Lewis. "When I met George Wallace, I had to forgive him," wrote Lewis, "because to do otherwise – to hate him – would perpetuate the evil system we sought to destroy." See John Lewis, "Forgiving George Wallace," *New York Times* (September 16, 1998).

[35] Quoted from Hornsby, "Martin Luther King," 41.   [36] Lewis, *King*, 180.

Mutinous Uprisings within Business

Prior to the opening kickoff at an August 2016 preseason football game of the San Francisco 49ers, the crowd spotted an unusual event during the playing of the "Star-Spangled Banner."[37] Rather than standing for the anthem, 49er quarterback Colin Kaepernick remained seated on the players' bench.[38] Following the game, he explained to the press, "I'm not going to stand up to show pride in a flag for a country that oppresses black people and people of color." He would continue his refusal to stand until he believed the flag "represents what it's supposed to represent." Kaepernick constructed his refusal to stand as a purposeful provocation intended to induce consideration of a profoundly urgent situation: the oppression of "black people and people of color."[39]

Teammate Eric Reid immediately joined Kaepernick: "My faith moved me to take action. I looked to James 2:17, which states, 'Faith by itself, if it does not have works, is dead.' I knew I needed to stand up for what is right." The goal, said Kaepernick, was to incite "uncomfortable" conversations. The two had been, like much of the rest of the country, paying attention to reports about the disturbing number of unarmed black people being killed by the police.

According to FBI data, African Americans were 300 percent more likely than whites to be killed by police. The disparity became even starker for unarmed suspects. Moved by the frequency of fatal police shootings of unarmed black men and angered by the inability or unwillingness of the justice system to find accountability, activists organized a direct-action movement, #BlackLivesMatter, and mobilized social media as a way of "working for a world where Black lives are no longer systematically targeted for demise."[40]

The week following Kaepernick's press conference, he and Reid elected to kneel rather than sit. Their intent was to show respect for US

---

[37] In 1969, Dave Meggyesy of the St. Louis Football Cardinals refused to place his hand over his heart during the pregame playing of the National Anthem. He was protesting the war in Vietnam. By the end of the season, despite playing at a near-all-pro level, Meggyesy would be out of the league for good – "blackballed, he believes, for his stance." Quote from Adam Kilgore, "For Decades, the NFL Wrapped itself in the Flag. Now, That's Made Business Uneasy," *Washington Post* (September 6, 2018).

[38] Kaepernick had remained seated for two earlier games, but his gesture went unnoticed.

[39] Steve Wyche, "Colin Kaepernick Explains Why He Sat during the National Anthem," *NFL Media* (August 27, 2016).

[40] www.vox.com/cards/police-brutality-shootings-us/us-police-shootings-statistics; https://blacklivesmatter.com/about; see also Josh Saul, "Police Killed More Than 1,100 People This Year and a Quarter of Them Were Black," *Newsweek* (December 29, 2017).

service members while continuing to make their statement. They "took a knee" in the vernacular of football.[41] As black deaths continued into 2016, Kaepernick's gesture spread, first among teammates and then to athletes on other teams and in other sports. A West Seattle high school football team – the entire team, including coaches – joined in the protest. "Everybody wants to talk about how this is disrespectful to the American flag," West Seattle's head coach explained, "That's a smokescreen. How about we talk about the issues people are kneeling and fighting for? If we could start addressing the issues and finding solutions to the issues, we won't have to kneel."[42] This was a form of mutiny. At the professional level, it was mutiny unfolding within and threatening the prosperity of a multi-billion-dollar enterprise.

The taking a knee gesture seemed particularly defiant given the institutional context in which it occurred. The National Football League (NFL) is a single, giant, and hugely profitable business syndicate. Sure, teams compete. Team owners, however, cooperate. They share 70 percent of their revenue across all teams: popular and unpopular teams, successful teams and those with losing records. And that wasn't a petty amount, adding up to $7.8 billion in 2016.[43]

"32 fat-cat Republicans who vote socialist." That's how one owner referred to the league owner's revenue-sharing arrangement.[44] A strict salary cap, non-guaranteed contracts, and a compliant players' union limited the capacity of athletes to either share in the revenues or participate in decision making. That's not to say they were poorly paid. The average annual salary for professional football players, $1.9 million, was impressive compared with that of the typical wage earner. That amount, however, placed NFL players at the very bottom rung of the ladder compared with other professional athletes in basketball, baseball, and hockey. And remember, the NFL was the most profitable sports league not just in the United States but the world.[45] That salary discrepancy is compounded by the average career length of an NFL player of 3.3 years, significantly lower than basketball (4.8 years), hockey (5 years), and baseball players (5.6

---

[41] When the quarterback takes a knee after a snap, the game clock is purposefully brought to a halt and the quarterback is protected from being tackled.

[42] Jayda Evans, "Garfield Football Team Takes Knee during National Anthem Prior to Game Friday Night," *Seattle Times* (September 16, 2016).

[43] Frank Jozsa Jr., *Football Fortunes: The Business, Organization, and Strategy of the NFL* (Jefferson, NC: McFarland & Company, 2010).

[44] Art Modell quoted in "In a League of Its Own," *The Economist* (April 27, 2006).

[45] Jozsa, *Football Fortunes.*

years).[46] Injuries play havoc with football careers. All sports may be injurious to players, but the NFL is unique.

Football players regularly place their current and future health at risk by virtue of skull rattling (that's a literal description, not a metaphor) head-on collisions in a way that most professional team athletes do not. The enhanced risk faced by NFL players helps explain why their contracts are not guaranteed. Footballers were well-paid athletes and widely celebrated throughout society, for sure. They were also vulnerable, both to injuries and to owners' whim.[47] And then there was a contract with the US Department of Defense.

For years, the NFL collected millions of dollars from the Department of Defense in exchange for "patriotic displays" deemed to be helpful for military recruitment. The league responded to the money by having players stand on the sidelines for the playing of the anthem rather than waiting in their locker room for game time.[48] Colin Kaepernick's gesture exploded in that context. Teams and the league were being paid to have their players stand in a showy gesture of a type of patriotism. Kaepernick's gesture on behalf of his own understanding of patriotism posed a threat to a multi-billion-dollar business.

A number of NFL owners objected to players taking a knee, with one threatening to bench any player who declined to stand for the anthem. Even those less bellicose owners – there was not a single African American among them – complained about the bottom-line impact on paraphernalia sales and, most worrisome of all, declining television ratings.[49] Donald Trump chided owners for not being tough enough on protestors. He wanted owners to say, "Get that son of a bitch off the field right now, he's fired. Fired!"[50]

---

[46] www.statista.com/statistics/240102/average-player-career-length-in-the-national-football-league; the average career earnings for NFL players is $6.27 million, compared with $24.7 million for basketball professionals, $17.92 million for baseball players, and $12 million for players in the National Hockey League. The average American wage earner receives $1.4 million over a career; www.quora.com/How-much-money-does-the-average-American-make-in-their-lifetime.

[47] On the risks of football compared with other sports, see Chris Deubert et al., *Comparing Health-Related Policies & Practices in Sports: The NFL and Other Professional Leagues* (Cambridge, MA: Football Players Health Study at Harvard University, 2017).

[48] Payments were made to other professional sports leagues as well. See Paula Reed Ward, "DoD Paid $53 Million of Taxpayers' Money to Pro Sports for Military Tributes," *Pittsburgh Post-Gazette* (May 7, 2018).

[49] Ken Belson and Mark Leibovich, "Inside the Confidential NFL Meeting to Discuss National Anthem Protests," *New York Times* (April 25, 2018).

[50] Sophie Tatum, "Trump: NFL Owners Should Fire Players Who Protest the National Anthem," *CNN Politics* (September 23, 2017). This was an echo of a line that had helped

Behind closed doors, owners groused about Trump's use of kneeling as "fodder to do his mission."[51] Nonetheless, with a fan base that skewed heavily toward conservative-leaning Republicans (the National Basketball Association, by contrast, has "the most liberal fan base of any major sport"), owners worried about the financial impact of protests.[52] Would it adversely impact game attendance, television ratings, or paraphernalia sales?

A year after he had first taken a knee, Kaepernick found himself out of work. No team offered him a contract.[53] The same was true for Eric Reid. Owners now adopted a new policy insisting that "a club will be fined by the League if its personnel are on the field and do not stand and show respect for the flag and the anthem." The president, who was unhappy that the new policy would allow players to remain in their locker rooms, insisted, "You have to stand proudly for the National Anthem or you shouldn't be playing, you shouldn't be there, maybe they shouldn't be in the country."[54] Kaepernick's initial gesture and its spread had indeed provoked widespread discomfort. Such discomfort is the core intent of an apostle of crisis.

Kaepernick was insisting that the unit was flawed. In his claim, however, the unit in question was not so much the NFL but the country. Owners responded to an urgent situation instituted by Kaepernick, Reid, and their supporters. The mutineers were disrupting one unit, the NFL, as a way of directing attention to the underlying urgency extant in their broader community.

Unlike King's protests and the naval uprisings that I've recounted, the taking-a-knee mutiny unfolded within a billion-dollar business enterprise, the NFL. Like any other social unit, businesses face the pressures imposed by the need for voice. Probably the most common form of business mutinies over the years have been organized labor confrontations with management over rights and voice that had been denied to employees. In 1885, the Knights of Labor disrupted Jay Gould's

make Trump famous – "You're fired!" – from his popular reality TV show, *The Apprentice.*

[51] Belson and Leibovich, "Inside the Confidential NFL Meeting."

[52] Statistics on fan-base politics, as well as the quote on the NBA, come from Perry Bacon Jr., "Why LeBron Can Say Whatever He Wants About Politics," *FiveThirtyEight* (July 31, 2018).

[53] Kaepernick was never a top-tier quarterback, but he was certainly talented enough to deserve a spot on many teams as a backup player. That was the finding of Kyle Wagner, "Colin Kaepernick Is Not Supposed to Be Unemployed," *FiveThirtyEight* (August 9, 2017).

[54] Matthew Nussbaum, "NFL Caves to Trump," *Politico* (May 23, 2018); John Wagner and Mark Maske, "Trump: NFL Players Unwilling to Stand for Anthem Maybe 'Shouldn't Be in the Country,'" *Washington Post* (May 24, 2018).

Southern Railway System, involving more than half-a-million workers in labor actions that spread across the industrial landscape.[55] The rise of industrial unions in the Depression–era United States – notably the Congress of Industrial Organizations and the United Auto Workers – provoked frequent, often violent confrontations as owners waged occasionally quite literal war against organizers and members.[56] Whether on the farms of western Massachusetts, the streets of Birmingham, or the arenas of professional sports, mutinous disruptions depend on the existence of shared values.

Appeal to (It Is Hoped) Shared Values

In his "Letter from a Birmingham Jail," King appealed to a sense of shared purpose and common values. In writing to the moderate clergy urging an end to disruptive demonstrations, King asserted a shared belief in "what is best in the American dream." His purpose was to make good on the "great wells of democracy" endorsed by "the founding fathers in their formulation of the Constitution and the Declaration of Independence," not to mention the "sacred values in our Judeo-Christian heritage." King was not naively assuming that Bull Connor and his core segregationist supporters shared those values. Rather, his appeal was precisely to the moderates who claimed to be supporters of justice for all and believers in the rights guaranteed by the Constitution.

When a mutiny exploded in the front pages of a city newspaper in the spring of 2018 – this one instigated by the paper's reporters and staff – the hoped-for shared value was the need in a democracy for a free press capable of watching over and reporting on the mechanisms of local government. The claim was that another dynamic, one focused solely on market values of maximizing return on investment, represented an existential threat not to the paper but to the pursuance of that mission. But just how shared was that value? Journalists do not protest. They may carp about their bosses, their pay, unreasonable deadlines, and the deterioration of commitment to news. But their dissatisfaction is not meant to be front-page news. Not usually, anyway. This time was different. "I've never done this before," noted a protesting employee, "But I feel like if there's one thing a journalist can fight for it's for journalism. That's our blood."[57]

---

[55] Melvyn Dubofsky and Joseph McCartin, *Labor in America: A History* (Hoboken, NJ: Wiley Blackwell, 2017).

[56] Sydney Lens, *The Labor Wars: From the Molly Maguires to the Sitdowns* (New York: Doubleday, 1973).

[57] Quoted in Marc Stewart, "That's Our Blood: Denver Post Reporters, Staff Members Rally against Corporate Owner," *Denver Post* (May 8, 2018).

In April 2018, the editorial board of the *Denver Post* organized a mutiny. Under the front-page banner headline "News Matters," there was its statement of shared values. The threat was not being posed *to* the paper. Rather it came *from* the paper, in the form of the *Post*'s ownership, a hedge-fund management company.

It may seem like the story of the *Denver Post* is just one more example of an industry under stress. And there is something to that. Newspapers had faced threats from technological innovations – radio and television most prominently – for decades.[58] Perhaps the Internet would be the fatal blow. With daily sales of 134,537 papers (253,261 on Sundays) and nine Pulitzer Prizes to its credit by the turn of the twenty-first century, the *Denver Post* had weathered all of these existential threats since its founding in 1892. As part of the heavy consolidation of the newspaper industry, the *Post* fought off several take-over attempts, starting in 1960. Though it remained locally owned, the paper was no longer profitable after 1980. Then, local ownership ended, and a series of outside owner-ship groups trimmed budgets and cut back on news coverage, all in a futile effort to return profitability.

In 2008, the *Post*'s main competitor, the *Rocky Mountain News*, folded. Even then, the *Post* could not realize a profit. Sure, there was no more competition from the *News*. Yet, the *Post* continued to experience declining ad revenues, leading to regular newsroom staff reductions in 2006 and 2007.[59] The mood within the *Post*'s newsroom was gloomy.

When *Post* ownership partnered with Digital First Media for manage-ment services, the paper now faced an epic struggle with an especially profit-driven segment of the American economy: hedge funds. Often referred to an "alternative investments," hedge funds typically eschew stocks, bonds, commodities, and foreign currency exchange. Rather, they purchased existing, struggling companies with the goal of slashing costs, improving management, lowering debt, and generally making the com-pany attractive to future investors.[60] Although research has raised doubt about the real performance of hedge-fund investments, proponents insist that the unregulated nature of the investment and the willingness to use innovative strategies allow for a return superior to more traditional invest-ment approaches.[61]

---

[58] David Davis, *The Postwar Decline of American Newspapers, 1945–1965* (Westport, CT: Praeger, 2006).

[59] Robert Sanchez, "How Massive Cuts Have Remade the *Denver Post*," *Mile High Magazine* (October 2016).

[60] Kevin Mirabile, *Hedge Fund Investing: A Practical Approach to Understanding Investor Motivation, Manager Profits, and Fund Performance* (Hoboken, NJ: Wiley, 2013).

[61] Ilia Dichev and Gwen Yu, "Higher Risk, Lower Returns: What Hedge Fund Investors Really Earn," *Journal of Financial Economics* 100 (2011), 248–263.

Digital was owned by a hedge fund management company, Alden Global Capital. Determined to maximize return on invested capital, Alden moved into the *Post*'s daily operations, adopting a micromanagement approach and engaging in what *Post* editors insisted was censorship.[62] Tension erupted when the paper's opinion-page editor resigned in protest. Then, an additional round of layoffs led the *Post* editor to tell her staff that "these job losses are painful, and we know meaningful work will not get done because talented journalists have left the organization."[63] These were "desperate times," said one of the accompanying pieces, "If we don't speak up now, then we will be destined to witness the demise of our city's largest and most essential news-gathering operations." And there was much at stake: "What would happen to democracy then?" Who would hold the powerful "accountable in the absence of a major metropolitan daily newspaper?" The implied answer: no one.

Another headline used the metaphor of a vulture to attribute anti-democratic values to the new owners: "As Vultures Circle, The *Denver Post* Must Be Saved." The owners, the editorial writers argued, were siphoning off revenues from the paper to make investments in unrelated, risky enterprises: "When newsroom owners view profits as the only goal, quality, reliability and accountability suffer. Their very mission is compromised."[64]

"The @denverpost is being murdered by its owners," tweeted one reporter.[65] The front-page mutinous editorial agreed: "If Alden isn't willing to do good journalism here, it should sell the *Post* to owners who will." The "fundamental truth" that propelled the editorial board's act of mutiny was a plea on behalf of first principles of a free press that they held to be necessary to a well-functioning democracy.

Mutinies are always risky undertakings. Mutineers lack the institutional power of the status quo leaders. The values to which they appeal may not always be as widely shared as they hoped. It was, after all, the mutineers rather than the captains who were no longer aboard. The *Post* continues to be published by Digital.

Regardless of whether the uprising is a success or a failure, we can make judgments about the legitimacy of its claims and the impact of the claims

---

[62] Digital has purchased dozens of daily and weekly papers, making it the second largest newspaper owner by circulation in the country. See Ashley Dean, "*Denver Post* Employees Protest Ownership with Events in Denver and New York," *Denverite* (May 8, 2018).

[63] Sydney Ember, "*Denver Post* Rebels Against Its Hedge-Fund Ownership," *New York Times* (April 7, 2018).

[64] www.denverpost.com/2018/04/06/as-vultures-circle-the-denver-post-must-be-saved

[65] Ember, "*Denver Post* Rebels."

makers. It is important to recognize that mutinies, no less than the communities toward which the mutinies are directed, have leaders. Those leaders come in many varieties: intellectuals, social activists, professional athletes, workers and editors, and so on. And they all intend, in leading mutiny, to ferment an uprising on behalf of some deeply held values.

Leading a Mutiny

Fletcher Christian is perhaps the most famous of all naval mutiny leaders. He is a well-known figure in popular culture, having been portrayed in movies by Hollywood leading men Clark Gable, Marlon Brando, and Mel Gibson. Christian was the leader of the mutiny of the *Bounty*. At age 24, Christian was not the hierarchical head of the *Bounty* and its crew; William Bligh held that position. But he didn't lack hierarchical status; Christian was the master mate in service to Bligh. More significant than that official capacity, however, was the action he took on April 28, 1789. It was then that Christian led a small group of the *Bounty* crew in the famous mutiny.

Christian had become convinced that the abusive rule of the captain had made the situation on board intolerable. "Sir," he told Bligh, "your abuse is so bad that I cannot do my duty with any pleasure. I have been in hell for weeks with you."[66] Tensions flared during the ship's five-month layover on Tahiti, spurred by Bligh's hostile reaction to the Polynesian inhabitants and the relationships some crew members were forming with locals. Punishments for perceived misbehavior were harsh. Bligh's ire came down especially heavily on his protégé, Fletcher Christian, whom he condemned publicly as a "cowardly rascal."[67] Christian first toyed with desertion (exit) before settling on mutiny (voice *in extremis*).

Early that April morning, Christian first gathered some weapons and then brought together a small number of sympathetic crew members. After arming them and insisting that "there is to be no murder," he and his followers neutralized several guards, approached Bligh's cabin, then bound him and forced him to the deck.[68] During the initial hours on deck, as Bligh pleaded and threatened, Christian wore a heavy depth-sounding devise around his neck so he could jump overboard and drown should the

---

[66] Caroline Alexander, *The Bounty* (London: HarperCollins, 2003), p. 127. Quotes are from diaries and other contemporaneous records.

[67] Ibid., 133.

[68] Richard Hough, *Captain Bligh and Mr. Christian: The Men and the Mutiny* (London: Hutchinsons, 1972), p. 18. Regardless of whether "murder" was to occur in the course of the mutiny, Christian had already committed the capital offense of incitement to mutiny.

mutiny fail.[69] Bligh and approximately half of the crew who stood by him were soon cast adrift in a launch while Christian set the *Bounty*'s course for the small island of Tubuai.

In instigating mutiny and other forms of crises, individuals become leaders. These individuals may hold some lesser but still important positions. Fletcher Christian was an acting lieutenant, and Martin Luther King was head of the Southern Christian Leadership Conference. While positioning themselves in opposition to the extant power structure, these individuals emerged as leaders who asserted their own claims of urgency. That urgency arose not from threats to the status quo but from the status quo itself: from the command of Captain Bligh to the Jim Crow regime in Birmingham. To these insurgents, crisis is not an event to be managed but a force to be unleashed. And the hoped-for outcome was not the restoration of the once-glorious kingdom, because the kingdom was deemed to be profoundly flawed.

Apostles of crisis exchange order for resistance, demanding dynamism and change rather than stasis and conformity. The intentionally created situation arrays two systems in oppositional conflict. The intermediate goal is the fermentation of dialectic and urgent tension. The end game is the assertion and institutionalization of first principles. In forcing a crisis, mutinous leaders assert a misalignment. The regime imposed and enforced by Bull Connor, and allowed by Southern moderates, say, stood in stark contrast to the principles asserted in the Declaration of Independence. That was King's position. He would quote from the Declaration: "We hold these truths to be self-evident, that all men are created equal." And then, in the gender-biased language he adopted uncritically, he asserted what he took to be its first principles:

This is a dream. It's a great dream. The first saying we notice in this dream is an amazing universalism. It doesn't say, "some men"; it says, "all men." It doesn't say "all white men"; it says, "all men," which includes black men. It does not say "all Gentiles"; it says, "all men," which includes Jews. It doesn't say "all Protestants"; it says, "all men," which includes Catholics. It doesn't even say "all theists and believers"; it says, "all men," which includes humanists and agnostics.[70]

Unlike the US Constitution, the Declaration of Independence has no legal standing. It was meant as a statement of "natural law."[71] For that

---

[69] Alexander, *The Bounty*. Christian lived out his life in Tahiti.

[70] https://kinginstitute.stanford.edu/king-papers/publications/knock-midnight-inspiration-great-sermons-reverend-martin-luther-king-jr-4

[71] The US Citizenship and Immigration Services provides a booklet reprinting the Declaration and the Constitution, referring to them as the "two most important, and enduring documents in our Nation's history." Perhaps, but they are very different documents, written by different groups of men (with some overlap) for very different purposes.

reason, King had to rely on an appeal to principles; that tension under-lying urgency grew from a misalignment not between King and Bull Connor, but between foundational principles and de jure/de facto segre-gation. And like any other claim, we can and should evaluate its legitimacy.

What about the role of insurgents as leaders? Leaders are claims makers, including both those seeking preservation and those attempting a convulsive reorientation. So, I turn next to considering the role of leader as claims maker. My intention is not to determine which leaders were most effective in navigating through turbulent times. That's the territory of the crisis-as-event model. My intention, rather, is to consider the role *all* claims makers play when they determine the time has come to claim urgency.

9 Beyond Forged-in-Crisis Leadership

Crises were made for leaders. Leaders were made for crises. The crisis-as-event model is clear on that point. Leaders navigate their units through the turbulence wrought by crisis events. When companies face financial turmoil, the board hires a CEO to lead the organization to recovery and prosperity. Countries engulfed in war look to their leaders – think of the outsized roles played by Franklin Roosevelt and Winston Churchill during World War II – to offer guidance, strength, and a steady hand.[1] These are the folks who determine success or failure, rejuvenation or death. Leaders and leadership sit front and center in the crisis-as-event model. "Leading in crisis is the real test for leaders," asserts former CEO Bill George.[2] Likewise, having an effective leader is the real test for organizations in trouble.

The crisis-as-event model generates a seemingly unending stream of metaphors bolstering the view that crisis provides the opportunity for great leadership. Leaders guide their units through "the eye of the storm." They "ride the tiger" in turbulent times, "master" the requisite skills of crisis management, and ensure that their units will "survive disaster" when "it hits the fan" to emerge "stronger and better" and turn "losers into winners."[3] It is a potentially heroic interaction: leaders and crisis.

---

[1] As Churchill fought bitterly against England's appeasement faction in the debate over the 1939 Munich Pact, Lord Arthur Ponsonby lamented, "In a crisis, he [Churchill] is one of the first people who ought to be interred." Great leadership is always a matter of perspective. See Andrew Roberts, *Churchill: Walking with Destiny* (New York: Viking, 2018), p. 435.

[2] Bill George, "Seven Lessons for Leading in Crisis," *Wall Street Journal* (March 5, 2009).

[3] Donald Bibeault, *Corporate Turnaround: How Managers Turn Losers into Winners* (New York: McGraw-Hill, 1982); Harvard Business Essentials, *Crisis Management: Mastering the Skills to Prevent Disasters* (Boston: Harvard Business School Press, 2004); Meyers and Holusha, *When It Hits the Fan*; Mitroff, *Why Some Companies Emerge Stronger and Better from a Crisis*; Pricilla Nelson and Ed Cohen, *Riding the Tiger: Leading through Learning in Turbulent Times* (Alexandria, VA: American Society for Training and Development,

To be sure, there are plenty of examples of leaders who seemingly failed the "forged-in-crisis" test:

• Blockbuster CEO John Antioco's late and lame response to the competitive challenge posed by Netflix led the company into bankruptcy. He's hardly alone among CEOs who failed spectacularly to navigate their now-defunct businesses through trauma, turmoil, and competitive pressures. The same could be said of Borders Books CEO George Jones, Circuit City CEO Philip Schoonover, Compaq CEO Eckhard Pfeiffer, Enron CEO Ken Lay, and Lehman Brothers CEO Richard Fuld. No riding the tiger here.

• The list of leaders said to have failed in their efforts to deal with Hurricane Katrina and its impact on New Orleans is long and includes President George Bush, Undersecretary of Emergency Preparedness and Response Michael Brown, and New Orleans Mayor Ray Nagin. When "it" hit the fan, these leaders failed spectacularly.

It's a precarious perch, apparently: leaders attempting to steer from within the eye of a storm or whatever crisis-as-event metaphor might be preferred.

Operating strictly from within that model, crisis management experts offer a pretty standard checklist of what leaders should do in times of trouble. Perhaps they could follow this typical enumeration of suggestions:

• Encourage a proactive crisis culture.
• Establish and enforce standards and processes.
• Prioritize and set an example.
• Properly assess the full range of risks.
• Promote open upward communication.
• Build relationships before the crisis.
• Be ready to deal with the news media.
• Encourage a learning environment and shared experience.[4]

The idea is this: the capacity of the leader to perform these tasks impacts the degree to which the unit will weather the crisis. Will it survive, indeed flourish? That depends on leaders and what they do in response.

The crisis-as-claim model demands a new interpretation of leader behaviors. Leaders are now construed not as tiger riders but as claims makers. Sure, they will need to manage their units once urgency has been

2010); Bill Tribbo, *Leadership in the Eye of the Storm; Putting Your People First in a Crisis* (Toronto: University of Toronto Press, 2016).
[4] Jacques, "Crisis Leadership," 368.

declared, and they may even follow the checklist. And yes, some will do that more competently than others. But they all are claims makers of urgency, instigating crisis through their own declarations. Perhaps their claims are legitimate, perhaps not. Either way, what they do once they claim urgency follows a discernable pattern. Before identifying that pattern, we can look at a corporate chief executive and his response to what was heralded in the press variously as a "crisis," a "scandal," and even an "existential" threat to the company's survival.

Facebook – and Its Leader – under Fire

When Mark Zuckerberg, founder and CEO of Facebook, was called on to account publicly for a major scandal at his company, he did so before an angry congressional hearing in the spring of 2018. Facebook's "worse crisis yet" exploded in the aftermath of the 2016 US presidential campaign.[5] It began not at Facebook but with the revelation that Republican candidate Donald Trump had hired Cambridge Analytica, a British-based consulting firm, to provide data to aid his campaign.

There was really nothing unusual or particularly alarming in politicians leaning on social media. The gathering of demographic data to aid in the effectiveness of messages has become a regular feature of politics around the world. Barack Obama's 2008 campaign made highly effective use of targeted ads on Facebook.[6]

Social media generally has provided an especially fruitful platform for highly targeted ads based on in-depth knowledge of users: urging one profile of voters, for instance, to "vote early" while assuring another group that "we're going to say Merry Christmas again!"[7] Rather than spending large sums of money on television ads broadcast to all viewers, politicians and companies alike tailor specific appeals to targeted audiences.

That's where Cambridge Analytica came in. It could provide demographic data and even personality attributes for millions of potential consumers or voters, much of it originating from Facebook. Not everyone, for example, would be equally appreciative of the pledge to "say Merry Christmas again." But how, exactly, did Cambridge Analytica manage to get that data from Facebook? *That* was the key question.

---

[5] Quote from Seera Frankel and Kevin Roose, "Zuckerberg, Facing Facebook's Worst Crisis Yet, Pledged Better Privacy," *New York Times* (March 21, 2018).

[6] A key strategist for that Obama campaign, Chris Hughes, was a Facebook cofounder.

[7] The theme of a so-called War on Christmas in which "Happy Holidays" would be forced on people who wished to say "Merry Christmas" was promulgated by right-wing commentators and picked up by Donald Trump as part of his 2016 campaign.

Before answering that, however, it is necessary to appreciate the context in which Cambridge Analytica and Facebook operated.

In the thirteen years since its founding in 2004, Facebook grew to reach 2.2 billion active monthly users (including its WhatsApp and Instagram subsidiaries).[8] Facebook's revenue model – the manner in which it monetized its product – has always been "free-to-end-users." Rather than charging users, revenue is generated through selling ads, with the particular appeal of targeting those ads to specific customers based on demographic data provided to Facebook by those customers. To be sure, that model proved to be remarkably effective. Facebook's total revenue for the election year of 2016 was $27.6 billion.[9] This was a model, in other words, that was working extremely well for Facebook. It was a model that Zuckerberg had no intention of upending.

"If you're not paying for the product," a marketing adage goes, "you *are* the product." That is certainly the case at Facebook, which boasts to potential clients – politicians, businesses, marketing companies, or any other party seeking to reach specific groups – that "Your people are here." Facebook's "powerful audience selection tools" allow advertisers to match their customers on the basis of "demographics, interests, and behaviors" with Facebook's users.[10] Remember, Facebook reaches several billion users each month!

The company does *not* provide the data directly to advertisers and other outside parties. That, at least, was Facebook's stated policy. "What we allow is for advertisers to tell us who they want to reach, and then we do the placement," Zuckerberg explained.[11] It was true: Facebook had a specific policy that prohibited any personal data to be sold or given "to any ad network, data broker or other advertising or monetization-related service."[12] Sure, but not really.

Back in 2007, Facebook was fighting Google for web supremacy. Zuckerberg initiated a policy of sharing user data, including friends' lists, likes, and affinities, with outside developers.[13] Data sharing, in other words, was not a loophole or a glitch in Facebook's system.

---

[8] www.statista.com/statistics/264810/number-of-monthly-active-facebook-users-worldwide

[9] www.statista.com/statistics/277229/facebooks-annual-revenue-and-net-income

[10] www.facebook.com/business/products/ads/ad-targeting

[11] Quoted in Ben Gilbert, "How Facebook Makes Money from Your Data, in Mark Zuckerberg's Words," *Business Insider* (April 11, 2018).

[12] Ibid.

[13] Google, which collects copious amounts of personal data on users, certainly exploits that data but has not been known to share with or sell to external parties.

Rather, it was a conscious strategy by the company, one touted by Zuckerberg himself, to increase its Internet footprint.

Zuckerberg's strategy for Facebook also provided user data to mobile phone makers including Apple, Samsung, and Huawei, a Chinese telecommunications giant that had been flagged by US intelligence agencies as a national security threat. Again, this was a strategic move to encourage smart phone makers to install Facebook-friendly features on their products.[14] Special arrangements were reached with "favored companies" including Airbnb, Lyft, and Netflix to provide direct access to data.[15] Revelation of that strategy did not come from Zuckerberg. External investigators, mainly reporters, unearthed it.

Facebook's generous sharing policy ended in 2015. But that was after a Cambridge University psychologist had posted a personality test on Facebook, his "This Is Your Digital Life" app. More than a quarter million Facebook users took the "Digital Life" personality quiz, rating their response to statements including "I don't talk a lot," "I make a mess of things," "I do not have a good imagination," "I feel others' emotions," "I have frequent mood swings," and "I have difficulty understanding abstract ideas."[16] They then checked a box allowing their data to be shared for purposes of "research."

Data was also collected on the "friends" of those who filled out the form, a sharing allowed by Facebook's terms of agreement for purposes of improving the app. Even though Zuckerberg's policies barred such data from being used commercially, the information flowed from Cambridge University to Cambridge Analytica.

Despite sharing the name "Cambridge," the two institutions were not related. Aleksandr Kogan, a senior research associate in Cambridge University's Department of Psychology, provided the bridge between the two. When he posted his personality test on Facebook, he was simultaneously at work on a "Mechanical Turk" – an online crowdsourcing model – for Cambridge Analytica. That software was designed explicitly to harvest information from Facebook users' and their friends' profiles.[17]

Cambridge Analytica counted mainly politicians among its clients, not just Donald Trump but also the organizers of the Vote Leave campaign in

[14] This was before Facebook had developed its own fully functioning app. See Michael La Forgia and Gabriel Dance, "Facebook Gave Chinese Giants Access to Data," *New York Times* (June 6, 2018).
[15] Adam Satariano, "Facebook Gave Some Companies Special Access to Users' Data, Documents Show," *New York Times* (December 5, 2018).
[16] https://discovermyprofile.com/miniIPIP.html
[17] Flora Bowen, "How Is Cambridge University Linked to Cambridge Analytica and the Facebook Data Scandal?" *The Tab* (2018).

the United Kingdom. The company collected personal data that was exploited on behalf of the client.[18] It boasted of "psychographic" tools that it used to harvest personality profiles to help target specific messages to specific voters. It would later be revealed that Cambridge Analytica also touted its experience in entrapping and blackmailing politicians.[19]

Facebook knew as early as 2015 that Cambridge Analytica had gained access to user data through the personality test. No crisis was declared, no statements were released, no warnings sent out to users, and no internal policy changes occurred. In December 2017, a Cambridge Analytica whistle-blower contacted various British and European agencies, as well as the UK's *Observer*, saying, "We spent $1 million harvesting millions of Facebook profiles."[20] Uh-oh.

Facebook spokespeople at first issued denials, claiming that the company had complete control of its own user data. Facebook's UK policy director, for instance, insisted, that while Cambridge Analytica "may have lots of data," that would "not be Facebook user data. It may be data about people who are on Facebook, but it is not data that we provided."[21] That denial was accurate, but only in the narrowest possible sense. Facebook had not "provided" data to Cambridge Analytica but had allowed it to be collected by a university researcher who then turned it over to Cambridge Analytica. The company had not reported a "breach" because no breech had occurred. At this point, there was still no crisis claim. Everything was purportedly under control at Facebook.

As the public was to learn through whistle-blower revelations and press investigations, Facebook had indeed controlled the data. Then, it allowed the Cambridge University researcher access according to standard policies and procedures. And he wasn't alone. Thousands of developers had obtained personal data from Facebook. What made Aleksandr Kogan especially disruptive was that he had turned his data over to Cambridge Analytica, a particularly dubious enterprise.

With the 2018 investigations into Russian involvement in the US presidential election and criminal indictments against Russian individuals who had gained easy access to Facebook through the use of false identities, the company could no longer insist that nothing improper had

---

[18] Kevin Granville, "Facebook and Cambridge Analytica: What You Need to Know as Fallout Widens," *New York Times* (March 19, 2018).

[19] Issue Lapowsky, "Cambridge Analytica Execs Caught Discussing Extortion and Fake News," *Wired* (February 19, 2018).

[20] Carole Cadwalladr and Emma Graham-Harrison, "Revealed: 50 Million Facebook Profiles Harvested for Cambridge Analytica in Major Data Breach," *The Guardian* (March 17, 2018).

[21] Ibid.

happened.[22] Its story now shifted to an admission that Cambridge Analytica and its agents had violated company policy. The "This Is Your Digital Life" app was removed, and users were notified by Facebook that "we have banned the app" because it "may have misused some of your Facebook information by sharing it with a company called Cambridge Analytica."[23] *May* have?

Behind closed doors, Zuckerberg and his second-in-command, Chief Operating Officer Sheryl Sandberg, worked feverishly to contain the story. Public relations campaigns were launched to point fingers at rivals including Google, which were accused of similar privacy lapses. Facebook quietly hired a Republican opposition research firm with the intent of discrediting anti-Facebook activist protesters (a contact that Zuckerberg later denied any knowledge of). Sandberg was especially active in lobbying friendly (mainly Democratic) senators on the company's behalf.[24]

That frenzy of defensive activity did not show in public. Instead, company spokespeople continued to insist that there was nothing to be terribly worried about. In addition to the misleading qualifier that the researcher *may* have "misused" personal data, the company reassured users: "In most cases, the information was limited to public profiles, page likes, birthday, and current city." Still, Facebook's stock price took a beating, shedding billions of dollars in market value.

As pressure mounted, including a request to appear before a congressional committee, Zuckerberg issued an apology: "We have a responsibility to protect your data, and if we can't then we don't deserve to serve you. I've been working to understand exactly what happened and how to make sure this doesn't happen again." It was an apology that was, in no uncertain terms, a forces-beyond-our-control defense. Blame was still apportioned to the university researcher and Cambridge Analytica, not Facebook.

During his congressional appearance, Zuckerberg insisted that the company's revenue model and the notion of collecting personal data on the demographics, interests, and behaviors of Facebook friends – and on non-Facebook users as well – was not just valid but socially beneficial: "That's the only way that we can reach billions of people." The model of selling targeted ads was in no way implicated in the bad acts of the

---

[22] Mark Mazzetti and Katie Benner, "12 Russian Agents Indicted in Mueller Investigation," *New York Times* (July 13, 2018).
[23] www.facebook.com/help/1873665312923476?helpref=search&sr=1&query=cambridge
[24] Seera Fraenkel et al., "Delay, Deny and Deflect: How Facebook's Leaders Fought Through Crisis," *New York Times* (November 14, 2018).

Cambridge researcher and Cambridge Analytica.[25] Although apologizing and promising future (and unspecified) policy reforms, Zuckerberg pointed the finger of blame away from the core activities of Facebook.

Zuckerberg leaned heavily on the once-great-kingdom narrative trope. "My top priority," he told senators, "has always been our social mission of connecting people, building community and bringing the world closer together. Advertisers and developers will never take priority over that, as long as I am running Facebook." It may be that his socially oriented, community-building company had been threatened by forces-beyond-our-control. But don't worry, he assured his interrogators, that would change. Control would become stronger.

"We're getting to the bottom of exactly what Cambridge Analytica did," Zuckerberg explained. That was the outside force that "improperly accessed some information about millions of Facebook members by buying it from an app developer." Facebook had done its best to manage that force, the narrative continued. "When we heard back from Cambridge Analytica," Facebook was told, "they weren't using the data and had deleted it." It wasn't that Zuckerberg was unwilling to admit to some laxity on Facebook's part: "In retrospect, that was clearly a mistake. We shouldn't have taken their word for it."[26] The real fault, the bad actors, was external to Facebook.

It was a rickety narrative artifice that Zuckerberg built, omitting more than it included. The company, after all, had openly and strategically shared user data with outsiders, had pushed the boundaries on both collecting and commercializing that data, and then had blamed others for bad-faith actions when the negative publicity exploded. Would it be effective?

The press remained largely unmoved, blaring headlines such as "Facebook in crisis," "Facebook's two years in hell," "Facebook is facing an existential crisis," and "Facebook under fire."[27] Zuckerberg's testimony was deemed to have made things worse. Crisis experts insisted that "Facebook has mishandled the data scandal," and "Mark Zuckerberg lied

---

[25] In May 2018, Cambridge Analytica went out of business. While professing its innocence and professionalism, company statements said that adverse publicity had driven clients away. See Olivia Solon and Oliver Laughland, "Cambridge Analytica Closing after Facebook Data Harvesting Scandal," *The Guardian* (May 2, 2018).

[26] Zuckerberg quoted from www.washingtonpost.com/news/the-switch/wp/2018/04/10/transcript-of-mark-zuckerbergs-senate-hearing/?utm_term=.073847747fd0.

[27] Dylan Byers, "Facebook Is Facing an Existential Crisis," *CNN Money* (March 19, 2018); Christopher Carbone, "Facebook in Crisis," *Fox News* (April 12, 2018); Todd Spangler, "Facebook Under Fire: How Privacy Crisis Could Change Big Data Forever," *Variety* (2018).

to Congress."[28] And yet, within months, Facebook returned to its high-flying past. The company's stock price recovered, and its customer base continued to expand.[29]

How can we evaluate Zuckerberg's crisis leadership? Perhaps Zuckerberg's actions were more effective than critics understood. Facebook users did not share in the great fuss kicked up by the press and adopted by politicians. "You pay nothing for Facebook, they told you they were selling your data, where's the crisis?" asked one user, adding, "No harm, no foul. Big Fat Nothing Burger."[30] Most customers seemed content with the knowledge that Facebook was a public forum, and expectations for privacy were far different from what they would be from, say, a bank or hospital.[31] From the perspective of users, at least, Zuckerberg's response proved more satisfying than it was to the experts who decried Zuckerberg's lame excuses. To some, Zuckerberg even loomed as some sort of a nerdy superhero, working to connect the world, fending off disruptive forces, and becoming a billionaire in the process.[32]

Over the following year, problems continued to surface at Facebook. In October 2018, the company revealed a more straightforward breech: tens of millions of user accounts were exposed.[33] The next month, Facebook released a report commissioned by the company and undertaken by the independent Business for Social Responsibility finding that Facebook's platform had been used in Myanmar "to foment division and incite offline violence." Facebook had been used to spread hate speech and disinformation, resulting in a "negative impact on freedom of expression, assembly and association for Myanmar's most vulnerable users," the report concluded.[34] Alex Warofka, Facebook's corporate product policy manager, said, "We agree that we can and should do more."[35] Both instances were widely reported. No commentators declared a new existential crisis

---

[28] Associated Press, "Crisis Experts Say Facebook Had Mishandled the Data Scandal," *Snopes* (2018).

[29] Sarah Frier and Sarah Ponczek, "Facebook Shares Recover from Cambridge Analytica Scandal," *Bloomberg* (May 10, 2018).

[30] Spangler, "Facebook Under Fire."

[31] Ben Bajarin, "Survey: Most Facebook Users Don't Expect Much Privacy," *Fast Company* (April 20, 2018).

[32] The idea of a nerdy superhero, at least pre-crisis, is from Rebecca Greenfield, "Mark Zuckerberg: Super Hero?" *The Atlantic* (May 14, 2012). For evidence of his ongoing post-crisis appeal, see Shawn Langlois, "Mark Zuckerberg Is a 'Hero,' and D.C. Needs to Be More Careful, Says Venture Capitalist," *Marketwatch* (April 11, 2018).

[33] Farhad Manjoo, "How Mark Zuckerberg Became Too Big to Fail," *New York Times* (November 1, 2018).

[34] Alexandra Stevenson, "Facebook Admits It Was Used to Incite Violence in Myanmar," *New York Times* (November 6, 2018).

[35] https://newsroom.fb.com/news/2018/11/myanmar-hria

at Facebook, and no analysis of the effectiveness of the company's response took place.[36]

The Leader's Role Forged in Crisis

Navigating through a crisis is often seen as heroic. Martin Luther King, Franklin Roosevelt, even Fletcher Christian all came to be viewed by many as heroes. They had brought Birmingham segregation to its heels, seen a troubled nation through depression and war, and reclaimed dignified governance in the face of a tyrannical ship captain. Archie Norman won praise as a best-case example of turnaround leadership at the ailing ASDA grocery chain and carried those hopes with him to M&S. Individuals become designated as heroes only when the unit they lead faces a crisis. If you want to be seen as a hero, in other words, you'll need to construct a crisis and identify a role for yourself in response.[37]

But Crisis Heroes in Business?

Leaders who take on the role of defender of the status quo may be admired by those who approve of that status quo but will be "doomed to be viewed as non-heroic" by most others[38] No one writes celebrations of Birmingham civic leaders who counseled moderation or cast leading actors in the role of the crewmen who joined Captain Bligh in his forced exile. Leading a nation through war, facing down terrorists, overseeing economic recovery all offer fertile grounds for leaders to claim a mantle of heroism. Those opportunities exist in the business world as well. It's just that, in that world, heroism and corporate stewardship make for an uneasy fit.

Let's face it: the notion of a heroic CEO is a stretch. CEOs occupy a position of power within their organizations. Admittedly, they often follow a challenging, obstacle-filled path in their rise to the top. We know, however, that it is not a strictly meritorious ascension. Some are part of a family business that builds its executive pipeline based on a form of corporate nepotism. Additionally, decades of research have demonstrated the persistence of bias – prominently, racial- and gender-based bias – in the selection and promotion of corporate executives. And it is not

---

[36] Several human rights groups weighed in, saying, in essence, "better late than never," and also pointing out how Facebook was being used to spread hate speech in other countries. See Stevenson, "Facebook Admits It Was Used to Incite Violence."

[37] Dermot O'Reilly et al., "Leadership, Authority and Crisis: Reflections and Future Directions," *Leadership* 11 (2015), 489–499.

[38] Allison and Goethals, *Heroes*, 133.

obvious that the journey to the top was untaken on behalf of some greater good, especially as the material rewards have grown more disproportionate over time. The work itself is not apparently heroic, either. In truth, much of the daily life of a corporate CEO amounts to mundane, even trivial chores.[39] When Henry Mintzberg clinically analyzed the daily lives of working CEOs, he found little that was exciting, let alone heroic.[40] Meetings, public appearances, planning, making decisions on resource allocation – these are the kinds of activities that dominate a CEO's calendar. And then there is dealing with shareholders.

Ever since the rise of shareholder activism in the 1970s, the main focus of a CEO's job has been on the decidedly unheroic task of driving up the company's stock price. That's where Zuckerberg's crisis leadership, after all, had its greatest impact; Facebook's share price recovered and then grew. That market success hasn't won Zuckerberg any kudos as a "forged-in-crisis" leader. Yet he did his job. Shareholders – through his own stock, Zuckerberg controls more than 53 percent of the company's voting rights and added significantly to his personal wealth in the aftermath of his congressional appearance – seemed pleased.[41] Other CEOs focus on cost cutting, divestitures, stock buybacks, and various other schemes all with the goal of enriching shareholders. As CEO compensation has increasingly been tied to stock price, it is difficult to find traces of motivation beyond a drive for individual power and immense wealth.

Responding to shareholders, constantly cutting costs, and attending to bottom-line performance, all while being lavishly paid, is hardly the stuff of heroic leadership. That's where the forged-in-crisis image of leaders can be useful as an ego builder, reputation enhancer, and wealth provider. By placing their own role front and center in responding to crises, CEOs can enhance their self-esteem and justify exalted power and prestigious (and prodigious) rewards.[42] Failures, in turn, can be blamed on outside forces such as unfair foreign competition, crippling state regulation, and world economic trends. In McDonald's 2014 annual report, executives

[39] Matts Alvesson and Stefan Sveningsson, "Managers Doing Leadership: The Extraordinization of the Mundane," *Human Relations* 56 (2003), 1435–1459.

[40] Henry Mintzberg, *The Nature of Managerial Work* (Englewood Cliffs, NJ: Prentice Hall, 1973).

[41] On Zuckerberg's stock ownership, see J. M. Maverick, "The Top 6 Shareholders of Facebook," *Investopedia* (October 30, 2018).

[42] Judy Gray and Iain Densten, "How Leaders Woo Followers in the Romance of Leadership," *Applied Psychology: An International Review* 56 (2007), 558–581; Gerald Salancik and James Meindl, "Corporate Attributions as Strategic Illusions of Management Control," *Administrative Science Quarterly* 29 (1984), 238–254; Barry Staw et al., "The Justification of Organizational Performance," *Administrative Science Quarterly* 28 (1983), 582–600.

improbably blamed bad winter weather – forces-beyond-our-control – for an earnings downturn in their stores, even though rival fast-food chains experienced no such downturn in the same quarter.[43]

By placing their own role front and center in responding to crises, CEOs anoint themselves as heroes. That self-proclamation can occur in the form of a best-selling memoir. The prototype for such CEO self-promotion appeared in 1984 with the publication of *Iacocca*. Lee Iacocca, then CEO of the Chrysler Corporation, was widely heralded for his apparent turnaround of this ailing automotive giant. The book was a stunning success, topping the *New York Times* annual best-selling nonfiction book list for two years running. Iacocca became the first CEO ever to enter the Gallup Poll's annual most admired person list, and his name was soon bandied about as a potential presidential candidate.[44] Iacocca was unabashed in his claim that the crisis leadership he had exhibited at Chrysler had been exceptional. "Today I am a hero," he stated matter of factly.[45] And descriptively, he was right. His was an appealing narrative that was widely celebrated at the time.

Any assertion of a central and unequivocal role in guiding the organization to recovery makes the leader attractive to others who seek guidance in times of turbulence.[46] People prefer an interpretation of the world in which individuals are the prototype of origin, that is, the individual cause of outcomes, the prime mover in events.[47]

Iacocca is certainly not alone among CEOs who strove to depict themselves as heroes navigating their companies through crisis. Al Dunlap, who earned the nickname "Chainsaw Al" in the 1990s for his relentless cost trimming at nine separate corporations, insisted that he was a hero not of "Wall Street fat cats," but of "working people and retired men and women" who "have entrusted us with their 401Ks and pension plans for their children's college tuition and their own long-term security."[48] Carly Fiorina leveraged her "heroic" efforts to turn around Hewlett-Packard into her own best seller and a bid for the 2016 Republican presidential

[43] Ben Rooney, "Blaming Poor Performance on Weather? Nice Try," *CNN Money* (May 2, 2014).

[44] Bert Spector, "Flawed from the 'Get-Go': Lee Iacocca and the Origins of Transformational Leadership," *Leadership* 10 (2014), 361–379.

[45] Lee Iacocca, *Iacocca: An Autobiography* (New York: Bantam, 1984), p. xv.

[46] Judy Gray and Iain Densten construct this as a wooing process. See Gray and Iain, "How Leaders Woo Followers in the Romance of Leadership."

[47] The phrase "prototype of origin" is from Fritz Heider, "Social Perception and Phenomenal Causality," *Psychological Review* 51 (1944), 358–374.

[48] Albert Dunlap, *Mean Business: How I Save Bad Companies and Make Good Companies Great* (New York: Simon & Schuster, 1996), p. ix.

nomination.[49] Donald Trump's 1987 *Art of the Deal* helped solidify his image as a master negotiator. And Mark Zuckerberg promised to make Facebook more effective than ever at knitting together a better world.

In the corporate sphere, the image of a CEO as crisis hero attracts benefits, both tangible and intangible. When employees are able to attribute "heroism" to their leaders, they tend to imbue those leaders with the characteristics of charisma, strength, and decisiveness.[50] Shareholders (both current and potential future investors), board members, fellow executives, and employees at all levels are assured that their companies are overseen by worthy individuals and that their executives have earned the hierarchical power, prestige, and monetary rewards bestowed upon them by the organization. Investors drive up stock prices when corporations hire heroes as their CEOs. It's a comforting delusion. There is ample evidence to suggest that the subsequent performance of hero CEOs often lags behind that of rival companies led by less celebrated executives.[51]

Once individuals attract the prestigious status of hero, their derived power becomes generalizable.[52] Now, the anointed heroes – perhaps *self-anointed* through their own telling – are able to exert influence beyond the specific accomplishment and setting that attracted prestige in the first place. The result is a self-reinforcing cycle in which the designation "hero" confers power, and that act of conferment accumulates additional power. Ever since the glory days of Lee Iacocca, extraordinarily successful business leaders find their names on "most admired" lists, the subject of political speculation, and, for a time anyway, presumed fonts of wisdom on myriad issues beyond business. And, let's be honest, leaders may actually welcome crisis as a vehicle for earning hero status.

[49] Peter Burrows, *Backfire: Carly Fiorina's High-Stakes Battle for the Soul of Hewlett-Packard* (San Francisco: Wiley, 2003) and Carly Fiorina, *Tough Choices: A Memoir* (New York: Portfolio, 2006). A number of observers have questioned the business results achieved by Dunlap, Iacocca, and Fiorina. On Dunlap, see Byrne, *Chainsaw*; on Iacocca, see Spector, "Flawed from the 'Get-Go'"; and on Fiorina, see Geoff Colvin, "Carly Fiorina's Disastrous Record as HP's CEO," *Fortune* (September 21, 2015); Steve Rattner, "Carly Fiorina Really Was That Bad," *New York Times* (September 25, 2015); Jeffrey Sonnenfeld, "Why I Still Think Fiorina Was a Terrible CEO," *Politico* (September 20, 2015).

[50] Carmeli and Schaubroeck, "Organizational Crisis-Preparedness"; Meindl, "On Leadership"; Rajnandini Pillai and James Meindl, "Context and Charisma: A 'Meso' Level Examination of the Relationship of Organic Structure, Collectivism, and Crisis to Charismatic Leadership," *Journal of Management* 24 (1998), 643–671.

[51] Rakesh Khurana, *Searching for the Corporate Savior: The Irrational Quest for Charismatic CEOs* (Princeton: Princeton University Press, 2002); Ulrike Malmendier and Geoffrey Tate, *Superstar CEOs* (NBER Working Paper, 2008); Larry Yu, "The Superstar CEO Curse," *MIT Sloan Management Review* 48 (2007), 4.

[52] John Spanier, *Games Nations Play: Analyzing International Politics* (New York: Holt, 1984).

"Exquisite Agony"

Part of what we admire about crisis leaders is their performance under tremendous pressure. In the crisis-as-event model, stories of leading through a crisis emphasize the stressfulness and risk of the situation. Leaders who lack "character" respond to stress by "panicking" or "cracking." Great crisis leaders, conversely, respond with "moral purpose," evidencing their own "core values."[53]

That stress should not be minimized. But there is another aspect of crisis leadership that is never admitted in the crisis-as-event model: leaders may relish the opportunity to be seen as heroic rescuers. President Theodore Roosevelt spoke admirably about the individual "in the arena whose face is marred by dust and sweat and blood."[54] Richard Nixon, perhaps more candidly and completely than any other politician, assessed the "exquisite agony" of a politician leading in times of crisis. He did so, fittingly, in a memoir titled *Six Crises*:

> One man may have opportunities that others do not. But what counts is whether the individual used what chances he had. Did he risk all when the stakes were such that he might win or lose all? Did he affirmatively seek the opportunities to use his talents to the upmost in causes that went beyond personal and family situations?[55]

As Nixon and Theodore Roosevelt suggested, the opportunity to forge a reputation as a heroic crisis leader can be difficult but can be intensely rewarding.

Heroism can offer a powerful symbol to a unit in crisis. Although Roosevelt and Nixon, in their own (and different) ways, relished the opportunity to be taken as heroes, perhaps no twentieth-century figure welcomed and molded the symbolic grandeur of heroism forged in crisis more emphatically than France's Charles de Gaulle.

A decorated officer and prisoner of war in World War I, de Gaulle became the self-proclaimed leader of the Free French government-in-exile during World War II. Dispirited by his country's quick surrender to German invaders in 1940 and subsequent collaboration with Nazi occupiers (the so-called Vichy government), de Gaulle moved to London. From there, he encouraged French resistance in radio broadcasts full of

---

[53] Mark Evans, "The Importance of Grace Under Pressure," *Forbes* (March 28, 2012); Doris Kearns Goodwin, *Leadership in Turbulent Times* (New York: Simon & Schuster, 2018).

[54] Theodore Roosevelt, "Citizenship in the Republic; A Speech Delivered at the Sorbonne, Paris, April 23, 1910." www.theodore-roosevelt.com/trsorbonnespeech.html

[55] Richard Nixon, *Six Crises* (New York: Doubleday, 1962), pp. xv–xvi.

promises of eventual liberation.[56] As he did so, he insisted on being taken as the legitimate head of the non-Vichy Free French.

Often finding ways around the wishes of Allied leaders – both Winston Churchill and Franklin Roosevelt viewed his claims and aspirations with suspicion while attempting to minimize his leadership role – de Gaulle engineered a triumphant return to the French capital after D-Day.[57] The Allied military commander, Dwight Eisenhower, proved more empathetic than political leaders, allowing de Gaulle the opportunity to lead a triumphant parade down Paris's Champs-Élysées days after the city's liberation in late August.

Particularly during the traumatic years of Nazi occupation and Vichy collaboration, de Gaulle sought the opportunity to create a "perpetual illusion."[58] That was his term, and it was precisely what he continued to do on that August day as he led a march from the Arc de Triomphe to Notre Dame Cathedral. Active German snipers still operated from Paris buildings, and Communist resistance leaders complained that their own more direct and immediate role in resisting German occupation was being (purposefully) marginalized. And yet, there was de Gaulle, pompously, audaciously, and bravely providing his fellow citizens with "the appearance of a solid, firm, confident, and expanding country."[59] Even his political foes were impressed.

With gunshots ringing "all over the place," according to a contemporaneous BBC account, de Gaulle marched "straight ahead without hesitation, his shoulders flung back, and walked right down the center aisle" of the parade route.[60] Determined to be seen as well as held to be heroic, he arranged for fellow marchers – including those who had remained in France to resist German occupation – to walk several feet behind him. By inserting himself as the hero first of resistance and then of liberation, de Gaulle advanced the cause of "*liberté, égalité, fraternité*," as well as his own prominence.[61]

Who wouldn't welcome the opportunity to be seen as a hero? The act of certification of an individual as a hero involves an inherent grant of social

---

[56] It is doubtful that many in France actually heard his pro-resistance speeches. Information on de Gaulle is largely from Julian Jackson, *De Gaulle* (Cambridge, MA: Belknap Press, 2018).

[57] June 6, 1944, the day of the Allied landing in France.

[58] Quoted in Adam Gopnik, "How Charles de Gaulle Rescued France," *New Yorker* (August 20, 2018).

[59] Ibid.

[60] BBC account quoted in Charles Wertenbaker, "Paris Is Free. Merci! Merci! Merci!" *Time* (September 4, 1944).

[61] De Gaulle was, at best, an uneasy ally of Republicanism, even in its most conservative form. He remained a general, not at home with the necessary give-and-take of Republican-styled governance. See Jackson, *De Gaulle*.

prestige.[62] When the designation of hero is bestowed on an individual already in a position of hierarchical power, the status of that individual is further enhanced. But while being seen as a hero comes with its benefits – power, prestige, rewards – the process of anointing leaders as crisis heroes poses a risk to their units.

The Hero Trap

We *think* we want our leaders to "save us" in tough times, to rise to the occasion and master the skills so we can emerge stronger and better. That's natural, even basic. There may well be a primal drive to identify a hero / savior.[63]

Still, there are more than a few downsides to that desire for forged-in-crisis leaders to save the day. Buying into grand expectations about what it means to be a hero has been linked to narcissistic attitudes and behaviors by leaders, risky decision making, the emergence of cult-like cultures where basic freedoms of thought and expression are stifled, and to individuals who are dangerously out of touch with the daily realities of life.[64,65]

Once the leader is designated as the savior of the unit in crisis, dissenting voices are problematized, depicted as obstacles to be overcome rather than perspectives to be considered. The very act of overcoming such contrary opinions provides further evidence of a heroic journey by the leader. Look at the opposition they had to face down to be successful. The opportunity to learn from dissent or of incorporating any opinion other than the crisis leaders is diminished. The act of infusing leaders with heroic qualities during a crisis may be "seductive" and "enticing," but those very characteristics raise the danger of increasing dependency and passivity.[66]

The crisis-as-claim model scuttles all talk of crisis leaders as heroes. Instead of separating the heroes from the scamps, the effective from the ineffective, the crisis-as-claim model positions leaders as claims makers and invites analysis on how that role is played out.

---

[62] William Goode, *The Celebration of Heroes: Prestige as a Social Control System* (Berkeley: University of California Press, 1978).

[63] Sigmund Freud, *Group Psychology and the Analysis of the Ego* (New York: Liveright Publishing, 1921 / 1967).

[64] Jackie Ford et al., *Leadership as Identity: Constructions and Deconstructions* (London: Palgrave, 2008).

[65] Michael Honey, *To the Promised Land: Martin Luther King and the Fight for Economic Justice* (New York: Norton, 2018).

[66] Deborah Frieze and Margaret Wheatley, "It's Time for the Heroes to Go Home," *Leader to Leader* 62 (2011), 28.

Leaders as Claims Makers

Whether a leader is attempting to overturn Jim Crow segregation in Birmingham, oversee a financial turnaround, or seize control of a ship on the high seas, the act of claiming urgency follows a particular pattern. Rather than asking what it is that separates effective crisis leaders from ineffective ones, those who pass the forged-in-crisis test from those who flunked, we need to ask a different question. What is it that *all* leaders do – regardless of judgments about their ultimate effectiveness – when they claim urgency?

"I Have Not Heard Him Express Anything. Sorry."

Leaders have the power and influence to assert a crisis and to allocate attention and resources to resolving the matter. They have the power either to declare urgency or to decline to do so. The failure to apply the crisis label doesn't make the brute facts go away, but it does ensure that those facts will not be treated with urgency.

Let's look at how a US president responded to an emergent health pandemic, even after becoming aware of it, with what might charitably be called a lack of urgency. In this case, with brute facts available to him and everyone else, and with the full resources of the federal government at his command, the president's failure to claim urgency had real conse-quences. It cost lives.

Friday, October 15, 1982, proved to be a moment of historical import in the White House pressroom. It was at that day's press conference that a reporter posed, for the first time ever, a question about AIDS (Acquired Immune Deficiency Syndrome). San Francisco–based jour-nalist Lester Kinsolving asked: "Larry," he said, addressing Larry Speakes, President Ronald Reagan's deputy press secretary, "does the president have any reaction to the announcement by the Center for Disease Control [CDC] in Atlanta that AIDS is now an epidemic in over 600 cases?"[67]

The first case of AIDS was diagnosed in the United States the previous year.[68] There is no reason to believe that Reagan was aware of that 1981 diagnoses. Nonetheless, he certainly knew about the spreading disease and its deadly impact long before he responded with the President's

---

[67] Quotes from Scott Calonico, "When AIDS Was Funny," *Vanity Fair* (2015). At the time, AIDS was pronounced by spelling it out – A-I-D-S – rather than as a single word.

[68] For a history of the early years of the AIDS pandemic, see Lawrence Gostin, *The AIDS Pandemic: Complacency, Injustice, and Unfulfilled Expectations* (Chapel Hill: University of North Carolina Press, 2004).

Commission on the HIV Epidemic in 1987. A family friend, actor Rock Hudson, suffered from and died of AIDS, communicating about his disease directly with First Lady Nancy Reagan. Newspaper reports, congressional hearings, and the federal government's own CDC had issued multiple reports on the disease and its fatal consequences. By 1985, the year of Rock Hudson's well-publicized death, the federal budget included funding for AIDS research.

Despite all that, the White House declined to treat the AIDS pandemic as a crisis, framing it not as an urgent situation but as a laughing (or perhaps a better term is "snickering") matter. That approach has been captured on videotape and compiled in Scott Calonico's 2015 documentary, *When AIDS Was Funny*.

At the point of the 1982 press conference when AIDS was first broached, the disease was associated almost entirely with two stigmatized communities: gay men and intravenous drug users.[69] It was the homosexual connection that elicited that day's snickering. In his question, Lester Kinsolving referenced a four-month-old CDC "Morbidity and Mortality Weekly Report" that drew attention to what seemed to be a rare lung infection spreading among previously healthy males. There had already been stories in the popular press of a "rare and often rapidly fatal form of cancer" among gay men.[70] After the CDC's report, doctors flooded the agency with information on additional cases. The CDC would soon estimate that perhaps tens of thousands of gay men had already been infected. The first AIDS clinic was still three months away from opening when Kinsolving raised the matter at the press conference.

Here is how the exchange unfolded between Kinsolving and Press Secretary Larry Speakes concerning the president's reaction:

SPEAKES: AIDS? I haven't got anything.
KINSOLVING: Over one-third of them have died. It's known as "gay plague."
             [Press pool laughter]. No, it is – it's a pretty serious thing. One in
             every three people that get this have died, and I wondered if the
             president was aware of this?
SPEAKES: I don't have it [presumably referring to the disease]. Are you
             [press pool laughter], do you?
KINSOLVING: You don't have it? Well, I'm relieved to hear that, Larry.
SPEAKES: Do you?
KINSOLVING: No, I don't.

---

[69] When eighteen-year-old Ryan White died of an AIDS-related respiratory infection in 1990 – he contracted the disease through a blood transfusion – public awareness of the broader dimensions of the disease's impact increased considerably.

[70] Lawrence Altman, "Rare Cancer Seen in 41 Homosexuals," *New York Times* (July 3, 1981).

SPEAKES:	You didn't answer my question. How do you know?
KINSOLVING:	Does the president, in other words, the White House look on this as a great joke?
SPEAKES:	No, I don't know anything about it, Lester.
KINSOLVING:	Does the president, does anybody in the White House know about this epidemic, Larry?
SPEAKES:	I don't think so, I don't think there's been any ...
KINSOLVING:	Nobody knows?
SPEAKES:	There's been no personal experience here, Lester.
KINSOLVING:	No, I mean, I thought you were keeping ...
SPEAKES:	Doctor ... I checked thoroughly with Dr. Ruge [physician to the president] this morning and he said no. [Press pool laughter] No patient suffered from AIDS, or whatever it is.
KINSOLVING:	The president doesn't have gay plague? Is that what you're saying, or what?
SPEAKES:	No, didn't say that.
KINSOLVING:	Didn't say that?
SPEAKES:	I thought I heard you in the State Department over there? Why didn't you stay over there? [Press pool laughter].
KINSOLVING:	Because I love you, Larry.
SPEAKES:	Oh, I see ... well, I don't. ... Let's don't put it in those terms, Lester.
KINSOLVING:	I retract that.
SPEAKES:	I hope so.

Much transpired following that exchange to make clear the seriousness of AIDS. The Gay Men's Health Crisis Center – perhaps the first to affix the term "crisis" to the disease – opened in New York City. Henry Waxman, chair of the House Subcommittee on Health and the Environment convened a congressional hearing on "gay cancer." An additional CDC report highlighted the transmission of the disease largely within the gay community through both sexual activity and exposure to blood. Congress allocated $12 million – not a large sum but a token recognition of the problem – for research.

By the time of this next exchange between Kinsolving and Speakes about AIDS, taking place two years after the first question, an estimated 4,200 people had died from the disease. The snickering, however, continued:

SPEAKES:	Lester is beginning to circle now. He's moving up front. Go ahead.
KINSOLVING:	Since the Centers for Disease Control in Atlanta report is going to ... [Press pool laughter.]
SPEAKES:	This is going to be an AIDS question.
KINSOLVING:	... that an estimated ...
SPEAKES:	You were close.

KINSOLVING: Can I ask the question, Larry? That an estimated 300,000 people have been exposed to AIDS, which can be transmitted through saliva.[71] Will the president, as commander-in-chief, take steps to protect armed forces, food, and medical services from AIDS patients or those who run the risk of spreading AIDS in the same manner that they ban typhoid fever people from being involved in the health or food services? [Continuous laughter].

SPEAKES: I don't know.

KINSOLVING: Is the president concerned about this subject, Larry?

SPEAKES: I haven't heard him express concern. [Press pool laughter.]

KINSOLVING: That seems to have evoked such jocular reaction here. [More laughter]. No, but I mean, is he going to do anything, Larry?

SPEAKES: Lester, I have not heard him express anything. Sorry.

KINSOLVING: You mean he has expressed no opinion about this epidemic?

SPEAKES: No, but I must confess I haven't asked him about it.

KINSOLVING: Will you ask him, Larry?

SPEAKES: Have *you* been checked? [Press pool laughter.]

UNIDENTIED: Is the president going to ban mouth-to-mouth kissing?

KINSOLVING: What? Pardon? I didn't hear your answer.

SPEAKES: [Laughs.] Ah, it's hard work. I don't get paid enough. Um. Is there anything else we need to do here?

Speakes's admission that he had not heard Reagan "express concern" was reinforced by the president's ongoing silence. Reagan would, in fact, make no public response to AIDS until 1987 when he created the Presidential Commission.[72] That delay, suggested Dennis Altman, helped "prevent a full-scale national response to AIDS and made it that much easier to see AIDS as the concern of a particular pressure group rather than a health crisis."[73] People died.

The objective realities of a situation – the spread of a virulent disease, the sharing of user data with outside agencies, and so on – often unfold over time, sometimes, an unconscionably long time. They simmer below the surface unless and until someone in a position of authority, with access to resources, declares a crisis. The first step of leaders as claims makers then is to determine if the unit faces an urgent situation. The next step, once leaders decide to proclaim a crisis, is to explain the meaning of

---

[71] This was not true.

[72] Even then, there were delays in staffing the Commission. James Watkins, appointed as commission chair, recounted a story in which, after being asked to serve, he told Reagan's chief of staff, "I'm a sailor and a submariner, and I know nothing about medicine." The chief of staff responded, "You're exactly who we're looking for." See T. Reed Shapiro, "James D. Watkins, Who Led Reagan's Commission on AIDS in the 1980s, Dies at 85." *Washington Post* (July 27, 2012).

[73] Dennis Altman, *AIDS in the Mind of America: The Social, Political, and Psychological Impact of a New Epidemic* (New York: Anchor Books, 1987), p. 178.

that crisis to others. This is an activity that has been called "framing" or "sense making."[74]

"Americans Have Known Wars"

Frame making and sense making are not precisely the same constructs. Gary Klein and colleagues define sense making as "a motivated, continuous effort to understand connections (which can be among people, places and events) in order to anticipate their trajectories and act effectively."[75] Erving Goffman analyzed the process of frame construction in an essay on the organization of experience, positing frames as a structure for determining meaning, for including or excluding interpretations, and for directing an appropriate response.[76] John Kolko added that frame making involves "an *active* perspective that both describes and perceptually changes a given situation."[77] The accent on the word "active" is mine, emphasizing a leader actively applying a perspective intended to reshape people's understanding.

Gail Fairhurst and Robert Sarr wrote about the task of leaders to manage meaning: "We must make sense of a situation before we can know how to respond."[78] Once an event has been called a crisis, there is a need to attach additional meaning. Given the ubiquitous ambiguity and uncertainty of a dynamic world, there is typically "considerable maneuverability with respect to 'the facts.'" How will the "brute facts" of the world be represented? Which will be included and excluded? When leaders manage meaning, they assert that their "interpretations should be taken as real over other possible interpretations."[79] And leaders will always have options in how they frame that meaning. Let's return to the 9/11 attacks, the defining traumatic event of the early twenty-first century in the United States, to understand the power and importance of framing.

---

[74] Frame making and leadership have been explored by, for example, Gail Fairhurst and sense making and leadership by, for example, Karl Weick. See Fairhurst, "Leadership and the Power of Framing," *Leader to Leader* 61 (2011), 43–47; Weick, *Sensemaking in Organizations*.

[75] Gary Klein et al., "Making Sense of Sensemaking 1: Alternative Perspectives," *IEEE Intelligent Systems* 21 (2006), 71.

[76] Erving Goffman, *Frame Analysis: An Essay on the Organization of Experience* (New York: Harper & Row, 1974).

[77] Jon Kolko, "Sensemaking and Framing: A Theoretical Reflection on Perspective in Design Synthesis," a paper presented at the Design Research Society Conference (2010).

[78] Gail Fairhurst and Robert Sarr, *The Art of Framing: Managing the Language of Leadership* (San Francisco: Jossey-Bass, 1996), p. 2.

[79] Ibid., 3–4.

By the time of George W. Bush's first public statement on the evening of September 11, 2001, everyone knew that hijacked airplanes had been deliberately crashed into the World Trade Center twin towers and the Pentagon. Although the number of deaths was not yet precisely known (2,700 people died as the towers collapsed, 184 perished in the Pentagon attack, and 40 more were killed in the plane crash in Pennsylvania), it was clear that this was the largest loss of life on American soil since Pearl Harbor.

But what did it *mean*? Bush searched for a frame. Perhaps the attack could be represented as mass murder, presented as a monstrous criminal act. Perhaps something else. On the night of 9/11, Bush leaned toward criminality: "These acts of mass murder were intended to frighten our nation into chaos and retreat." The notion of "mass murder" references crime, albeit on a large scale, while evoking the possibility of a police response, seeking to capture and punish all responsible parties. It is *not* a declaration of war. The final words of that night's speech – "we stand together to win the war on terrorism" – suggested some uncertainty as to what the nature of the frame that Bush and the federal government would adopt: law enforcement or war.

Nine days later, as Bush stood before the joint houses of Congress, all ambiguity vanished. He unequivocally framed the situation as *war*. "On September 11," the president asserted, "enemies of freedom committed an act of war against our country."[80] With an implicit reference to Pearl Harbor – "Americans have known wars ... Americans have known surprise attacks" – Bush framed the events as an "act of war" rather than of mass murder.

Did Bush have a choice? Of course he did. The response of Bush's predecessor, Bill Clinton, to an earlier attack on the same World Trade Center towers illustrates an alternative path. The February 1993 detonation of a 606-kg urea-nitrate-hydrogen gas explosive mixture in the World Trade Center garage was intended to send one tower crashing into the other. That did not happen. Nonetheless, six people were killed, and more than a thousand injured.[81]

The attack was a "tragedy" that had cost "a number of people" their lives, Clinton noted. In a response attached to the opening of a radio address "on our economic program," Clinton promised to deploy "the full measure of federal law enforcement resources," specifically mentioning

---

[80] George Bush, *Address to Joint Session of Congress Following 9/11 Attacks* (September 20, 2001).

[81] Lawrence Wright, *The Looming Tower: Al-Qaeda and the Road to 9/11* (New York: Knopf, 2006).

the FBI and the Treasury Department.[82] No military was involved, no joint sessions of Congress convened, no references made to Pearl Harbor, no soundings of war were invoked, and no response suggested beyond law enforcement. Clinton's remarks were not even televised. Given the scope of the 9/11 attack, Bush needed to do more. But how he framed his response: *that* was his choice.

We can and should debate the consequences of these two choices. We know that in the aftermath of Bush's declaration, more than 6,800 Americans died in the subsequent Afghanistan and Iraq wars that followed in the wake of his militaristic framework.[83] About 104,000 Afghans, 31,000 of them civilians, were killed, as were 260,000 Iraqis.[84] We also know that no massive terrorist attack occurred in the United States since Bush's response. The same cannot be said about Clinton's. Both framings rested on legitimate claims – accurate and plausible – even though they were significantly different, and open to hearty debate as to which was "right" and "wrong."[85]

When a leader frames a crisis in one way, the consequences will follow in the same frame. A law enforcement frame creates an expectation of arrests, criminal trials, and prison time. A war frame demands a military response. Indeed, the response that unfolded within Bush's war frame was militaristic and included prolonged conflicts in both Afghanistan and Iraq.[86]

Even considering the vastly different scope of the two attacks, both Clinton and Bush had a choice of frame. Mark Zuckerberg made a choice as well. *All* leaders make a choice about how to frame their claim of urgency. It is the act of framing *by* the leader that provides the language of the crisis.

Leaders determine meaning, character, and significance by selecting a framework. When leaders communicate that frame to others, they assert that their "interpretations should be taken as real over other possible interpretations."[87] The verb "assert" in the previous sentence deserves special attention. Framing is for everyone, Fairhurst and Sarr insist. That may be. But when it comes to making assertions that matter, not every

---

[82] William Clinton, "Clinton on the 1993 World Trade Center Bombing," *History.com* (1993).
[83] Casualty figures from Department of Defense Casualty Report (2017, June 12). www .defense.gov/casualty.pdf
[84] http://watson.brown.edu/costsofwar; www.iraqbodycount.org
[85] For a flavor of this debate, see Phillip Gordon, "Can the War on Terror Be Won?" *Brookings* (November 1, 2007), and Zachary Laub, "Debating the Legality of the Post-9/11 'Forever War,'" *Foreign Affairs.com* (September 1, 2016).
[86] Can the war in Iraq be conflated with the war on terror launched after 9/11? President Bush certainly thought so, referring to Iraq as a "central front" in the war on terrorism. See Daniel Byman, "Iraq and the Global War on Terrorism," *Brookings* (July 1, 2007).
[87] Fairhurst and Sarr, *Art of Framing*, 3.

claims maker is equal. Leaders retain hierarchical power to transform their frames into the defining "truth" of the prevailing crisis narrative. Much of that power derives from their capacity to define the parameters of the crisis "event."

"Begin at the Beginning"

"Where shall I begin, please, your Majesty?" the White Rabbit asks the King of Hearts in *Alice's Adventures in Wonderland*. "Begin at the beginning," the King sagely orders, "and go on till you come to the end. Then stop." Would that it was so easy, so obvious. Lewis Carroll knew better, as should we.

As claims maker, the leader determines what constitutes the "event" that has presented the threat. We saw in Chapter 7 how framing the crisis that unfolded in the aftermath of the flooding of New Orleans shifted dramatically based on how the parameters of the crisis event were framed. As a narrative initiated by the flooding, New Orleans and its citizens (and local government) were victimized by an act of nature combined with a number of "bad apples," ranging from corrupt and poorly trained police officers to top government officials (the head of FEMA and perhaps even the president). A long-term historical view implicates larger socioeconomic issues and implicates some of those same officials – most prominently, the city's mayor – in earlier decisions that made a tragedy nearly inevitable.

In identifying a crisis event, the leader as claims maker makes a choice that involves constructing a timeline, most particularly, identifying the initiating event said to constitute the "beginning"? That is the prerogative of the claims maker as narrator-in-chief.[88] Mark Zuckerberg apologized for an event that was kicked off by a rogue university researcher sharing data with a shady consulting firm. That choice made some sense. It focused on the main dynamic that attracted press attention: the use of personal data in a political campaign without user knowledge. But like all crisis narratives, it was one that could be told differently. Zuckerberg's timetable excluded early decisions that made data sharing not the act of an outside bad player but a core strategy of the company.

Taking a crisis to be an event requires human construction, even manipulation, of the narrative. Is the event sudden or long simmering, internal or external, human or naturally caused? These distinctions that attract so much interest and study in the crisis-as-event model become nonsensical in the crisis-as-claim model. Was the disaster in New Orleans

---

[88] Paul Ricoeur, *Time and Narrative* (Chicago: University of Chicago Press, 1984).

after the hurricane the result of an act of nature or a string of human decisions played out over decades? Within the crisis-as-claim model, the only possible answer to those questions is this: it depends on who's telling the story. The crisis "event" is nothing more or less than a story, a narrative that is always the result of interpretation. It is the storyteller, the White Rabbit rather than the King of Hearts, who gets to determine where the beginning is.

A "Reprehensible Outcome"

When it comes to declaring a crisis, leaders include an assessment of responsibility. What and who are responsible for this particular crisis? Where will they point the finger? Zuckerberg attempted an uncomfortable balancing act: pointing the blame finger at external bad actors while insisting that Facebook would improve. Deciding where to point the finger of responsibility is a choice that leaders make when they declare a crisis.

Blame is fundamentally a judgment or evaluation that assigns either causal or explanatory responsibility to some person, group, or force. When blame is aimed at people, it amounts to an accusation targeting the responsible agent.[89] In the immediate aftermath of Union Carbide's horrific 1984 chemical leak at its Bhopal plant, corporate executives in Houston blamed the management at the Indian subsidiary as well as local regulators. Perhaps it had been "sabotage," executives immediately suggested. In any event, the American corporation "owned just 51 percent" of the Indian subsidiary and had delegated oversight to local management. An identical facility in the United States had been run effectively and safely, so don't blame *us*.[90]

For a rather dramatic contrast, we should consider the case of Starbucks' CEO Kevin Johnson who learned of an incident kicked off with the following phone message: "I have two gentlemen in my cafe that are refusing to make a purchase or leave. I am at the Starbucks at 18th and

---

[89] Bertram Malle et al., "A Theory of Blame," *Psychological Inquiry* 25 (2014), 147–186.

[90] Richard Ice, "Corporate Publics and Rhetorical Strategies: The Case of Union Carbide's Bhopal Crisis," *Management Communication Quarterly* 4 (1991), 341–362 and Douglas Martin, "Warren Anderson, 92, Dies; Faced India Plant Disaster," *New York Times* (October 30, 2014). The "owned just 51 percent" statement is a meaningless denial. As a subsidiary (in which the parent corporation holds a majority interest), Union Carbide India was under corporate control. The subsidiary structure shields the parent from most legal liability (even when ownership is 100 percent). The parent corporation did eventually pay the Indian government $470 million. Union Carbide's CEO Warren Anderson visited Bhopal immediately after the leak. He was arrested by local authorities, posted bail, and then left the country for good. The Indian courts referred to him as a fugitive and an "absconder."

Spruce." Those words, spoken by an employee for a Philadelphia Starbucks to a police dispatcher in the late Thursday afternoon of April 12, 2018, sparked turmoil for both the local café and the national chain. It would be up to Johnson to figure out what had happened.

A *USA Today* reporter related the immediate story of that call:

At the Starbucks store that afternoon, the two men explained they were waiting for a friend. One had asked for access to a restroom and was denied because he hadn't bought anything. The manager then called police even though Starbucks, with its comfy chairs and usually ample electric outlets for computers, has never shunned being a community meeting spot.[91]

Starbucks' founder Howard Schultz had long boasted that his stores offered a "third place" – besides home and office – to sit, meet, and enjoy coffee.[92] It was hoped, of course, that customers would also order coffee, but that did not seem to be a hard-and-fast expectation. In this particular case, however, the two men were black; the employee was white.[93] When the police arrived, the men said they were sitting in the shop waiting for a colleague. They were arrested anyway and held until the early hours of the morning. Customers videoed the incident and released the recording on social media.

On the following Saturday, Starbucks corporate public relations department tweeted a short apology. It was, perhaps, less cold than the one made by United's Oscar Munoz (Chapter 3), but still rather terse, starting with, "We apologize to the two individuals and our customers and are disappointed this led to an arrest."[94] The following day, CEO Kevin Johnson labeled the arrest a "reprehensible outcome" and promised to meet "with partners, customers and community leaders as well as law enforcement."[95]

Public relations professionals weighed in, largely commending Johnson for his robust response. Wrote one:

---

[91] Chris Woodyard, "Starbucks' 911 Call That Led to Philadelphia Arrests of Two Black Men," *USA Today* (April 17, 2018).

[92] Schultz is not, strictly, the founder of Starbucks. Rather, he purchased the chain in 1987, rebranded and expanded it, becoming, perhaps I can say, its *re*-founder.

[93] A writer at *The Root* commented on this phenomenon of white people calling the police on black people and having police respond to the complaint. "We are living in very scary times," wrote Monique Judge. "Every little thing black people do is being policed by white people – walking, breathing, talking, swimming, having fun, shopping, driving – everything. We aren't safe in a coffee shop, at the community pool, at work, on vacation, in the park – nowhere." Judge, "Why Do White People Feel Entitled to Police Black People?" *The Root* (October 15, 2018).

[94] https://twitter.com/Starbucks/status/985200942030012416

[95] Justin Joffee, "Starbucks' Late Crisis Response Offers PR Pros a Lesson in Social Listening," *PR News* (April 15, 2018).

Johnson was accountable, involving himself in the dialogue and conversations about unconscious bias and policy reform at Starbucks. Earlier today it was reported Johnson already was in Philadelphia and the manager and the company agreed to part ways. It wasn't too little, but time will tell if it was too late.[96]

Later in the week, Johnson announced that all of the chain's US stores would be closed for a single afternoon in May for a "training program designed to address implicit bias, promote conscious inclusion, prevent discrimination, and ensure everyone inside a Starbucks store feels safe and welcome."[97] In doing so, he passed another test for the crisis professionals: "When dealing with a crisis, it's important not only to acknowledge it and apologize, but also to demonstrate your organization is taking action to rectify the situation and ensure it doesn't occur again."[98]

What moved the experts the most seemed to be Johnson's commitment to active listening. Once the video spread, protesters raced to the store. Johnson met with their leaders, as well as representatives of the community, the police, and employees, including the originator of the call (who was no longer employed by Starbucks a week after the incident, although the exact circumstances of her departure were not disclosed). "I've spent the last few days in Philadelphia with my leadership team listening to the community, learning what we did wrong and the steps we need to take to fix it," Johnson announced.[99]

The pros were impressed. "This move goes far beyond the playbook" of what a normal crisis response would be, noted the president of one crisis management firm.[100] If Starbucks could "leverage its reputation for social listening to function as an active conduit for meaningful discussions about race, class and 'otherness' in modern society, then the brand can also position itself as the catalyst for conversations about corporate America that many believe are long overdue."[101] All leaders, once they have

---

[96] Ibid.

[97] Starbucks closed all of its stores once before, in 2008, to discuss how to get back to company basics. Another chain, Chipotle, did the same in 2016 to discuss food safety after a widespread outbreak of salmonella, norovirus, and E. coli. Like Starbucks, virtually all Chipotle stores in the United States are company owned. It would be very difficult to pull off such a massive store closing if the outlets were franchised.

[98] Hayley Jennings, "Starbucks Doubles Down on Its Philly Incident Apology," *PR News* (April 18, 2018).

[99] Rachael Abrams et al., "Starbucks's Tall Order: Tackle Systemic Racism in 4 Hours," *New York Times* (May 29, 2018).

[100] Ibid.

[101] Joffee, "Starbucks' Late Crisis Response Offers PR Pros a Lesson in Social Listening."

identified an urgent situation and attached meaning to that situation, will determine how their units should respond.

"We Are Sorry"

In the crisis-as-event model, leaders are expected to make a public accounting of incidents caused by the actions of the business that had a broader, negative impact. These accountings typically come in the form of apologies.[102] "Before we start or as we start," Wells Fargo CEO Jim Stumpf told a TV interviewer as he introduced his apology, "I want to tell you, your audience and our customers that we are sorry." Defensive discourses "are persuasive attempts to reshape the audience's attitudes."[103] That discourse can come in a wide range of postures, moving from denial (Johnson & Johnson assuring customers in 1982 that it wasn't the company that had laced Tylenol tablets with potassium cyanide) to minimization (Exxon insisting that its massive 1989 oil spill had not killed many animals) to mortification (Starbucks CEO calling the arrest of a customer a "reprehensible outcome").[104]

The crisis-as-event model holds defensive discourse from leaders in a particular regard. Disclaimers are positioned as post-event add-ons. From the crisis-as-claim model, on the other hand, disclaimers need to be considered as organic to the narrative being offered by the claims maker.

In his "Letter from a Birmingham Jail," Martin Luther King explicitly and defiantly declined to apologize for stirring up tension in the segregated city. "My citing the creation of tension as part of the work of the nonviolent resister may sound rather shocking," he informed the local clergy, "But I must confess that I am not afraid of the word 'tension.' I have earnestly opposed violent tension, but there is a type of constructive, nonviolent tension which is necessary for growth." In his alternative narrative, it was only the defenders of the status quo who should be apologetic.

We can now see how apology is used as a devise for advancing a particular narrative. Even as executives at Tokyo Electric Power

---

[102] Owen Hargie and colleagues conducted a discursive analysis of the public apologies offered by UK bankers in the wake of the financial industry collapse. See Hargie et al., "Interpretations of CEO Public Apologies for the Banking Crisis: Attributions of Blame and Avoidance of Responsibility," *Organization* 17 (2010), 721–742.

[103] Benoit, *Accounts, Excuses, and Apologies*, 3.

[104] William Benoit and Anne Czerwinski, "A Critical Analysis of USAir's Repair Discourse," *Communication Quarterly* 60 (1997), 38–57. The Starbucks example is not from the article.

"sincerely" apologized, they consistently labeled the nuclear meltdown an "accident." The disaster was a force beyond their control. Mark Zuckerberg apologized for not being vigilant enough in protecting Facebook users from external bad actors. For both Tokyo Electric and Power Company and Facebook, apology became part of the blame-shifting narrative.

Claims makers are always spinning a story, and there is always a purpose to the way in which they construct that story. Disclaimers are not responses to crisis events so much as devices meant to advance a particular narrative, presenting rhetorical cues designed to tell the audience how to think about urgent events and the leader's response.

A New Understanding of Crisis Leadership

As should be apparent at this point, the understanding of leadership in times of claimed urgency depends on the governing crisis model. In both models, the leader assumes a central position. But where in the crisis-as-event model, the leader is the first and chief responder *to* a crisis, the leader in the crisis-as-claim model becomes the prime mover *of* the crisis. That's the distinction between leader as dependent variable in the first model and as independent variable in the second.

In the crisis-as-claim model, we seek not heroism. We evaluate the content of the claim and the interests of the claims maker. We never dismiss the possibility that the claim is legitimate, but neither do we

Table 9.1 *Two approaches to leadership*

LEADERSHIP IN CRISIS-AS-EVENT MODEL	LEADERSHIP IN CRISIS-AS-CLAIM MODEL
Leader as responder (dependent variable)	Leader as first mover (independent variable)
Recognize urgency	Assert urgency
Explain the event	Create the event
Take ownership of events (apologize sincerely when appropriate)	Help advance a narrative designed to shape audience response to leaders' actions
Opportunity for heroism but no guarantee Test character	Opportunity for legitimacy but no guarantee Express interests
Still need to manage	Still need to manage

take any claim as innocent of interpretation, construction, and assertions of power. Table 9.1 draws that contrast.

These contrasting images of leadership derive directly from the contrasting crisis models presented in *Constructing Crisis*. In my concluding chapter, I return to the question evoked in Chapter 1: why is it important to consider an alternative model in the first place? In other words, why should anyone care?

10 So What?

Constructing Crisis was conceived and executed under the assumption that ideas have consequences, that how we think helps shape how we act. The goal throughout has been to prompt a rethinking of the notion of crisis, with particular focus on the relationship between leaders and their claims of urgency.

Whether as members of a group, employees of an organization, or citizens of a country, we face numerous and varied claims on our attention by leaders. Focus on this, we are urged. Ignore that. *Constructing Crisis* advocates for a deliberative, critical response to all such claims. Crises are not things to be managed; they are claims to be appraised thoughtfully and critically.

Given the deluge of crisis claims with which we are greeted virtually daily – business crises, constitutional crises, natural crises, humanitarian crises, environmental crises, and crises in legitimacy, in democracy, and even in civilization – it is useful to get the concept right. And there is something else adding weight to the importance of appreciating just what it means when our leaders claim urgency. If people believe those claims and accept that their units face an urgent situation, they respond in predictable ways: predictable and potentially worrying ways. So do their leaders. "The 'crisis situation' allows for the bypassing of the usual protocols of democratic control, decision-making, or public debate," observed Stijn De Cauwer.[1] That should serve as both an observation and a warning.

Getting the concept of crisis right, in other words, is important. It matters. *Constructing Crisis* suggests that we often get the concept wrong. Let's look at how the CEO of General Motors constructed a crisis claim, and then analyze how the two models – crisis-as-event and crisis-as-claim – will understand that claim differently.

---

[1] Stijn De Cauwer, "Introduction: Resistance in Times of Crisis," in *Critical Theory at a Crossroads: Conversations on Resistance in Times of Crisis* (New York: Columbia University Press, 2018), p. xv.

"Not Just Another Business Crisis"

"The daughter of a retired blue-collar GM veteran and herself a one-time 'factory rat' who started working at a GM plant as a student," Mary Barra had spent her life with General Motors (GM).[2] Her remarkable ascension included managing the Detroit/Hamtramck assembly plant, serving as vice president of global manufacturing engineering, vice president of global human resources, and executive vice president of global product development. That career culminated in her appointment as CEO in January 2014, a promotion that came at a propitious moment for GM.

The global recession of 2008 forced GM to prune its broad brand offerings (shuttering Pontiac, discontinuing Cobalt and Saturn, and selling off Opal and Vauxhall, for example), declare bankruptcy, and accept a $500 billion bailout from the federal government. The CEO who led GM to bankruptcy, Rick Wagoner, was "asked" by the Obama administration to step down.

But it was less GM's roller coaster financial performance than an uncorrected and long-standing safety problem – faulty ignition switches linked to 124 deaths, 17 serious and 258 less-serious injuries – that attracted Barra's attention when she stood before employees five months after her appointment and declared a crisis.[3] The problem, the installation of a fatally flawed ignition switch within millions of GM cars, had not erupted suddenly. Rather it was a situation that unfolded over nearly twelve years. By 2014 Barra had no choice but to address the issue. *How* she addressed it was a matter of choice. It always is.

This was what might be referred to as a long-simmering crisis. Delphi Systems, an independent supplier, sold the part to GM starting in 2002. GM engineers approved the installation of the Delphi ignition switch in several car models. They made that decision in full awareness that the switch was "far below GM's own specifications."[4] That conclusion came

---

[2] Paul Eisenstein, "From Factory Floor to Corner Office, Mary Barra Is a Rule Breaker," *NBCNews.com* (August 4, 2017).

[3] Those numbers represent the compensation claims that GM settled, which were less than 10 percent of the total claims filed. A report in the *Detroit News* concluded, "Because accident investigators, for a decade, didn't know of the flaw and may have attributed wrecks to other factors, it's impossible to say how many accidents, deaths and injuries were truly the result of the bad part." Furthermore, the burden of proof was placed on the claimants. Therefore, if anything, these numbers represented an underestimation of the human cost of GM's decisions. See David Shepardson, "GM Compensation Fund Completes Review with 124 Deaths," *Detroit News* (August 24, 2015).

[4] Anton Valukas, *Report to Board of Directors of General Motors Company regarding Ignition Switch Recalls* (May 29, 2014), 1.

from an internal probe conducted by an outside attorney, Anton Valukas.[5]

True, the switch was not made in house. However, the decision to install the part with full awareness that it was designed poorly was internal. The switch's flaw arose from a combination of two factors: a metal plunger designed to activate the starter and the level of compression engineered into the internal spring that governed the plunger. Those two details interacted in such a way that, if jostled, the driver's key could accidently turn off the engine while moving, an event labeled, rather innocuously considering the resulting fatalities, as a "moving stall."

Between the plunger and the spring, the force needed to turn the engine off was dangerously low. A bump of the driver's knee against the ignition switch, or even the key chain – the kind of bump that might occur, say, when the car was swerving to avoid an accident and the driver was tossed about – could shut off the engine. Power steering would be lost.

The decision to install that faulty switch was not a misunderstanding or an oversight. It was an action taken by GM engineers knowingly, in the hope that a moving stall would occur rarely, and that the defect would quickly be corrected. The engineer responsible for that decision would, years later, explained, "I did what I was supposed to do."[6]

Yet another design choice needs to be added to the mix before we can appreciate the full impact of that moving stall danger. Automobile airbags are designed to be turned off when the car is not running. By itself, that design feature makes sense. Airbag deployment carries its own risks to drivers and front-seat passengers. The calculation is this. If you are rammed while sitting in a parked car, it will be less risky if the airbag does not deploy. The chance of injury is higher from airbag deployment than from the impact of a sitting collision. Fair enough. The decision had a broader, more deadly implication, however. Under conditions of a highway accident in which the driver might be tossed about, the airbags meant to protect driver and passengers would fail to deploy if the engine shut down. By design.

Was that danger the unintended consequence of two independent sets of decisions? Or were the two groups of decision makers – those who decided to install the faulty switch and those who installed airbags designed to not deploy when the engine was turned off – fully aware of the deadly synergy? The internal report remained ambiguous on that point.

[5] Mary Barra, "Extremely Thorough, Brutal, Tough and Deeply Troubling," *Vital Speeches of the Day* 80 (2014), 287.
[6] Quoted in Bill Vlasic, "A Fatally Flawed Switch, and a Burdened GM Engineer," *New York Times* (November 13, 2014).

At best, GM personnel failed to understand how their cars were built. Employees who installed the switch may have seen their decision as causing inconvenience to drivers only under rare circumstances rather than as a potentially fatal safety threat. They may have simply been doing what they were "supposed to do." Even so, people were going to die.

This problem of accidental shutdowns was not a secret. Customers, dealers, the press, state agencies, and employees knew that the ignition switch led to moving stalls.[7] As early as 2006, GM issued a technical service bulletin to dealers warning of the tendency for ignition switches on six models to suddenly and unexpectedly turn off. A "heavy key chain hanging from the ignition," the bulletin informed dealers, could trigger the moving stall. The solution was relatively simple: tell customers to remove "unessential items from their key chain."[8] There was no a proclamation of a crisis, no claim of urgency. The bulletin shifted the "blame" for the problem, as well as responsibility for its solution, from the company to the driver. Stop adorning your key chains with charms and trinkets!

That directive was, at the very least, misleading. GM engineers fully understood that the source of the problem lay in the inner working of the Delphi-supplied switch, not with key chains and dangling trinkets. We know that because, in 2006, GM corrected that problem. From then on, bumping the key would not lead to a moving stall. However, customers driving cars with the uncorrected ignition switch – and there were millions – were *not* notified. No recall occurred. Still no declaration of crisis was issued. Resulting injuries, including fatalities, mounted.

One phrase that recurred throughout the Valukas report refers to the lack of any "sense of urgency" in GM's response.[9] "Throughout the entire odyssey, there was no demonstrated sense of urgency, right to the very end," the report noted, "Everyone had responsibility to fix the problem, [but] nobody took responsibility."[10] GM's recall committee, charged with issuing product recalls, deferred decisions to gather "yet more information." The problem was not considered urgent enough to be raised to "the highest levels of the company."[11] No claims of urgency from leadership, no urgent response from within the company, no crisis.

Mary Barra, then executive vice president for global product development, purchasing, and supply chain, heard about the safety concerns only

---

[7] Matthew Wald, "GM Report Illustrates Managers' Disconnect," *New York Times* (June 8, 2014).

[8] Christopher Jensen, "GM Recalls Some Cars, but Not All with Ignition Switch Problem," *New York Times* (February 20, 2014).

[9] Valukas, *Report to Board of Directors*, 3.   [10] Ibid., 2.

[11] Ibid., 4. This finding supports the report's contention, and Mary Barra's insistence, that top executives were kept in the dark concerning this long-simmering problem.

in December 2013. That's what she said. Her position as head of development, purchasing, and supply chain at that time involved direct oversight of "many of the personnel" involved in the long and long-delayed review process.[12] Yet, her story, supported by the report, was that she was uninformed until the end of 2013.

It was on January 15, 2014, that the GM board promoted Barra to be CEO. On the way home from headquarters in one of the first days of her tenure, she received a call from the executive director of product development providing her with a head's up. "He said he'd just learned we had this problem with the vehicles," Barra recalled, "and that we had to do a recall and that it was large."[13]

A week later, GM notified the National Highway Safety Administration of the faulty ignition switch installed in millions of cars built between 2002 and 2006. Although the company claimed to be aware of six deaths in which airbags failed to deploy, spokespeople insisted that "some" of the fatalities had been due to driver failures: alcohol use, not using seat belts, and high speeds. Now, GM was recalling 619,000 cars spread across two product lines.

That was a fraction of the vehicles assembled with the faulty switch. There were still millions of impacted cars not covered in that initial recall. When asked why only a small portion of the implicated vehicles had been recalled, a company spokesperson provided a non-answer: "GM has devoted significant time and resources to evaluating this issue" and concluded that only these models should be included.[14] Eventually bowing to public pressure, GM extended that recall. "Today's GM is fully committed to learning from the past," said a spokesperson.[15]

By the time Barra addressed GM employees on June 5, nearly six million cars had been recalled (there would be still more in the weeks ahead). The company had been fined $35 million and the internal report had been delivered.[16] The Valukas report had been "extremely thorough, brutally tough, and deeply troubling," Barra told employees that day. It revealed "a pattern of management deficiencies and misjudgments – often based on incomplete data – that were passed off at the time as business as usual." To be sure, "this is not just another business crisis." Rather, the failure to address and correct faulty ignition switches

---

[12] Ibid., 228.
[13] Quoted in Rana Foroohar, "Mary Barra's Bumpy Ride," *Time* (October 6, 2014), 34.
[14] Jensen, "GM Recalls Some Cars, but Not All."
[15] Tom Krisher, "GM Excluded Crash Deaths from Inquiry into Ignition Switches, Company Document [*sic*] Say," *Driving* (March 13, 2014).
[16] Penalties would eventually balloon to $900 million. See Drew Harwell, "Why General Motors' $900 Million Fine for a Deadly Defect Is Just a Slap on the Wrist," *Washington Post* (September 17, 2015).

represented a failure "in our system." GM as a company "didn't do our job. We failed these customers." GM's pride and reputation had been undermined. People had died. Barra added, "I know many of you are saying to yourselves that this problem isn't a fair reflection of the company as a whole. I know it's not. We are better than this."

Barra's crisis leadership, she declared, "would be guided by two principles. First, that we do the right thing for those who are harmed; and second, that we accept responsibility for our mistakes and commit to doing everything within our power to prevent this problem from ever happening again."[17] Mary Barra's response won her kudos from many sides. "Instead of stonewalling the issue (which appears to have been the approach of some of GM's so-called leaders)," wrote a business commentator, "Barra is meeting it head on with large doses of honesty. And she's doing it in front-and-center fashion."[18] Another expert pointed to three characteristics of Barra's response – take ownership, recognize the human angle, and recognize the corporate culture angle – that should be taken as best-practice lessons for all crisis leaders.[19] And *Fortune* named Barra "Crisis Manager of the Year."[20] It was an honor she probably would have gladly done without. Still, it was a recognition that she had performed admirably, at least from within the crisis-as-event model.

Sure, It Matters

For ideas to matter, they must at the very least alter the way in which we understand the world. The crisis-as-event model offers a straightforward understanding of the "more than a business crisis" at GM. There was a real crisis, an objective threat to GM's well-being. The crisis event occurred in 2002 – the installation of a fatally flawed part – and then simmered for more than a decade. Although unacknowledged at the time, that decision posed a threat to General Motors. Over the next twelve years, steps were taken, inadequate steps to be sure, that allowed passengers to continue to drive with the part and, in so doing, risk their lives. More than 100 people died as a result.

When Mary Barra, the hero of this crisis-as-event narrative, ascended to the CEO office, she first learned about the decision and its consequences, and then moved vigorously to take change. Determined to

[17] Ibid.

[18] Geoff Loftus, "Mary Barra's Leadership Legacy," *Fortune* (March 19, 2014).

[19] Mark Athitakis, "Three Lessons from Mary T. Barra's Crisis at GM," *Now Associations* (2014).

[20] Ben Geier, "GM's Mary Barra: Crisis Manager of the Year," *Fortune* (December 28, 2015).

"own" the crisis before it owned her, Barra commissioned an internal investigation, leaving no stone unturned in her search for the truth. Then, facts in hand, she addressed GM employees, and the public, with her blunt assessment: a "pattern of management deficiencies and misjudgments" had created a failure "in our system." That's what made her the "Crisis Manager of the Year."

Barra's claim of urgency – the "more than a business crisis" claim – can be judged as legitimate. Even so, the crisis-as-claim model challenges every assumption about how the crisis-as-event model understands the dynamic by which Barra constructed her claim. Rather than debating if Barra deserves kudos as a hero or vilification as a villain, the crisis-as-claim model challenges the underlying assumptions on which those judgments are embedded. Neither hero nor villain, Barra was a leader operating from a position of power and authority asserting a claim. In that regard, she was like all the previous crisis leaders we have encountered: Nissan's Carlos Ghosn and M&S's Archie Norman no less that Wells Fargo's Jim Stumpf and Border Book's George Jones. She was constructing a claim, wanting to be believed, and expecting to be followed.

Let's consider the GM story from the perspective of the crisis-as-claim model. Now, there is no specific event that should be taken, per se, to be a crisis. There *were* several events: a real ignition switch, the uncontested reality of a decision to install that switch, an interaction between the part and the design of the airbags to shut down when the car was off, and real deaths, 124 at a minimum. There was also a correction of the part along with a decision not to notify drivers of the potential danger. Yet there was no urgency. That was the finding of GM's own report: no urgency until Mary Barra became CEO, commissioned an internal study, and made a statement to employees.

And then there is the whole notion of an "event." What was the crisis event anyway?

Constructing the Event

The very foundation of the crisis-as-event model is the acceptance of an event as an objective reality. The model offers no critical assessment of what an event is, what the concept suggests, and how an understanding of an event is constructed.

For the crisis-as-event model to maintain its positivist posture, it must insist on events as objective clusters of dynamics: prepackaged bundles in possession of objective characteristics that can and should be understood and responded to. And yet, the lumping together and naming of ambiguous, complex dynamics is a human endeavor, not a natural phenomenon. It is a construction of meaning that is imposed on the world. Just as there is no such thing as a crisis, there is no such thing as an event. And because there is no such thing as an event, the structure of the crisis-as-event model is revealed as a flawed edifice that collapses under its own weight.

As claims maker, the leader determines what constitutes the "event" and what is included in any timeline that defines the temporal boundaries of that event. Neither is a natural, objective construction. It is the prerogative of the claims maker as narrator-in-chief of the story of the crisis to determine just what the crisis event is and, by implication, what it is not.[21]

Mary Barra used that power as narrator of GM's crisis story to establish the 2002 installation of the faulty part as the initiating event in her crisis narrative. "Our job is clear: To build high quality, safe vehicles," she told employees. The installation of the part represented a failure: "We didn't do our job."

Now, operating from the crisis-as-claim model, let's reconsider the notion of the crisis event as constructed by GM's leader. Remember how historian Douglas Brinkley started his analysis of New Orleans and Hurricane Katrina by looking back decades before the storm? Or how I examined the privacy crisis at Facebook as stretching back far beyond the manipulation of a university researcher? I can do the same thing with GM's faulty switch crisis. By relocating the initiating event from 2002 to 1960, for example, I present a very different view of the crisis and the company's role.

If I decided to open my narrative of the crisis in 1960, I could point out that it was then that GM introduced its new Chevrolet Corvair with an unusual rear-mounted engine. That design was unsafe from the very beginning. The company knew that, based on internal warnings issued and distributed by its own engineers. "Despite the fact that the Corvair demonstrated itself to be unsafe almost immediately, and despite the fact that a stabilizer bar costing only $15 a car would have provided a solution," wrote Howard Schwartz, "GM did not correct the problem until the release of the 1964 models, by which time numerous lives had been lost."[22]

The Corvair, noted automotive writer Paul Niedermeyer, "was the product of GM's repeated tendencies to go off in directions that were an engineer's dream, but were either flawed from the initial concept, or

---

[21] Ricoeur, *Time and Narrative*.

[22] Howard Schwartz, "Narcissism Project and Organizational Decay: The Case of General Motors," *Business Ethics Quarterly* 1 (1991), 249. Television comedian Ernie Kovacs was killed in a Corvair crash related to its design, as was the son of a GM Cadillac general manager.

diminished by the bean counters. In the case of the Corvair, it was both."[23] Sound familiar: knowingly allowing drivers to operate their cars with a faulty part, delaying correction, and sacrificing lives?

To be sure, GM was hardly unique within the industry for compromising the safety of its passengers in the name of driving down costs. Ford's Pinto model released in the 1970s (and "honored" as the most dangerous car ever made) had a poorly conceived fuel tank design that was linked to fiery deaths in the event of rear-end collisions.[24]

The GM case, however, generated a great amount of publicity when Ralph Nader's best-selling *Unsafe at Any Speed* (1965) criticized the Corvair design as well as management's handling of the safety issue. Then GM attracted special attention when a lawsuit revealed that the company had hired a private detective to dig up dirt on Nader to discredit his work.[25]

This is not who we are, Barra had insisted in 2014. GM is "better than this." Really? Wasn't the promotion of economics over passenger service a deep and abiding part of GM's and the auto industry's history? The answer to that question resides in which story you choose to tell. Did this crisis event really start in 2002 as Barra constructed the event? Why not 1960?

To be clear, *both* are arbitrary, human choices: one Barra's and one mine. That point is fundamental to the crisis-as-claim model. Events do not exist objectively. They come into being only when constructed as events through human authorship. All authors of a claim of urgency make a choice concerning how to define the temporal boundaries of their claimed crisis event. When does it start? When does it end?

It's a purposeful choice. Leaders make that choice to control the narrative and protect interests. Barra's choice served her purposes. She wanted, perhaps needed, to insist that GM was "better than this." My

[23] Paul Niedermeyer, "Automotive History: 1960–1963 Chevrolet Corvair – GM's Deadliest Sin?" *Curbside Classic* (November 30, 2015).

[24] Douglas Birsch and John Fielder, *The Ford Pinto Case: A Study in Applied Ethics, Business, and Technology* (Albany: State University of New York Press, 1994). The "most dangerous car" designation comes from Car Insurance Quotes, "5 of the Most Dangerous Cars Ever Made" (no date). GM's Corvair ranked third.

[25] Jerry Bauich, "GM's Head Apologizes to 'Harassed' Car Critic," *Washington Post* (March 28, 1966). In 2018, Facebook admitted that Chief Operating Officer Sheryl Sandberg had sicced company investigators on billionaire George Soros after Soros delivered a speech at the World Economic Forum attacking Facebook and Google as "menaces" to society. And this was before Facebook hired a private opposition research firm to dig into Soros's finances. See Nicholas Confessore and Matthew Rosenberg, "Sheryl Sandberg Asked for Soros Research, Facebook Acknowledges," *New York Times* (November 29, 2018).

choice of turning the pages back to 1960 was purposeful as well, intended to demonstrate a longer history of flawed decision making.

The "we're better than this" assertion that Barra employed is always a decoy, a deflection by a leader from reality. When Barra made the statement, GM was neither better nor worse than "this." It *was* "this": a company that had spent twelve years allowing people to die, that had knowingly produced and sold an unsafe car in the 1960s, and that had hired a private detective to dig up dirt on a critic.

"We're better than this" is an aspirational representation. It may also be a public relations ploy or a sentimental interpretation. It is never an objective description.[26] But Barra wanted to make it so; to accomplish that, she needed her version of the event to be initiated in 2002 and not 1960.

We've seen that dynamic of selecting an initiating point that helped spin a particular story and worked to reinforce a desired interpretation unfold in the hands of other leaders. Mark Zuckerberg started his crisis narrative with the leakage of user data from a Cambridge University researcher to Cambridge Analytica and then to the 2016 Trump campaign. His narrative was one of a force-beyond-our-control story in which a bad apple had acted corruptly. No need to dig into past strategic decisions that opened up user data to numerous external players. Zuckerberg, like Barra – like any leader making a claim of urgency – was exercising the power inherent in frame making and amplified by narrative construction.

It is precisely the exercise of power inherent in narrative authorship that represents a significant blind spot in the crisis-as-event model. What is a blind spot in one model becomes a core component of the other.

Power as a Component of All Claims

Critique is inherently seditious of accepted wisdom.[27] Through surfacing its subject's uncontested (and often unacknowledged) assumptions, critique clears a path toward a new interpretive effort. One of the core intents of offering a critique of the crisis-as-event model and proposing an alternative is to highlight the insufficient attention paid in traditional crisis

---

[26] GM trotted out the "this is not who we are" trope again in January 2019 in response to reports of rampant racism in a Toledo, Ohio plant. I'm reminded of the famous quote from sports coach Bill Parcels when asked if his team was, in reality, "better" than its current woeful won-loss record suggested. "You are what your record says you are," he insisted. That's a kind of realism missing from all the hollow "we're better than this" proclamations. GM statement quoted in Mallory Simon and Sara Sidner, "GM Responds to Backlash after Racism Allegations: 'This Is Not Who We Are,'" *CNN* (January 22, 2019).

[27] Raffnsøe, "What Is Critique?" 42.

analysis to power and control or the expression of interests embedded in each and every claim of urgency.

All social units generate endless pathologies. The matter of which ones come to be labeled as crises resides in the hands of the leaders of those units. There is nothing inherent in any dynamic that automatically acquires that crisis label, no meaning that resides outside of human interpretation.

Of course, there *are* brute facts and dynamics at play – storms forming in the Atlantic, faulty parts installed in millions of cars, a nascent AIDS epidemic, "White-Only" signs in Birmingham storefronts – that could potentially be called urgent. By opting to name some of these as crises and not others, leaders exercise their power to raise awareness, focus attention, and devote resources toward some matters and away from others.

We've come across examples – Hurricane Maria on its approach to Puerto Rico – where the crisis label was applied without much controversy.[28] Claiming that the approach of a Category 5 hurricane is an urgent situation makes a great deal of sense. We've also seen times when the label was applied in questionable, even objectionable ways. The claim that the United States and its allies needed to respond urgently and militaristically to Iraq's alleged accumulation of weapons of mass destruction – a reckless claim that was plausible but inaccurate – led to a military response with its inevitably lethal outcomes.

In all cases of claims of urgency, interests were served. When Bush and Powell claimed that Iraq possessed weaponry that posed a direct threat to US national security, they were advancing a particular interest in ousting Iraq's leadership from power. Bush's interest in removing the Iraqi dictator was served by his reckless claim that Iraq possessed weapons of mass destruction.

That assertion of interests is fundamental to all claims. Woodrow Wilson downplayed the attack on the *Lusitania* and Franklin Roosevelt did the same with the Japanese sinking of the *Panay* because of the interest of these two chief executives in promoting military neutrality.[29] Lyndon Johnson, conversely, leaped at the opportunity to claim an attack in the

---

[28] Do you believe that the approach of a Category 5 hurricane provides a real threat? That seems like a no-brainer. Who wouldn't be worried? And yet, in reference to an earlier storm, Rush Limbaugh offered an alternative ascription: that hurricane warnings were conspiratorial plots by local news media and businesses. "I explained how severe weather events are opportunities for big ratings boosts in the media and explained how it happens. I explained how severe weather events impact retailers and how some retailers are smart enough to coordinate advertising with television stations. It happens!" Quoted in Callum Borchers, "Rush Limbaugh Indicates He's Evacuating Palm Beach Days after Suggesting Hurricane Irma Is Fake News," *Washington Post* (September 8, 2017).

[29] Peifer, *Choosing War*.

Gulf of Tonkin based on his interest in escalating America's war effort against North Vietnam.[30]

The same dynamic gets played out in a business setting. Borders Books' George Jones had an interest in continuing his company's commitment to bricks-and-mortar stores even in the face of burgeoning online competition from Amazon. That interest was based on his view of what retailing was – selling stuff from stores – built up over a lifetime in the bricks-and-mortar–denominated industry.[31] It was also a claim that defended his own past strategic decisions. Ken Lay had a decidedly more corrupt interest in denying the fragility and fraud that was fundamental to Enron's image as a high-flying company. In these, as in all determinations about what constitutes an urgent situation and what does not, the interests of leaders shape their construction of the dynamics their units face.

Most CEOs have an institutional interest in preserving and growing their companies. There can also be a bundle of more self-aggrandizing goals, however. They may enjoy the admiration and rewards that come with being seen as a crisis hero.

Another inherent component of a claim of urgency is that while advancing interests, claims simultaneously and inevitably assert the leader's power. This is the way the threat should be understood and how the unit must respond. The claim, in turn, triggers a demand for greater power and control on the part of that leader, typically accompanied by an enhanced willingness on the part of followers to grant that enlargement in power. With that enhanced power, leaders advance interests with a claim that seeks to shape the crisis response. By placing the claim and the claims maker center stage in an analysis, power and interests are not afterthoughts; rather, they are organically and inevitably intertwined.

The crises-as-event model conflates the label with the thing. As a direct result, we forgo the responsibility for asking about the legitimacy of the label. We focus our analysis away from interrogating the motives of the claims maker and seek instead recipes for guiding an effective response. The crisis-as-claim model insists that the label *is* the thing. Now, we must inquire as to why a crisis label is being applied (or withheld).

---

[30] Richard Cherwitz, "Lyndon Johnson and the 'Crisis' of the Tonkin Gulf: A President's Justification of War," *Western Journal of Speech Communication* 42 (1978), 93–104.

[31] C. K. Prahalad and Richard Bettis noted how executives formed a "dominant logic" that referred to "a mind set or a world view or conceptualization of the business and the administrative tools to accomplish goals and make decisions in that business." The danger comes when that logic is set in the past and constricts the capacity of leaders to respond to a new logic demanded by environmental changes. See Prahalad and Bettis, "The Dominant Logic: A New Linkage between Diversity and Performance," *Strategic Management Journal* 7 (1986), 491.

As claims makers, leaders have power to impose meaning but no special privilege to understand the world. The "winning" claim in a tournament of competing claims – that is, the claim that establishes and then enforces a dominant definition of the meaning of an event on a social unit – will be determined by a number of factors, most particularly the relative power of the competing claims makers. And that power will always be asserted – not sometimes or often, but *always* – on behalf of the interests of the claims maker.

When embedding a claim into a constructed narrative, leaders assert their hierarchical power. My story is the "authoritative" version of events. Mary Barra had both the responsibility and the power to frame her public admission of the long-standing faculty ignition switch in terms of "a pattern of management deficiencies and misjudgments – often based on incomplete data – that were passed off at the time as business as usual." This was a failure "in our system." GM as a company "didn't do our job. We failed these customers."

That phrase, "we failed these customers," might be read as a rather bland and jarringly bloodless way to frame GM's actions. The lives of millions of customers were placed in jeopardy. The company delayed its response and misled dealers and drivers when it did issue warnings. At least 127 people died. Those are the outcomes she framed with the phrase, "We failed these customers," rather than saying, for instance, "We recklessly and purposefully risked the lives of millions of customers and killed more than 100 of them." Barra's assessments were tough, to be sure. They were accompanied by "my deepest sympathies." They could have been much tougher. But this was a story that she was telling, and she constructed it in a particular way. Experts operating from within the crisis-as-event model praised her as a crisis manager to be emulated. But from within the crisis-as-claim model, we can – indeed must – adopt a more critical posture toward any and all constructions of crisis.

The failure of the company as a system was included in the frame that Barra created to communicate urgency. That decision to go beyond the few-bad-apples narrative favored by a number of other CEOs we have encountered (most prominently, Facebook's Mark Zuckerberg and Wells Fargo's Jim Stumpf) won her lavish praise from spokespeople for the crisis-as-event model. She had taken ownership in a "front-and-center fashion," recognized the "human angle," and acknowledged "the corporate culture."

The crisis-as-claim model does not criticize those conclusions. Rather, it critiques the failure of that "crisis manager of the year" interpretation to take into account Barra's assertion of power and advancement of interests inherent in her framing of the claim.

By focusing on the claim as opposed to the event and by remaining ever-vigilant to the exercise of power, we should recognize that something important *was* left out of Barra's claim. She had been in charge of the production unit prior to becoming CEO, after all. Fifteen senior legal and engineering executives were fired and five others (unidentified) were disciplined.[32] Yet, her narrative excluded her own actions or inactions as well as those of any other high-ranking GM executive.

It is impossible, currently, to offer an independent assessment of the accuracy of the claim that no top executive, Barra included, knew of the ignition switch problem. It does seem implausible, however. What is clear, even indisputable, is that (a) as leader, Barra took an active role in framing the crisis in a way intended to shape the response of others to that crisis; (b) her frame excluded GM top executives from responsibility; and (c) her frame was endorsed by an internal report that was made public.

The crisis-as-claim model insists that all components of the claim itself be scrutinized. So, what about the claim that an internal investigation held GM top executives blameless? How does that report and its exculpatory conclusions fit into the crisis narrative constructed by Barra?

Barra's narrative attempted to build source credibility for Valukas and his findings. "On Monday," she said in her address to employees, "former US Attorney Anton Valukas presented the findings of his investigation into our ignition switch recall to the Board of Directors."[33] There were some powerful terms in that description, most notably an "investigation" by "US Attorney" Valukas. Barra invited credibility, virtually insisted on it. Who wouldn't trust a "former US Attorney" – prosecutors appointed by the US attorney general to represent the government in federal courts – to conduct a full and fair "investigation"? Of course, as Barra admitted, Valukas wasn't a US attorney; he was a *former* US attorney. So, what was the implication of the word "former" attached to Valukas's title?

The crisis-as-claim model demands critical analysis of Barra's description of the Valukas report. That was, after all, part of her claim and, crucially, the source of confirming evidence for her insistence that top management was kept in the dark. Analysis can start with this: just how accurate were those labels: "former US attorney" and "investigation"?

Well, to start, there was *no* investigation, at least not in the sense of an independent fact-finding research intervention. Valukas was *not* a US attorney when he undertook his inquiry. He had been, but he was no longer one. Barra's description of Valukas as a former US attorney was

---

[32] Tom Krisher and Dee-Ann Dubin, "GM Ousts 15 Employees over Ignition-Switch Scandal," *San Diego Union-Tribune* (June 5, 2014).

[33] Barra, "Extremely Thorough, Brutal, Tough and Deeply Troubling," 287.

accurate but not fulsome. She hadn't lied but omitted explaining what role he had played while conducting research for his report. What, exactly, was he if he wasn't a current US attorney and what, exactly, was he doing at GM? The answer was there, "hiding" in plain sight on the cover of his report.

At the time of the report, the former US attorney was a senior partner at the law firm of Jenner & Block. Current US attorneys are, of course, not for hire to conduct internal investigations. Private law firms are. Jenner & Block had been engaged by GM for the explicit purpose of offering advice to its client on how to respond to potential criminal and civil actions. The law firm was not investigating GM in the sense of making an official external inquiry. It was *representing* a client, and that client was GM itself.[34]

The resulting report was unquestionably "brutally tough" and "deeply troubling," as Barra noted. But was it – the version that was made public – "extremely thorough"? Perhaps.[35] However, Barra framed the report as an independent investigation, and the description she gave of Valukas referred to what he *used* to do, not what he was doing. To evaluate Valukas's credibility as a source for the finding that GM top brass did not participate in any cover-up in the deadly parts scandal, one has to assume that a law firm working on behalf of its client would make an "extremely thorough" report available to both that client and the public.

Barra was framing the Valukas report, indeed her entire claim, in a purposeful way. All claims makers do that; that's a process inherent in the staking of a claim. In this case, she framed the Valukas report as a credible, honest, and thorough inquiry into just what happened at GM. *Caveat emptor*, the crisis-as-claim model urges the claim's audience. Buyer (of the claim) beware.

Barra was calling on a commonly used strategy, hiring law firms to conduct an internal report intended to help the organization avoid (or at least diminish) legal liability. Caution is always called for when assessing claims of independent investigations. A 2017 report on long-standing sexual abuse in the gymnastics program at Michigan State University, for example, absolved top university officials, including Michigan State's

---

[34] The report, as well as the collected documents said to number 41 million and the transcripts of more than 200 employee interviews were all made available to the government as well as plaintiffs' lawyers in ensuing civil cases. GM balked only at allowing the release of the lawyers' notes, citing attorney-client privilege.

[35] I have been told by lawyers involved in such internal investigations that it is not uncommon for the most troubling findings – those with the most immediate opportunity for claims of liability – to be withheld from the final report and communicated to top management and / or the board in confidence. I have no knowledge, of course, that this is what happened between Jenner & Block and GM.

president, of any prior knowledge of the abuse. A "former federal prosecutor," the university proudly noted, undertook that investigation.[36]

There's that word again: *former*. At the time the report was compiled, the *former* prosecutor was a *current* private practice attorney, engaged by the university to protect the school from any damage in the courts.[37] Although cleared of wrongdoing by the report, the university's president resigned under pressure.[38]

Then in 2018, an internal report absolved top executives at NBC News of any complicity or wrongdoing in the years-long sexual harassment campaign waged by *Today Show* host Matt Lauer. The general corporate counsel at NBC-Universal wrote that report with the assistance of two outside law firms.[39] In all these cases – NBC and Michigan State no less than GM – leaders worked to frame internal inquiries as independent investigations to gain credibility for their denials of complicity. That's their prerogative, of course. It is also an illustration of the power of claims makers as constructors of frames of meaning.[40]

As we have seen, much of the asserted power of the claims maker derives from the narratives they devise to communicate that claim. They determine if the crisis is understood as sudden or long simmering,

---

[36] Justin Hinkley, "Who Is William Forsyth, the Man Investigating Michigan State's Handling of Larry Nassar?" *Lansing State Journal* (January 28, 2918).

[37] A Michigan state senator made note of this very contradiction: "Michigan State led the public to believe that there had been an independent investigation. And then as we continued to dig into this, we found out it was not an independent investigation. It was an internal investigation to shield them from liability." See Monica Davey and Mitch Smith, "In Nassar Case, Michigan State Wanted Famed Ex-Prosecutor to Both Examine and Defend It," *New York Times* (January 27, 2018).

[38] The by-then former president Lou Anna Simon was subsequently charged with two felony counts of lying to police as part of the investigation. Her successor was subsequently forced to resign after he publicly suggested that some victims of sexual abuse were "enjoying" the spotlight. See Eliott McLaughlin, "Michigan State President Resigns after He Claimed Nassar Victims Were 'Enjoying' the Spotlight," *CNN* (January 17, 2019), and Matt Mencarini et al., "Ex-MSU President Lou Anna Simon Charged with Lying to Police about Nassar Investigation," *Lansing State Journal* (November 20, 2018).

[39] Stephen Battaglio, "Internal Review Says NBC News Didn't Know of Any Sexual Harassment Involving Matt Lauer Before His Firing," *Los Angeles Times* (May 9, 2018).

[40] An internal investigation of Leslie Moonves, the chief executive of CBS accused of multiple and long-running incidents of sexual abuse, unfolded in a somewhat different manner. Two separate law firms were hired; they were hired by and reported to the independent members of the CBS board. And the incentives were significantly different in this case. CBS had agreed to pay Moonves a $120 million severance package, an agreement that could be abrogated if it was learned that Moonves lied to investigators. CBS, in other words, could save a lot of money if the investigating attorneys discovered such lies. And their internal report concluded that Moonves had lied, repeatedly. Rachel Abrams and Edmund Lee, "Les Moonves Obstructed Investigation into Misconduct Claims, Report Says," *New York Times* (December 4, 2018), and James Stewart et al., "'If Bobbie Talks, I'm Finished': How Les Moonves Tried to Silence an Accuser," *New York Times* (November 28, 2018).

internal or external, human or naturally caused, an accident or a disaster. The crisis-as-event model builds topologies based on the assumption that the proposed distinctions are objectively real.

Within the crisis-as-claim model, either / or questions about the nature of a crisis are rendered nonsensical. External or internal? Human engineered or forces of nature? The only possible answer to those questions is that it depends on who's telling the story. The crisis "event" is nothing more or less than a story, a constructed narrative that is always the result of interpretation.

Evaluating Performance

We can see the unanimous praise heaped on Barra by crisis management experts. This was Mary Barra's "Pearl Harbor moment," and she had responded heroically.[41] GM escaped criminal charges when the US Department of Justice instead levied a $900 million fine, a hefty amount to be sure, but less than a third of the company's annual profits. Shareholders had reason to be pleased as well. Three years of record earnings following her rocky inaugural months, driven by Barra's tough cost cutting combined with higher prices "on strong-selling SUVs and crossovers."

As CEO, "Barra demonstrates a mix of discipline and vision, adroitly balancing GM's immediate imperatives – producing vehicles people want at a profitable price – and its longer-term challenges – ensuring GM's future in the face of unprecedented industry upheaval," enthused a *Forbes* writer.[42] In late 2018, she announced the idling of five factories and the elimination of 14,000 jobs to reduce costs while focusing on electric and self-driving cars.[43] Although it is true that GM stock price had gained little under Barra's leadership, "the company she leads today is vastly different from the one she inherited: more decisive, focused, responsive and responsible."[44]

The crisis-as-event model lends itself to performance evaluation. The threat was real, the crisis needed to be managed, the leader responded, and the threatened unit either recovered admirably (Nissan, for example), faltered noticeably (Wells Fargo), or failed

---

[41] Joann Muller, "Mary Barra's Pearl Harbor Moment: 'I Never Want You to Forget' How GM Failed Customers," *Forbes* (June 5, 2014).

[42] Joann Muller, "Mary Barra Is Running GM with a Tight Fist and an Urgent Mission," *Forbes* (May 2, 2017).

[43] Neal Boudette and Ian Austen, "GM to Idle Plants and Cut Thousands of Jobs as Sales Slow," *New York Times* (November 26, 2018).

[44] Mark Phelan, "Mary Barra Shapes a New GM: Fast, Focused, and Decisive," *Detroit Free Press* (June 3, 2017).

entirely (Borders Books). Those are roughly the three major classifications of evaluation. Are disruptions and losses minimized? If the crisis
is managed properly, threats become opportunities, learning occurs so
that lessons are transferred to future incidents, and the unit goes on,
stronger than ever.

Organizational performance is an outcome of many factors. Dynamics
in the larger industry and the wider economy play a major role in shaping
performance outcomes of any particular business.[45] Furthermore, the act
of defining performance is a fundamentally human activity, fraught with
contention and conflict. There is no possibility of defining performance in
the aftermath of a crisis without imposing a specific definition of performance and denying competing definitions. The crisis-as-event model
simply elides the matter of who gets to determine what performance is.
If the firm is performing well post crisis, then the crisis leader performed
well. *Post hoc ergo propter hoc.*

Measuring the performance of a business is a surprisingly tricky business. There are yardsticks, a lot of them. Profitability, revenue growth,
earnings-before-interest-taxes-amortization, stock price, economic-
value-added, and return-on-equity are among the many. Even with myriad measures, corporations are not quite the transparent containers
amenable to a detached, focused accounting appraisal that they like to
suggest to investors. But there is an inevitable bottom line. Shareholders
insist on seeing a statement of net income and calculating the price-to-
earnings ratio to help shape future investments.

But how do we measure effectiveness when we leave business organizations? There is no real bottom line for societies, and no report certified by
independent auditors that accounts for costs and benefits of social policies. That isn't to say that there aren't plenty of non-governmental organizations conducting their own audits. But there is ample opportunity
and powerful motivation for interest groups to skew findings in a particular direction.[46] Still, there is no doubting the underlying premise: to
judge the leader's response to a crisis event, we look at the ensuring
performance of the unit.

---

[45] A number of empirical studies have suggested that "firm effects" account for little more
than half of a firm's performance. Other studies suggest that CEOs account for between
20 and 36 percent of firm performance. Industry dynamics, customer preferences,
demographic shifts, and macro-economic trends are hugely influential. See Frank
Rothaermel, *Strategic Management* (New York: McGraw-Hill, 2017), and Edward
Zajac, "CEO Selection, Succession, Compensation and Firm Performance: A
Theoretical Integration and Empirical Analysis," *Strategic Management Journal* 11
(1990), 217–230.

[46] Joel Best, *Damned Lies, and Statistics: Untangling the Numbers from the Media, Politicians
and Activists* (Berkeley: University of California Press, 2012).

The performance orientation embedded in the crisis-as-event model shouldn't come as a surprise. As a society, we seek to evaluate and measure everything. Perhaps this is an inevitable outcome of the reigning ideology of usefulness. In business especially, financial growth has become the dominant regime for judging effectiveness.[47]

Given its origins in the Hippocratic formulation of crisis – as the tipping point in the body's struggle with disease – it is to be expected that the crisis-as-event model takes recovery as the end point of any crisis response. There's no disputing that performance metrics can be useful if appropriately defined, calibrated, and strategically integrated into the activities of the unit and motivation of its members. But the act of defining performance is a fundamentally human activity, an activity fraught with contention and conflict.

When the event is replaced by the claim as the focal unit of analysis, a different evaluation must be applied. The crisis-as-claim model considers the content of the claim and offers an evaluation based on accuracy and plausibility. Was Barra's claim legitimate – that is, both objectively accurate and subjectively plausible? I would argue that yes, it was generally legitimate, but that no, it wasn't on a more specific level. There was little question that her assertion about GM's failures related to the faulty part was legitimate. Her insistence that she had no knowledge of the problem – nor had any other top GM executive – is far less plausible, despite being vouched for by the Valukas report.[48]

The contrasting views of the GM crisis, as summarized in Table 10.1, suggest how models and theories can and do shape our understanding of the world. The crisis-as-claim model evaluates the legitimacy of the claim, redefines the role of the leader, and focuses on the process by which power is asserted and interests are advanced. The final question to ask is this: how and why does that matter?

---

[47] Robert Boyer, "Is a Finance-led Growth Regime a Viable Alternative to Fordism? A Preliminary Analysis," *Economy and Society* 29 (2000), 111–145.

[48] When Barra asserted her lack of knowledge in a congressional hearing, Representative Diana DeGette expressed doubts. "The report singles out many individuals at GM who made poor decisions or failed to act, but it doesn't identify one individual in a position of high leadership who was responsible for these systemic failures," she told Barra, "The report absolves previous CEOs, the legal department, Ms. Barra and the GM Board from knowing about the tragedy beforehand." Was it possible that Barra would remain so ill informed of more than a decade of intense activity, much of it taking place in her own department, that discussed the problem and corrected it in 2006? The implausibility of that aspect of Barra's claim led Representative DeGette to conclude that her claim "smacked of a cover up." Top executives either knew or didn't know. Either way, Valukas report or no Valukas report, "this is a remarkable failure on the part of those running the corporation." See Jerry Hirsch and Jim Puzzanghera, "Lawmaker: GM Response to Ignition Switch Issue 'Smacks of Cover-Up,'" *Los Angeles Times* (June 18, 2014).

Table 10.1 *The GM crisis from two models*

CRISIS-AS-EVENT MODEL	CRISIS-AS-CLAIM MODEL
Smoldering crisis triggered by 2002 installation of faulty part	Urgency instigated by Barra's 2014 claim of a crisis
Internal investigation conducted to get facts	Internal report conducted to get facts tempered by need to protect company
As leader, Barra responded to crisis by taking ownership	As leader, Barra took ownership by shaping and controlling the crisis narrative.
Sees Barra as hero	Sees Barra as claims maker
Barra's response revealed "best practices" of crisis management	Barra's response revealed underlying power and interests of claims maker
Effective response as measured by GM financial recovery	Legitimate claim on a general level but with an implausible assertion that no one in GM's upper ranks knew about the problem

The Importance of Getting It Right

It was during the months between his 1932 election and swearing in for his first presidential term that Franklin Roosevelt met with the prominent newspaper columnist Walter Lippmann. Labels like "most influential journalist" of the twentieth century and the "Father of Modern Journalism" have often been attached to Lippmann. He was a towering twentieth-century figure.

Long before the 1929 stock market crash, Lippmann had become a prominent journalist as co-founder in 1914 of the *New Republic* and author of numerous volumes on the role of media in public life. In *Public Opinion*, considered to be his masterwork, Lippmann proposed that citizens of the United States were ill equipped to participate in informed policy debates, hampered as they were by uninformed, stereo-typical thinking. Although that argument reeks of elitism, he was equally dubious of the capacity of elites to possess more than a passing glimpse of reality.[49]

At the point of the Roosevelt-Lippmann meeting in Warm Springs, Georgia, on February 1, 1933, the crash had devastated investors while leaving the larger economy shaken but not decimated. The banking system was under great strain but had not yet crumbled (as it would in the following month). Still, faith in the economy's future was seriously eroded.

[49] Susan Herbst, "Walter Lippmann's *Public Opinion*, Revisited," *Harvard International Journal of Press/Politics* 4 (1999), 88–93; Walter Lippmann, *Public Opinion* (New York: Macmillan, 1922).

Presciently, Lippmann saw worse times ahead: not pie-in-the-sky hopes for recovery but massive devastation. He was, of course, correct. By the end of that year, with the banking system in shambles, unemployment topped a quarter of the labor force. It was in that context of looming disaster that Lippmann offered advice to President-elect Franklin Roosevelt.

"The situation is critical, Franklin," Lippmann told his fellow traveler in the American sociopolitical elite, "You may have no alternative but to assume dictatorial power."[50] His next newspaper column followed along the same line of advocating for a kind of dictatorship. Congress should not be allowed to "obstruct, to mutilate, and to confuse." Rather, it should give Roosevelt a free hand for his first year.[51]

There may be no such thing as a crisis, but that doesn't imply that people don't believe that their social unit – their community, organization, country, and so forth – is threatened. There was certainly a broad sense of unease and pending threat in February 1933 on the eve of Roosevelt's inauguration. Lippmann believed that, and Roosevelt concurred.

What people believe to be real becomes real in its consequences. With perceived threat comes a desire for "strong" leadership. Governments seek to build authority to respond effectively.[52] Individual leaders believe they must demonstrate resolve, determination, courage, and decisiveness. Followers tend to agree, seeking just those qualities from a crisis leader. As understandable as that dynamic may be, it holds the potential for grave danger captured by the phrase "threat-rigidity effect."

What Could Go Wrong?

The "threat-rigidity effect": that's the label applied to the dynamic interplay between leader and follower by Barry Staw and colleagues. What they noted was "a general tendency for individuals, groups, and organizations to behave rigidly in threatening situations."[53] And that's what a

---

[50] Quoted in Ronald Steel, *Walter Lippmann and the American Century* (Boston: Little, Brown, 1980), p. 300.
[51] Ibid. Lippmann was not alone. "For Dictatorship if Necessary" ran a headline in the *New York Daily News*.
[52] Hui Zhao, "Constructing Authority in Times of Crisis: A Genre Analysis of Government Crisis Communication in China," *Journal of Communication Management* 22 (2018), 346–360.
[53] Barry Staw et al., "Threat-Rigidity Effects in Organizational Behavior: A Multi-Level Analysis," *Administrative Science Quarterly* 26 (1981), 502. These findings are consistent with those of Jane Dutton, "The Processing of Crisis and Non-Crisis Strategic Issues," *Journal of Management Studies* 23 (1986), 501–517; Hermann, "Some Consequences of

crisis is taken to be by those who believe the claim of urgency: a threatening situation.

When people believe that their social unit faces a threat, two separate but interrelated reactions are likely: "First, the threat may result in restriction of information processing, such as a narrowing in the field of attention, a simplification of information codes, or a reduction in the number of channels used."[54] This constriction of information and attention is a serious matter for all organizations under any circumstances. Now, just when dangers are believed to be most acute and when the need for bountiful information from and about the outside world becomes most pressing, the reaction is perverse.

Rather than opening up, crisis leaders begin to shut down – not completely, of course. But fewer people are listened to and those who are heard tend to be those who agree with the leaders' views of the world, and their interpretation of the nature and causes of the threat. Fewer channels of communication are accessed; consideration of alternative options for response narrows. So, the idea of crisis, and the degree to which that idea is applicable at any given moment, has profound consequences.

And there's more, Staw and colleagues tell us: "When a threat occurs, there may be a constriction in control, such that power and influence can become more concentrated in higher levels of a hierarchy."[55] That desire for centralized control was what Lippmann seemed to be getting at in his advice to Roosevelt. He was not advocating for the establishment of a totalitarian police state so much as expressing a preference for "a strong leader unfettered by Congress or the other inconveniences of democracy."[56] That centralization of power and authority, unhampered by prevailing norms and institutions, was necessary to meet the threatening demands of a crumbling economy.

During urgent times, leaders narrow their attention while consolidating their power. "The ability of managers to process information and make well-reasoned choices," noted Matthew Seeger and colleagues, "is often seriously reduced during crisis."[57] Stressful situations lead to further isolation by decision makers who, as a consequence, become increasing

Crisis Which Limit the Viability of Organizations"; Jackson and Jane Dutton, "Discerning Threats and Opportunities." The phenomenon is essentially the same as Jeffrey Pfeffer's "centralization theses." See Pfeffer, "The Micropolitics of Organizations," in *Environments and Organizations* (San Francisco: Jossey-Bass, 1978), pp. 29–50.

[54] Staw et al., "Threat-Rigidity Effects," 502.   [55] Ibid.

[56] Jonathan Atler, *The Defining Moment: FDR's Hundred Days and the Triumph of Hope* (New York: Simon & Schuster, 2006), p. 5.

[57] Matthew Seeger et al., *Communication and Organizational Crisis* (Westport, CT: Praeger, 2013), p. 9.

unwilling and unable to consider additional, especially disconfirming, information.[58] Karl Weick added the observation that the centralization of decision making in increasingly fewer hands undermines competency by shutting down communications from valuable advisors.[59]

Perceptions of great threat lead to fewer decision makers paying attention to fewer sources of information while expecting enhanced loyalty and obedience from followers. Those followers, in turn, seek strong, decisive leaders. Stress is ramped up; the expectations placed on leaders to respond heroically multiply significantly.[60]

What could go wrong?

Political scientists have long noted the same troubling dynamics at governmental levels. When heads of state claim a crisis – the country has been attacked, the economy is in serious decline, terrorists are endangering innocent civilians – the leader typically makes a decisive determination about how to respond and then expects to be supported. Justificatory rhetoric is deployed to explain and justify an already determined course of action. *This* is the definitive explanation of what has caused the declared crisis. *This* is the course of action to be undertaken in response.

Time for discussion and debate about options – both for interpretation of the situation and for the adoption of a particular response – has now passed. It is time to get on board and pull together in the face of an existential threat. Dissent from the leader's narrative is denounced as disloyalty, not to the leader but to the country.[61] Under Woodrow Wilson's wartime presidency, opposition was, indeed, criminalized.[62]

---

[58] Dennis Gouran, *Making Decisions in Groups: Choices and Consequences* (Glenview, IL: Scott, Foresman, 1982).

[59] Weick, "Enacted Sensemaking in Crisis Situations."

[60] There is empirical evidence to suggest that powerful CEOs – that is, executives who amass enhanced centralized control – undermine firm performance during periods of extreme turbulence. See Vishal Gupta et al., "When Crisis Knocks, Call a Powerful CEO (or Not): Investigating the Contingent Link between CEO Power and Firm Performance during Industry Turmoil," *Group & Organization Management* 41 (2016), 1–28.

[61] Richard Cherwitz and Kenneth Zagacki, "Consummatory versus Justificatory Crisis Rhetoric," *Western Journal of Speech Communication* 50 (1986), 307–324; Michael Genovese, "Presidential Leadership and Crisis Management," *Presidential Studies Quarterly* 16 (1986), 300–309; Pitirim Sorokin, *Man and Society in Calamity: The Effects of War, Revolution, Famine, Pestilence upon Human Mind, Behavior, Social Organization, and Cultural Life* (New York: Greenwood Press, 1942); Theodore Windt, "The Presidency and Speeches on International Crisis: Repeating the Rhetorical Past," *Speaker and Gavel* 2 (1973), 6–14; Dror Yuravlivker, "'Peace without Conquest': Lyndon Johnson's Speech of April 7, 1965," *Presidential Studies Quarterly* 36 (2006), 457–481.

[62] Wilson urged passage of the Espionage Act of 1917 and the Sedition Act the next year because, he told Congress, "If there should be disloyalty, it will be dealt with a firm hand of repression." Michael Beschloss tells us that almost 1,000 people were convicted for

That dynamic is often tolerated, even applauded by followers. During the Vietnam War years, President Johnson denounced war protestors as "cut-and-run people" – essentially, unpatriotic cowards. His followers paraded with "Love it or Leave it" placards, demanding either obedience or exit.[63] That's an unwelcomed but predictable dynamic.

The Double-Edged Sword

Based on a shared belief that their unit is under threat, followers "become increasingly susceptible to the leader and his or her vision."[64] When people believe they are facing a crisis, they want to be led; they expect their leaders to *do something*, to make quick, decisive, even unilateral decisions.[65] Dissent is marginalized, perhaps even punished.[66]

Again, what could possibly go wrong?

To be fair, rigidity and centralization are not entirely maladaptive responses. Since it is unlikely that there will be a unity of purpose among all stakeholders, a degree of centralization may be functionally required. It is also more likely that members will tolerate and support what is perceived to be "strong" leadership.[67] But while it may not be entirely maladaptive, it is not entirely adaptive either.

There is a double-edged sword, after all, one buried just beneath the surface of a crisis. Leaders first proclaim a crisis and then insist on

using "disloyal, profane, scurrilous, or abusive language" directed against the government, the military, or the flag. See Beschloss, "On This World War I Anniversary, Let's Not Celebrate Woodrow Wilson," *Washington Post* (November 11, 2018). Although revised many times, the Espionage Act is still on the books. It has been used to prosecute Daniel Ellsberg, author and whistleblower / leaker of the Pentagon Papers; actual spies including Aldrich Ames and Robert Hansen; and more recent disseminators of documents, including Chelsea Manning and Edward Snowden. On the use of the act, see George Anastaplo, *Reflections on Freedom of Speech and the First Amendment* (Lexington: University Press of Kentucky, 2007).

[63] www.presidentprofiles.com/Kennedy-Bush/Lyndon-B-Johnson-Protest-at-home.html.

[64] Michelle Bligh et al., "Charisma under Crisis: Presidential Leadership, Rhetoric, and Media Responses Before and After the September 11th Terrorist Attacks," *Leadership Quarterly* 15 (2004), 215.

[65] Arjen Boin and Paul 't Hart, "Public Leadership in Times of Crisis: Mission Impossible?" *Public Administration Review* 63 (2003), 544–553; S. Alexander Haslam et al., "Social Identity and the Romance of Leadership: The Importance of Being Seen to Be 'Doing It for Us,'" *Group Processes & Intergroup Relations* 4 (2001), 191–205; James Meindl, "On Leadership: An Alternative to the Conventional Wisdom," *Research in Organizational Behavior* 12 (1990), 159–203; B. Dan Wood, "Presidential Rhetoric and Economic Leadership," *Presidential Studies Quarterly* 34 (2004), 573–606.

[66] Much of the classical intergroup conflict literature points to similar dynamics. See, for example, Muzafer Sherif, *In Common Predicament: Social Psychology of Intergroup Conflict and Cooperation* (Boston: Houghton Mifflin, 1966).

[67] Mauk Mulder et al. "An Organization in Crisis and Non-Crisis Situations," *Human Relations* 24 (1971), 19–41.

consolidating their power and control. Followers tend to accede. *Our country is in a disreputable state of carnage. I alone can fix it* says the leader. *Go to it,* cheer the followers. *Our company's financial state is non-sustainable. Get on board and follow me as we fix it* says the leader. *We're on your team* proclaim the followers. Those who don't accede may be asked (or forced) to leave. Overdependence on charismatic leaders with the potential rise of would-be authoritarians represents that barely concealed undercurrent of the response to threat.

For these reasons, it becomes vital to think carefully and critically about the process that gets initiated once a leader claims urgency. The intent in offering a new crisis model is to help influence how people think about such claims. And perhaps, as a result of rethinking, behaviors will be impacted as well.

Impacting Thinking about Acting

Social scientists, at least those with a theoretical inclination, are fond of quoting psychologist Kurt Lewin. "There is nothing as practical as a good theory," he wrote, adding that the source of the quote was an otherwise unidentified "business man."[68] Predictably, Lewin's admonition is especially taken to heart by business school academics who insist that their research can and should be both academically rigorous and directly relevant to practitioners.[69]

In direct contraposition to Lewin's practical "business man," there is an argument to be made that conceptual thinking should not concern itself with the world of application at all. Sociologist Peter Berger advanced that argument, insisting that there was no "intrinsic necessity" for theorists to take on a dialogue with practitioners. Only other theorists should engage questions raised by theorists.[70] Theorists and practitioners live in two different, and not necessarily overlapping, worlds.

The intention for theoretical work to be explicitly meaningful to other academics is by no means trivial. Researchers can advance knowledge of claims of urgency by studying the interactive dynamics between claim content, claim maker, and intended audience. They may analyze the discursive devices called upon in various claims of urgency. My proposed typology for classifying claims can be parsed into testable hypotheses and

---

[68] Kurt Lewin, "Psychology and the Process of Group Living," *Bulletin of the Society for the Psychological Study of Social Issues* 17 (1943), 118.

[69] Mark Saunders et al., "Concepts and Theory Building," in *A Guide to Professional Doctorates in Business and Management* (Los Angeles: Sage, 2015).

[70] Peter Berger, *The Sacred Canopy: Elements of a Sociological Theory of Religion* (Garden City: Doubleday, 1967), p. 181.

subjected to empirical rigor. Are the four offered classifications both all inclusive and mutually exclusive? And what is the relationship, for example, between claim classification and claim believability?

Discourse draws its strength from links to institutionalized practice.[71] Even the wary Peter Berger held out the tantalizing additional prospect that in the absence of a direct academic-practitioner dialogue, theorizing could be impactful in the world beyond the ivory tower. Okay, but how? In particular, how does new interpretation move from some academic setting to the world at large and become inscribed, somehow, in systems of practice?

Theory Talk and Beyond

When, in the 1990s, Al Dunlap closed operations, sold off assets, decimated his companies' workforce, and auctioned off the remaining assets of his many companies (he moved around a lot in the 1990s, from Scott Paper to Crown Zellerbach and Sunbeam, a testament to the attractiveness of his approach to corporate boards), he did so in the name of a particular academic theory. "It's the shareholders" – holders of a company's stock – "who own the company," he insisted. No one else mattered.[72] This was the shareholder primacy theory formulated most notably by the university economics professors Milton Friedman (University of Chicago) and Michael Jensen (University of Rochester).

Because shareholders "owned" public corporations, a contested view but fundamental to shareholder theory, they were entitled to the full scope of its benefits. All executives, from the CEO down, were mere agents expected to conduct business "in accordance with their [shareholders'] desires," which, to Milton Friedman, meant "make as much money as possible."[73] Dunlap agreed, defending his efforts as directed precisely toward the goal celebrated in the theory: the maximization of shareholder wealth.

Shareholder primacy is far from the only academic theory to find its way into practitioners' talk. Listen to Steven Spinner, CEO of United Natural Foods, articulate the goal of his company: to meet and exceed "the needs and expectations of all our stakeholders: our customers, associates, natural and specialty product consumers, suppliers, shareholders,

---

[71] Michel Foucault, *Discipline and Punish: The Birth of the Prison* (New York: Vintage, 1979).
[72] Quoted in John Byrne, *Chainsaw: The Notorious Career of Al Dunlap in the Era of Profit at Any Price* (New York: HarperCollins, 1999), pp. xiv–xv.
[73] Milton Friedman, "The Social Responsibility of Business Is to Increase Its Profits," *New York Times Magazine* (September 13, 1970).

communities, the environment, and the planet."[74] Spinner was channeling a different academic model from the one called on by Dunlap: stakeholder theory, with its emphasis on myriad groups beyond shareholders who are said to hold a legitimate stake in the business's functioning. Like shareholder primacy, stakeholder theory also emerged from a university, in this case University of Virginia business school professor R. Edward Freeman.[75]

There are many other theories – transformational leadership, activity-based management, channel marketing, and blue ocean strategy among them – whose ideas and rhetoric have been developed by academics and deployed by practitioners. "Ideals truly do change the world," insisted Michael Porter, a Harvard Business School professor who made seminal contributions to the fields of industry analysis, competitive advantage, and corporate strategy.[76] Sure, he may have been engaging in no small amount of self-promotion. Even so, his industrial economics perspective on strategy came to dominate "the language and practices of strategy emanating from the corporate boardroom, consultancy firms, and business schools," basically permeating "all facets of society."[77] That is noteworthy. Still, we need to be cautious in drawing conclusions about causation.

Literary theorist Stanley Fish diminished the capacity of a good theory to fully engage individuals in a critical analysis of their own assumptions. The actual impact of theories, he insisted, was far more superficial: to provide "theory talk" to practitioners who called on theory "as an ornament, one thought to confer cachet and status on the practitioner."[78] Michael Porter's industrial economics theories didn't so much change the world as offer a sophisticated set of tools and vocabulary to support how businesspeople already saw and understood their world. When a theory conforms to our a priori assumptions, we are only too happy to adopt it.

Participating in ornamental theory talk is not the same as engaging in theoretical discourse. Most of the theories listed earlier do not demand a fundamental rethinking of the role of corporations in a democratic society. Transformational leadership, for instance, provided academic credence for what was, in fact, a century-old notion of heroic leaders

---

[74] www.unfi.com/Company/Pages/VisionAndMission.aspx

[75] R. Edward Freeman, *Strategic Management: A Stakeholder Approach* (Boston: Pitman, 1984).

[76] Porter quoted in www.topmba.com/why-mba/faculty-voices/worlds-most-influential-management-concepts-acknowledged-ranking.

[77] Chris Carter and Andrea Whittle, "Making Strategy Critical?" *Critical Perspectives on Accounting* 53 (2018), 1.

[78] Stanley Fish, *Doing What Comes Naturally: Change, Rhetoric, and the Practice of Theory in Literary and Legal Studies* (Durham: Duke University Press, 1989).

reshaping the world.[79] If you wanted to be thought of as a great leader, you could make a claim to being transformational. *Stake*holder, in contrast to *share*holder, theory comes the closest in leveling a critique at the order of things. But it really isn't possible to know the degree to which any of these ideas directly and fundamentally changed the world, or even the views of their individual proponents.[80]

Had Al Dunlap even read Milton Friedman or Michael Jensen? Was Steven Spinner familiar with the work of R. Edward Freeman? Perhaps not. Might either have made precisely the same decisions even if the theories had not been developed on a university campus? Quite possibly. We shouldn't draw an inference of direct causality between theory and action.

What is demonstrably true is that Dunlap and Spinner couched their statements of business goals in the language of academic doctrine. From their perspective, that's not such a bad idea. Practitioners can claim virtue for their ideas by attaching them to a discourse that has been anointed as legitimate, even true, by prestigious academic thinkers. Treating shareholders as owners with sole claim to the rewards of the corporation, for instance, could be embedded as "objective," even commonsensical by reference to an academic theory:[81] *It's well known that …*

Fish used ornamentation as a metaphor for what he believed was the superficiality of the theory talk engaged in by practitioners. Leaders call on theory talk as a way of justifying their previously formed and deeply held assumptions. But Fish is overemphasizing the superficiality of theory talk. There is a not-so-superficial value beyond ornamentation.

Unless we assume that there is nobody out there harboring deep doubts or engaging in critical thinking – that would be a rather arrogant assumption, no? – then we need to recognize the possibility of some people searching for a new framework, an alternative model that can both guide and justify their thoughts. In abandoning a priori assumptions, it is useful – and I deploy that term "useful" purposefully – to have a new destination, one based on new definitions and propositions. Kuhn

[79] Bert Spector, *Discourse on Leadership: A Critical Appraisal* (Cambridge: Cambridge University Press, 2016); Dennis Tourish, *The Dark Side of Transformational Leadership* (London: Routledge, 2013); Suze Wilson, *Thinking Differently About Leadership: A Critical History of Leadership Studies* (London: Edward Elgar, 2016).

[80] Fish did accept a possibility, however remote, of individual beliefs being changed by theory. Stanley Fish, "Consequences," *Critical Inquiry* 11 (1985), 433–458.

[81] Michel Foucault, *"Society Must Be Defended": Lectures at the College de France, 1975–76* (New York: Picador, 1976); Kathleen McCormick, "On a Topic of Your Own Choosing," in *Writing Theory and Critical Theory: Research and Scholarship in Composition* (New York: Modern Language Association of America, 1994), pp. 33–52.

Table 10.2 *The implications of a new model*

	CRISIS-AS-EVENT MODEL	CRISIS-AS-CLAIM MODEL
Ontology	Crisis are material events with objective elements that pose a threat to a social unit.	Claims are human interpretations of ambiguous dynamics in which events are constructed, meaning is imposed, and threat is ascribed.
Cause and effect	Crisis events are independent variables; leader responses are dependent variables.	Leader claims are independent variables; crisis situations are the dependent variable.
Crisis narrative	Leaders narrate a crisis story to enhance effective communication.	Leaders narrate a crisis story to frame, control, and shape understanding.
Evaluation	Effective crisis response leads to recovery and improvement.	Legitimate crisis claims are based on objective description and subjective ascription.
Disruption	Crisis events are threats because of their inherent potential for disruption.	Crisis claims may be opportunities because of their inherent potential for disruption.
Power	Leaders need power to respond to crisis.	Leaders gain power through their claims of urgency.
Role of leader	Leaders are crisis responders.	Leaders are claims makers.

recognized that people do not abandon old paradigms without having a new one to turn to. The non-ornamental value of new models is to offer people an alternative landing spot for their thinking.

Constructing Crisis has presented two contrasting models of crisis, summarized in Table 10.2. The intention in so doing is to provoke not superficial talk about crisis but rather a critical reappraisal of the approach taken by academics, by practitioners, and by all of those who are the intended audience for claims of urgency made by leaders.

Each element of the crisis-as-claim model offers challenges to the way of thinking about crisis embedded in the crisis-as-event model:

- By shifting *ontological assumptions* from positivism to constructionism, the crisis-as-claim model demands that all claims be treated with critical skepticism. Positioning crisis as a claim does not inherently delegitimize the content of that claim. But it does insist that no claim is legitimate per se and thus awaits evaluation.
- The two models *reverse cause and effect*. In the crisis-as-event model, the event is an independent variable, an objective event that shapes the leader's response. In the crisis-as-claim model, the leader's claim is the independent variable, shaping the official narrative of the crisis and determining how resources will be deployed to respond.

- Using *narrative theory* to analyze claims allows us to appreciate the degree to which the stories told by leaders are just one way to understand events. There will always be competing and alternative narratives. Beliefs in one or another narrative may be shaped by the power of those narrative structures.
- The focus of *evaluation* shifts. Rather than using a performance evaluation – how well did the unit perform after the crisis – we now evaluate the legitimacy of the claim.
- The two models take different stances on *disruption*. Because the crisis-as-claim model does not inherently problematize disruption, we need to analyze critically the status quo that is the target of the urgency and the potential for disruption to lead to rather than away from progress.
- *Power* becomes an inherent component of the crisis-as-claim model. Although power as a force is taken to be neutral, with potential for both benefit and harm, it is recognized that power is never distributed evenly within a social unit and that claims are both reflections and reinforcers (or, potentially, disrupters) of that power hierarchy.
- In the crisis-as-event model, *leaders* are, at least potentially, the heroes of the narrative, rescuing the unit from the objective threats posed by the crisis. Or they are the villains, responding ineptly. The crisis-as-claim model insists on removing considerations of heroic leadership, positioning leaders as claims makers intent on advancing interests and enhancing power.

An alternative model offers the opportunity for rethinking the idea of crisis and reflecting on practice.

Battling a Priori Assumptions

We all confront the ambiguous dynamics of the world armed with assumptions and heuristics to help navigate complexity. It is only when those a priori assumptions fail to satisfy our own thought processes and thus create disequilibrium in our reasoning that we are motivated to search for alternative models. Those new models may be, in fact most likely *must* be, unsettling. But they may also provide the relief of ultimately offering greater insight into the dynamics that we are experiencing and have experienced repeatedly.[82]

A practitioner may, insisted MIT urban affairs professor Donald Schön, "reflect on the tacit norms and applications which underlie a

---

[82] I'm borrowing here from Melvin Pollner and his notion of "unsettling" reflexivity. See Pollner, "Left of Ethnomethodology: The Rise and Decline of Radical Reflexivity," *American Sociological Review* 56 (1991), 370–380.

judgment, or on the strategies and theories implicit in a pattern of behavior."[83] What was it in this particular situation that elicited my response? What, if any, were my alternatives? And how did the manner in which I defined a situation impact the outcomes I experienced?

Deliberative, critical thinking, if and when it is engaged, will always do battle with a priori assumptions. Rather than falling back on those givens, reflective practitioners can move on to new assumptions. Moving on does not happen easily, however. It can only happen when there is a coherent set of principles to move to.[84] Reflective practitioners are able, now, to see new categories and take conceptual U-turns. That's where academic models become useful.

Note that the word "useful" has been embraced, but with a particular meaning. It is likely the case that critiques, concepts, models, theories, and frameworks emanating from academic thought do not, cannot, motivate people to seek new answers and understanding. That motivation, rather, arises from an engagement between individuals and their world. And this is precisely where the opportunity for genuine usefulness lies.

Theorists grapple with a world germane to them. Reflective practitioners puzzle over their own pertinent sphere of action. When overlap occurs between the relevant domains of practitioners and theorists, both parties have the opportunity to engage, not necessarily directly or immediately but conceptually. One's idea can become an aid not in directing the action of practitioners but in guiding the way practitioners *think* about acting.[85] That's the route theory can take to achieving relevancy: to impact thinking about acting.

A Bottom-line Assessment

In the world of business schools, we always like to ask: what's the bottom line? My final statement of bottom-line implications is straightforward. Rigorous research on the impact of different responses to and preparation

---

[83] Donald Schön, *The Reflective Practitioner: How Professionals Think in Action* (New York: Basic Books, 1983), p. 62.

[84] Wim De Neys, "Heuristic Bias, Conflict and Rationality in Decision Making," in *Towards a Theory of Thinking: Building Blocks for a Conceptual Framework* (Berlin: Springer, 2010), pp. 23–33; Markus Graf, "Categorization and Object Shape," in *Towards a Theory of Thinking*, 73–101; Daniel Kahneman, "Maps of Bounded Rationality: A Perspective on Intuitive Judgement and Choice," *Nobel Prize Lecture* (2002); Helge Ritter, "Models as Tools to Aid Thinking," in *Towards a Theory of Thinking*, 347–374.

[85] Keith Grint and Brad Jackson make that important distinction between impacting action versus impacting thinking about action. See Grint and Jackson, "Toward 'Socially Constructive' Social Constructions of Leadership," *Management Communication Quarterly* 24 (2010), 348–355.

for threatening contingencies will always be valued. The crisis-as-claim model offers leaders, followers, and those of us who analyze their interactions a framework for thinking differently about the process of constructing crisis. It presents crisis not as an objective condition but as a subjective claim. These claims may be legitimate, but not always. When we recognize that all claims are constructed as exercises in power and influence, we do so not to automatically delegitimize the claim. We do so to invite scrutiny and hearty debate. Immediate action may well be required, but critical thinking is always advised.

References

Abbott, H. Porter. *The Cambridge Introduction to Narrative*. Cambridge: Cambridge University Press, 2008.

Abrams, Rachel and Lee, Edmund. "Les Moonves Obstructed Investigation into Misconduct Claims, Report Says." *New York Times* (December 4, 2018). www.nytimes.com/2018/12/04/business/media/les-moonves-cbs-report.html?action=click&module=Top%20Stories&pgtype=Homepage

Abrams, Rachel, Hsu, Tiffany, and Eligon, John. "Starbucks's Tall Order: Tackle Systemic Racism in 4 Hours." *New York Times* (May 29, 2018). www.nytimes.com/2018/05/29/business/starbucks-closing-racial-bias-training.html

Adame, Alexandra L. and Knudson, Roger M. "Beyond the Counter-Narrative: Exploring Alternative Narratives of Recovery from the Psychiatric Survivor Movement." *Narrative Inquiry* 17 (2007): 157–178.

Adubato, Steve. *What Were They Thinking? Crisis Communication – The Good, the Bad and the Totally Clueless*. New Brunswick: Rutgers University Press, 2008.

Agai, Jock M. "Resurrection Imageries: A Study of the Motives for Extravagant Burial Rituals in Ancient Egypt." *Verbum et Ecclesia* 36 (2015): 1–7.

Agazzi, Evandro. "Consistency, Truth, and Ontology." *Studia Logica: An International Journal for Symbolic Logic* 97 (2011): 7–29.

Aguilera, Donna C. *Crisis Intervention: Theory and Methodology*. St. Louis: Mosby, 1986.

Aguirre, Abby. "He Fixes the Worst PR Crises Imaginable." *New York Times* (June 1, 2018). www.nytimes.com/2018/06/01/style/michael-sitrick-harvey-weinstein-crisis-management.html

Albright, Madeline. *Fascism: A Warning*. New York: HarperCollins, 2018.

Alexander, Caroline. *The Bounty*. London: HarperCollins, 2003.

Allen, Myria Watkins and Caillouet, Rachel H. "Legitimation Endeavors: Impression Management Strategies Used by an Organization in Crisis." *Communication Monographs* 61 (1994): 45–62.

Allison, Scott T. and Goethals, George. *Heroes: What They Do and Why We Need Them*. Oxford: Oxford University Press, 2011.

Altman, Dennis. *AIDS in the Mind of America: The Social, Political, and Psychological Impact of a New Epidemic*. New York: Anchor Books, 1987.

Altman, Lawrence K. "Rare Cancer Seen in 41 Homosexuals." *New York Times* (July 3, 1981). www.nytimes.com/1981/07/03/us/rare-cancer-seen-in-41-homosexuals.html

Alvesson, Matts and Sveningsson, Stefan. "Managers Doing Leadership: The Extra-ordinization of the Mundane." *Human Relations* 56 (2003): 1435–1459.

Anastaplo, George. *Reflections on Freedom of Speech and the First Amendment.* Lexington: University Press of Kentucky, 2007.

Anderson, Carol. *One Person, No Vote: Suppression Is Destroying Our Democracy.* New York: Bloomsbury, 2018.

Anderson, David L. *The Columbia Guide to the Vietnam War.* New York: Columbia University Press, 2002.

Anderson, Douglas M. (Ed.). *Mosby's Medical, Nursing, & Allied Health Dictionary.* Cambridge, MA: Elsevier Health Sciences, 2001.

Ansoff, H. Igor. "Conceptual Underpinnings of Systemic Strategic Management." *European Journal of Operational Research* 19 (1985): 2–19.

Archer, Patrick. "Towards a Theory of Interest Claims in Constructing Social Problems." *Quantitative Sociology Review* 11 (2015): 46–60.

Arendt, Hannah. *The Origins of Totalitarianism.* New York: Harcourt, Brace, 1958.

Argenti, Paul. "Crisis Communication: Lessons from 9/11." *Harvard Business Review* 80 (2002): 103–119.

Ariely, Dan. *Predictably Irrational: The Hidden Forces That Shape Our Decisions.* New York: HarperCollins, 2008.

Armenakis, Achilles A. and Fredenberger, William B. "Organizational Change Readiness Practices of Business Turnaround Change Agents." *Knowledge and Process Management* 4 (1997): 143–152.

Armenakis, Achilles A., Fredenberger, William B., Cheronnes, Linda, Field, Hubert, Gibbs, William, and Holley, William. "Symbolic Actions Used by Business Turnaround Change Agents." *Academy of Management Journal* 38 (1994): 229–233.

Associated Press. "Crisis Experts Say Facebook Had Mishandled the Data Scandal." *Snopes* (2018). www.snopes.com/ap/2018/03/21/crisis-experts-say-facebook-mishandled-data-scandal

Athitakis, Mark. "Three Lessons from Mary T. Barra's Crisis at GM." *Now Associations* (2014). https://associationsnow.com/2014/03/three-lessons-from-mary-t-barras-crisis-at-gm

Atler, Jonathan. *The Defining Moment: FDR's Hundred Days and the Triumph of Hope.* New York: Simon & Schuster, 2017.

Augustine, Norman R. "Managing the Crisis You Tried to Prevent." *Harvard Business Review* 73 (1995): 147–158.

Baca, George. *Conjuring Crisis: Racism and Civil Rights in a Southern Military City.* New Brunswick, NJ: Rutgers University Press, 2010.

Bacon, John. "President Donald Trump on Kim Jong Un: 'We Fell in Love' Over 'Beautiful Letters.'" *USA Today* (September 30, 2018). www.usatoday.com/story/news/politics/2018/09/30/trump-north-koreas-kim-love-beautiful-letters/1478834002

Bacon, John. "What United Airlines Must Do after PR Nightmare to Win Back Customers." *USA Today* (April 12, 2017). www.usatoday.com/stor

y/news/2017/04/12/how-united-must-make-their-skies-friendly-again/100365668

Bacon, Perry, Jr. "Why LeBron Can Say Whatever He Wants About Politics." *FiveThirtyEight* (July 31, 2018). https://fivethirtyeight.com/features/why-lebron-can-say-whatever-he-wants-about-politics

Bailey, Kenneth D. *Typologies and Taxonomies: An Introduction to Classification Techniques*. Thousand Oaks: Sage, 1994.

Bajarin, Ben. "Survey: Most Facebook Users Don't Expect Much Privacy." *Fast Company* (April 20, 2018). www.fastcompany.com/40561281/survey-most-facebook-users-dont-expect-much-privacy

Baker, Peter. "Unlike His Brother, George W. Bush Stands by His Call to Invade Iraq." *New York Times* (May 15, 2015). www.nytimes.com/2015/05/16/us/politics/some-ask-what-george-w-bush-would-have-done-with-different-iraq-data.html

Baldoni, John. "How a Good Leader Reacts to a Crisis." *Harvard Business Review Web* (January 4, 2011). https://hbr.org/2011/01/how-a-good-leader-reacts-to-a

Bandyopadhyay, Sanghamitra and Saha, Sriparna. *Unsupervised Classification: Similarity Measures, Classical and Metaheuristic Approaches and Applications*. Heidelberg: Springer, 2013.

Banet, Remi. "Brexit and EU Bans on Bananas." *Yahoo* (May 22, 2016). www.yahoo.com/news/brexit-eu-bans-bananas-032855692.html

Baran, Benjamin E. and Adelman, Marisa. "Preparing for the Unthinkable: Leadership Development for Organizational Crisis." *Industrial and Organizational Psychology* 3 (2010): 45–47.

Barra, Mary. "Extremely Thorough, Brutal, Tough and Deeply Troubling." *Vital Speeches of the Day* 80 (2014): 287–289.

Barthes, Roland. *Mythologies*. New York: Noonday Press, 1957/1972.

Battaglio, Stephen. "Internal Review Says NBC News Didn't Know of Any Sexual Harassment Involving Matt Lauer Before His Firing." *Los Angeles Times* (May 9, 2018). www.latimes.com/business/hollywood/la-fi-ct-nbc-lauer-20180509-story.html

Bauchner, Howard, Rivara, Frederick P., Bonow, Robert O. et al. "Death by Gun Violence – A Public Health Crisis." *The JAMA Network* (November 14, 2017). jamanetwork.com/journals/jama/fullarticle/2657417

Bauman, David C. "Evaluating Ethical Approaches to Crisis Leadership: Insights from Unintentional Harm Research." *Journal of Business Ethics* 98 (2011): 281–295.

Bausch, Jerry T. "GM's Head Apologizes to 'Harassed' Car Critic." *Washington Post* (March 28, 1966): A1, A6.

Becker, Ernest. *The Denial of Death*. New York: Free Press, 1997.

Becker, Howard S. "Whose Side Are We On?" *Social Problems* 14 (1967): 239–247.

Becker, Howard S. *Outsiders: Studies in the Sociology of Deviance*. New York: Free Press, 1973.

Belson, Ken and Leibovich, Mark. "Inside the Confidential NFL Meeting to Discuss National Anthem Protests." *New York Times* (April 25, 2018). www.nytimes.com/2018/04/25/sports/nfl-owners-kaepernick.html

Bennis, Warren G. and O'Toole, James. "How Business Schools Lost Their Way." *Harvard Business Review* 83 (2005): 95–104.

Benoit, William. *Accounts, Excuses, and Apologies: A Theory of Image Restoration Strategies*. Albany: State University of New York Press, 1995.

Benoit, William L. and Czerwinski, Anne. "A Critical Analysis of USAir's Repair Discourse." *Communication Quarterly* 60 (1997): 38–57.

Berger, Peter L. *The Sacred Canopy: Elements of a Sociological Theory of Religion*. Garden City, NY: Doubleday, 1967.

Berger, Peter L. and Luckmann, Thomas. *The Social Construction of Reality: A Treatise in the Sociology of Knowledge*. New York: Anchor Books, 1966.

Berkelaar, Brenda and Dutta, Mohan. "A Culture-Centered Approach to Crisis Communication." A paper presented at the annual meeting of the NCA 93rd annual convention, Chicago, 2007.

Berliner, David C. and Biddle, Bruce J. *The Manufactured Crisis: Myths, Fraud, and the Attack on America's Public Schools*. Reading, MA: Addison-Wesley, 1995.

Bernstein, Richard B. *Thomas Jefferson*. New York: Oxford University Press, 2003.

Beschloss, Michael. "On This World War I Anniversary, Let's Not Celebrate Woodrow Wilson." *Washington Post* (November 11, 2018). www.washingtonpost.com/opinions/on-this-world-war-i-anniversary-lets-not-celebrate-woodrow-wilson/2018/11/09/1c7ca77c-e456-11e8-b759-3d88a5ce9e19_story.html?utm_term=.3b8bb8c8f0a8

Beschloss, Michael. *Presidents of War*. New York: Crown, 2018.

Best, Joel. *Threatened Children: Rhetoric and Concern about Child-Victims*. Chicago: University of Chicago Press, 1990.

Best, Joel. "But Seriously Folks: The Limitations of the Strict Constructionist Interpretation of Social Problems." In J.A. Holstein and G. Miller (Eds.), *Reconsidering Social Constructionism: Debates in Social Problems Theory* (pp. 129–147). New York: Aldine De Gruyter, 1993.

Best, Joel. "Constructionism in Context." In J. Best (Ed.), *Images of Issues: Typifying Contemporary Social Problems* (pp. 337–354). New York: Aldine de Gruyter, 1995.

Best, Joel. *Dammed Lies, and Statistics: Untangling the Numbers from the Media, Politicians and Activists*. Berkeley: University of California Press, 2012.

Best, Joel. "The Social Construction of a Mass Shooting Epidemic." *Reason: Free Minds and Free Market* (July 16, 2013). http://reason.com/archives/2013/06/16/the-politics-of-gun-violence

Best, Joel. Personal correspondence with author, 2017. Used by permission.

Bevin, Judi. *The Rise and Fall of Marks & Spencer*. London: Profile Books, 2007.

Bhatnagar, Parija. "The Kmart-Sears Deal." *CNN Money* (November 14, 2004). http://money.cnn.com/2004/11/17/news/fortune500/sears_kmart

Bibeault, Donald B. *Corporate Turnaround: How Managers Turn Losers into Winners*. New York: McGraw-Hill, 1982.

Bigelow, John. "Presentism and Properties." *Philosophical Perspectives* 10 (1966): 35–52.

Birsch, Douglas and Fielder, John H. *The Ford Pinto Case: A Study in Applied Ethics, Business, and Technology.* Albany: State University of New York Press, 1994.

Bischoff, Laura A. (2017, October 21). "Ohio Upgrades Drug Trafficking System to Help Fight Opiate Addiction Crisis." *Dayton* (Ohio) *Daily News* (October 21, 2017): B1.

Bitektine, Alex. "Toward a Theory of Social Judgments of Organizations: The Case of Legitimacy, Reputation, and Status." *Academy of Management Review* 36 (2011): 151–179.

Bligh, Michelle C., Kohles, Jeffrey C., and Meindl, James R. "Charisma under Crisis: Presidential Leadership, Rhetoric, and Media Responses Before and After the September 11th Terrorist Attacks." *Leadership Quarterly* 15 (2004): 211–239.

Blumer, Herbert. "Social Problems as Collective Behavior." *Social Problems* 18 (1971): 298–306.

Boin, Arjen and 't Hart, Paul. "Public Leadership in Times of Crisis: Mission Impossible?" *Public Administration Review* 63 (2003): 544–553.

Boin, Arjen, 't Hart, Paul, McConnell, Allan, and Preston, Thomas. "Leadership Style, Crisis Response, and Blame Management: The Case of Hurricane Katrina." *Public Administration* 88 (2010): 706–723.

Borchers, Callum. "Rush Limbaugh Indicates He's Evacuating Palm Beach Days after Suggesting Hurricane Irma is Fake News." *Washington Post* (September 8, 2017). www.washingtonpost.com/news/the-fix/wp/2017/09/06/rush-limbaughs-dangerous-suggestion-that-hurricane-irma-is-fake-news/?utm_term=.0d1f3208c4dc

Boren, Cindy. "Donald Trump: NFL Has Become Soft Like Our Country Has Become Soft." *Washington Post* (January 10, 2016). www.washingtonpost.com/news/early-lead/wp/2016/01/10/donald-trump-nfl-football-has-become-soft-like-our-country-has-become-soft/?utm_term=.fddb5566a905

Borhek, James T. and Curtis, Richard F. *A Sociology of Belief.* New York: John Wiley & Sons, 1975.

Bornstein, Robert F. "An Interactionist Perspective on Interpersonal Dependency." *Current Directions of Psychological Science* 20 (2011): 124–128.

Bourdieu, Pierre. "What Makes a Social Class? On the Theoretical and Practical Existence of Groups." *Berkeley Journey of Sociology* 32 (1987): 1–17.

Bovasso, Gregory. "A Network Analysis of Social Contagion Processes in an Organizational Intervention." *Human Relations* 49 (1996): 419–435.

Bowen, Flora. "How Is Cambridge University Linked to Cambridge Analytica and the Facebook Data Scandal?" *The Tab* (2018). https://thetab.com/uk/cambridge/2018/04/13/how-is-cambridge-university-linked-to-cambridge-analytica-and-the-facebook-data-scandal-110205

Bowers, Melissa R., Hall, J. Reggie, and Srinivasan, Mandyam. "Organizational Culture and Leadership Style: The Missing Combination for Selecting the Right Leaders for Effective Crisis Management." *Business Horizons* 60 (2017): 551–563.

Boyer, Robert. "Is a Finance-led Growth Regime a Viable Alternative to Fordism? A Preliminary Analysis." *Economy and Society* 29 (2000): 111–145.

Bracken, Joseph. "Being: An Entity, an Activity, or Both an Entity and an Activity?" *Journal of Religion* 96 (2016): 77–93.

Bradner, Eric. "Conway: Trump White House Offered 'Alternative Facts' on Crowd Size." *CNN* (January 23, 2017). www.cnn.com/2017/01/22/politics/ke llyanne-conway-alternative-facts/index.html

Branch, Taylor. *Parting the Waters: America in the King Years, 1954-63*. New York: Simon & Schuster, 1988.

Breslow, Jason M. "Speech 'Was a Great Intelligence Failure.'" *PBS Frontline* (May 17, 2016). www.pbs.org/wgbh/frontline/article/colin-powell-u-n-speech-was-a-great-intelligence-failure

Brinkley, Douglas. *The Great Deluge: Hurricane Katrina, New Orleans, and the Mississippi Gulf Coast*. New York: Harper, 2007.

Brockner, Joel and James, Erika H. "Toward an Understanding of When Executives See Crisis as Opportunity." *Journal of Applied Behavioral Science* 44 (2008): 94–115.

Brooks, David. "The Crisis of Western Civ." *New York Times* (April 21, 2017). www.nytimes.com/2017/04/21/opinion/the-crisis-of-western-civ.html

Bruner, Jerome. *Making Stories: Law, Literature, Life*. New York: Farrar, Straus & Giroux, 2002.

Buckwalter, Wesley, Rose, David, and Turri, John. "Belief through Thick and Thin." *Noûs* 49 (2015): 748–775.

Burawoy, Michael. "For Public Sociology." *American Sociological Review* 70 (2005): 4–28.

Burke, Monte. "Average Player Salaries in the Four Major American Sports Leagues." *Forbes* (December 7, 2012). www.forbes.com/sites/monteburke/20 12/12/07/average-player-salaries-in-the-four-major-american-sports-leagues /#763417035e86

Burke, Peter. "The Crisis in the Arts of the Seventeenth Century: A Crisis of Representation?" *Journal of Interdisciplinary History* 40 (2009): 239–261.

Burns, Ken and Novick, Lynn. *The Vietnam War*. Produced by Florentine Films and WETA (2017).

Burr, Vivian. *Social Constructionism*. London: Routledge, 2015.

Burrows, Peter. *Backfire: Carly Fiorina's High-Stakes Battle for the Soul of Hewlett-Packard*. San Francisco: Wiley, 2003.

Bush, George W. "Speech" (September 11, 2001). www.youtube.com/watch? v=XbqCquDl4k4

Bush, George W. *Address to Joint Session of Congress Following 9/11 Attacks* (September 20, 2001). www.americanrhetoric.com/speeches/gwbush911joint sessionspeech.htm

Bush, George W. *Decision Points*. New York: Crown, 2010.

Butler, Nick, Delaney, Helen, and Spoelstra, Sverre. "Risky Business: Reflections on Critical Performativity in Practice." *Organization* 25 (2018): 428–445.

Byers, Dylan (2018, March 19). "Facebook Is Facing an Existential Crisis." *CNN Money* (March 19, 2018). https://money.cnn.com/2018/03/19/technology/busi ness/facebook-data-privacy-crisis/index.html

Byman, Daniel L. "Iraq and the Global War on Terrorism." *Brookings* (July 1, 2007). www.brookings.edu/articles/iraq-and-the-global-war-on-terrorism

Byrne, John A. *Chainsaw: The Notorious Career of Al Dunlap in the Era of Profit at Any Price.* New York: HarperCollins, 1999.

Cadden, Michael. *Telling Children's Stories: Narrative Theory and Children's Literature.* Lincoln: University of Nebraska Press, 2011.

Cadwalladr, Carole and Graham-Harrison, Emma. "Revealed: 50 Million Facebook Profiles Harvested for Cambridge Analytica in Major Data Breach." *The Guardian* (March 17, 2018). www.theguardian.com/news/2018/mar/17/cambridge-analytica-facebook-influence-us-election

Calonico, Scott. "When AIDS Was Funny." *Vanity Fair* (2015). www.vanityfair.com/news/2015/11/reagan-administration-response-to-aids-crisis

Carbone, Christopher. "Facebook in Crisis." *Fox News* (April 12, 2018). www.foxnews.com/tech/2018/04/12/facebook-in-crisis-mark-zuckerbergs-testimony-reveals-massive-problems-remain.html

Car Insurance Quotes. "5 of the Most Dangerous Cars Ever Made" (no date). Car Insurance Quotes.net. www.carinsurancequotes.net/5-of-the-most-dangerous-cars-ever-made

Carlyle, Thomas. *On Heroes, Hero-worship, and the Heroic in History.* New Haven: Yale University Press, 1841/2013.

Carmeli, Abraham and Schaubroeck, John. "Organizational Crisis-Preparedness: The Importance of Learning from Failures." *Long-Range Planning* 41 (2008): 177–196.

Carp, Alex. "History for a Post-Fact America." *NYR Daily* (October 19, 2018). www.nybooks.com/daily/2018/10/19/history-for-a-post-fact-america/?utm_medium=email&utm_campaign=NYR%20Daily%20Alex%20Carp&utm_content=NYR%20Daily%20Alex%20Carp+CID_ac1dbeb6636ffb5049e6f2120148de07&utm_source=Newsletter&utm_term=History%20for%20a%20Post-Fact%20America

Carpenter, Daniel. *Reputation and Power: Organizational Image and Pharmaceutical Regulation at the FDA.* Princeton: Princeton University Press, 2010.

Carter, Bill. "Chevy Chase's Show Canceled after 6 Weeks." *New York Times* (October 18, 1993). www.nytimes.com/1993/10/18/arts/chevy-chase-s-show-canceled-after-6-weeks.html

Carter, Chris and Whittle, Andrea. "Making Strategy Critical?" *Critical Perspectives on Accounting* 53 (2018): 1–15.

Case, Anne and Deaton, Angus. "Rising Morbidity and Mortality in Midlife among White Non-Hispanic Americans in the 21st Century." *Proceedings of the National Academy of Sciences of the United States of America* 112 (2015): 15078–15083.

Ceaser, James W. "The Social Construction of Ronald Reagan." In C. W. Dunn (Ed.), *The Enduring Ronald Reagan* (pp. 37–50). Lexington: University Press of Kentucky, 2009.

Cherwitz, Richard A. "Lyndon Johnson and the 'Crisis' of the Tonkin Gulf: A President's Justification of War." *Western Journal of Speech Communication* 42 (1978): 93–104.

Cherwitz, Richard A. and Zagacki., Kenneth S. "Consummatory versus Justificatory Crisis Rhetoric." *Western Journal of Speech Communication* 50 (1986): 307–324.

Chin, Rita. *The Crisis of Multiculturalism in Europe*. Princeton: Princeton University Press, 2017.

Chisholm, Roderick. "Referring to Things That No Longer Exist." *Philosophical Perspectives* 4 (1990): 545–556.

Chrisman, James J., Hofer, Charles W., and Boulton, William R. "Toward a System for Classifying Business Strategies." *Academy of Management Review* 13 (1988): 413–428.

Christensen, Sandra L. and Kohls, John. "Ethical Decision Making in Times of Organizational Crisis." *Business & Society* 42 (2003): 328–358.

Chua, Amy. *Political Tribes: Group Instinct and the Fate of Nations*. New York: Penguin, 2018.

Cleghorn, Reese. "Apostle of Crisis." *Saturday Evening Post* 236 (1963): 15–20.

Clinton, Hilary Rodham. "American Democracy Is in Crisis," *The Atlantic* (September 16, 2018). www.theatlantic.com/ideas/archive/2018/09/american-democracy-is-in-crisis/570394

Clinton, William J. "Clinton on the 1993 World Trade Center Bombing." History.com (1993). www.history.com/speeches/clinton-on-the-1993-world-trade-center-bombing

Cohen, Stanley. *Folk Devils and Moral Panics*. London: Routledge, 2011.

Collignon, Richard A. "The 'Holistic' and 'Individualistic' Views of Organizations." *Theory and Society* 18 (1989): 83–123.

Collins, Randall. "On the Microfoundations of Macrosociology." *American Journal of Sociology* 86 (1981): 984–1014.

Colvin, Geoff. "Carly Fiorina's Disastrous Record as HP's CEO." *Fortune* (September 21, 2015). http://fortune.com/2015/09/21/carly-fiorina-hp-ceo-business-record

Confessore, Nicholas and Rosenberg, Matthew. "Sheryl Sandberg Asked for Soros Research, Facebook Acknowledges." *New York Times* (November 29, 2018). www.nytimes.com/2018/11/29/technology/george-soros-facebook-sheryl-sandberg.html

Connors, Michael H. and Halligan, Peter W. "A Cognitive Account of Belief: A Tentative Roadmap." *Frontiers of Psychology* 5 (2014): 1–14.

Coombs, W. Timothy. *Ongoing Crisis Communication: Planning, Managing, and Responding*. Los Angeles: Sage, 2007.

Cooter, Roger. "Historical Key Words: Crisis." *The Lancet* 373 (2009): 887.

Coulson, Andy. "How United Airlines Should Have Handled this PR Crisis." *GQ* (April 12, 2017). www.gq-magazine.co.uk/article/united-airlines-stock

Coye, Ray W., Murphy, Patrick J., and Spencer, Patricia E. "Using Historic Mutinies to Understand Defiance in Modern Organizations." *Journal of Management History* 16 (2010): 270–287.

Czarnecki, Sean. "Timeline of a Crisis." *PR Week* (June 6, 2017). www .prweek.com/article/1435619/timeline-crisis-united-airlines#RqzfmsZlKtMX WgdK.99.

Czarniawska, Barbara. *Writing Management: Organization Theory as a Literary Genre*. Oxford: Oxford University Press, 1999.

Daft, Richard L. and Weick, Karl E. "Toward a Model of Organizations as Interpretation Systems." *Academy of Management Review* 9 (1984): 284–295.

Dahl, Robert A. "The Concept of Power." *Behavioral Science* 2 (1957): 201–215.

Davey, Monica and Smith, Mitch. "In Nassar Case, Michigan State Wanted Famed Ex-Prosecutor to Both Examine and Defend It." *New York Times* (January 27, 2018). www.nytimes.com/2018/01/27/us/michigan-state-nassar-fitzgerald.html

Davis, David R. The *Postwar Decline of American Newspapers, 1945–1965*. Westport, CT: Praeger, 2006

Davis, Lanny J. *Crisis Tales: Five Rules for Coping with Crisis in Business, Politics, and Life*. New York: Threshold, 2013.

Davis, Murray S. "That's Interesting! Towards a Phenomenology of Sociology and a Sociology of Phenomenology." *Philosophy of Social Sciences* 1 (1971): 309–344.

Dawson, Christopher. *Progress and Religion: An Historical Inquiry*. Washington, DC: Catholic University Press, 2001.

Dean, Ashley. "*Denver Post* Employees Protest Ownership with Events in Denver and New York." *Denverite* (May 8, 2018). denverite.com/2018/05/08/denver-post-protest-ownership

De Beauvoir, Simone. *The Second Sex*. New York: Knopf, 1952.

De Cauwer, Stijn. "Introduction: Resistance in Times of Crisis." In S. De Cauwer (Ed.), *Critical Theory at a Crossroads: Conversations on Resistance in Times of Crisis* (pp. xi–xxxv). New York: Columbia University Press, 2018.

Deephouse, David L. and Carter, Suzanne M. "An Examination of Differences between Organizational Legitimacy and Organizational Reputation." *Journal of Management Studies* 42 (2005): 329–360.

Dehghani, Morteza, Johnson, Kate, Hoover, Joe, Sagi, Eyal, Garten, Justin, Parmar, Nik, ... and Gauthier, Isabel. "Purity Homophily in Social Networks." *Journal of Experimental Psychology* 145 (2016): 366–375.

De Neys, Wim. "Heuristic Bias, Conflict and Rationality in Decision Making." In B. Glatzeder, V. Goel, and A. Müller (Eds.), *Towards a Theory of Thinking: Building Blocks for a Conceptual Framework* (pp. 23–33). Berlin: Springer, 2010.

De Rycker, Antoon and Zuraidah, Mohd Don. "Discourse in Crisis: Crisis in Discourse." In A. De Rycker and M. D. Zuraidah (Eds.). *Discourse and Crisis: Critical Perspectives* (pp. 3–65). Amsterdam: John Benjamins, 2013.

Desai, Vinit M. "Mass Media and Massive Failures: Determining Organizational Efforts to Defend Field Legitimacy During Crisis." *Academy of Management Journal* 54 (2011): 263–278.

Deubert, Chris, Cohen, I. Glenn, and Lynch, Holly Fernandez. *Comparing Health-Related Policies & Practices in Sports: The NFL and Other Professional*

Leagues. Cambridge: Football Players Health Study at Harvard University, 2017.

De Vries, Y. A., Roest, A. M., de Jonge, P., Cuijpers, P., Munafó, M. R., and Bestiaansen, J. A. "The Cumulative Effect of Reporting and Citation Biases on the Apparent Efficacy of Treatments: The Case of Depression." *Psychological Medicine* 1–3 (2018): 1–3.

Dewey, John. *How We Think*. Lexington: D.C. Heath, 1910.

Diamond, Larry. "The Liberal Democratic Order in Crisis." *American Spectator* (February 16, 2018). www.the-american-interest.com/2018/02/16/liberal-democratic-order-crisis

Dichev, Ilia and Yu, Gwen. "Higher Risk, Lower Returns: What Hedge Fund Investors Really Earn." *Journal of Financial Economics* 100 (2011): 248–263.

DiMaggio, Paul and Powell, Walter W. "The Iron Cage Revisited: Collective Rationality and Institutional Isomorphism in Organizational Fields." *American Sociological Review* 48 (1983): 147–160.

Douglass, Paul. *The Crisis in Modernism: Bergson and the Vitalist Controversy*. Cambridge: Cambridge University Press, 2010.

Dubin, Robert. *Theory Building*. New York: Free Press, 1978.

Dubofsky, Melvyn and McCartin, Joseph A. *Labor in America: A History*. Hoboken, NJ: Wiley Blackwell, 2017.

Ducachet, Henry W. *The Prognosis and Crisis of Hippocrates*. New York: J. Eastburn and Co., 1819.

Duncan, W. Jack, Yeager, Valeria A, and Rucks, Andrew C. "Surviving Organizational Disasters." *Business Horizons* 54 (2011): 135–142.

Dunlap, Albert J. *Mean Business: How I Save Bad Companies and Make Good Companies Great*. New York: Simon & Schuster, 1996.

Durkheim, Émile. *The Rules of Sociological Method*. New York: Free Press, 1966.

Duster, Troy. "Race and Reification in Science." *Science* 18 (2005): 1050–1051.

Dutton, Jane E. "The Processing of Crisis and Non-Crisis Strategic Issues." *Journal of Management Studies* 23 (1986): 501–517.

Economist. "In a League of Its Own." *The Economist* (April 27, 2006). www.economist.com/business/2006/04/27/in-a-league-of-its-own

Editors. "Case Against Iraq." *New York Times* (February 6, 2003). www.nytimes.com/2003/02/06/opinion/the-case-against-iraq.html

Editors. "From the Editors: The Times and Iraq." *New York Times* (May 26, 2004). www.nytimes.com/2004/05/26/world/from-the-editors-the-times-and-iraq.html

Editors. "Irrefutable." *Washington Post* (February 6, 2003). www.washingtonpost.com/archive/opinions/2003/02/06/irrefutable/e598b1be-a78a-4a42-8e1a-c336f7a217f4/?utm_term=.737a45605151

Editors. "Slandering the Unborn." *New York Times* (December 28, 2018). www.nytimes.com/interactive/2018/12/28/opinion/crack-babies-racism.html

Effron, Daniel A. "It Could Have Been True: How Counterfactual Thoughts Reduce Condemnation of Falsehoods and Increase Political Polarization." *Personality and Social Psychology Bulletin* 44 (2017): 729–745.

Effron, Daniel and Brewis, Kathy. "Politicians' Lies and the Power of Imagination." *London Business School* (May 2, 2018). www.london.edu/faculty-and-research/lbsr/politicians-lies-and-the-power-of-imagination

Egelhoff, W. G. and Sen, F. "An Information-Processing Model of Crisis Management." *Management Communication Quarterly* 5 (1992): 443–484.

Eisenstein, Paul A. "From Factory Floor to Corner Office, Mary Barra Is a Rule Breaker." *NBCNews.com.* (August 4, 2017). www.nbcnews.com/business/autos/factory-floor-corner-office-gm-s-mary-barra-rule-breaker-n789596

Ekirch, A. Roger. *American Sanctuary: Mutiny, Martyrdom, and National Identity in the Age of Revolution.* New York: Pantheon, 2017.

Ember, Sydney. "*Denver Post* Rebels against Its Hedge-Fund Ownership." *New York Times* (April 7, 2018). www.nytimes.com/2018/04/07/business/media/denver-post-opinion-owner.html

Emerson, Robert M. and Messinger, Sheldon L. "The Micro-Politics of Trouble." *Social Problems* 25 (1977): 121–134.

Erikson, Erik H. "Autobiographic Notes on the Identity Crisis." *Daedalus* 99 (1970): 730–759.

Evans, Jayda. "Garfield Football Team Takes Knee during National Anthem Prior to Game Friday Night." *Seattle Times* (September 16, 2016). www.seattletimes.com/sports/high-school/garfield-football-team-takes-knee-prior-to-game-friday-night

Evans, Mark. "The Importance of Grace Under Pressure." *Forbes* (March 28, 2012). www.forbes.com/sites/markevans/2012/03/28/the-importance-of-grace-under-pressure/#260a1e6e1228

Everest, Larry. *Behind the Poison Cloud: Union Carbide's Bhopal Massacre.* Chicago: Banner Press, 1985.

Fainaru-Wada, Mark and Fainaru, Steve. *League of Denial: The NFL: Concussions, and the Battle for Truth.* New York: Crown, 2013.

Fairhurst, Gail T. "Leadership and the Power of Framing." *Leader to Leader* 61 (2011): 43–47.

Fairhurst, Gail T. and Sarr, Robert A. *The Art of Framing: Managing the Language of Leadership.* San Francisco: Jossey-Bass, 1996.

Falkheimer, Jesper and Heide, Mats. "Multicultural Crisis Communication: Towards a Social Constructionist Perspective." *Journal of Contingencies and Crisis Management* 14 (2006): 180–189.

Falkheimer, Jesper and Heide, Mats. "Crisis Communicators in Charge: From Plans to Improvisation." In W.T. Coombs and J. Holladay (Eds.), *The Handbook of Crisis Communication* (pp. 511–526). Hoboken, NJ: Wiley-Blackwell, 2010.

Farley, Robert. "Trump's Bogus Voter Fraud Claims." *FactCheck.org* (October 19, 2016). www.factcheck.org/2016/10/trumps-bogus-voter-fraud-claims

Fauconnier, Giles. *Mental Spaces: Aspects of Meaning Construction in Natural Language.* Cambridge, MA: MIT Press, 1985.

Fauconnier, Giles and Turner, Mark. *The Way We Think: Conceptual Blending and the Mind's Hidden Complexity.* New York: Basic Books, 2002.

Fearn-Banks, Kathleen. *Crisis Communications: A Casebook Approach*. New York: Routledge, 2011.

Feeley, Francis. "The New Republican Man and the Role of Women in the New Republic. In F. Feeley (Ed.), *Comparative Patriarchy and American Institutions: The Language, Culture, and Politics of Liberalism* (pp. 10–38). Newcastle upon Tyne: Cambridge Scholars Publishing, 2010.

Ferrante, Joan and Brown, Prince, Jr. *The Social Construction of Race and Ethnicity in the United States*. New York: Longman, 1998.

Field, Kelly. "Obama Plan to Tie Student Aid to College Ratings Draws Mixed Reviews." *Chronicle of Higher Education* (August 22, 2013). www .chronicle.com/article/obama-plan-to-tie-student-aid/141229

Finkelman, Paul. "Voters and Voices: Reevaluations in the Aftermath of the 2000 Presidential Election: The Proslavery Origins of the Electoral College." *Cardozo Law Review* 23 (2002): 1145–1157.

Fiorina, Carly. *Tough Choices: A Memoir*. New York: Portfolio, 2006.

Fish, Stanley. "Consequences." *Critical Inquiry* 11 (1985): 433–458.

Fish, Stanley. *Doing What Comes Naturally: Change, Rhetoric, and the Practice of Theory in Literary and Legal Studies*. Durham: Duke University Press, 1989.

Fisher, Marc, Cox, John W., and Hermann, Peter. "Pizzagate: From Rumor to Hashtag to Gunfire in DC." *Washington Post* (December 6, 2016). www .washingtonpost.com/local/pizzagate-from-rumor-to-hashtag-to-gunfire-in-dc /2016/12/06/4c7def50-bbd4-11e6-94ac-3d324840106c_story.html?utm_ term=.8f9d47b62a9c

Fisher, Walter. *Human Communication as Narration: Toward a Philosophy of Reason, Value, and Action*. Columbia: University of South Carolina Press, 1987.

Flamm, Michael W. *Law and Order: Street Crime, Civil Unrest, and the Crisis of Liberalism in the 1960s*. New York: Columbia University Press, 2007.

Foley, John Miles. *Oral Tradition and the Internet: Pathways of the Mind*. Urbana: University of Illinois Press, 2012.

Follmer, Max. "The Reporting Team That Got Iraq Right." *Huffington Post* (May 25, 2011). www.huffingtonpost.com/2008/03/17/the-reporting-team- that-g_n_91981.html

Ford, Jackie, Harding, Nancy, and Learmonth, Mark. *Leadership as Identity: Constructions and Deconstructions*. London: Palgrave, 2008.

Foroohar, Rana. "Mary Barra's Bumpy Ride." *Time* (October 6, 2014): 32–38.

Foucault, Michel. *"Society Must Be Defended." Lectures at the College de France*, 1975–76. New York: Picador, 1976.

Foucault, Michel. *Discipline and Punish: The Birth of the Prison*. New York: Vintage, 1979.

Foucault, Michel. *The History of Sexuality*. New York: Vintage, 1980.

Fowler, Karen L., King, Nathan D., and Larson, Milan D. "Organizational Preparedness for Coping with a Major Disaster." *Business & Society* 46 (2007): 88–103.

Frank, L. K. "Social Problems." *American Journal of Sociology* 30 (1925): 462–473.

Frankel, Seera and Roose, Kevin. "Zuckerberg, Facing Facebook's Worst Crisis Yet, Pledged Better Privacy." *New York Times* (March 21, 2018). www .nytimes.com/2018/03/21/technology/facebook-zuckerberg-data-privacy.html

Frankel, Todd C. "Why Gun Violence Research Has Been Shut Down for 20 Years." *Washington Post* (October 4, 2017). www.washingtonpost.com/news/ wonk/wp/2017/10/04/gun-violence-research-has-been-shut-down-for-20- years/?utm_term=.b4d7024c7a34.

Freedman, James O. *Crisis and Legitimacy: The Administrative Process and American Government.* Cambridge: Cambridge University Press, 1978.

Freeman, R. Edward. *Strategic Management: A Stakeholder Approach.* Boston: Pitman, 1984.

French, John R. P., Jr. and Raven, Bertram. "The Bases of Social Power." In D. Cartwright (Ed.), *Studies in Social Power* (pp. 150–167). Ann Arbor: Institute for Social Research, 1959.

Freud, Sigmund. *Group Psychology and the Analysis of the Ego.* New York: Liveright Publishing, 1921/1967.

Friedman, Milton. "The Social Responsibility of Business Is to Increase Its Profits." *New York Times Magazine* (September 13, 1970). www .colorado.edu/studentgroups/libertarians/issues/friedman-soc-resp- business.html 2

Frier, Sarah and Ponczek, Sarah. "Facebook Shares Recover from Cambridge Analytica Scandal." *Bloomberg* (May 10, 2018). www.bloomberg.com/news/a rticles/2018–05-10/facebook-shares-recover-from-cambridge-analytica-crisis

Frieze, Deborah and Wheatley, Margaret. "It's Time for the Heroes to Go Home." *Leader to Leader* 62 (2011): 27–32.

Frymer, Paul. *Building an American Empire: The Era of Territorial and Political Expansion.* Princeton: Princeton University Press, 2017.

Funk, Cary, Kennedy, Brian, and Hefferon, Meg. "Vast Majority of Americans Say Benefits of Childhood Vaccines Outweigh Risis." *Pew Research Center* (February 2, 2017). www.pewinternet.org/2017/02/02/vast-majority-of- americans-say-benefits-of-childhood-vaccines-outweigh-risks

Geier, Ben. "GM's Mary Barra: Crisis Manager of the Year." *Fortune* (December 28, 2015). http://fortune.com/2014/12/28/gms-barra-crisis- manager

Genovese, Michael A. "Presidential Leadership and Crisis Management." *Presidential Studies Quarterly* 16 (1986): 300–309.

George, Alice L. *The Cuban Missile Crisis: The Threshold of Nuclear War.* New York: Routledge, 2013.

George, Bill. "Seven Lessons for Leading in Crisis." *Wall Street Journal* (March 5, 2009). www.wsj.com/articles/SB123551729786163925

George, Bill. "What Mark Zuckerberg Can Learn About Crisis Leadership from Starbucks." *Harvard Business School's Working Knowledge* (April 24, 2018). https://hbswk.hbs.edu/item/op-ed-what-mark-zuckerberg-can-learn-about-cri sis-leadership-from-starbucks?cid=spmailing-19871858-WK%20Newsletter %2004–25-2018%20(1)-April%2025,%202018

Gerber, Jeffrey S. and Offit, Paul A. "Vaccines and Autism: A Tale of Shifting Hypotheses." *Clinical Infectious Diseases* 48 (2009): 456–461.

Gerbre, Tefere. "Voter Suppression Is the Problem, Not Voter Fraud." *Huffingt onPost.com* (May 24, 2017). www.huffingtonpost.com/entry/voter-suppression -the-problem-not-voter-fraud_us_592598bae4b09c5b6bf92d81

Getus, Arie de. *The Living Company*. Boston: Harvard Business School, 1997.

Ghosn, Carlos. "We Don't Have a Choice." *Automotive News* (November 8, 1999). www.autonews.com/article/19991108/ANA/911080721/ghosn:we-dont-have-a-choice

Gilbert, Ben. "How Facebook Makes Money from Your Data, in Mark Zuckerberg's Words." *Business Insider* (April 11, 2018). www.businessinsider.com/how-facebook-makes-money-according-to-mark-zuckerberg-2018-4

Gilpin, Dawn R. and Murphy, Pricilla J. *Crisis Management in a Complex World*. Oxford: Oxford University Press, 2008.

Gioia, Dennis A. and Sims, Henry P., Jr. "Introduction: Social Cognition in Organizations." In H.P. Sims and D.A. Gioia (Eds.), *The Thinking Organization* (pp. 1–19). San Francisco: Jossey-Bass, 1986.

Giroux, Henry. *The University in Chains: Confronting the Military-Industrial-Academic Complex*. Boulder: Paradigm Publishers, 2007.

Gnyawali, Devi R. and Song, Yue. "Pursuit of Rigor in Research: Illustration for Coopetition Literature." *Industrial Marketing Management* 57 (2016): 12–22.

Goffman, Erving. *Frame Analysis: An Essay on the Organization of Experience*. New York: Harper & Row, 1974.

Goldee, Fiona. "The Fraud Behind the MMR Scare." *British Medical Journal* 342 (2011). www-bmj-com.ezproxy.neu.edu/content/342/bmj.d22

Goldman, Lynn R. "We Calculated the Deaths from Maria. Politics Played No Role." *Washington Post* (September 15, 2018). www.washingtonpost.com/opi nions/we-calculated-the-deaths-from-hurricane-maria-politics-played-no-role /2018/09/15/2b765b26-b849-11e8-94eb-3bd52dfe917b_story.html?utm_ term=.45c896cfc25f

Gomez, Melissa. "Giuliani Says 'Truth Isn't Truth' in Defense of Trump's Legal Strategy." *New York Times* (August 19, 2018). www.nytimes.com/2018/08/19/ us/giuliani-meet-the-press-truth-is-not-truth.html

Goode, William J. *The Celebration of Heroes: Prestige as a Social Control System*. Berkeley: University of California Press, 1978.

Goodwin, Doris Kearns. *Leadership in Turbulent Times*. New York: Simon & Schuster, 2018.

Gopnik, Adam. "How Charles de Gaulle Rescued France." *New Yorker* (August 20, 2018). www.newyorker.com/magazine/2018/08/20/how-charles-de-gaulle-rescued-france

Gostin, Lawrence O. *The AIDS Pandemic: Complacency, Injustice, and Unfulfilled Expectations*. Chapel Hill: University of North Carolina Press, 2004.

Gould-Wartofsky, Michael. "The Crisis of Liberal Democracy." *Huffington Post* (December 6, 2017). www.huffingtonpost.com/michael-gouldwartofsky/the-crisis-of-liberal-dem_b_6782558.html

Gouldner, Alvin W. *The Coming Crisis of Western Sociology*. New York: Basic Books, 1970.

Gouran, Dennis S. *Making Decisions in Groups: Choices and Consequences.* Glenview: Scott, Foresman, 1982.

Graf, Markus. "Categorization and Object Shape." In B. Glatzeder, V. Goel, and A. Müller (Eds.), *Towards a Theory of Thinking: Building Blocks for a Conceptual Framework* (pp. 73–101). Berlin: Springer, 2010.

Grant, Joseph M. and Mack, David A. "Healthy Leadership during Organizational Crisis." *Organizational Dynamics* 33 (2004): 409–425.

Granville, Kevin. "Facebook and Cambridge Analytica: What You Need to Know as Fallout Widens." *New York Times* (March 19, 2018). www .nytimes.com/2018/03/19/technology/facebook-cambridge-analytica-explained.html

Graves, Allison and Moorthy, Neelesh. "Fact-Checking Donald Trump on the Final Night of the Republican Convention." *Politifact* (July 21, 2016). www .politifact.com/truth-o-meter/article/2016/jul/21/fact-checking-final-night-rncincle

Gray, Judy H. and Densten, Iain L. "How Leaders Woo Followers in the Romance of Leadership." *Applied Psychology: An International Review* 56 (2007): 558–581.

Green, Melanie C. "Transportation into Narrative Worlds: The Role of Prior Knowledge and Perceived Realism." *Discourse Processes* 38 (2004): 247–266.

Green, Melanie C. and Brock, Timothy C. "The Role of Transportation in the Persuasiveness of Public Narratives." *Journal of Personality and Social Psychology* 79 (2000): 701–721.

Greenfield, Rebecca. "Mark Zuckerberg: Super Hero?" *The Atlantic* (May 14, 2012). www.theatlantic.com/technology/archive/2012/05/mark-zuckerberg-super-hero/328178

Grint, Keith. *Management: A Sociological Introduction.* Cambridge: Polity Press, 1995.

Grint, Keith and Jackson, Brad. "Toward 'Socially Constructive' Social Constructions of Leadership." *Management Communication Quarterly* 24 (2010): 348–355.

Gryboski, Michael. "7 Reactions to the Las Vegas Shooting Massacre." *Christian Post* (October 3, 2017). www.christianpost.com/news/7-reactions-to-the-las-vegas-shooting-massacre-201479/page8.html

Gubrium, Jaber F. and Holstein, James A. *Analyzing Narrative Reality.* Thousand Oaks: Sage, 2009.

Guilbert, Alain "Crisis Communications." *Ivey Business Journal* 64 (1999): 78–89.

Gupta, Vishal, Seonghee, Han, Vikram, Nanda, and Sabatino (Dino), Silveri. "When Crisis Knocks, Call a Powerful CEO (or Not): Investigating the Contingent Link between CEO Power and Firm Performance during Industry Turmoil." *Group & Organization Management* 41 (2016): 1–28.

Gusfield, Joseph R. "Conversation." *Addiction* 101 (2006): 481–490.

Gusfield, Joseph R. *The Culture of Public Programs: Drinking-Driving and the Symbolic Order.* Chicago: University of Chicago Press, 1981.

Gusfield, Joseph R. *Symbolic Crusade: Status Politics and the American Temperance Movement.* Urbana: University of Illinois Press, 1963.

Haass, Richard N. *War of Necessity, War of Choice: A Memoir of Two Iraq Wars*. New York: Simon & Schuster, 2009.

Habermas, Jürgen. *Legitimation Crisis*. Boston: Beacon Press, 1975.

Hahn, Dan F. "Corrupt Rhetoric: President Ford and the Mayaguez Affair." *Communication Quarterly* 28 (1980): 38–43.

Hahs, Adam and Colic, Milan. "Truth-Making in a World Made Up of Stories." *Explorations: An E-Journal of Narrative Practice* 1 (2010): 72–77.

Halbach, Volker and Horsten, Leon. *Principles of Truth*. Frankfurt: Ontos Verlag, 2004.

Halligan, Peter W. "Belief and Illness." *Psychologist* 20 (2007): 358–361.

Hambrick, Donald C. and Quigley, Timothy J. "Toward More Accurate Contextualization of the CEO Effect on Firm Performance." *Strategic Management Journal* 35 (2014): 473–491.

Hannah, Sean T., Uhl-Bien, Mary, Avolio, Bruce J., and Cavarretta, Fabrice L. "A Framework for Examining Leadership in Extreme Contexts." *Leadership Quarterly* 20 (2009): 897–919.

Harcourt, Bernard E., Meares, Tracey L., Hagan, John, and Morrill, Calvin. "Seeing Crime and Punishment through a Sociological Lens: Contributions, Practices, and the Future." *University of Chicago Law School Legal Forum* (2005): 289–323.

Hardin, Russell. "The Economics of Religious Belief." *Journal of Institutional and Theoretical Economics* 153 (1997): 259–278.

Hargie, Owen, Stapleton, Karyn, and Tourish, Dennis. "Interpretations of CEO Public Apologies for the Banking Crisis: Attributions of Blame and Avoidance of Responsibility." *Organization* 17 (2010): 721–742.

't Hart, Paul and Boin, Arjen. "Between Crisis and Normalcy: The Long Shadow of Post-Crisis Politics." In U. Rosenthal, A. Boin, and L. K. Comfort (Eds.), *Managing Crisis: Threats, Dilemmas, Opportunities* (pp. 28–46). Springfield, IL: Charles C. Thomas, 2001.

Harvard Business Essentials. *Crisis Management: Mastering the Skills to Prevent Disasters*. Boston: Harvard Business School Press, 2004.

Harwell, Drew. "Why General Motors' $900 Million Fine for a Deadly Defect Is Just a Slap on the Wrist." *Washington Post* (September 17, 2015). www .washingtonpost.com/news/business/wp/2015/09/17/why-general-motors-900 -million-fine-for-a-deadly-defect-is-just-a-slap-on-the-wrist/?utm_term= .e4e0bc69b26a

Haslam, S. Alexander, Platow, Michael J., Turner, John C., Reynolds, Katherine J., Megarty, Craig, Oakes, Penelope J. … and Veenstra, Kristine. "Social Identity and the Romance of Leadership: The Importance of Being Seen to Be 'Doing It for Us.'" *Group Processes & Intergroup Relations* 4 (2001): 191–205.

Haun, Daniel and Over, Harriet. "Like Me: A Homophily-Based Account of Human Culture." In T. Breyer (Ed.), *Epistemological Dimensions of Evolutionary Psychology* (pp. 117–130). New York: Springer, 2015.

Haydock, Michael D. "The Dark Side of Normalcy: The U.S. under President Warren Harding." *American History* 34 (1999): 16–25.

Hearit, Keith Michael and Courtright, Jeffrey L. "A Social Constructionist Approach to Crisis Management: Allegations of Sudden Acceleration in the Audi 5000." *Communication Studies* 54 (2003): 79–95.

Heath, Robert L. and Millar, Dan P. *Responding to Crisis: A Rhetorical Approach to Crisis Communication.* New York: Routledge, 2003.

Hefferman, George. "The Concept of Krisis in Husserl's *The Crisis of the European Sciences and Transcendental Phenomenology.*" *Husserl Studies* 33 (2017): 229–257.

Heider, Fritz. "Social Perception and Phenomenal Causality." *Psychological Review* 51 (1944): 358–374.

Heifetz, Ronald, Grashow, Alexander, and Linsky, Marty. "Leadership in a (Permanent) Crisis." *Harvard Business Review* 87 (2009): 62–70.

Heinrich, Michael. "Crisis Theory, the Law of the Tendency of the Profit Rate to Fall, and Marx's Studies in the 1870s." *Monthly Review* 64 (2013): 15–31.

Heracleous, Loizos. *Discourse, Interpretation, Organization.* Cambridge: Cambridge University Press, 2006.

Herbst, Susan. "Walter Lippmann's *Public Opinion,* Revisited." *Harvard International Journal of Press/Politics* 4 (1999): 88–93.

Hermann, Charles F. "Some Consequences of Crisis Which Limit the Viability of Organizations." *Administrative Science Quarterly* 8 (1963): 61–82.

Hipwell, Deirdre. "Toblerone 'Crisis' Was Never a Case of Biting Off More Than You Can Chew." *The Times* (London) (October 21, 2017). www.thetimes.co.uk/article/the-cadbury-crisis-that-was-never-a-case-of-biting-off-more-than-you-can-chew-6t0bz6zcl

Hirsch, Jerry and Puzzzanghera, Jim. "Lawmaker: GM Response to Ignition Switch Issue 'Smacks of Cover-Up.'" *Los Angeles Times* (June 18, 2014). www.latimes.com/business/autos/la-fi-hy-barra-congressional-testimony-20140617-story.html

Hirschman, Albert O. *Exit, Voice, and Loyalty: Responses to Decline in Firms, Organizations, and States.* Cambridge, MA: Harvard University Press, 1970.

Hirschman, Albert O. "Exit, Voice, and the State." *World Politics* 31 (1978): 90–107.

Hiyama, Hiroshi. "Fukushima Was 'Man-Made' Disaster: Japanese Probe." *Phys.org* (July 4, 2012). https://phys.org/news/2012-07-japan-diet-publish-fukushima-disaster.html

Hodgson, Godfrey. *The Myth of American Exceptionalism.* New Haven: Yale University Press, 2009.

Hofstadter, Richard. *Anti-Intellectualism in American Life.* New York: Knopf, 1966.

Hofweber, Thomas. "Logic and Ontology." *Stanford Encyclopedia of Philosophy* (2017). https://plato.stanford.edu/entries/logic-ontology/#DifConOnt

Honneth, Alex. *Reification: A New Look at an Old Idea.* New York: Oxford University Press, 2008.

Hooijberg, Robert, Hunt, James G., and Dodge, George E. "Leadership Complexity and Development of the Leaderplex Model." *Journal of Management* 23 (1997): 375–408.

Hornsby, Alton, Jr. "Martin Luther King, Jr. – Letter from a Birmingham Jail." *Journal of Negro History* 71 (1986): 38–44.

Hoshi, Masamichi. "Carlos Ghosn's Short-Term Mindset Puts Nissan in a Fix." *Nikkei Asian Review* (February 19, 2018). https://asia.nikkei.com/Sp otlight/Comment/Carlos-Ghosn-s-short-term-mindset-puts-Nissan-in -a-fix2

Hough, Richard. *Captain Bligh and Mr. Christian: The Men and the Mutiny.* London: Hutchinsons, 1972.

Huang, Li and Murnighan, J. Keith. "Why Everybody Trusted Madoff." *Forbes* (December 22, 2010). www.forbes.com/2010/12/22/bernard-madoff-trust-psychology-leadership-managing-ponzi.html#6e543f571de9

Hughes, Alan, Kitson, Michael, Probert, Jocelyn, Bullock, Anna, and Milner, Isobel. *Hidden Connections: Knowledge Exchange Between the Arts and Humanities and the Private, Public, and Third Sectors.* Cambridge: Arts & Humanities Research Council, 2011.

Hughes, Brent L. and Zaki, Jamil. "The Neuroscience of Motivated Cognition." *Science and Society* 19 (2015): 62–64.

Hunt, Lynn A. *The Family Romance of the French Revolution.* Berkeley: University of California Press, 1992.

Hunt, Ronald J. "The Crisis of Liberal Democracy." *Polity* 13 (1980): 312–326.

Iacocca, Lee with Novak, William. *Iacocca: An Autobiography.* New York: Bantam, 1984.

Ibarra, Herminia. "Homophily and Differential Returns: Sex Differences in Network Structure and Access in an Advertising Firm." *Administrative Science Quarterly* 37 (1992): 422–447.

Ice, Richard. "Corporate Publics and Rhetorical Strategies: The Case of Union Carbide's Bhopal Crisis." *Management Communication Quarterly* 4 (1991): 341–362.

Inhorn, Marcia C. "A Male Infertility Crisis Is Coming: The Middle East Can Help." *New York Times* (October 21, 2017). www.nytimes.com/2017/10/21/o pinion/sunday/male-infertility-middle-east.html

Irion, Robert. "What Proxmire's Golden Fleece Did For and To Science." *The Scientist* (December 12, 1988). www.the-scientist.com/?articles.view/articleN o/10030/title/What-Proxmire-s-Golden-fleece-Did-For–And-To–Science

Isabella, Lynn A. "Managing the Challenges of Trigger Events: The Mindsets Governing Adaptation to Change." *Business Horizons* 35 (1992): 59–66.

Israel, Jonathan I. *Radical Enlightenment Philosophy and the Making of Modernity, 1650–1950.* Oxford: Oxford University Press, 2001.

Israel, Jonathan I. *A Revolution of the Mind: Radical Enlightenment and the Intellectual Origins of Modern Democracy.* Princeton: Princeton University Press, 2010.

Jackson, Julian. *De Gaulle.* Cambridge, MA: Belknap Press, 2018.

Jackson, Susan E. and Dutton, Jane E. "Discerning Threats and Opportunities." *Administrative Science Quarterly* 33 (1988): 370–387.

Jacques, Tony. "Crisis Leadership: A View from the Executive Suite." *Journal of Public Affairs* 12 (2012): 366–372.

Jacques, Tony. *Crisis Proofing: How to Save Your Company from Disaster.* New York: Oxford University Press, 2017.

Jacquette, Dale. *Ontology.* London: Routledge, 2002.

James, Erika H. and Wooten, Lynn P. "Leadership as (Un)Usual: How to Display Competence in Times of Crisis." *Organizational Dynamics* 34 (2005): 141–152.

James, Erika H. and Wooten, Lynn P. "Diversity Crises: How Firms Manage Discrimination Lawsuits." *Academy of Management Journal* 49 (2006): 1103–1118.

James, Erika H., Wooten, Lynn P., and Dushek, Kelly. "Crisis Management: Informing a New Leadership Research Agenda." *Academy of Management Annals* 5 (2011): 455–493.

Jasanoff, Sheila. *Leaning from Disaster: Risk Management After Bhopal.* Philadelphia: University of Pennsylvania Press, 1994.

Jenkins, Scott. "Nietzsche's Questions Concerning the Will to Truth." *Journal of the History of Philosophy* 50 (2012): 265–289.

Jennings, Hayley. "Starbucks Doubles Down on Its Philly Incident Apology." *PR News* (April 18, 2018). www.prnewsonline.com/starbucks-doubles-down-on-apology

Jensen, Christopher. "GM Recalls Some Cars, but Not All with Ignition Switch Problem." *New York Times* (February 20, 2014). www.nytimes.com/2014/02/21/automobiles/gm-recalls-some-cars-but-not-all-with-ignition-switch-pro blem.html

Joffee, Justin. "Starbucks' Late Crisis Response Offers PR Pros a Lesson in Social Listening." *PR News* (April 15, 2018). www.prnewsonline.com/starbucks-late-crisis-response-offers-pr-pros-a-lesson-in-social-listening.

John, Sue Lockett, Domke, David, Coe, Kevin, and Graham, Erica S. "Going Public, Crisis after Crisis: The Bush Administration and the Press from September 11 to Saddam." *Rhetoric and Public Affairs* 10 (2007): 195–219.

Johnson, Jenna. "Trump Calls for 'Total and Complete Shutdown of Muslims Entering the United States.'" *Washington Post* (December 7, 2015). www.washingtonpost.com/news/post-politics/wp/2015/12/07/donald-trump-calls-for-total-and-complete-shutdown-of-muslims-entering-the-united-states/?ut m_term=.fd6da98bd1b4

Johnson, Lyndon B. *Report on the Gulf of Tonkin Incident* (August 4, 1964). http://millercenter.org/president/speeches/speech-3998

Johnson, Richard. "Defending Ways of Life: The (Anti-) Terrorist Rhetorics of Bush and Blair." *Theory, Culture & Society* 19 (2002): 211–231.

Johnson, Robert David. "Ernest Gruening and the Tonkin Gulf Resolution: Continuities in American Dissent." *Journal of American – East Asian Relations* 2 (1993): 111–135.

Jones, Brian J., McFalls, Joseph A., Jr., and Gallagher, Bernard J., III. "Toward a Unified Model for Social Problems Theory." *Journal for the Theory of Social Behavior* 19 (1989): 337–356.

Jordheim, Helge and Wigen, Einar. "Conceptual Synchronization: From *Progress* to *Crisis*." *Millennium* 46 (2018): 421–439.

Jozsa, Frank P., Jr. *Football Fortunes: The Business, Organization, and Strategy of the NFL*. Jefferson, NC: McFarland & Company, 2010.

Judge, Monique. "Why Do White People Feel Entitled to Police Black People?" *The Root* (October 15, 2018). www.theroot.com/why-do-white-people-feel-entitled-to-police-black-peopl-1829766307

Kahn, William A., Barton, Michelle A., and Fellows, Steven. "Organizational Crises and the Disturbance of Relational Systems." *Academy of Management Review* 38 (2013): 377–396.

Kahneman, Daniel. "Maps of Bounded Rationality: A Perspective on Intuitive Judgement and Choice." *Nobel Prize Lecture* (2002). http://nobelprize.org/nob el_prizes/economics/laureates/2002/kahnemann-lecture.pdf

Kallet, Lisa. "The Diseased Body Politic, Athenian Public Finance, and the Massacre at Mykalessos (Thucydides 7.27–29)." *American Journal of Philology* 120 (1999): 223–244.

Kanter, Rosabeth Moss. "Leadership and the Psychology of Turnarounds." *Harvard Business Review* 81 (2003): 3–11.

Kantor, Jodi and Twohey, Megan. "Harvey Weinstein Paid Off Sexual Harassment Accusers for Decades." *New York Times* (October 5, 2017). www.nytimes.com/2017/10/05/us/harvey-weinstein-harassment-allegations.html

Keen, Suzanne. *Narrative Form*. New York: Palgrave Macmillan, 2013.

Kenny, Michael. "Back to the Populist Future? Understanding Nostalgia in Contemporary Ideological Discourse." *Journal of Political Ideologies* 22 (2017): 256–273.

Kessler, Glenn and Lee, Michelle Y. H. (2016, July 22). "Fact-Checking Donald Trump's Acceptance Speech at the 2016 RNC." *Washington Post* (July 22, 2016). www.washingtonpost.com/news/fact-checker/wp/2016/07/2 2/fact-checking-donald-trumps-acceptance-speech-at-the-2016-rnc/?utm_ term=.c45ef519d961

Kessler, Ronald C., Warner, Christopher H., Ivany, Christopher, Petukhova, Maria V., Rose, Sherri, Bromet, Evelyn J. . . . and Ursano, Robert J. "Predicting Suicides after Psychiatric Hospitalization in US Army Soldiers: The Army Study to Assess Risk and Resilience in Service Members (Army STARRS). *JAMA Psychiatry* 72 (2015): 49–58.

Ketchen, David J., Jr. "How Penn State Turned a Crisis into a Disaster: An Interview with Crisis Management Pioneer Steven Fink." *Business Horizon* 57 (2014): 667–675.:

Khaldarova, Irma and Pantti, Mervi. "Fake News." *Journalism Practice* 19 (2016): 891–901.

Khurana, Rakesh. *Searching for the Corporate Savior: The Irrational Quest for Charismatic CEOs*. Princeton: Princeton University Press, 2002.

Kielkowski, Robin. "Leadership during Crisis." *Journal of Leadership Studies* 7 (2013): 62–65.

Kieser, Alfred. "Rhetoric and Myth in Management Fashion." *Organization* 4 (1997): 49–74.

Kilgore, Adam. "For Decades, the NFL Wrapped Itself in the Flag. Now, That's Made Business Uneasy." *Washington Post* (September 6, 2018). www

.washingtonpost.com/sports/for-decades-the-nfl-wrapped-itself-in-the-flag-now-thats-made-business-uneasy/2018/09/06/bc9aab64-b05d-11e8-9a6a-56
5d92a3585d_story.html

Kimes, Mina. "At Sears, Eddie Lampert's Warring Divisions Model Adds to Trouble." *Bloomberg Business Week* (July 11, 2013). www.bloomberg.com/ne
ws/articles/2013–07-11/at-sears-eddie-lamperts-warring-divisions-model-adds-to-the-troubles

Klein, Gary, Moon, Brian, and Hoffman, Robert R. "Making Sense of Sensemaking 1: Alternative Perspectives." *IEEE Intelligent Systems* 21 (2006): 70–74.

Klein, Joe. *Woody Guthrie: A Life.* New York: Knopf, 1980.

Knapp, Stan J. "Critical Theorizing: Enhancing Theoretical Rigor in Family Research." *Journal of Family Theory & Review* 1 (2009): 133–145.

Koehn, Nancy. *Forged in Crisis: The Power of Courageous Leadership in Turbulent Times.* New York: Scribner, 2017.

Kolko, Jon. "Sensemaking and Framing: A Theoretical Reflection on Perspective in Design Synthesis." A paper presented at the Design Research Society Conference (2010). www.jonkolko.com/writingSensemaking.php

Kolodny, Andrew. Personal correspondence with author (2017). Used by permission.

König, Andreas, Graf-Vlachy, Lorenz, Bundy, Jonathan, and Little, Laura M. "A Blessing and a Curse: How CEOs Trait Empathy Affects Their Management of Organizational Crises." *Academy of Management Review* (2018). Advanced online publication. https://journals.aom.org/doi/10.5465
/amr.2017.0387

Kramer, Larry. "Harvards Fight Fiercely Over the Business School." *Washington Post* (June 8, 1979). www.washingtonpost.com/archive/business/1979/06/08/h
arvards-fight-fiercely-over-the-business-school/3c824a7f-af1d-4c26-8294-fdc791282189/?utm_term=.3b0f08536957

Krepinevich, Andrew F., Jr. *The Army and Vietnam.* Baltimore: Johns Hopkins University Press, 1988.

Krisher, Tom. "GM Excluded Crash Deaths from Inquiry into Ignition Switches, Company Document [sic] Say." *Driving* (March 13, 2014). https://driving.ca
/auto-news/news/gm-excluded-crash-deaths-from-inquiry-into-ignition-switches-company-document-say

Krisher, Tom and Dubin, Dee-Ann. "GM Ousts 15 Employees over Ignition-Switch Scandal." *San Diego Union-Tribune* (June 5, 2014). www
.sandiegouniontribune.com/sdut-gm-incompetence-negligence-led-to-delayed-recall-2014jun05-story.html

Kuhn, Thomas S. *The Structure of Scientific Revolutions.* Chicago: University of Chicago Press, 1962.

Kulicha, Clara, Iacovielloa, Vincenzo, and Lorenzi-Cioldia, Fabio. "Solving the Crisis: When Agency Is the Preferred Leadership for Implementing Change." *Leadership Quarterly* 29 (2018): 295–308.

Labov, William. "Where Should I Begin?" In D. Schiffrin, A. De Fina, and A. Nylund (Eds.), *Telling Stories: Language, Narrative, and Social Life* (pp. 7–22). Washington, DC: Georgetown University Press, 2010.

La Forgia, Michael and Dance, Gabriel J. K. "Facebook Gave Chinese Giants Access to Data." *New York Times* (June 6, 2018). www.nytimes.com/2018/06/05/technology/facebook-device-partnerships-china.html

Langley, G.H. "Belief." *Philosophy* 8 (1933): 66–76.

Langlois, Shawn. "Mark Zuckerberg Is a 'Hero,' and D.C. Needs to Be More Careful, Says Venture Capitalist." *Marketwatch* (April 11, 2018). www.marketwatch.com/story/mark-zuckerberg-is-a-hero-and-dc-needs-to-be-more-careful-says-venture-capitalist-2018-04-11

Lapowsky, Issie. "Cambridge Analytica Execs Caught Discussing Extortion and Fake News." *Wired* (February 19, 2018). www.wired.com/story/cambridge-analytica-execs-caught-discussing-extortion-and-fake-news

Larson, Lars L. and Rowland, Kendrith M. "Leadership Style and Cognitive Complexity." *Academy of Management Journal* 17 (1974): 37–45.

Latour, Bruno. "Postmodern? No, Simply Amodern! Steps toward an Anthropology of Science." *Studies in the History and Philosophy of Science* 21 (1990): 145–171.

Lawrence, Paul R. and Lorsch, Jay W. "Differentiation and Integration in Complex Organizations." *Administrative Science Quarterly* 12 (1967): 1–47.

Lay, Ken. "Speaking to Enron All-Employees Meeting." *YouTube* (August 16, 2001). www.youtube.com/watch?v=6svTm7zC50w

Leader-Chivée, Lauren. "CEOs: Own the Crisis Or It Will Own You." *Harvard Business Review Web* (March 26, 2014). https://hbr.org/2014/03/ceos-own-the-crisis-or-it-will-own-you

Learmonth, Mark, Lockett, Andy, and Dowd, Kevin. "Promoting Scholarship That Matters: The Uselessness of Useful Research and the Usefulness of Useless Research." *British Journal of Management* 23 (2011): 35–44.

Lefebvre, Georges. *The Coming of the French Revolution, 1789.* Princeton: Princeton University Press, 1947.

Lens, Sidney. *The Labor Wars: From the Molly Maguires to the Sitdowns.* New York: Doubleday, 1973.

Leonhardt, David. "Puerto Rico's Crisis by the Numbers." *New York Times* (October 17, 2017). www.nytimes.com/2017/10/17/opinion/puerto-ricos-crisis-by-the-numbers.html

Lepore, Jill. *These Truths: A History of the United States.* New York: Norton, 2018.

Levine, Matt. "Wells Fargo Opened a Couple Million Fake Accounts." *Bloomberg Opinion* (September 9, 2016). www.bloomberg.com/view/articles/2016-09-09/wells-fargo-opened-a-couple-million-fake-accounts

Levitsky, Steven and Ziblatt, Daniel. *How Democracies Die.* New York: Penguin, 2018.

Lewin, Kurt. "Psychology and the Process of Group Living." *Bulletin of the Society for the Psychological Study of Social Issues* 17 (1943): 113–131.

Lewis, Alain A. *On the Formal Character of Plausible Reasoning.* Santa Monica: Rand Corporation, 1980.

Lewis, David L. *King: A Biography.* Urbana: University of Illinois Press, 2013.

Lewis, John. "Forgiving George Wallace." *New York Times* (September 16, 1998). www.nytimes.com/1998/09/16/opinion/forgiving-george-wallace.html

Lewy, Guenter. *America in Vietnam*. New York: Oxford University Press, 1978.

Limerick, Patricia N. *The Legacy of Conquest: Unbroken Past of the American West*. New York: Norton, 1987.

Lippmann, Walter. *Public Opinion*. New York: Macmillan, 1922.

Littlefield, Robert S. and Quenette, Andrea M. "Crisis Leadership and Hurricane Katrina: The Portrayal of Authority by the Media in Natural Disasters." *Journal of Applied Communication Research* 35 (2007): 26–47.

Littlejohn, Robert F. *Crisis Management: A Team Approach*. New York: American Management Association, 1983.

Loftus, Geoff. "Mary Barra's Leadership Legacy." *Fortune* (March 19, 2014). www.forbes.com/sites/geoffloftus/2014/03/19/mary-barras-leadership-legacy/#559eb2c05301

Lombardi, Doug, Nussbaum, E. Michael, and Sinatra, Gale M. "Plausibility Judgments in Conceptual Change and Epistemic Cognition." *Educational Psychologist* 51 (2016): 35–56.

Lopach, James J. and Luckowski, Jean A. *Jeannette Rankin: A Political Woman*. Boulder: University of Colorado Press, 2005.

Lucero, Mercela, Kwang, Alywin Tan Teng, and Pang, Augustine. "Crisis Leadership: When Should the CEO Step Up?" *Corporate Communications: An International Journal* 14 (2009): 234–248.

Luxon, Nancy. *Crisis in Authority: Politics, Trust, and Truth-Telling in Freud and Foucault*. Cambridge: Cambridge University Press, 2015.

Lyons, Peter and Rittner, Barbara. "The Construction of the Crack Babies Phenomenon as a Social Problem." *American Journal of Orthopsychiatry* 68 (1998): 313–320.

MacAskill, Ewen and Borger, Julian. "Iran War Illegal and Breached UN Charter, Says Annan." *The Guardian* (September 15, 2004). www.theguardian.com/world/2004/sep/16/iraq.iraq

Maddaus, Gene. "Harvey Weinstein's Crisis Response 'One of the Worst' Experts Have Seen." *Variety* (October 11, 2017). https://variety.com/2017/biz/news/harvey-weinstein-scandal-crisis-response-worst-1202582850

Madera, Juan M. and Smith, D. Brent. "The Effects of Leader Negative Emotions on Evaluations of Leadership in a Crisis Situation: The Role of Anger and Sadness." *Leadership Quarterly* 20 (2009): 103–114.

Malmendier, Ulrike and Tate, Geoffrey. *Superstar CEOs*. NBER Working Paper No. 14140 (June 2008). www.nber.org/papers/w14140

Malle, Betram F., Guglielmo, Steve, and Monroe, Andrew E. "A Theory of Blame." *Psychological Inquiry* 25 (2014): 147–186.

Manjoo, Farhad. "How Mark Zuckerberg Became Too Big to Fail." *New York Times* (November 1, 2018). www.nytimes.com/2018/11/01/technology/mark-zuckerberg-facebook.html?action=click&module=Top%20Stories&pgtype=Homepage

Mannarelli, Thomas. *The World Wrestling Federation*. Fontainebleau, France: INSEAD, 2000.

March, James G. "A Scholar's Quest." *Journal of Management Inquiry* 20 (2011): 355–357.

Marcus, Alfred A. and Goodman, Robert S. "Victims and Shareholders: The Dilemmas of Presenting Corporate Policy during a Crisis." *Academy of Management Journal* 34 (1991): 281–330.

Marcus, David D. "The Carlylean Vision of *A Tale of Two Cities*." *Studies in the Novel* 8 (1976): 56–68.

Markopolos, Harry. *No One Would Listen: A True Financial Thriller*. Hoboken, NJ: Wiley, 2010.

Martin, Douglas. "Warren Anderson, 92, Dies; Faced India Plant Disaster." *New York Times* (October 30, 2014). www.nytimes.com/2014/10/31/business/w-m-anderson-92-dies-led-union-carbide-in-80s-.html

Marzilli, Ted. "United Airlines Hits Lowest Consumer Perception in 10 Years." *YouGovBrandIndex* (April 13, 2017). www.brandindex.com/article/united-airlines-hits-lowest-consumer-perception-10-years

Maverick, J. M. "The Top 6 Shareholders of Facebook." *Investopedia* (October 30, 2018). www.investopedia.com/articles/insights/082216/top-9-shareholders-facebook-fb.asp

May, Gary. *Bending Toward Justice: The Voting Rights Act and the Transformation of American Democracy*. Durham: Duke University Press, 2014.

Mayr, Ernst. "Biological Classification: Toward a Synthesis of Opposing Methodologies." *Science* 214 (1981): 510–516.

Mazzetti, Mark and Benner, Katie. "12 Russian Agents Indicted in Mueller Investigation." *New York Times* (July 13, 2018). www.nytimes.com/2018/07/13/us/politics/mueller-indictment-russian-intelligence-hacking.html

McCormick, Kathleen. "On a Topic of Your Own Choosing." In J. Clifford and J. Schilb (Eds.), *Writing Theory and Critical Theory: Research and Scholarship in Composition* (pp. 33–52). New York: Modern Language Association of America, 1994.

McDonald, Duff. *The Golden Passport: Harvard Business School, the Limits of Capitalism, and the Moral Failure of the MBA Elite*. New York: Harper Business, 2017.

Mckie, Robin. "The Infertility Crisis Is Beyond Doubt: Now Scientists Must Find a Case." *The Guardian* (July 29, 2017). www.theguardian.com/science/2017/jul/29/infertility-crisis-sperm-counts-halved

McKinnon, Neil and Bigelow, John. "Presentism, and Speaking of the Dead." *Philosophical Studies* 160 (2012): 253–263.

McLaughlin, Eliott C. "Michigan State President Resigns after He Claimed Nassar Victims Were 'Enjoying' the Spotlight." *CNN* (January 17, 2019). www.cnn.com/2019/01/16/us/michigan-state-president-nassar-victims/index.html

McNichol, Tom. "God and Baseball." *Huffington Post* (May 25, 2011). www.huffingtonpost.com/tom-mcnichol/god-and-baseball_b_71753.html

McNulty, Eric J., Dorn, Barry C., Serino, Richard, Goralnick, Eric, Grimes, Jennifer O., Flynn, Lisa B., . . . and Marcus, Leonard J. "Integrating Brain Science into Crisis Leadership Development." *Journal of Leadership Studies* 11 (2018): 7–20.

McPherson, Miller, Smith-Loving, Lynn, and Cook, James M. "Birds of a Feather: Homophily in Social Networks." *Annual Review of Sociology* 27 (2001), pp. 415–444.

Meindl, James R. "On Leadership: An Alternative to the Conventional Wisdom." *Research in Organizational Behavior* 12 (1990): 159–203.

Menza, Kaitlin. "Can This Woman Save Weinstein?" *The Cut* (November 10, 2017). www.thecut.com/2017/11/sallie-hofmeister-harvey-weinstein-sitrick-crisis-management.html

Mercier, Hugo and Sperber, Dan. *The Enigma of Reason*. Cambridge, MA: Harvard University Press, 2017.

Merkin, Daphine. "Shaken." *New York Times Book Review* (October 21, 2018): 21.

Mermin, David. "Is the Moon There When Nobody Looks? Reality and Quantum Theory." *Physics Today* 38 (1985): 38–42.

Merton, Robert K. "The Unanticipated Consequences of Purposeful Social Action." *American Sociological Review* 1 (1936): 894–904.

Merton, Robert K. and Nisbet, Robert A. "Preface." In R. K. Merton and R. A. Nisbet (Eds.), *Contemporary Social Problems* (pp. vii–xi). New York: Harcourt Brace, 1961.

Meyer, John P. *Handbook of Employee Commitment*. Cheltenham, UK: Edward Elgar, 2016.

Meyers, Gerald C. with Holusha, John. *When It Hits the Fan: Managing the Nine Crises of Business*. Boston: Houghton Mifflin, 1986.

Midgley, Neil. "Word of the Year 2016 Is . . ." *Oxford Dictionary* (2016). https://en.oxforddictionaries.com/word-of-the-year/word-of-the-year–2016

Mikušová, Marie and Čopiková, Andrea. "What Business Owners Expect from a Crisis Manager? A Competency Model Survey Results from Czech Businesses." *Journal of Contingencies and Crisis Management* 24 (2016): 162–180.

Milburn, Thomas W., Schuler, Randall S., and Watman, Kenneth H. "Organizational Crisis. Part I: Definition and Conceptualization." *Human Relations* 36 (1983): 1141–1160.

Milburn, Thomas W., Schuler, Randall S., and Watman, Kenneth H. "Organizational Crisis. Part II: Strategies and Responses." *Human Relations* 36 (1983): 1161–1180.

Miller, Gale and Holstein, James A. "Reconsidering Social Constructionism." In G. Miller and J. A. Holstein (Eds.), *Reconsidering Social Constructionism: Debates in Social Problems* (pp. 5–24). New York: Aldine de Gruyter, 1993.

Miller, Mike. "How Brad Pitt Threatened Harvey Weinstein After He Allegedly Harassed Gwyneth Paltrow." *People* (October 10, 2017). https://people.com/movies/inside-story-how-brad-pitt-threatened-harvey-weinstein-with-a-missouri-whooping-after-gwyneth-paltrow-incident

Mills, C. Wright. "The Professional Ideology of Social Pathologists." *American Journal of Sociology* 49 (1943): 165–180.

Minder, Raphael. "A Year After Catalonia Secession Vote, New Unrest and Still No Resolution." *New York Times* (October 1, 2018). www.nytimes.com/2018/10/01/world/europe/spain-catalonia-independence.html

Mintzberg, Henry. *The Nature of Managerial Work*. Englewood Cliffs, NJ: Prentice Hall, 1973.

Mirabile, Kevin. *Hedge Fund Investing: A Practical Approach to Understanding Investor Motivation, Manager Profits, and Fund Performance.* Hoboken, NJ: Wiley, 2013.

Mitchell, Linda E. "The Enlightenment." In F. W. Thackeray and J. E. Findling (Eds.), *Events That Changed the World in the Eighteenth Century* (pp. 77–96). Westport, CT: Greenwood Press, 1998.

Mitroff, Ian I. *Why Some Companies Emerge Stronger and Better from a Crisis: Seven Essential Lessons for Surviving Disaster.* New York: American Management Association, 2005.

Mitroff, Ian I. and Anagnos, Gus. *Managing Crises Before They Happen: What Every Executive and Manager Needs to Know about Crisis Management.* New York: AMACON, 2001.

Mitroff, Ian I. and Pearson, Christine M. *Crisis Management: A Diagnostic Guide for Improving Your Organization's Crisis-Preparedness.* San Francisco: Jossey-Bass, 1993.

Mnookin, Seth. *The Panic Virus: A True Story of Medicine, Science, and Fear.* New York: Simon & Schuster, 2011.

Mollica, Kelly A., Gray, Barbara, and Treviño, Linda K. "Racial Homophily and Its Persistence in Newcomers' Social Networks." *Organization Science* 14 (2003): 123–136.

Morehouse, Ward and Subramaniam, M. Arun. *The Bhopal Tragedy: What Really Happened and What It Means for American Workers and Communities at Risk.* New York: Council on International and Public Affairs, 1986.

Mosse, George L. *The Crisis of German Ideology: Intellectual Origins of the Third Reich.* New York: Grosset & Dunlap, 1964.

Mowday, Richard T., Porter, Lyman W., and Steers, Richard. *Employee-Organization Linkages: The Psychology of Commitment, Absenteeism, and Turnover.* New York: Atlantic Press, 1982.

Mueller, Chris. "Why Do People Watch the WWE if They Know It's Fake?" *Bleacher Report* (January 25, 2010). https://bleacherreport.com/articles/33268 6-why-do-people-watch-wwe-knowing-its-fake

Mulder, Mauk, Ritema van Eck, Jan R., and de Jong, Rendel D. "An Organization in Crisis and Non-Crisis Situations." *Human Relations* 24 (1971): 19–41.

Muller, Joann. "Mary Barra's Pearl Harbor Moment: 'I Never Want You to Forget' How GM Failed Customers." *Forbes* (June 5, 2014). www .forbes.com/sites/joannmuller/2014/06/05/mary-barras-pearl-harbor-moment-i-never-want-you-to-forget-how-gm-failed-customers /#1f2445ba6b2d

Muller, Joann. "Mary Barra Is Running GM with a Tight Fist and an Urgent Mission." *Forbes* (May 2, 2017). www.forbes.com/sites/joannmuller/2017/05/ 02/mary-barra-is-running-gm-with-a-tight-fist-and-an-urgent-mission /#2c5535911bdb

Murphy, Patrick J. and Coye, Ray W. *Mutiny and Its Bounty: Leadership Lessons from the Age of Discovery.* New Haven: Yale University Press, 2013.

Mustow, David F. "Evolution of American Attitudes toward Substance Abuse." *Annals of the New York Academy of Science* 562 (1988): 3–7.

Nelson, Pricilla and Cohen, Ed. *Riding the Tiger: Leading through Learning in Turbulent Times*. Alexandria: American Society for Training and Development, 2010.

Niedermeyer, Paul. "Automotive History: 1960–1963 Chevrolet Corvair – GM's Deadliest Sin?" *Curbside Classic* (November 30, 2015). www.curbsideclassic.com/automotive-histories/automotive-history-1960-1963chevrolet-corvair-gms-deadliest-sin

Nikolskaya, Polina. "Russia's Putin Calls to Resolve North Korean Crisis via Dialogue." *Reuters* (October 19, 2017). www.reuters.com/article/northkorea-putin/russias-putin-calls-to-resolve-n-korea-crisis-via-dialogue-idUSR 4N1KN027

Nixon, Richard M. *Six Crises*. New York: Doubleday, 1962.

Nunberg, Geoff. "Bad Apple Proverbs: There's One in Every Bunch." *National Public Radio* (May 5, 2011). www.npr.org/2011/05/09/136017612/bad-apple-proverbs-theres-one-in-every-bunch

Nussbaum, Matthew. "NFL Caves to Trump." *Politico* (May 23, 2018). www.politico.com/story/2018/05/23/nfl-kneeling-anthem-policy-trump-604497

Ogden, Emily. *Credulity: A Cultural History of U.S. Mesmerism*. Chicago: University of Chicago Press, 2018.

Ogden, Emily. "Donald Trump, Mesmerist." *New York Times* (August 4, 2018). www.nytimes.com/2018/08/04/opinion/sunday/donald-trump-mesmerist.html

Ohlsson, Stellan. *Deep Learning: How the Mind Overrides Experience*. Cambridge: Cambridge University Press, 2011.

O'Keefe, Daniel J. *Persuasion: Theory and Research*. Thousand Oaks: Sage, 2002.

Olive, Jacqueline K., Hotez, Peter J., Damania, Ashish, and Nolan, Melissa. "The State of the Antivaccine Movement in the United States: A Focused Examination of Nonmedical Exemptions in States and Counties." *PLOS Medicine* 15 (June 12, 2018). http://journals.plos.org/plosmedicine/article?id=10.1371/journal.pmed.1002578

Öniş, Ziya. "The Age of Anxiety: The Crisis of Liberal Democracy in a Post-Hegemonic Global Order." *The International Spectator: Italian Journal of International Affairs* 52 (2017): 18–35.

O'Reilly, Dermot, Leitch, Claire M., Harrison, Richard T., and Lamprou, Eleni. "Introduction: Leadership in a Crisis-Constructing World." *Leadership* 11 (2015): 387–395.

O'Reilly, Dermot, Leitch, Claire M., Harrison, Richard T., and Lamprou, Eleni. "Leadership, Authority, and Crisis: Reflections and Future Directions." *Leadership* 11 (2015): 489–499.

Orillia, Francesco. "Dynamic Events and Presentism." *Philosophical Studies* 160 (2012): 407–414.

Parker, Ashley and Warner, John. "Trump Retweets Inflammatory and Unverified Anti-Muslim Videos." *Washington Post* (November 29, 2017). www.washingtonpost.com/news/post-politics/wp/2017/11/29/trump-retweets-inflammatory-and-unverified-anti-muslim-videos/?utm_term=.0ac01129 2bce

Parker, Martin. *Shut Down the Business School*. London: Pluto Press, 2018.

Parker, Theodore. *Ten Sermons on Religion*. London: Trübner & Co.,1853.

Parris, Matthew. "Catalans Don't Really Want Independence." *The Times* (London) (October 21, 2017): 25.

Parrochia, Daniel and Neuville, Pierre. *Towards a General Theory of Classifications*. Basel: Springer, 2013.

Parsons, Elaine Frantz. *Ku-Klux: The Birth of the Klan during Reconstruction*. Chapel Hill: University of North Carolina Press, 2015.

Patterson, Molly and Monroe, Kristen R. "Narrative in Political Science." *Annual Review of Political Science* 1 (1998): 315–331.

Pauchant, Thierry C. and Mitroff, Ian I. *Transforming the Crisis-Prone Organization: Preventing Individual, Organizational, and Environmental Tragedies*. San Francisco: Jossey-Bass, 1992.

Paul, Deanna. "Trump May Declare a National Emergency in the Border Wall Battle. Here's What That Means." *Washington Post* (January 12, 2019). www .washingtonpost.com/politics/2019/01/12/trump-may-declare-national-emerg ency-border-wall-battle-heres-what-that-means/?utm_term=.efe3625e3b7c

Pearson, Christine M. and Clair, Judith A. "Reframing Crisis Management." *Academy of Management Review* 23 (1998): 59–76.

Peifer, Douglas C. *Choosing War: Presidential Decisions in the Maine, Lusitania, and Panay Incidents*. New York: Oxford University Press, 2016.

Peltz, James F. "Wells Fargo Launches Ad Campaign to Leave Accounts Scandal Behind. Not Everyone Is Buying It." *Los Angeles Times* (May 9, 2018). www .latimes.com/business/la-fi-wells-fargo-ad-campaign-20180509-story.html

Perrow, Charles. *Normal Accidents*. New York: Basic Books, 1984.

Petroff, Alanna. "United Airlines Shows How to Make a PR Crisis a Total Disaster." *CNN Money* (April 17, 2017). http://money.cnn.com/2017/04/11/ news/united-passenger-pr-disaster/index.html

Pfeffer, Jeffrey. "The Micropolitics of Organizations." In M. W. Meyer (Ed.), *Environments and Organizations* (pp. 29–50). San Francisco: Jossey Bass, 1995.

Phelan, Mark. "Mary Barra Shapes a New GM: Fast, Focused, and Decisive." *Detroit Free Press* (June 3, 2017). www.freep.com/story/money/cars/mark-phelan/2017/06/04/mary-barra-general-motors/352853001

Phillip, Abbey and Sun, Lena H. "Vaccine Skeptic Robert Kennedy Jr. Says Trump Asked Him to Lead Commission on 'Vaccine Safety.'" *Washington Post* (January 10, 2017). www.washingtonpost.com/politics/tru mp-to-meet-with-proponent-of-debunked-tie-between-vaccines-and-autis m/2017/01/10/4a5d03c0-d752-11e6-9f9f-5cdb4b7f8dd7_story.html? utm_term=.0b8c7b7d90f5

Piche, Michel T., Van der Heyden, Ludo, and Harle, Nicholas. *Marks & Spencer and Zara: Process Competition in the Textile Apparel Industry*. Fontainebleau, France: INSEAD, 2002.

Pihlaimen, Kallie. *The Work of History: Constructivism and the Politics of the Past*. New York: Routledge, 2017.

Pillai, Rajnandini and Meindl, James R. "Context and Charisma: A 'Meso' Level Examination of the Relationship of Organic Structure, Collectivism, and Crisis to Charismatic Leadership." *Journal of Management* 24 (1998): 643–671.

Pinciotti, Caitlin M. and Orcutt, Holly K. "Understanding Gender Differences in Rape Victim Blaming: The Power of Social Influence and Just World Beliefs." *Journal of Interpersonal Violence* 1 (2017): 1–21.

Pollner, Melvin. "Left of Ethnomethodology: The Rise and Decline of Radical Reflexivity." *American Sociological Review* 56 (1991): 370–380.

Prahalad, C. K. and Bettis, Richard A. "The Dominant Logic: A New Linkage between Diversity and Performance." *Strategic Management Journal* 7 (1986): 485–501.

Presidential Advisory Commission on Election Integrity (2017, July 13). www .whitehouse.gov/articles/presidential-advisory-commission-election-integrity

Propp, Vladimir. *Morphology of the Folktale*. Austin: University of Texas Press, 1968.

PR Week Staff. "United Airlines CEO Oscar Munoz Named PR Week US Communicator of the Year." *PR Week* (March 9, 2017). www.prweek.com/ar ticle/1426909/united-airlines-ceo-oscar-munoz-named-prweek-us-communi cator-year

Priestly, Jamie. "A Paradoxical Approach to Crisis." In A. De Rycker and M. D. Zuraidah (Eds.), *Discourse and Crisis: Critical Perspectives* (pp. 465–475). Amsterdam: John Benjamins, 2013.

Puckett, Kent. *Narrative Theory: A Critical Introduction*. Cambridge: Cambridge University Press, 2016.

Quarantelli, Enrico L. "Disaster Crisis Management: A Summary of Research Findings." *Journal of Management Studies* 25 (1988): 373–385.

Quinney, Richard. *The Social Reality of Crime*. Boston: Little, Brown, 1970.

Raffnsøe, Sverre. "What Is Critique? Critical Turns in the Age of Criticism." *Critical Practice Studies* 18 (2017): 28–60.

Rampton, Roberta. "'We Fell in Love': Trump Swoons over Letters from North Korea's Kim." *Reuters* (September 20, 2018). www.reuters.com/article/us-northkorea-usa-trump/we-fell-in-love-trump-swoons-over-letters-from-north-koreas-kim-idUSKCN1MA03Q

Rascher, Daniel A. "Revenue and Wealth Maximization in the National Football League: The Impact of Sadia." *Kinesiology*. Paper 12. University of San Francisco, 2004.

Ratcliffe, David T. "The 9–11 Bombings Are Not Acts of War: The 9–11 Bombings Are Crimes Against Humanity." *Crimes Against Humanity* (2003). https://ratical.org/ratville/CAH/intro2cah.html.

Rattner, Steve. "Carly Fiorina Really Was That Bad." *New York Times* (September 25, 2015). www.nytimes.com/2015/09/27/opinion/carly-fiorina-really-was-that-bad.html

Reagan, Ronald. "Address on Behalf of Senator Barry Goldwater: 'A Time for Choosing.'" *The American Presidency Project* (October 27, 1964). www .presidency.ucsb.edu/ws/?pid=76121

Reagan, Ronald. "Address Accepting the Presidential Nomination at the Republican National Convention in Detroit." *The American Presidency Project* (July 17, 1980). www.presidency.ucsb.edu/ws/?pid=25970

Reagan, Ronald. "Transcript of Reagan's Farewell Address to American People." *New York Times* (1989). www.nytimes.com/1989/01/12/news/transcript-of-reagan-s-farewell-address-to-american-people.html

Reed, Mike and Burrell, Gibson. "Theory and Organization Studies: The Need for Contestation." *Organization Studies* 40 (2019): 39–54.

Reich, Robert. "The New Tribalism and the Decline of the Nation State." *Huffington Post* (March 24, 2014). www.huffingtonpost.com/robert-reich/the-new-tribalism-and-the_b_5020469.html

Reinberg, Steven. "Measles Making a Comeback in the United States." *Heath Day* (October 3, 2017). https://consumer.healthday.com/kids-health-information-23/measles-news-464/measles-making-a-comeback-in-the-united-states-727165.html

Renshon, Jonathan. "Assessing Capabilities in International Politics: Biased Overestimation and the Case of the Imaginary 'Missile Gap.'" *Journal of Strategic Studies* 32 (2009): 115–147.

Rex, Justin. "The President's War Agenda: A Rhetorical View." *Presidential Studies Quarterly* 41 (2011): 93–118.

Rich, Motoko. "Japan and Utility Are Found Negligent Again in Fukushima Meltdowns." *New York Times* (October 10, 2012). www.nytimes.com/2017/10/10/world/asia/japan-fukushima-lawsuit.html

Rich, Motoko. "Carlos Ghosn Emerges to Say He was 'Wrongly Accused and Unfairly Detained." *New York Times* (2019, January 7). www.nytimes.com/2019/01/07/business/ghosn-nissan-court.html

Richards, Leonard. *Shays' Rebellion: The American Revolution's Final Battle.* Philadelphia: University of Pennsylvania Press, 2003.

Ricoeur, Paul. *Time and Narrative.* Chicago: University of Chicago Press, 1984.

Rigney, Daniel. "Three Kinds of Anti-Intellectualism: Rethinking Hofstadter." *Sociological Inquiry* 61 (1991): 434–451.

Ritter, Helge. "Models as Tools to Aid Thinking." In B. Glatzeder, V. Goel, and A. Müller (Eds.), *Towards a Theory of Thinking: Building Blocks for a Conceptual Framework* (pp. 347–374). Berlin: Springer, 2010.

Roberts, David. "America Is Facing an Epistemic Crisis." *Vox* (November 2, 2017). www.vox.com/policy-and-politics/2017/11/2/16588964/america-epistemic-crisis

Roig-Franzia, Manuel. "Lanny Davis, the Ultimate Clinton Loyalist, Is Now Michael Cohen's Lawyer. But Don't Call It Revenge." *Washington Post* (August 23, 2018). www.washingtonpost.com/lifestyle/style/lanny-davis-the-ultimate-clinton-loyalist-is-now-michael-cohens-lawyer-but-dont-call-it-revenge/2018/08/23/e1550056-a6b9-11e8-97ce-cc9042272f07_story.html?utm_term=.c921dfec8fb8

Roll-Hansen, Nils. *Why the Distinction between Basic (Theoretical) and Applied (Practical) Research Is Important in the Politics of Science.* London: London School of Economics, 2009.

Roochnik, David. *Retrieving Aristotle in an Age of Crisis.* Albany: State University of New York Press, 2013.

"Room for Debate: Should the Electoral College Be Abolished?" *New York Times* (November 16, 2016). www.nytimes.com/roomfordebate/2016/11/16/should-the-electoral-college-be-abolished

Rooney, Ben. "Blaming Poor Performance on Weather? Nice Try." *CNN Money* (May 2, 2014). http://money.cnn.com/2014/05/02/investing/weather-earnings

Roosevelt, Theodore. "Citizenship in the Republic: A Speech Delivered at the Sorbonne, Paris, April 23, 1910." www.theodore-roosevelt.com/trsorbonne speech.html

Rose, David. "Bush and Blair Made Secret Pact for Iraq War." *The Guardian* (April 4, 2004). www.theguardian.com/politics/2004/apr/04/iraq.iraq

Rosillo, Francisco. *Determination of Value: Guidance on Developing and Supporting Credible Opinions.* Hoboken, NJ: Wiley, 2008.

Rothaermel, Frank. *Strategic Management.* New York: McGraw-Hill, 2017.

Rycroft-Malone, Jo and Bucknall, Tracey. "Theory, Frameworks, and Models Laying Down the Groundwork." In J. Rycroft and T. Bucknall (Eds.), *Models and Frameworks for Implementing Evidence-Based Practice: Linking Evidence to Action* (pp. 23–50). Somerset: John Wiley, 2011.

Salancik, Gerald R. and Meindl, James R. "Corporate Attributions as Strategic Illusions of Management Control." *Administrative Science Quarterly* 29 (1984): 238–254.

Sanchez, Robert. "How Massive Cuts Have Remade the *Denver Post.*" *Mile High Magazine* (October 2016). www.5280.com/2016/09/how-massive-cuts-have-remade-the-denver-post

Sartre, Jean-Paul. *Being and Nothingness: An Essay on Phenomenological Ontology.* New York: Washington Square Press, 1943/1966.

Satariano, Adam. "Facebook Gave Some Companies Special Access to Users' Data, Documents Show." *New York Times* (December 5, 2018). www.nytimes.com/2018/12/05/technology/facebook-documents-uk-parliament.html

Sato, Akiko and Lyamzina, Yuliya. "Diversity of Concerns in Recovery after a Nuclear Accident: A Perspective from Fukushima." *International Journal of Environmental Research and Public Health Review* 15 (2018): 1–20.

Saul, Josh. "Police Killed More than 1,100 People This Year and a Quarter of Them Were Black." *Newsweek* (December 29, 2017). www.newsweek.com/police-shootings-killings-us-unarmed-black-reform-michael-brown-764787

Saunders, Mark N. K., Gray, David E., Tosey, Paul, and Sadler-Smith, Eugene. "Concepts and Theory Building." In L. Anderson, J. Gold, J. Stewart, and R. Thorpe (Eds.), *A Guide to Professional Doctorates in Business and Management* (pp. 35–56). Los Angeles: Sage, 2015.

Scarry, Eddie. "Trump's Election Shows the Constitution May Be a 'Suicide Pact.'" *Washington Examiner* (September 25, 2017). www.washingtonexaminer.com/new-york-times-columnist-trumps-election-shows-the-constitution-may-be-a-suicide-pact

Schneider, Joseph W. "Social Problems Theory: The Constructionist View." *Annual Review of Sociology* 11 (1985): 209–229.

Schön, Donald A. *The Reflective Practitioner: How Professionals Think in Action.* New York: Basic Books, 1983.

Schwartz, A. Brad. *Broadcast Hysteria: Orson Welles' War of the Worlds and the Art of Fake News.* New York: Hill & Wang, 2015.

Schwartz, Howard S. "Narcissism Project and Organizational Decay: The Case of General Motors." *Business Ethics Quarterly* 1 (1991): 249–268.

Scott, Joan W. "History-writing as Critique." In K. Jenkins, S. Morgan, and A. Munslow (Eds.), *Manifestos for History* (pp. 19–38). London: Routledge, 2007.

Scott, Robert A. *The Gothic Enterprise: A Guide to Understanding the Medieval Cathedral.* Berkeley: University of California Press, 2011.

Searle, John R. *The Construction of Social Reality.* New York: Free Press, 1995.

Sechrest, L. B. "Research on Quality Assurance." *Professional Psychology: Research and Practice* 18 (1987): 113–116.

Seeger, Matthew W. and Sellnow, Timothy L. *Narratives of Crisis: Telling Stories of Ruin and Renewal.* Stanford: Stanford University Press, 2016.

Seeger, Matthew, Sellnow, Timothy, and Ulmer, Robert. *Communication and Organizational Crisis.* Westport, CT: Praeger, 2013.

Senier, Laura. "'It's Your Most Precious Thing': Worst-Case Thinking, Trust, and Parental Decision Making about Vaccines." *Sociological Inquiry* 78 (2008): 207–229.

Sexton, Jay. *A Nation Forged by Crisis: A New American History.* New York: Basic Books, 2018.

Shank, J. B. "Crisis: A Useful Category of Post-Social Scientific Historical Analysis?" *American Historical Review* 113 (2008): 1090–1099.

Shapiro, T. Rees. "James D. Watkins, Who Led Reagan's Commission on AIDS in the 1980s, Dies at 85." *Washington Post* (July 27, 2012). www.washingtonpost.com/local/obituaries/james-d-watkins-who-led-reagans-commission-on-aids-in-the-1980s-dies-at-85/2012/07/27/gJQA4LSpEX_stor y.html?utm_term=.2438366cb43a

Shenhav, Shaul R., Oshri, Odelia, Ofek, Dgani, and Sheafer, Tamir. "Story Coalitions: Applying Narrative Theory to the Study of Coalition Formation." *Political Psychology* 35 (2014): 661–678.

Shepardson, David. "GM Compensation Fund Completes Review with 124 Deaths." *Detroit News* (August 24, 2015). www.detroitnews.com/story/busi ness/autos/general-motors/2015/08/24/gm-ignition-fund-completes-review /32287697

Sherif, Muzafer. *In Common Predicament: Social Psychology of Intergroup Conflict and Cooperation.* Boston: Houghton Mifflin, 1966.

Shermer, Michael. *The Believing Brain: From Ghosts and Gods to Politics and Conspiracies – How We Construct Beliefs and Reinforce Them as Truths.* New York: Times Books, 2011.

Shrivastava, Paul. *Bhopal: Anatomy of a Crisis.* London: Paul Chapman Publishing, 1992.

Shrivastava, Paul. "Crisis Theory and Practice: Towards a Sustainable Future." *Industrial and Environmental Crisis Quarterly* 7 (1993): 23–42.

Shrivastava, Paul, Mitroff, Ian, Miller, Danny, and Miglani, Anil. "Understanding Industrial Crises." *Journal of Management Studies* 25 (1988): 285–303.

Sillence, Elizabeth. "Seeking Out Very Likeminded Others: Exploring Trust and Advice Issues in an Online Health Support Group." *International Journal of Web Based Communities* 6 (2010): 376–394.

Silva, Daniella. "President Trump Says He'll Ask for 'Major Investigation' into Unsubstantiated Allegations of Voter Fraud." *NBCNews.com* (January 25, 2017). www.nbcnews.com/politics/politics-news/president-donald-trump-says-he-will-ask-major-investigation-allegations-n711956

Simon, Mallory and Sidner, Sara. "GM Responds to Backlash after Racism Allegations: 'This Is Not Who We Are.'" *CNN* (January 22, 2019). www .cnn.com/2019/01/21/us/gm-response-racism-story/index.html

Siniff, John. "By Any Definition, 9/11 Was an 'Act of War.'" *USA Today* (September 10, 2014). www.usatoday.com/story/news/nation/2014/09/10/voi ces-911-act-of-war/15385439

Sitaraman, Ganesh. "The Three Crises of Liberal Democracy." *The Guardian* (March 17, 2018). www.theguardian.com/commentisfree/2018/mar/17/the-three-crises-of-liberal-democracy

Slaikeu, Karl A. *Crisis Intervention: A Handbook for Practice and Research.* Englewood Cliffs, NJ: Pearson, 1986.

Sloman, Steven A. and Fernbach, Phillip. *The Knowledge Illusion: Why We Never Think Alone.* New York: Riverhead Books, 2017.

Slotkin, Richard. *Regeneration through Violence: The Mythology of the American Frontier, 1600–1860.* Middletown: Wesleyan University Press, 1973.

Smith, Frances L. M. and Dougherty, Debbie S. "Revealing a Master Narrative: Discourses of Retirement throughout the Working Life." *Management Communication Quarterly* 26 (2012): 453–478.

Smock, Charles D. "The Influence of Psychological Stress on the 'Intolerance of Ambiguity.'" *Journal of Abnormal Psychology* 50 (1955): 177–182.

Snow, Charles C. and Ketchen David J., Jr. "Typology-Driven Theorizing: A Response to Delbridge and Fiss." *Academy of Management Review* 39 (2013): 231–233.

Solon, Olivia and Laughland, Oliver. "Cambridge Analytica Closing after Facebook Data Harvesting Scandal." *The Guardian* (May 2, 2018). www .theguardian.com/uk-news/2018/may/02/cambridge-analytica-closing-down-after-facebook-row-reports-say

Sonnenfeld, Jeffrey. "Why I Still Think Fiorina Was a Terrible CEO." *Politico* (September 20, 2015). www.politico.com/magazine/story/2015/09/carly-fiorina-ceo-jeffrey-sonnenfeld-2016-213163

Sorokin, Pitirim A. *Man and Society in Calamity: The Effects of War, Revolution, Famine, Pestilence upon Human Mind, Behavior, Social Organization, and Cultural Life.* Westport, CT: Greenwood Press, 1942.

Spangler, Todd. "Facebook Under Fire: How Privacy Crisis Could Change Big Data Forever." *Variety* (2018). https://variety.com/2018/digital/features/face book-privacy-crisis-big-data-mark-zuckerberg-1202741394

Spanier, John W. *Games Nations Play: Analyzing International Politics*. New York: Holt, 1984.

Spector, Bert. "HRM at Enron: The Unindicted Co-conspirator." *Organizational Dynamics* 32 (2003): 207–220.

Spector, Bert. *Implementing Organizational Change: Theory into Practice*. Boston: Pearson, 2013.

Spector, Bert. "Flawed from the 'Get-Go': Lee Iacocca and the Origins of Transformational Leadership." *Leadership* 10 (2014): 361–379.

Spector, Bert. "Using History Ahistorically: Presentism and the Tranquility Fallacy." *Management & Organizational History* 9 (2014): 305–313.

Spector, Bert. "Carlyle, Freud, and the Great Man Theory More Fully Considered." *Leadership* 12 (2015): 250–260.

Spector, Bert. *Discourse on Leadership: A Critical Appraisal*. Cambridge: Cambridge University Press, 2016.

Spector, Malcom and Kitsuse, John I. "Social Problems: A Reformulation." *Social Problems* 21 (1973): 145–159.

Spector, Malcom and Kitsuse, John I. *Constructing Social Problems*. New York: Walter de Gruyter, 1987.

Spector-Merseel, Gabriela. "Narrative Research: Time for a Paradigm." *Narrative Inquiry* 20 (2010): 204–224.

Spicer, André, Alvesson, Mats, and Kärrenanm Dan. "Critical Performativity: The Unfinished Business of Critical Management Studies." *Human Relations* 62 (2009): 537–560.

Spiliopoulos, Leonidas. "Pattern Recognition and Subjective Belief Learning in a Repeated Constant-Sum Game." *Games and Economic Behavior* 75 (2012): 921–935.

Spoelstra, Sverre and Svensson, Peter. "Critical Performativity: The Happy End of Critical Management Studies?" In A. Prasad, P. Prasad, A. J. Mills, and J. H. Mills (Eds.), *The Routledge Companion to Critical Management Studies* (pp. 69–79). London: Routledge, 2016.

Stanley, Jason. *How Fascism Works: The Politics of Us and Them*. New York: Random House, 2018.

Starbuck, William H. and Milliken, Frances J. "Executives Perceptual Filters: What They Notice and How They Make Sense." In D. C. Hambrick (Ed.), *The Executive Effect: Concepts and Methods for Studying Top Managers* (pp. 35–65). Greenwich: JAI Press, 1988.

Starn, Randolph. "Historians and 'Crisis.'" *Past and Present* 52 (1971): 3–22.

Statement by the Press Secretary on the Presidential Advisory Commission on Election Integrity (January 3, 2018). www.whitehouse.gov/briefings-statements/statement-press-secretary-presidential-advisory-commission-election-integrity

Staw, Barry M., McKechnie, Pamela L., and Puffer, Shelia M. "The Justification of Organizational Performance." *Administrative Science Quarterly* 28 (1983): 582–600.

Staw, Barry M., Sandelands, Lance E., and Dutton, Jane E. "Threat-Rigidity Effects in Organizational Behavior: A Multi-Level Analysis." *Administrative Science Quarterly* 26 (1981): 501–524.

Steckelberg, James M. "Measles Vaccine: Can I Get the Measles if I've Already Been Vaccinated?" *Mayo Clinic* (no date). www.mayoclinic.org/diseases-conditions/measles/expert-answers/getting-measles-after-vaccination/faq-20125397

Steel, Ronald. *Walter Lippmann and the American Century.* Boston: Little, Brown, 1980.

Stevens, Mitchell L. *Creating a Class: College Admissions and the Education of Elites.* Cambridge, MA: Harvard University Press, 2007.

Stewart, Marc. "That's Our Blood: *Denver Post* Reporters, Staff Members Rally against Corporate Owner." *Denver Post* (May 8, 2018). www.denverpost.com/2018/05/08/denver-post-alden-global-capital-protest

Straumann, Benjamin. *Crisis and Constitutionalism: Roman Political Thought from the Fall of the Republic to the Age of Revolution.* New York: Oxford University Press, 2016.

Stuart, Gisela, Johnson, Boris, and Gove, Michael. "Vote Leave for a Fairer Britain." *Voteleavetakecontrol.org* (June 22, 2016). www.voteleavetakecontrol.org/news.html

Sugrue, Thomas J. *The Origins of the Urban Crisis: Race and Inequality in Postwar Detroit.* Princeton: Princeton University Press, 1996.

Sun, Lena H. "Percentage of Young US Children Who Don't Receive Any Vaccines Has Quadrupled Since 2001." *Washington Post* (October 11, 2018). www.washingtonpost.com/national/health-science/percentage-of-young-us-children-who-dont-receive-any-vaccines-has-quadrupled-since-2001/2018/10/11/4a9cca98-cd0d-11e8-920f-dd52e1ae4570_story.html?utm_term=.14d054f8bf23

Szasz, Thomas S. *The Manufacture of Madness.* New York: Delta Books, 1970.

Tannen, Deborah. "'We've Never Been Close, We're Very Different': Three Narrative Types in System Discourse." *Narrative Inquiry* 18 (2008): 206–222.

Tatum, Sophie. "Trump: NFL Owners Should Fire Players Who Protest the National Anthem." *CNN Politics* (September 23, 2017). www.cnn.com/2017/09/22/politics/donald-trump-alabama-nfl/index.html

Tavana, Art. "People Are Making Tons of Money Betting on (Fake) Pro Wrestling." *Vice.com* (January 31, 2014). www.vice.com/en_us/article/4w7w33/people-are-making-tons-of-money-betting-on-fake-pro-wrestling

Taylor, Ian, Walton, Paul, and Young, Jock. *The New Criminology: For a Social Theory of Deviance.* New York: Harper & Row, 1973.

Taylor, Simon. *Defending Your Reputation: A Practical Guide to Crisis Communications.* London: Thorogood, 2001.

Tesich, Steve. "A Government of Lies." *The Nation* (January 1992). www.highbeam.com/doc/1G1-11665982.html

Thompson, Derek. "What in the World Is Causing the Retail Meltdown of 2017?" *The Atlantic* (April 10, 2017). www.theatlantic.com/business/archive/2017/04/retail-meltdown-of-2017/522384

Thompson, Nicholas and Vogelstein, Fred. "Inside the Two Years That Shook Facebook – and the World." *Wired* (February 12, 2018). www.wired.com/story/inside-facebook-mark-zuckerberg-2-years-of-hell

Tieying Yu, Sengul, Metin, and Lester, Richard H. "Misery Loves Company: The Spread of Negative Impacts Resulting from an Organizational Crisis." *Academy of Management Review* 33 (2008): 452–472.

Tjosvold, Dean. "Effects of Crisis Orientation on Managers' Approach to Controversy in Decision Making." *Academy of Management Journal* 27 (1984): 130–138.

Tobak, Steve. "How to Manage a Crisis, Any Crisis." *CNet* (August 23, 2008). www.cnet.com/news/how-to-manage-a-crisis-any-crisis

Toffler, Alvin. *Future Shock.* New York: Random House, 1970.

Tornoe, Rob. "Trump to Veterans: Don't Believe What You're Reading or Seeing." *Philadelphia Inquirer* (July 24, 2018). www2.philly.com/philly/news/politics/presidential/donald-trump-vfw-speech-kansas-city-what-youre-seeing-reading-not-whats-happening-20180724.html

Torres-Spelliscy, Clara. "Corporate Democracy from Say-on-Pay to Say-on-Politics." *Constitutional Commentary* 30 (2015): 431–462.

Tourish, Dennis. *Dark Side of Transformational Leadership: A Critical Perspective.* London: Routledge, 2013.

Tribbo, Bill. *Leadership in the Eye of the Storm; Putting Your People First in a Crisis.* Toronto: University of Toronto Press, 2016.

Trump, Donald. "2016 RNC Draft Speech Transcript." *Politico* (July 21, 2016). www.politico.com/story/2016/07/full-transcript-donald-trump-nomination-acceptance-speech-at-rnc-225974

Trump, Donald J. "Inauguration Speech." *Politico* (2017). www.politico.com/story/2017/01/full-text-donald-trump-inauguration-speech-transcript-233907

Turner, Frederick J. *The Frontier in American History.* New York: H. Holt, 1920.

"Vaccines: An Unhealthy Skepticism." *Times Video* (February 2, 2015). www.nytimes.com/video/us/100000003485198/vaccines-an-unhealthy-skepticism.html

Valukas, Anton R. *Report to Board of Directors of General Motors Company regarding Ignition Switch Recalls* (May 29, 2014). www.projectauditors.com/Papers/GM_investigation_report_Valukas_ignition_switch.pdf

Varotsis, George. *Screenplay and Narrative Theory: The Screenplectics Model of Complex Narrative Systems.* Lanham: Lexington Books, 2015.

Vatz, Richard E. "The Myth of the Rhetorical Situation." *Philosophy & Rhetoric* 8 (1973): 154–161.

Vernon, Pete. "The Media Today: The John Kelly Narrative Takes Hold." *Columbia Journalism Review* (August 3, 2017). www.cjr.org/the_media_today/the-media-today-the-john-kelly-narrative-takes-hold.php

Victor, Daniel and Stevens, Matt. "United Airlines Passenger Is Dragged from an Overbooked Flight." *New York Times* (April 10, 2017). www.nytimes.com/2017/04/10/business/united-flight-passenger-dragged.html

Vlasic, Bill. "A Fatally Flawed Switch, and a Burdened GM Engineer." *New York Times* (November 13, 2014). www.nytimes.com/2014/11/14/business/a-fatally-flawed-switch-and-a-burdened-engineer.html

Von der Mühlen, Sarah, Richter, Tobias, Schmid, Sebastian, Schmidt, Elisabeth Marie, and Schmid, Kirsten Berthold. "Judging the Plausibility of Arguments in Scientific Texts: A Student–Scientist Comparison." *Thinking & Reasoning* 22 (2016): 221–249.

Von Foerster, Heinz. "On Constructing a Reality." In H. von Foerster (Ed.), *Observing Systems* (pp. 288–309). Seaside, CA: Intersystems, 1973.

Waddock, Sandra. *Intellectual Shamans: Management Academics Making a Difference.* Cambridge: Cambridge University Press, 2015.

Wagar, Elizabeth A. "Credibility." *Archives of Pathology & Laboratory Medicine* 138 (2014): 873–875.

Wagner, John and Achenbach, Joel. "Trump Is Rebuked after Questioning Number of Deaths Attributed to Hurricane Maria." *Washington Post* (September 13, 2018). www.washingtonpost.com/politics/trump-questions-number-of-deaths-attributed-to-hurricane-maria-falsely-says-democrats-created-a-higher-count-to-make-him-look-bad/2018/09/13/9519308a-b73b-11e8-a7b5-adaaa5b2a57f_story.html?noredirect=on&utm_term=.05114021e9cd

Wagner, John and Maske, Mark. "Trump: NFL Players Unwilling to Stand for Anthem Maybe 'Shouldn't Be in the Country.'" *Washington Post* (May 24, 2018). www.washingtonpost.com/politics/trump-nfl-owners-doing-the-right-thing-on-national-anthem-policy/2018/05/24/cdd66490-5f36-11e8-a4a4-c07 0ef53f315_story.html?utm_term=.be07d859e2f3

Wagner, Kyle. "Colin Kaepernick Is Not Supposed to Be Unemployed." *FiveThirtyEight* (August 9, 2017). https://fivethirtyeight.com/features/colin-kaepernick-is-not-supposed-to-be-unemployed

Wagner-Pacifici, Robin. *What Is an Event?* Chicago: University of Chicago Press, 2017.

Wakefield, A. J., Murch, S. H., Anthony, A., Linnell, J., Casson, D. M., Malik, M., ... and Walker-Smith, J. A. "Ileal-Lymphoid-Nodular Hyperplasia, Non-Specific Colitis, and Pervasive Developmental Disorder in Children." *Lancet* 351 (1998): 637–641.

Walby, Sylvia. *Crisis.* Malden, MA: Polity, 2015.

Wald, Matthew L. "GM Report Illustrates Managers' Disconnect." *New York Times* (June 8, 2014). www.nytimes.com/2014/06/09/business/gm-report-illustrates-managers-disconnect.html

Walsh, John. "Ireland Must Get a Grip on Its Identity Crisis." *The Times* (London) (October 21, 2017): 23.

Walsh, Margaret. "Women's Place on the American Frontier." *Journal of American Studies* 29 (1995): 241–255.

Walsh, Richard. *The Rhetoric of Fictionality; Narrative Theory and the Idea of Fiction.* Columbus: Ohio State University Press, 2007.

Walters, J. Donald. *Crisis in Modern Thought.* Nevada City: Chrystal Clarity Publishers, 1987.

Ward, Paula Reed. "DoD Paid $53 Million of Taxpayers' Money to Pro Sports for Military Tributes." *Pittsburgh Post-Gazette* (May 7, 2018). www.post-gazette.com/news/nation/2015/11/06/Department-of-Defense-paid-53-million-to-pro-sports-for-military-tributes-report-says/stories/201511060140

Wechsler, Harold S. *The Qualified Student: A History of Selective College Admission in America.* New York: John Wiley & Sons, 1977.

Weick, Karl E. *Sensemaking in Organizations.* Thousand Oaks: Sage, 1995.

Weick, Karl E. "Enacted Sensemaking in Crisis Situations." *Journal of Management Studies* 25 (1998): 305–317.

Weinberg, Darin. "On the Social Construction of Social Problems and Social Problems Theory: A Contribution to the Legacy of John Kitsuse." *American Sociologist* 40 (2009): 61–78.

Weinstein, Harvey. "Statement." *The Cut* (October 5, 2017). www.thecut.com /2017/11/sallie-hofmeister-harvey-weinstein-sitrick-crisis-management.html

Weisman, Steven R. "Powell Calls His UN Speech a Lasting Blot on His Record." *New York Times* (September 9, 2005). www.nytimes.com/2005/09/0 9/politics/powell-calls-his-un-speech-a-lasting-blot-on-his-record.html

Weissman, David. *A Social Ontology*. New Haven: Yale University Press, 2000.

Wertenbaker, Charles C. "Paris Is Free. Merci! Merci! Merci!" *Time* (September 4, 1944). http://content.time.com/time/magazine/article/0,9171,8 85688,00.html

Whitehead, Alfred North. *Science and the Modern World*. Cambridge: Cambridge University Press, 1925.

Whitehead, Alfred North. *Process and Reality: An Essay in Cosmology*. New York: Free Press, 1929/1978.

Wickert, Christopher and Schaefer, Stephan M. "Towards a Progressive Understanding of Performativity in Critical Management Studies." *Human Relations* 68 (2015): 107–130.

Wilkie, Christina. "White House: It Doesn't Matter if Anti-Muslim Videos Are Real Because the 'Threat Is Real.'" *CNBC* (November 29, 2017). www .cnbc.com/2017/11/29/white-house-it-doesnt-matter-if-anti-muslim-videos- are-real-the-threat-is-real.html.

Williams, Ethlyn, Pillai, Rajnandini, Lowe, Kevin B., Jung, Dongil, and Herst, David. "Crisis, Charisma, Values, and Voting Behavior in the 2004 Presidential Election." *Leadership Quarterly* 20 (2009): 70–86.

Wilson, Suze. *Thinking Differently About Leadership: A Critical History of Leadership Studies*. London: Edward Elgar, 2016.

Windt, Theodore O. "The Presidency and Speeches on International Crisis: Repeating the Rhetorical Past." *Speaker and Gavel* 2 (1973): 86–14.

Wines, Frederick H. *The New Criminology*. New York: James Kempster, 1904.

Wolcott, James. "The Fraudulent Factoid That Refuses to Die." *Vanity Fair* (October 23, 2012). www.vanityfair.com/culture/2012/10/The-Fraudulent- Factoid-That-Refuses-to-Die

Wolff, Michael. "GM's Barra Shames Voiceless CEOs." *USA Today* (March 23, 2014). www.usatoday.com/story/money/columnist/wolff/2014/03/23/gms- mary-barra-takes-ownership-of-crisis/6656729

Wood, B. Dan. "Presidential Rhetoric and Economic Leadership." *Presidential Studies Quarterly* 34 (2004): 573–606.

Wood, Zoe. "Not Just for Over-55s! M&S Chairman Says Chain Needs Younger Clothing." *The Guardian* (November 5, 2017). www.theguardian.com/busi ness/2017/nov/05/not-just-for-over-55s-ms-chairman-says-chain-needs- younger-clothing

Woodyard, Chris. "Starbucks' 911 Call That Led to Philadelphia Arrests of Two Black Men." *USA Today* (April 17, 2018). www.usatoday.com/story/money/b

usiness/2018/04/17/hear-911-call-led-starbucks-arrests-two-african-americans/526255002

Wozniak, John F. with Cullen, Francis T. and Platt, Tony. "Richard Quinney's *The Social Reality of Crime:* A Marked Departure from and Reinterpretation of Traditional Criminology." *Social Justice* 41 (2015): 197–216.

Wren, Daniel A. "American Business Philanthropy and Higher Education in the Nineteenth Century." *Business History Review* 57 (1983): 321–346.

Wright, Lawrence. *The Looming Tower: Al-Qaeda and the Road to 9/11.* New York: Knopf, 2006.

Wyche, Steve. "Colin Kaepernick Explains Why He Sat during the National Anthem." *NFL Media* (August 27, 2016). www.nfl.com/news/story/0a p3000000691077/article/colin-kaepernick-explains-protest-of-national-anthem

Yaco, Sonia and Hardy, Beatriz Betancourt. "Historians, Archivists, and Social Activism." *Archival Science* 13 (2013): 253–272.

Young, Kevin. *Bunk: The Rise of Hoaxes, Humbug, Plagiarists, Phonies, Post-Facts, and Fake News.* Minneapolis: Graywolf Press, 2018.

Yu, Larry. "The Superstar CEO Curse." *MIT Sloan Management Review* 48 (2007): 4.

Yuravlivker, Dror. "'Peace without Conquest': Lyndon Jonson's Speech of April; 7, 1965." *Presidential Studies Quarterly* 36 (2006): 457–481.

Zajac, Edward J. "CEO Selection, Succession, Compensation and Firm Performance: A Theoretical Integration and Empirical Analysis." *Strategic Management Journal* 11 (1990): 217–230.

Zarefsky, David. "Making the Case for War: Colin Powell at the United Nations." *Rhetoric & Public Affairs* 10 (2007): 275–302.

Zaremba, Alan J. *Crisis Communication: Theory and Practice.* Armonk, NY: M.E. Sharpe, 2010.

Zdanowicz, Christina and Grinberg, Emanuella. "Passenger Dragged Off Overbooked United Flight." *CNN.com* (April 10, 2017). www.cnn.com/2017 /04/10/travel/passenger-removed-united-flight-trnd/index.html

Zhao, Hui. "Constructing Authority in Times of Crisis: A Genre Analysis of Government Crisis Communication in China." *Journal of Communication Management* 22 (2018): 346–360.

Index